URBAN REGENERATION

OTHER TITLES FROM E & FN SPON

Rebuilding the City
Property-led urban regeneration
P. Healey, S. Davoudi, M.O. Toole, S. Tavsanoglu and D. Usher

Industrial Property Markets in Western Europe
Edited by B. Wood and R. Williams

Property Development
3rd Edition
D. Cadman and L. Austin-Crowe
Edited by R. Topping and M. Avis

Industrial and Business Space Development
Implementation and urban renewal
S. Morley, C. Marsh, A. McIntosh and H. Martinos

International Real Estate Valuation, Investment and Development
V.J. Nurcombe

Property Investment and the Capital Markets
G.R. Brown

Property Investment Decisions
A quantitative approach
S. Hargitay and M. Yu

National Taxation for Property Management and Valuation
A. MacLeary

Risk, Uncertainty and Decision-making in Property Development
P.J. Byrne and D. Cadman

Property Valuation
The five methods
D. Scarrett

Microcomputers in Property
A surveyor's guide to Lotus 1-2-3 and dBASE IV
T.J. Dixon, O. Bevan and S. Hargitay

Effective Writing
Improving scientific, technical and business communication
2nd Edition
C. Turk and J. Kirkman

Good Style
Writing for science and technology
J. Kirkman

Effective Speaking
Communicating in speech
C. Turk

Journals

Journal of Property Research (Formerly Land Development Studies)
Editors: B.D. MacGregor, D. Hartzell and M. Miles

Planning Perspectives
An international journal of planning, history and the environment
Editors: G. Cherry and A. Sutcliffe

For more information on these and other titles please contact:
The Promotion Department, E & FN Spon, 2–6 Boundary Row,
London SE1 8HN   Telephone 071 865 0066

URBAN REGENERATION

Property investment and development

Edited by

Jim Berry, Stanley McGreal and Bill Deddis
Department of Surveying, University of Ulster, Jordanstown

E & FN SPON
An Imprint of Chapman & Hall

London · Glasgow · New York · Tokyo · Melbourne · Madras

Published by
E & FN Spon, an imprint of Chapman & Hall, 2–6 Boundary
Row, London SE1 8HN

Chapman & Hall, 2–6 Boundary Row, London SE1 8HN, UK

Blackie Academic & Professional, Wester Cleddens Road, Bishopbriggs, Glasgow G64 2NZ, UK

Chapman & Hall Inc., 29 West 35th Street, New York NY10001, USA

Chapman & Hall Japan, Thomson Publishing Japan, Hirakawacho Nemoto Building, 6F, 1-7-11 Hirakawa-cho, Chiyoda-ku, Tokyo 102, Japan

Chapman & Hall Australia, Thomas Nelson Australia, 102 Dodds Street, South Melbourne, Victoria 3205, Australia

Chapman & Hall India, R. Seshadri, 32 Second Main Road, CIT East, Madras 600 035, India

First edition 1993

1 0 6 4 8 7 4 7

© 1993 E & FN Spon

Typeset in 10/12pt Garamond by Graphicraft Typesetters Ltd, Hong Kong
Printed in Great Britain by St Edmundsbury Press, Bury St Edmunds, Suffolk

ISBN 0 419 18310 8

A catalogue record for this book is available from the British Library

Library of Congress Cataloging-in-Publication data available.

♾ Printed on permanent acid-free text paper, manufactured in accordance with the proposed ANSI/NISO Z 39.48-199X and ANSI Z 39.48-1984

Contents

Contributors

Alastair Adair is a senior lecturer in the Department of Surveying, University of Ulster and senior course tutor for the BSc (Hons) estate management programme. Research interests include property market analysis, urban regeneration and the financing of property development.

Jim Berry is a lecturer in estate management in the Department of Surveying, University of Ulster and consultant town planner. His main areas of research are within urban economic policy, urban regeneration and property investment performance.

Marie Bintley is the principal of Marie Bintley Associates (Chartered Town Planners) and part-time lecturer in town planning. She is currently secretary of the north-west branch of the Royal Town Planning Institute.

Stuart Black is a lecturer in the Department of Land Economy, University of Aberdeen. He was formerly a property research analyst with Hillier Parker Chartered Surveyors, London.

Michael Brodtman is a partner at St Quintin, Chartered Surveyors and a director of St Quintin Property Finance. His areas of professional expertise include the financing of properties both inside and outside Enterprise Zones.

Maxwell Cowan is a chief planning officer with Strathclyde Regional Council, Scotland. He has worked in local authority planning departments for 25 years.

Bill Deddis is a senior lecturer in the Department of Surveying, University of Ulster. He specializes in urban economics, property development and valuation. Current research includes the monitoring of regeneration initiatives in Northern Ireland.

Arnost Diamant worked as technical director of a state planning organization in Czechoslovakia specializing in the design and implementation of large construction projects. Current interests include the analysis of trends in the housing market.

Nicholas Falk is founder director of URBED (Urban and Economic Development Group), consultants and project managers in urban regeneration and local economic development. He was a member of the Department of the Environment's Property Advisory Group for ten years.

James Gahan is group property manager with Coras Iompair Eireann, Dublin. A surveyor/valuer by profession he was commercial director of Custom House Docks Development Authority, Dublin from 1987 to 1992.

Robin Goodchild is partner and head of the Investment Department of Gerald Eve, Chartered Surveyors, London. He is visiting professor at Nottingham Polytechnic and an editorial member of the *Journal of Property Valuation and Investment.*

Richard Grover is principal lecturer in economics in the School of Estate Management, Oxford Brookes University. He has specialist interest in European Community policy.

Nicholas Hanley is in the Urban Environment Unit, Directorate General Environment, Commission of the European Communities. He is responsible for urban environmental policy and had a major input into the Commission's Green Paper on Urban Environment.

Philip Hudson is a founding partner of East 8. He was previously an associate with Covell Matthews Wheatley. Since 1989 he has been exclusively involved in eastern Europe and has written on real estate opportunities in several leading journals.

Richard Johnson is a property analyst with St Quintin, Chartered Surveyors, London. He has specialized in working with Enterprise Zones projects and investment matters throughout the United Kingdom. In 1991 he was awarded a Jones Lang Wootton Travelling Scholarship.

Paul Jorna is a financial analyst working with the Amsterdam Waterfront Financieringsmaatschappij. Previously he conducted financial appraisals on large scale urban projects for the public sector in Amsterdam.

Paul Kohnstamm is professor of real estate studies, University of Amsterdam and managing director of the Centre for Investment and Real Estate, Amsterdam. He is a member of the Netherlands Advisory Council for Housing and adviser to the board of the Netherlands Association of Project Developers.

Rob Lawton is project leader of the Brigg Regeneration Project and formerly town centre manager in Scunthorpe. His career also included the position of lecturer in Kaduna Polytechnic, Nigeria.

Craig Lindsay is a principal planning officer with Strathclyde Regional Council. He has worked in planning since 1974 and was previously with a New Town Development Corporation.

Colin Lizieri is director of the Property Investment Research Centre at City University Business School, London. He is a member of the research committee of the Royal Institution of Chartered Surveyors and is chair of the Society of Property Researchers.

Greg Lloyd is a senior lecturer in the Department of Land Economy, University of Aberdeen. He has published widely and is currently researching the impact of development agencies on local economic and property development.

John Lockwood is director of the Inheritance Project with Calderdale Metropolitan Council. A chartered town planner, he has experience of both the public and private sectors; his specific expertise includes urban design, planning policy and economic development initiatives.

Kamila Matouskova is involved in research and design work at the State Institute for the Restoration of Historical Monuments and at the Institute for Construction and Architecture, Prague. She has specialist interests in the urban development of Czechoslovakia.

Stanley McGreal is reader in the Department of Surveying, University of Ulster. His main areas of research incorporate property market analysis, urban regeneration and housing issues.

Paul McNamara is property research manager at Prudential Portfolio Managers (PPM) Ltd. Before joining PPM in 1987 he was a senior lecturer in the Department of Estate Management, Oxford Brookes University. In 1992 he returned to the department part time as a visiting professor.

Paul Syms is the principal of Paul Syms Associates, Urban Economists. He was formerly an associate senior lecturer in the School of Urban and Regional Studies, Sheffield City Polytechnic. His areas of particular expertise include urban renewal projects, grant mechanisms and financial incentives.

Gerjan Vos is a senior lecturer in the Department of Real Estate Economics, University of Amsterdam. His research interests include valuation and investment analysis, market research, feasibility studies and sector studies.

Frank Witbraad is project manager with the Amsterdam Waterfront Financieringsmaatschappij. He has worked in urban planning in The Netherlands for over 20 years with particular responsibility for urban planning in new towns.

Preface

Urban regeneration has been high on the political agenda for the past two decades. In Great Britain the 1977 White Paper highlighted the nature and extent of the inner city problem and outlined possible remedial action. Subsequently the causes of decline have been the subject of several extensive studies providing considerable insight into urban issues. A key element to emerge from these studies has been the loss of employment in the manufacturing sector due to extensive corporate restructuring and rationalization. In addition, the mismatch between skills and jobs meant that the inner city became increasingly unattractive to residents and investors.

The prescription advocated in the 1977 White Paper was to target resources, through the Urban Programme, towards specific inner city areas, to strengthen their economics through industrial and regional policy, to terminate the dispersal to new and existing towns and to form partnership arrangements between central and local government based on a comprehensive co-ordinated regeneration strategy. However, by the early 1980s achieving consensus within partnership arrangements was becoming increasingly problematic. In many instances partnerships moved away from the central concept of defining a coherent strategy to an *ad hoc* spending of funds, with the result that Urban Programme expenditure was not always allocated to areas prioritized for economic development.

The Conservative administrations elected in 1979, 1983 and 1987 advanced the partnership concept to the extent that it encouraged co-operation with and assistance from the private sector. Consequently, the City Action Teams and Task Forces were established to take a more pragmatic and proactive approach by concentrating on large scale catalytic schemes and by targeting private sector investment. As part of the process to resolve the difficulties stemming from the Urban Programme, Enterprise Zones and Urban Development Corporations (UDCs) were established under the Local Government, Planning and Land Act (1980). The former included areas within which relaxed planning and financial regimes were to operate with the intention of boosting industrial output and jobs. Urban Development Corporations as centrally appointed bodies were given wide powers of land acquisition and development enabling them to pursue an entrepreneurial approach to urban renewal strategies. Financial incentives, initially in the form of the Urban Development Grant and Urban Renewal Grant and the subsequent City Grant, were introduced to lever resources from the market in the implementation of schemes which would not otherwise have occurred at economic cost given expected out-turn performance.

In assessing the degree of change which has taken place in urban regeneration policy over the last decade, three key characteristics are apparent: the focus on economic-led solutions, the concentration on supply side measures and the predominance of public–private partnership arrangements. The economic dimension has become prevalent as political concern for employment creation and training has replaced initial anxieties about social malaise and community development. Within the twin aims of sustaining and strengthening the economy of local areas on the one hand, and helping the disadvantaged on the other, policy directions in the 1980s favoured the market by emphasizing national efficiency and competitiveness, the argument being that through getting the urban economy working, social and environmental improvements would follow.

With respect to the second issue, the supply side approach acquired increasing relevancy in the 1980s due to the reduction in public sector funding. The budget for the Urban Programme itself grew in the early 1980s but subsequently decreased in real terms after 1984. In essence, supply side economics encourages the stimulation of growth not by demand management but by improvements in the supply of production factors – land, labour, capital and entrepreneurship. In the case of land the transfer of property from statutory authorities onto the market, the improvement of infrastructure, access and environment, the upgrading of the building stock for industrial and commercial use and deregulating of planning controls were successively advanced throughout the 1980s. Measures to improve labour markets included training of the unemployed, introducing regional differentials to pay and using the housing market to encourage labour mobility. With respect to capital mechanisms, provision for tax relief on investments in Enterprise Zones and the reduction of the financial burden through the rating system were the principal initiatives targeted to the end-user. By cushioning risk, conditions favourable to entrepreneurship were created with developers also achieving benefits from these supply side measures.

Thirdly, the concept of partnership changed dramatically in the 1980s. The original concept of linking central government departments, local authorities, health authorities and voluntary organizations together to produce urban regeneration programmes gave way to partnership arrangements between the public and private sectors. One of the key reasons for this switch in strategy was the disdain of central government to the bureaucracy and commercial insensitivity of local government, with the consequence that new entrepreneurial agencies such as UDCs emerged to entice private sector investment into inner city locations, levered if necessary by public resources.

'Action for Cities', the Government's statement on urban policy objectives and spending, stresses the importance of partnership with the private sector shifting closer to the centre of policy as both target and targeter. The public sector, having ceded some authority as the instigator and implementor of development, has moved towards ensuring a greater focusing of the urban funding programme and a better local delivery of policy. In this context 'City Challenge' and the principle of competitive bidding is galvanizing towns and cities into bringing forward imaginative proposals for regeneration. This initiative has improved co-ordination, secured better value for money and encouraged programmes which tackle local problems on a number of fronts.

The 1990s seem likely to be characterized by a continuation of current initiatives but with the added feature of a new urban regeneration agency, which once constituted will in all likelihood take over the administration of the Urban Programme from the Department of the Environment. The 1992 Conservative manifesto sees the agency operating outside the areas covered by UDCs and having two key functions: the reclamation of derelict land/ assembly of sites for redevelopment, and development of the land itself in partnership with the private sector. As the new agency evolves, its role and remit may conceivably spread into inward investment, UDC co-ordination and the development of the east Thames corridor initiative.

Policy and mechanisms are thus aimed at physical development and financial investment. This book, adopting a property perspective, seeks to evaluate linkages between urban regeneration and the development and investment processes. As events in the economic cycle have indicated, the risk element in major development schemes (e.g. Canary Wharf) can be high to both financiers and developers. In this context the cushioning of risk and more effective public–private sector partnerships are likely to set the agenda for regeneration mechanisms in the 1990s. Furthermore, greater consideration needs to be placed on European policy and practice. Two key factors are important with respect to Europe, namely the Single Market within the existing, and probably enlarged, European Community and the opening up of market economies in eastern Europe. Depending on the outcome of these processes, which currently display considerable uncertainty, regeneration policy in the 1990s may become more hierarchically based with tiers comprising the European perspective and embodying national, regional and local influences. In such a scenario the networking of urban areas seems destined to be an emerging theme.

In considering property investment and development this book seeks to appraise existing initiatives, mechanisms and approaches to urban regeneration at differing spatial levels in the United Kingdom and Europe. It is argued that only by evaluating current practice can a better understanding of factors, including market behaviour and the impact of policy directions, be assessed. The structuring of this text into three parts reflects these (current and future) core areas of debate spanning property financing and investment, policy and practice, and regeneration mechanisms.

PART ONE ──────────

PROPERTY FINANCE
AND INVESTMENT

──────────────────

Editorial

Urban development is linked inextricably with the health of regional and national economies, and increasingly to the influence of European economic performance. The process of urban change is characterized by fluctuating cycles of growth, decline and regeneration. With respect to the latter, successful regeneration, although not synonymous with property development, requires a tangible outcome in the form of real estate. Furthermore the development of land, particularly in an urban context, necessitates the use of capital resources and raises the question of access to and the availability of finance. The more intensive the level of development, the more that process is dependent on the financial and investment markets for its capital requirements.

In Part One of this book the means of financing property development, the role of the financial institutions and their investment into urban property are some of the key issues explored. The urban regeneration process is both complex and lengthy, with large scale funding essential to pump prime redevelopment. Public capital or fiscal measures often act as the lever which attracts such injections of private sector monies to targeted urban areas in need of regeneration. The methods of financing and the sources from which funds are procured are becoming increasingly sophisticated to meet changing needs. Furthermore, in eastern Europe, where the requirement for urban regeneration is significantly greater than that faced by many western cities, financial arrangements necessitate internationally co-ordinated inputs.

Emphasis in this opening section is therefore placed on the private sector, market forces and the role of institutions. Concerning the latter, McNamara stresses the responsibilities of long term financial institutions, indicating that they are not entirely free agents and are restricted in their ability to take risks. Investments are seen to be characterized by differing risk/reward profiles with investors requiring a higher rate of return from assets exhibiting risk. Inner city areas, for several reasons, are perceived as risky locations. Although government has taken measures to adjust the risk/reward framework in such areas – for example, through grant provisions, tax relief and partnership schemes – McNamara argues the need for better quality information on the performance of inner city property assets to enable financial institutions to more accurately price such assets and give an adequate return for known risks.

Pursuing further the theme of property investment, Vos examines the role of institutional investors within an international property portfolio context. It is observed that most institutional investors in continental Europe maintain a conservative investment style seeking to combine the highest return with a low risk level. Vos argues that through international diversification portfolio risk is further reduced, relative to that possible in a diversified national portfolio, due to a lower volatility of return. With respect to risk reduction it is argued that investors should seek to identify important diverging markets. Rental growth is seen as a key determinant of investment value reflecting the diversity of the economy, quality elements of the market and net absorption of space. In evaluating the investment performance of different European cities Vos forwards examples of conservative, medium and aggressive portfolios using a risk/return trade-off model.

Lizieri and Goodchild, in their discussion of the impact of the Single European Market on industrial property, consider how the dismantling of barriers is likely to generate economic restructuring with spatial and property market outcomes. It is argued that the process of restructuring is set to intensify merger and acquisition activity as firms seek to benefit from economies of scope. Furthermore, it is suggested that industrial change is likely to provoke shifts in demand in the office sector. The importance of ownership patterns is stressed, with increasing internationalization leading to capital flows towards financial markets and away from peripheral regions. However, Lizieri and Goodchild also comment on how the larger institutional investors have tended to limit investment in industrial property, partly due to high perceived risk; furthermore, it is contended that the industrial requirement for small flexible units with flexible lease terms is unlikely to appeal to the major institutions. In conclusion they suggest that inertia and inflexibility in development, funding and financing may limit gains from market completion.

The growing sophistication and complexity of property financing over the past two decades is stressed in a detailed consideration of funding sources and techniques. In this discussion, Adair examines the economic context of financing with particular attention given to debt and equity sources of finance as the principal methods of funding development and investment in the private sector. The role of tax based methods, grants and incentives are considered in relation to urban regeneration projects for which development finance is more limited and lenders more cautious. In discussing the historical perspective Adair traces the active financing role of institutions from the late 1950s through to the 1980s and the shift, during the last decade, from institutional to bank finance. Implications arising from debt and the over-geared market of the early 1990s are assessed in terms of a move back to traditional forms of finance, the need to introduce liquidity to the market and the transfer of short-term financed projects to long-term investors.

The potential and challenges of eastern Europe are assessed by Hudson in the context of the international real estate market. It is argued that, in contrast with the poor state of mature western markets in the early 1990s, eastern Europe is a high demand, low supply market with commercial real estate booming. However, high returns need to be balanced against political, currency and title risks which are perceived to figure highly in the concerns of investors. Hudson discusses the type of financial packages which are being assembled, but notes a lack of activity by institutional investors due to problems of matching projects to the onerous conditions of particular funds. This in turn is seen to impose constraints on the secondary real estate market. Hudson also makes the interesting, though qualified, analogy between the United Kingdom in the early 1980s and current conditions in eastern Europe with respect to local authorities and state companies starved of monies but possessing assets in the form of real estate. It is argued that the development competition approach, as utilized in Britain, may find similar application in eastern Europe. In essence the property sector is seen as having scope to generate benefits from the proceeds of commercial real estate.

A further European perspective is provided by Gahan, who outlines the economic benefit which has flowed to Ireland as a result of membership of the European Community. Generally considered one of the poorer and more peripheral members of the European Community, Ireland's membership of the European Monetary System has resulted in a period of real economic growth, and together with significant transfer of resources through the European Regional and Social Fund has promoted business confidence. Gahan observes how economic growth has been translated into significant property development, a process enhanced by government policy to promote the redevelopment of cities by means of special taxation incentives within designated areas. Using the example of one such area, the Custom House Docks in Dublin, Gahan examines different phases of the development process with particular emphasis placed on financial arrangements and the need, in large scale projects, to avoid the tumble effect whereby a decrease in rental levels and an increase in investment yields can make a project uneconomic and unviable in a short space of time. The success of the Custom House Docks project is seen as a combination of factors incorporating financial and fiscal incentives aimed at the occupiers of buildings, most notably a rate of corporation tax of 10% for companies licensed to trade in the development's International Financial Services Centre.

1

Parameters for institutional investment in inner city commercial property markets

———————— *P. McNamara*

The focus of urban regeneration policy in the United Kingdom since the Second World War has evolved slowly from a concentration on environmental quality in the 1950s, through an emphasis on social policy in the 1960s, to a clear and lasting focus on economic issues in the 1970s and beyond (Healey, 1990). In the 1980s, emphasis was given to the stimulation of commercial confidence and environmental transformation through property development. In particular, considerable attention was paid by the Government to the involvement of major long term financial institutions and property companies in the United Kingdom in this process. Specific emphasis was given to the role of insurance companies and pension funds in supporting the property development process, deemed by many as a block on economic development. However, given their immense financial resources, there have been expressions of disappointment at the level of activity in which the long term financial institutions have engaged.

This chapter outlines the criteria which influence the investment policies of long term financial institutions and, in that context, examines the features of the inner city land market *vis-à-vis* those of other land related investment opportunities. In conclusion, it examines areas of policy that have not yet been fully explored by policymakers which, if implemented, should begin to place inner city land markets on an even playing field with other segments of the market and attack the continuing problem of 'hope value' which stultifies many development initiatives in the inner city. Emphasis is placed on property development. However, this is done in recognition that such investment is only one of many possible forms of investment that long term financial institutions might make to support inner city regeneration.

1.1 FINANCIAL INSTITUTIONS, CONSTITUENCIES AND INVESTMENT CRITERIA

The prevailing pressures that affect the nature and composition of the investment portfolios of long term financial institutions vary. Different forms of institution service different forms of clients or constituencies. In nearly all instances some form of payment, in the form of contributions, premia or investments, is made to the financial institution concerned in the expectation of return at some later date, either when or if some prespecified event occurs. Insurance and assurance companies therefore have responsibilities to policyholders; depending on whether they are public companies or mutual companies they may also have responsibilities to shareholders. Similarly, pension funds have responsibilities to provide for existing and prospective pension holders. In the implementation of their investment policy, they also have responsibilities to current employers and employees in terms of minimizing the level of extra contributions required to meet promised pension commitments.

Given these constituencies, long term financial institutions such as pension funds and life insurance companies should not be seen as entirely free agents in terms of the investments they can make. They are restricted in their ability to take risks. They must select assets which not only produce returns in a manner that broadly matches the incidence of the liabilities to which they are exposed but, in the case of life insurance companies, there is strict legislative control to ensure that the companies are secure from insolvency. It is imprudent and, in some instances, illegal for such institutions to expose themselves to undue risk.

Life insurance companies compete with each other for market share in the same way as companies do in any other industry. The performance of investments will influence both the scale of eventual policy payouts and the level of dividends paid to shareholders. To perform poorly would risk losing policyholders to other life companies, poor share performance and limiting the level of capital for reinvestment in the company. Hence, in brief, such investors are concerned with both the absolute and the relative performance of their investments.

There are, therefore, two major concerns facing long term financial institutions when purchasing investment assets with the prospect of future liabilities and payouts. Competitive levels of return are required. However, undue risk has to be avoided. Long term financial institutions are under a duty to respect these parameters. The options available to them are briefly reviewed here.

Increasing flows of information, improving technology and liberalization in terms of the movement of money across international boundaries mean that financial institutions now have a wider array of assets in which they can invest. A simple classification of investment types open to institutional investors in the United Kingdom would identify company shares, derivatives (options and futures), government and corporate bonds, and property. There is the opportunity to invest in any or all of these across the world. Each of these different forms of asset has a unique potential for income or capital return, or both; each has a unique profile of attendant risk attached to it. In short, each can be characterized by a different risk/reward profile. The investment community will review the risk/reward profile of this universe of assets and calibrate the price it will pay for each asset in a manner which reflects its perceived risks.

Without seeking to enter a detailed debate about investment theory, this idea can be explored a little further by way of example. The Government in the United Kingdom periodically raises money by issuing bonds. Investors purchasing such bonds usually receive a steady income and a final lump sum payment. Returns on the bonds are guaranteed by the funds raised by the Government through taxation and other means. If the returns from investing in bonds are fixed (i.e. they are the same each year), then unanticipated bouts of inflation will undermine the value of those assets. (An anticipated level of inflation will have been incorporated in the original pricing of the assets by the investor.) Hence, they are said to carry an 'inflation risk'. However, if returns from such bonds are index linked (i.e. they rise to take account of inflation), then the investor has a doubly secure investment. In some ways such an asset could almost be considered 'riskless'.

The concept of a riskless asset is an important foundation to how investors review different asset types. Clearly, on a like for like basis, an investor would pay more for an asset that is guaranteed against inflation than one that is not because there is no risk that income and final payments will be eroded by unanticipated inflation. The investor is therefore demanding a premium for investing in an asset that exhibits risk. This will come in the form of a higher rate of return and will be achieved by reducing the price for the asset until it will give sufficient return to compensate for the perceived risk of the asset.

The corollary of this is clear. An investor considering an asset that exhibits risk will naturally require a higher return from that asset (i.e. will adjust his purchase price downwards) compared to a riskless asset. Risk in this context can be seen as receiving less than was anticipated from the asset. The vast majority of investment opportunities open to investors, including financial institutions, exhibit risks of one form or another. Manifestly, returns from company shares depend significantly on how a company will perform. If economic conditions have been poor or the management of the company has taken bad decisions, or both, company dividend payouts and corresponding returns from such investments will be poor. The price of company shares is, therefore, adjusted by investors to try and best reflect not only the anticipated levels of return from those shares, but also the level of risk attached to that 'central estimate' of returns.

Explicitly or implicitly, investors considering investment in commercial property as a whole, or individual properties in particular, will similarly adopt a central view of returns from the investment and then adjust the price (or establish the risk premium) to take account of the many different forms of risk to which properties are exposed. As with company shares, economic conditions may prove worse than anticipated, making rental growth from properties less easy to achieve; tenants may even go bankrupt leaving a period of no income. More longstanding risks exist for commercial property. For example, new work practices or technological advances may render certain types of property obsolete.

Given that the risks of different types of asset, whether they are company shares, government bonds or different types of property, relate to different economic pressures, an investor can reduce risk by constructing portfolios of different asset types. This investment equivalent of 'not placing all one's eggs in one basket' means that, typically, long term financial institutions would have an exposure of 10–20% of their assets in commercial property.

Hence, in summary, when considering an investment a financial institution will want to consider both its risks and return profile. When considering commercial property, a risk premium will be added to the expected returns from riskless assets to establish a 'target' rate of return. This will be the level of return which an investor will need to receive from investing in an asset of given characteristics. When combined with a view about how the income from the asset might grow, this helps to determine the price that the investor will pay for that asset. It is in this context that investment in inner city properties, either as standing investments or in the form of development projects, must be considered. The following two sections consider the return prospects for properties in the inner city and the risk profile of such properties.

1.2   INNER CITY PROPERTY: PROSPECTS FOR RETURN

The total return from an investment relates to both the income received from the asset and to changes in the capital value of the asset. Clearly, with changing economic conditions both the income and the capital value will vary over time. Rents will be influenced by the relative balance between the demand and the supply of a given form of property in a given location. This balance will vary over time. Rents will also tend to rise naturally with inflation.

Likewise, the capital value of an asset is influenced by a range of factors. Brett (1990) suggests that there are two main factors which influence capital values. Firstly, if future rental growth prospects increase, capital values increase because the yield at which the current rental income is capitalized decreases. A second factor is the relative attractiveness to investors of commercial property compared with other asset types. If investors as a group consider that commercial property is, in general, attractively priced in that it will deliver target returns or above, then a 'weight of money' from the institutions will attempt to enter the commercial property market putting upward pressure on property prices (or downward pressure if the opposite circumstances apply).

Given these two features of return, it is pertinent to assess realistically the characteristics of commercial property in the inner city in terms of what it offers to long term financial institutional investors. The evolution and current situation concerning the problems of the inner city have been documented elsewhere (Lawless, 1989). However, in essence, the general perception of the cycle of decline faced by inner cities in the United Kingdom relates to a number of mutually reinforcing economic, environmental and socio-demographic processes. Inner city areas, being the historical locus for industrial activity, have a much higher than average number of traditional industries, often producing increasingly obsolete products using increasingly dated and uncompetitive techniques. Not surprisingly, it is therefore the inner city which has experienced the greatest impact of industrial decline throughout the post-war period. These economic structural problems have been exacerbated by many other firms finding expansion difficult on landlocked sites and resolving their growth problems through relocation (Fothergill and Gudgin, 1982). Furthermore, as economic activity has graduated from an urban to a regional, national and international scale, the natural location for industrial activity has moved to the edge of urban areas rather than in difficult to access inner city areas. This has rendered inner city locations increasingly obsolete *per se*.

Historically low standards of concern for environmental conditions have meant that these inner city areas have tended to suffer from poor environmental conditions. Factories and housing have located cheek-by-jowl in some instances since the industrial revolution. This situation has been exacerbated as companies in financial difficulties have had less and less to invest in the upkeep of properties and diminishing enthusiasm to respond to initiatives to combat general environmental decay. Failed firms have left a legacy of derelict sites, sometimes corporately vandalized to avoid rate liabilities, and often contaminated with deleterious by-products from the production process. Many inner city areas are traversed by major infrastructure corridors linking city centres with suburbs and beyond. All of these factors combine to create and maintain a very poor quality of environment.

Integral to these processes of economic and environmental decline are crucial socio-demographic processes. As traditional industries have failed, unemployment in the inner city has increased. Furthermore, as the importance of manufacturing industries has declined and service industries increased, the skills of the inner city labour force have become less relevant and long term unemployment has materialized. Over and above personal hardship, households have less to spend on maintaining properties. Similarly, increasing stringencies on local authority expenditure have resulted in a parallel process of poorer upkeep for council-owned property. Poverty and poor domestic, economic and environmental conditions have grown worse through time.

As employment opportunities migrate or start up elsewhere, those able and willing to move have tended to relocate. These pull factors are reinforced by push factors as people seek to escape an increasingly depressed economic, physical and social environment. Over time, as the more skilled and more mobile have migrated, the population takes on a more residual structure of those less able to move (for example, the elderly and the low skilled). Also, inner city locations have long formed a natural destination for newly arrived immigrant families. Often initially poor, taking employment in traditional industries and poorer paid services, and facing prejudice in seeking to mirror the aspirations of the indigenous population, such groups have tended to be restricted in their opportunities to leave inner city areas. The enforced self-help which these immigrant communities engage in provides a significant source of the remaining energy to be perceived in inner city areas.

Clearly, there are fundamental forces at work restructuring cities in the UK. In general, inner city locations *qua* locations have become increasingly unattractive for economic activity through the post-war period. There is little reason to suggest that, without significant government intervention to disrupt these natural spatial processes, this is going to change. Indeed, it is only through major government expenditure on infrastructure to 'open up' access to such areas that they are not currently more isolated. Even then, it is only selected parts of the inner city that experience such relief.

Since the 1960s local and central government have employed a wide range of measures to improve both the environment and the skills of the workforce to try and make inner city locations more attractive for employers. It is not the intention to review these measures. However, at best, policies can only be described as having had a modicum of success.

Looking dispassionately at inner city property markets which, given that long term financial institutions are not urban aid agencies is how they must be reviewed, the decreasing relative attractiveness of such areas should mean that rental growth prospects, in the long run, will be poorer for inner city locations than for those in city centres and on the urban fringes. The relative demand for and the level of rent users are willing to pay for inner city land is weakening against that for other areas. This is almost certainly the case for industrial property, though probably less strong for retail and office property. (The fact that there is little information to test these assertions is, in itself, an issue which is addressed later in this chapter.)

However, as should be clear from the discussion of how investors will assess the price to pay for assets, this relatively poor rental growth performance should not be seen as a problem *per se*. Providing it is discounted in the price paid for the investments, it should still prove possible for long term financial institutions to make investments in such areas. Rather, it is the uncertainties that surround this already poor prospect for rental growth that pose the biggest problems for institutions and potentially form a key part of the problem (and solution) for some of these issues.

Poor rental growth prospects will naturally mean that capital growth is restrained. In terms of capital growth occurring through a weight of money entering the property market and inflating prices, it is clear that inner city locations have not proved natural foci for institutional investment. This may be entirely justifiable or may reflect prejudice and ignorance. However, it remains true that locations such as central London, provincial capitals, market towns and cathedral cities would form the initial focus for institutional attention. Inner city areas would generally be among the last places to benefit from institutional investment surges into commercial property. However, given the low level of inner city values, any competition for such sites can cause a significant percentage increase in asset capital values.

1.3 INNER CITY PROPERTY: RISK PROFILE

As suggested, risk in the investment sense relates to not receiving what was expected from a given investment. In addition to poor return prospects, inner city areas are generally perceived as risky. Perceived as being at the 'margins' of acceptability for land users, inner city areas may be brought into use, usually through development, when there is an excess of short term demand for land. In such circumstances, land values in these 'secondary locations' can increase dramatically. However, when the supply of land begins to outstrip demand, it is these relatively less attractive sites that will fall fastest from favour. This results in substantial volatility of land values which, for an investor, represents substantial uncertainty about what returns might be achieved from such holdings.

The need to access inner city markets through the development process is itself a major source of risk. Property development is much more risky than simply investing in existing buildings (otherwise known as 'standing investments'). The complications associated with assembling land rights, obtaining planning permission and successfully implementing the project to meet the demands of tenants in what is primarily a cyclical investment market is fraught with danger. If projects take longer to complete than planned then market conditions may be on a downturn rather than the upturn hoped for. On the assumption that inner city land markets are the last to react to upturns and the first to fall, the risks of inner city development are even more acute. In addition, inner city locations are often highly complex in terms of their land rights (Healey *et al.*, 1988). Problems of fragmented ownership, dependence on local authorities for site assembly and non-uniform site areas can all combine to cause delays in the development process and undermine the security of return from that process.

Over and above the risk presented by the volatility of returns, the very nature of inner city properties and their tenants will cause investors to raise the risk premium they would require before committing themselves to investment. For example, completed inner city properties are likely to attract weaker tenancy covenants (e.g. small and newly formed firms) that are less able to afford accommodation in preferred locations. These firms are among the most prone to failure and, hence, cause disruption to income flow.

A further risk apparent in inner city property markets is self perpetuating to a certain extent. The fact that there are not many other active participants in the inner city land market means that those who do get involved may experience difficulties in disengaging. This means that inner city assets are relatively illiquid and, as a consequence, investors will demand an illiquidity premium. As more participants became involved, this risk and the required premium for investing in such locations would disappear.

Given the magnitude of some investment funds of long term financial institutions, there is a natural tendency not to wish to get involved in small value projects because they carry a disproportionate management cost. Furthermore, the level of inner city land values probably means that such investors would need to commit themselves to fairly sizeable projects to match the 'lot sizes' of other investment opportunities. The fragile nature of inner city land markets also carries risks of its own for which a discount on price would be required.

Market related risks are accompanied by a number of other uncertainties. Healey *et al.* (1988) reported the flexibility which local authorities require to 'plan' for inner city areas. Arising from the involvement of multiple public sector agencies at local, regional and national levels in inner city areas, and the desire to ensure that any positive initiatives from the private sector likely to assist regeneration objectives are not missed, circumstances require that the land use planning system remains responsive to capitalize on all opportunities. This results in plans and initiatives being amended, redirected or possibly reversed, often at short notice. The impact of this is that the context for appraising the prospects of inner city assets and making investment decisions is uncertain. The understandable lack of policy stability at the local level in inner city areas creates uncertainty. Also, recent policy discussions about the registration and possible remedial action by landowners required to repair land contaminated through a wide range of environmentally damaging industrial processes has created further risks to those considering investment in inner city locations. An investor in such areas may well be required to pay large amounts to substantially decontaminate the land. The existence or potential existence of such legislation will naturally increase the risk premium for investing in all land that might be exposed to such contaminants. (Clearly, this also affects many urban fringe sites.)

Finally, the fact that there is very little information available to investors about the rates of return from inner city investment or how they have varied over time is, in itself, a risk. Investors being asked to consider any market or investment where there is no existing track record of information will require some extra safety margin, by way of risk premium, for the uncertainty of investing in an unknown entity. This applies to property investment in inner city areas and is largely an unnecessary risk which could be substantially reduced by concerted action by those with knowledge of the inner city land market.

1.4   POTENTIAL FOR IMPROVING THE PROFILE OF INNER CITY LAND MARKETS FOR LONG TERM FINANCIAL INSTITUTIONS

The above discussion has detailed the reasons why inner city property markets are likely to offer investors relatively poor and uncertain prospects for investment returns. As such, it is not surprising that, other than at the height of property booms when the levels of perceived returns more than compensate for the perceived risks, long term financial institutions and property investment companies have refrained from making substantial investments (CASCO, 1989). Furthermore, it is apparent that many of the risks to inner city investment exist by virtue of the nature of inner city locations. However, it should also be clear that there are some dimensions of risk that continue to frustrate investment activity in inner city areas which are capable of reduction.

The fact that the levels of income and capital growth from inner city investments are likely to be limited should not, in itself, be a problem to those contemplating investment. Appropriate valuation techniques should, as suggested, be able to adjust the price paid for such assets to ensure that the return received from the investment is reasonable given the perceived levels of risk. Hence, much of the problem concerning long term financial institutional investment in inner city areas relates to the risks to those returns.

Several measures have been introduced by government bodies to adjust the risk/reward framework to make inner cities more appealing to investors. Funds have been provided to increase the level of returns to investors. Measures to improve returns to the investor have included 'top up' grants for developers to make schemes viable, grants and increased tax relief to lower the costs of development, and subsidies in the form of cheap land. Measures to reduce risk have included prior assembly of development sites, financial support for tenants and a range of joint venture partnerships between local authorities and investors. Clearly, continuing investment in infrastructure to redress the declining relative attractiveness of inner city locations both increases the prospects for rental growth and reduces some of the risks attendant to such areas. All of these measures have had a level of success and will naturally, in one form or another, be continued as long as the general approach towards assisting inner city areas persists.

However, one further key area of risk which should prove capable of being addressed by local authorities and private sector agencies active in inner city markets, and where little action has been undertaken to date, relates to the provision of information on the long term level and volatility of returns to inner city investment. Currently, many investors and institutions are being invited to consider inner city locations, with all their known unattractive features, with almost no knowledge of the level and volatility of returns they are likely to experience. The absence of such information will automatically mean that a further risk premium will be added to inner city property, the effect of which will be to further reduce the price that investors will pay for such assets. This unnecessary extra risk factor may further erode what remaining value is left in the land or, in any event, push the price below that which more informed local landowners and developers feel the land is worth.

Hence, one action that local authorities might pursue to aid inner city investment is to provide or even promote carefully prepared information on the performance of inner city property assets. Close liaison with locally operative chartered surveying practices and other business services, public reviews of the investment performance of government owned property assets in inner city areas and use of relevant information on commercial property databases such as the Investment Property Databank, should allow at least a general picture to be built up of the level and volatility of returns to inner city investments. The only review of such issues known to the author is that performed by CASCO (1989) which identified that, of all the projects contained in their detailed survey of 120 urban renewal schemes, nearly two-thirds of all schemes achieved their financial objectives. Such a high level of success might surprise some investors. Unfortunately, it is not clear what those objectives were or what levels of absolute returns were achieved. (The same study identified which factors lay behind the successes and the failures, many of which relate to containing and controlling for some of the risks outlined above.) A concerted effort by relevant parties could significantly improve on the extent and quality of such information.

Whether the performance of inner city assets has been good or bad, public knowledge of good information on returns and risk will generally make the inner city land market more transparent. This should be almost universally beneficial. Financial institutions would then be able to more accurately price inner city assets in a way that allows them to feel that they will receive an adequate return for the known risks they are taking. Similarly, local owners will be clearer about the real rather than the perceived value of their assets. 'Hope value' would then be removed as a barrier to the transfer of assets and a realistic opportunity given for financial institutions to invest in the inner city without breaching the responsibilities they have towards their clients.

1.5 CONCLUSIONS

This discussion has shown that, in the light of processes used for evaluating all forms of investment opportunities, investment in inner city commercial property is liable to produce poor long term rates of rental growth and experience substantial risk. By themselves, these factors should not deter investment. However, to contemplate such investments, a clear context for pricing such assets should be set. Given the risk/reward framework that has been demonstrated, this may mean that much inner city land is rendered virtually valueless. Such an evaluation may not accord with that held by the current holders of such assets who may genuinely have a more optimistic perception of the risk/reward framework for their assets.

Attempts to improve returns and control risks form much of government strategy to foster urban regeneration. At key times in the history of recent property market cycles this has led to a modicum of investment by long term financial institutions. However, there is clear merit in trying to evaluate inner city property investment opportunities in the language that institutional investors understand. To facilitate this, it has been argued that a major initiative is required to determine the historical levels of return to properties in inner city locations.

REFERENCES

Brett, M. (1990) *Property and Money*, Estates Gazette, London.

CASCO (1989) *Financing Inner Cities*, Price Waterhouse and Chesterton, London.

Fothergill, S. and Gudgin, G. (1982) *Unequal Growth*, Heinemann, London.

Healey, P. (1990) Urban regeneration and the development industry, *Regional Studies*, **25**(2), 97–110.

Healey, P., McNamara, P.F., Elson, M.J. and Doak, A.J. (1988) *Land Use Planning and the Mediation of Urban Change: the British Planning System in Practice*, Cambridge University Press, Cambridge.

Lawless, P. (1989) *Britain's Inner Cities*, Harper and Row, London.

The views expressed in this chapter are entirely those of the author. They do not represent the views of the Prudential Corporation or Prudential Portfolio Managers Ltd.

2

International real estate portfolios

G. Vos

Local governments planning large urban projects require an insight into how investors and institutions operate. A primary reason for this is that the performance and expectations of regional economies and property markets are of crucial importance with respect to the willingness to invest. As argued by MacIntosh and Sykes (1985), 'over the last 20 years there has been a revolution in the ownership of property in almost all large cities. Financial institutions have expanded as the new urban landlords of offices, retail centres and industrial units'. Therefore it is necessary to pay attention to institutional investors, including an understanding of their behaviour in making investment decisions within an international property portfolio context.

2.1   INVESTORS AND POLICY

When considering property assets, institutional investors (such as pension funds, insurance companies, and open-end and closed-end investment companies) are primarily interested in commercial real estate. These are properties that produce an income and are traded in a free market. In contrast, social housing does not fall into this category; although producing an income it is not priced and traded in a free market. Equally mortgage loans attached to real property belong to the asset category of long fixed loans, such as state bonds and private placements. Thus, in practice, the important property types in the commercial sector are offices, retail, industrial units and sometimes land.

Considering the long term perspective, institutional capital has expanded enormously in the post-war period. Since 1945 and the emergence of inflationary economies the investment market has experienced a growing interest in property. This is illustrated by data showing specific investment characteristics of this asset class relative to other categories such as stocks and bonds. Although many doubts exist about the correct measurement of the appropriate figures, especially the risk element of property, diversification and inflation hedging are nevertheless considered to be good practice. In this context the continuing attention of institutions towards real estate can be expected.

Most institutional investors in continental Europe maintain a conservative investment style, trying to combine the highest return with a low risk level in the investment portfolio. In practice this results in the selection of those market areas which meet the criteria of such an investment policy. Thus investment projects which tend to promise both high returns and a high risk are not attractive for most institutional investors, particularly as the success or failure of the management policy is expressed by the performance of the fund. Interestingly, market reports of international cities contain most of the investment return components (rental income, change in market value) which are required for the judgement of the management's investment policy.

The operational management tasks of a property fund can be divided into the following components: (1) market research – distinguishing in-time market trends with the aim of carrying out in-time mutations in the investment portfolio; (2) investment policy – making decisions on which markets the company will operate in and investment selection about individual buildings; (3) property management – marketing, tenant policy, refurbishment and sales; and (4) financial policy – attracting equity or debt money in a certain combination as a base for expansion of the portfolio.

Institutions possess the knowledge, time and money to develop detailed financial analysis and market area studies, with financial projections incorporated into their operating budgets and property management programmes. In this context two major information processing areas relate to a knowledge of the relevant markets covering an economic–geographical analysis of agglomerations, and expertise of asset management incorporating portfolio analysis and property management.

2.2   INTERNATIONAL INVESTING

Diversification of risk and return

Through international diversification portfolio risk is reduced and invariably tends to be less than a diversified national portfolio (Figure 2.1). For example, after diversification over 20 assets the risk of a domestic portfolio stays constant, but if investment opportunities in other countries are added this will result in a lower volatility of return. Several reasons can be proposed to account for this reduced volatility.

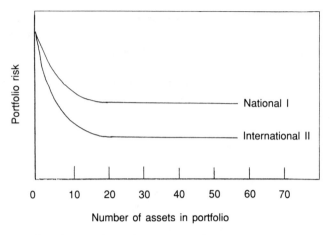

Figure 2.1 Risk reduction through international investing

Firstly, there are a number of heterogeneous economic blocs in the world, e.g. Europe, North America and the Far East. Thus there is diversity in the world economy and furthermore countries can experience a different economic phase at the same point in time. Hence the timing characteristics of investment, as one country tends to move into recovery and another country enters recession, mean that it becomes attractive to diversify internationally. Investment markets can also offer different qualities. A Spanish investor, for example, can find assets outside Spain which cannot be bought within the country, thus providing diversification opportunities. Incidental factors can also make a market temporally attractive; in this context the developments in eastern Europe provide a reason to diversify to these locations.

Secondly, theoretical arguments can be found in modern portfolio theory. These include different expected returns between countries and risk reduction; for example, foreign markets such as Hong Kong can produce relatively high returns. However, due to the lack of international property benchmarks for measuring returns, individual companies need to maintain in-house data systems as a basis for allocation (diversification). Time series returns for one country, relative to other countries, are analysed in an attempt to explain an exhibit pattern, for instance whether the high economic growth of countries is significantly reflected in their property markets. Another technique to determine whether actual properties are overpriced or underpriced is to analyse and compare the yields or the reversal 'multiples' of the investment markets for each country. In this respect the performance of countries over longer time periods could be used to explain the actual or future level of performance in one country relative to the average performance – for example, the extremely high multiples in Japan during the 1980s. Political, fiscal and legal changes, and the competitiveness of property to bond and stock markets, are other factors utilized in country analysis.

From the risk side investors consider the correlation between the markets of different countries, reflecting the relationship between quarterly or yearly returns. These statistics can show a close co-movement between some markets, indicating that for reasons of diversification it is of little benefit to hold or buy properties in all of these countries. The objective is to find important markets where diversification is achieved, as shown by low correlation coefficients between the respective countries. Such analysis is about risk reducing capacity, rather than return.

Currency risk

The total return on international portfolios incorporates three elements: current rental income, capital gains or losses and currency gains or losses. Changes in the rate of currencies can make a large contribution to the performance of foreign investments. Hence investors use several techniques to eliminate this type of risk. A prime mechanism is portfolio insurance, whereby the actual assets under management are unaffected by the insurance strategy, for instance the option hedge or selling the currency forward. Thus in practice the hedge is often implemented by using future currency contracts rather than moving a portion of the portfolio from property into cash and back again as the value changes in the market-place.

2.3   ASSET ALLOCATION

Decision hierarchy

The question as to how asset types and amounts are to be distributed at any moment in time, reflecting current investment objectives, is perhaps the most important aspect of portfolio management. Particularly relevant is the hierarchy of decisions which have to be made in portfolio allocation (Figure 2.2) including the following factors: choice between several asset categories; choice between countries and currencies; within a certain category, in this instance real estate, choice of the product market (location and property sector); and choice of a particular property within this market.

The selection between stocks, bonds and property is more important for return than the choice between individual properties within a market (or indeed between the shares of companies). Research has shown that in most cases differential performance is related to asset class selection, including correctly switching between asset classes, and to currency selection. Thus the difference in return between assets within a category is not as large at a national level relative to the international scale. This occurs because the appreciation/depreciation of investments is determined by market movement within a country – for example, if the German market is performing well then almost all assets will do likewise.

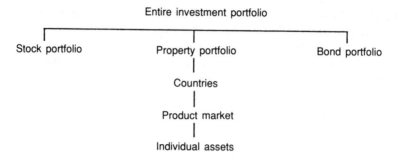

Figure 2.2   Portfolio allocation

Table 2.1   Average property returns (%) and standard deviation (%) for pension funds in the USA (1960–90). Reproduced with permission from Goslings and Petri (1991)

	Total return	*Standard deviation*
Direct real estate	8.67	4.83
Indirect real estate	10.79	13.39
Stocks	10.40	16.04
Bonds	7.04	4.84

Investment characteristics of real estate

Portfolio composition is based on, and importantly influenced by, expected rates of return, which in consequence shift as market levels fluctuate with the asset mix adjusted in the light of changed expectations (timing). Therefore the next step of the asset allocation problem is to analyse the investment characteristics of the main asset categories in different economic circumstances and relate them to the short term prospects for the economy. Initially it is important to consider the long term sensitivities of direct and indirect real estate to economic scenarios, then subsequently to look at the short term behaviour of the property cycle.

With respect to long term returns, these have been measured for the USA by Goslings and Petri (1991), with the return expected by real estate investors lying between stocks and bonds (Tables 2.1 and 2.2). Thus direct property is assumed to be less risky than stocks, resulting in a lower return. Regarding directly held property, the total rate of return is on average 8–9% per year; as a rule of thumb the return is built up from 2% real interest rate, 4–5% inflation and 2% risk premium. Inflation is particularly good for direct real estate as it is one of the few categories which offers a hedge against inflationary trends (Brown, 1991). This also explains the low correlation with stocks and bonds because inflation is detrimental to investment in bonds and generally also for stocks (the exception, perhaps, is the United

Table 2.2   Correlation matrix for the USA (1960–90). Reproduced with permission from Goslings and Petri (1991)

	Direct real estate	Indirect real estate	Stocks	Bonds	Inflation
Direct real estate	1.0	0.5	0.1	0.1	0.7
Indirect real estate		1.0	0.7	0.2	−0.1
Stocks			1.0	0.2	−0.2
Bonds				1.0	−0.1

Kingdom, which is used to high inflation). Thus investment in property is good for diversification. In a mixed portfolio and in circumstances of inflationary expectations, portfolios should consequently contain more property assets. In addition, economic growth has a positive influence on return because it increases the occupancy of buildings. Generally with economic growth, real estate offers capital appreciation and an inflation hedge. Furthermore, direct property returns are relatively insensitive to changes in monetary policy. In this context, if fluctuating interest rates only originate from inflation, property values will stay neutral because the valuation multiple will likewise be unaltered as both the discount rate and the annual rental growth rate are changed in a similar fashion.

Regarding indirect real estate (shares of closed-end investment companies valued on the stock exchange market), the correlation is stronger with stocks than with directly held property, although with respect to inflation little difference exists between stocks, bonds and indirect real estate (Goslings and Petri, 1991). Further research from these USA data suggests that indirect property returns show the same sensitivity to macroeconomic factors, as returns on stocks, and react strongly to stock market volatility. Finally, stocks and indirect real estate show the same reaction to a change in short and long term interest rates.

Evidence thus suggests the need to make a distinction between property categories in composing a mixed portfolio. Clearly both direct and indirect real estate categories show differing behaviour with respect to changes in economic circumstances, indirect real estate shows return characteristics commensurate with stock assets.

Allocation

Within the modern portfolio theory framework the optimum portfolio mix can be found with the help of the efficient frontier line based on risk/return profiles of asset categories and market expectations as shown with respect to European property portfolios. However, in practice, few property portfolios can be constructed on the result of modern portfolio theory outcomes because the technique is very sensitive to input information based on assumptions such as a stable correlation pattern and correctly measured return and risk factors. Nevertheless, the foregoing implies that in different economic scenarios there is no reason for over- or underweighting indirect real estate in an efficient portfolio. In contrast, direct real estate is overweighted in conservative portfolios (risk aversion to inflation). Considering the way investors compose their portfolios, in practice it is apparent that the property assets of pension funds vary from 5 to 20%, expressing not only the actual economic outlook for property investments but also a wide difference in investment style between investors in several countries.

2.4   MARKET CHOICE

The approach so far has been top-down in terms of portfolio construction with specific attention towards property and the economy on the national basis. However, of equal importance is the economic development of regions and cities in which property investors often follow a bottom-up approach assuming that the local supply and demand characteristics are more or less stable over time and to a large degree are independent of the short term business cycle. Hence the perception of investors that they can pick properties or select markets at the right time to form or enhance a portfolio. The basis of selection is normally that of the highest net present value and increasing portfolio wealth.

The two key sensitive economic variables for investment value in the market-place are the rental income and the required rate of return. As demonstrated, the expected long term return in a portfolio context will be known but in the shorter term and for specific markets or properties the risk premium can substantially deviate from the long term average. The underlying factors influencing rental income are a result of the changes in demand and supply of commercial space, area (regional) economic growth and inflation. Moreover, it is the rental growth of a property which appears to be important for its investment value. The rental level per unit of invested capital reflects the initial yield and if the expected growth rate is added a global indication of total return on investment can be achieved. An essential skill of a good property analyst is to understand the fundamentals of the market-place and the ability to estimate future figures. As average rental levels over time are influenced by market movement it is important to look at those variables determining the state of the market. In this respect critical factors determining whether a market will show a stable or fluctuating income include the following considerations.

1.   The diversity of the economy in the community can provide some protection against the risk of a strong depreciation of the market price of

Table 2.3   Net absorption of space in a year (m²), supply side/production figures

s1 Vacancy, beginning of the year	+
s2 Production	+
s3 Withdrawals	−
s4 Vacancy (end of the year)	−
Net absorption	+ or −

Rearranging: net production − net absorption = vacancy change

$$(s2 - s3) \quad - \text{net absorption} = \quad (s4 - s1) \quad \text{Eq. (1)}$$

property. Clearly the economic base of agglomerations is an important aspect of diversification.

2. The specific quality elements of the market – for example, many cities contain specific locations which are unique on a national or international scale such as the financial centre of London or shopping centres in Germany. On a smaller scale specific locations in cities can carry a certain reputation or prestige and can show a stable rise in value.

3. The expected change in the net absorption of rented space, or change in the net employment of tenants can be shown to have similar characteristics, producing the same effect on vacancy levels in the tenant market. The net absorption rate reflects the weakness or strength of the occupier's market as a result of economic growth of the community and activity in the developer's market. If the net absorption rate in time is rising, then it would be expected that vacancy levels would decline and rental levels increase (positive growth rate), resulting in an appreciation of capital values and lower yields (and vice versa).

Net absorption analysis

In this analytical technique the volume of supply and availability of development schemes play a crucial part which is illustrated by the simple rented space absorption model (Tables 2.3 and 2.4).

Assuming that the relocation surplus of tenants in the market is in balance and therefore zero, which is reasonable, it is evident that net absorption equals net employment growth in the occupier's market, the latter being the result of employment gains and losses in the community. By extending this analysis some simple observations about the commercial space market can be made.

1. Referring to Equation (1), if net production, mainly coming from new construction, is larger than the net absorption or net employment growth, then vacancy will increase and rental levels will decline, negatively affecting investment returns (and vice versa).

Table 2.4   Net absorption of space in a year (m²), demand side/transaction figures

d1 Take up from space expansion of tenants	+
d2 Take up from internal market relocation of tenants	+
d3 Supply from space reduction of tenants	−
d4 Supply from internal market relocations of tenants	−
Net absorption	+ or −

Rearranging: net absorption = net employment growth + relocation surplus

$$= \quad (d1 - d3) \quad + \quad (d2 - d4) \quad \text{Eq. (2)}$$

2. Combining Equations (1) and (2) it is evident that in circumstances of no economic growth ($d1 - d3 = 0$), there can still be high activity (high gross take-up) in the market coming from relocations. In this 'relocation market' locations are up- or downgraded and do not affect the investment market on average, but can create impacts, either positive or negative, on specific localities.
3. In circumstances where new construction activities are on a zero level, rental income from the occupier's market may decline if employment growth in the community is negative (and vice versa).

This type of analysis is extremely useful for practitioners (Detoy and Rabin, 1972); however, even more promising results can be expected if the model is translated into a more dynamic scenario and linked to macroeconomic variables. An illustration of the net absorption model is given for the office market in Amsterdam (Table 2.5). Changes in net absorption in the market result in reversal changes in vacancy levels (columns 11 and 12) and consequently in rental movement. These outcomes are reflected in the yield obtained (column 3), namely rising yields, with net absorption on average lower than the net production level during 1981–5 and the opposite during 1986–90. The analysis is completed by calculating the single year total returns. The Amsterdam office market also reflects the impact of the absorption rate compared with the inflation rate. In the first five years absorption levels relative to production levels were low and rental growth was lower than inflation (−0.6% average rental growth and 4.3% average inflation). In the second five year period absorption rates were relatively high resulting in rental growth rates (2.2% on average) significantly greater than the low level of average inflation (0.9%). Thus economic growth with low inflation can be particularly good for property showing real rental growth rates.

The property cycle

The absorption rate model is also useful in illustrating some peculiarities of the property investment cycle in relation to movements on the occupier's

Table 2.5 Amsterdam office market: agglomeration and total return per year (1980–90). Calculations based on data taken from office reports and *VastgoedMarkt* (a monthly property paper published in The Netherlands)

1 Year (ultimo)	2 Average gross rent (Dfl/m²)	3 Initial yield (%)	4 Capital value (2/3) (Dfl/m²)	5 Capital appreciation (Dfl/m²)	6 Indirect gross return (%)	7 Total gross return (3 + 6) (%)	8 Inflation (%)	9 Rental growth (%)	10 Net production (×1000 m²)	11 Net absorption (×1000 m²)	12 Vacancy level (%)
1980	264	7.3	3616								
1981	231	7.5	3080	−536	−14.8	−7.3	6.7	−12.5	80	60	4.4
1982	226	7.8	2897	−183	−5.9	1.9	6.0	−2.2	60	10	5.6
1983	231	8.0	2888	−11	−0.4	7.6	2.8	2.2	90	−30	8.3
1984	242	7.8	3103	215	7.4	15.2	3.3	4.8	50	100	7.0
1985	253	7.5	3373	270	8.7	16.2	2.5	4.6	70	50	7.4
1986	264	7.3	3616	243	7.2	14.5	0.3	4.4	20	80	6.0
1987	264	7.0	3771	101	2.8	9.8	−0.5	0.0	160	160	5.8
1988	270	6.8	3971	200	5.3	12.1	0.7	2.3	160	110	6.6
1989	286	6.2	4613	642	16.2	22.4	1.5	6.0	210	260	5.3
1990	281	6.7	4194	−419	−9.1	−2.4	2.5	−1.8	320	200	7.3

market and the development market. If tenant demand is increasing during the prosperity phase of the general economic cycle (9–11 years trough to trough), or is expected to increase, developers will react with new supply. At the moment when production exceeds the net absorption rate, rental levels will decline followed by capital values. The peak of development activity will be reached just after the turning point in the general economic cycle because, during the prosperity phase, market sentiment on the part of developers and bankers is optimistic based on the 'actual' high investment value of fully rented property compared with the cost price level of construction. Therefore finance is easy to achieve. In the recession phase, because of the 'pipeline effects', new buildings will still be completed, strongly competing and offering low rents to tenants (Jongejan, 1992). However, when construction has reached a low level at the end of the recession phase, rentals can still decline due to negative employment growth. In this depression scenario rental values will decrease in real terms, making investors very reluctant to invest.

With respect to the property investment market this means that perhaps the best time to sell property is just before and at the peak of the general economic cycle when economic growth and inflation are still high, and market values for property are buoyant. In a similar manner to the operation of the bond and stock market property investors are discounting future events, and investors expecting recession, with lower growth rates for rental income, will anticipate lower future investment values and sell. During the recession and depression phase investors stay away from the property market until there is an anticipated recovery in rental growth. The specific characteristics of property, a capital intensive product with an inelastic nature to market changes, means that the shocks in the property market can be relatively large and of long duration.

2.5 EUROPEAN PROPERTY PORTFOLIO

Calculation method

In evaluating European markets and the efficiency of portfolios, the key information includes the expected returns of the assets and the standard deviations and covariances of assets.

Analysis is based on historical data, and assuming that the risk/return profiles of the assets and their correlation structure is valid for a future period, then the modern portfolio theory method can have practical applications in terms of adjusting a European based investment portfolio.

Expected returns – that is, total return (TRR) in local currency in any year – is calculated as follows: TRR% = R1/Po% + P1 – Po/Po%. Information is based on market evidence using the rental levels (Rt) and the initial yields in any year to calculate the capital values (Pt). Return is denominated in the domestic currency, thus the return in local currency has to be translated into the domestic currency of the investor, in this instance Dutch guilders (Dfl). Thus, for instance, if the foreign currency of a certain asset has devaluated at 10% in a year and the total rate of return is 30.0%, then the 'translation' will take place as follows:

Return in Dfl = (1 + return in local currency)(1 + change in currency) − 1
$$= (1.30)(0.90) - 1 = 17.0\%$$

The standard deviations and correlation figures are calculated by reference to these total return figures.

Results of the calculations

The average total return in Dutch guilders of several European markets and the accompanying standard deviations of return as calculated by Bodewes (1990) are shown in Table 2.6. A comparison of the results for the period 1975–89 with 1979–89 indicates that in some markets the average returns in the second period are substantially higher (growth markets), namely the office market in Brussels, Paris, Madrid, London and Frankfurt, the industrial market in Paris, and the retail market in Frankfurt and Hamburg.

If performance over a shorter time span is considered (1984–9), then the average returns in all markets are better than in the period 1979–83, especially offices in Madrid, London (the West End) and Frankfurt, the retail markets in Paris and Frankfurt, and the market for industrial units in Paris and the Randstad (the western part of The Netherlands).

The currency effect of returns for some international markets was negative – that is, the return in local currency was higher than in Dutch guilders. Countries with a relatively weak currency included Spain, France, the United Kingdom and, to a lesser extent, Belgium. On the other hand returns in Germany showed the positive influence of the strong currency rate. The standard deviations of returns in Dutch guilders were also higher than those in the local currency caused by fluctuations, particularly in the Spanish peseta and sterling.

Positive correlation coefficients are calculated in most instances (Bodewes, 1990). Importantly, markets of the same property type within one country have a higher positive correlation than markets between different property types. Also, markets composed of differing categories within one country show a higher correlation than international markets of the same category, indicating that diversification does work in property markets. Currency effects have seemingly little influence on the correlation matrix.

Efficient portfolios

The modern portfolio theory optimization programme calculates for every desired portfolio returns the minimum portfolio risk (expressed in standard deviations) and the attached portfolio composition (quantities expressed in

Table 2.6 Average net returns (%) and standard deviations (%) in Dutch guilders for European markets. Reproduced with permission from Bodewes (1990)

Market	1975–89		1979–89	
	Return	Standard deviation	Return	Standard deviation
Brussels, office	9.8	12.3	15.3	8.2
Brussels, retail	6.6	8.5	6.5	7.7
Brussels, industrial	11.0	7.1	10.1	8.0
Paris, office	17.1	12.1	20.7	11.2
Paris, retail	15.1	9.8	15.9	10.2
Paris, industrial	17.5	24.6	22.2	26.6
Amsterdam, office	10.4	8.8	7.5	7.6
The Hague, office	8.6	7.6	5.5	5.8
Rotterdam, office	8.4	9.5	5.4	6.5
Rotterdam, retail	13.6	14.1	8.7	10.4
Randstad, industrial	9.4	10.6	8.1	11.7
Madrid, office	24.4	26.0	30.3	27.3
London (City), office	16.4	17.6	15.9	18.4
London (West End), office	21.4	24.8	19.7	24.3
Frankfurt, office	15.7	13.8	17.1	13.2
Frankfurt, retail	15.6	16.4	17.2	18.8
Frankfurt, industrial	11.7	9.2	11.4	9.7
Munich, retail	15.0	10.9	15.4	12.3
Munich, industrial	7.5	7.8	7.6	8.8
Hamburg, office	9.8	14.5	10.4	12.3
Hamburg, retail	11.7	6.5	13.7	6.5
Hamburg, industrial	9.8	6.6	8.7	6.4
Düsseldorf, office	8.3	9.8	7.7	4.5
Düsseldorf, retail	12.8	10.8	12.5	12.5

percentages). The efficient frontier line of the European property portfolios for the period 1975–89 shows the risk/return trade-off (Figure 2.3). The lowest risk level is 2.5% at a return of 11% and the highest possible portfolio return is 24% at a portfolio risk of 23.5%. The former is 2.5 times lower than the lowest risk of the individual market, namely the shopping centre in Hamburg (6.5%). Thus the portfolios are showing the risk reducing effect.

Combining market results in different types of property portfolio produces the following hypothetical examples of conservative, medium risk and aggressive portfolios, respectively.

1. Conservative portfolio (at 12% return level): industrial, Brussels 35%; offices, London (City) 14%, The Hague 15%; and retail, Hamburg 15%, Düsseldorf 6%.

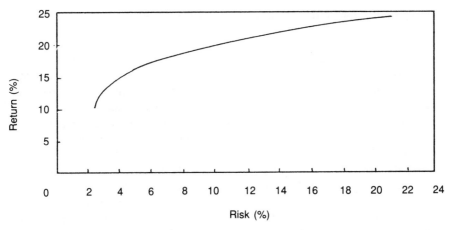

Figure 2.3   Efficient frontier line European market portfolios, no restrictions 1975–89. Reproduced with permission from Bodewes (1990)

2.   Medium risk portfolio (at 17% return level): offices, London 31%, Paris 28%; retail, Munich 28%.
3.   Aggressive portfolio (at 22% return level): offices, London (West End) 29%, Paris 21%, Madrid 50%.

It is remarkable that some countries or product markets do not play a part in such portfolios, namely: retail, Brussels, Paris; industrial, Randstad, Frankfurt, Munich, Hamburg; and offices, Düsseldorf, Hamburg. Also, the fraction of some property markets are very low: offices and shops in Brussels, Rotterdam and Frankfurt, industrial units in Paris and offices in Amsterdam.

The model allows differing portfolios and combinations of investments to be analysed; some of the more interesting to arise include the following observations (Bodewes, 1990).

1.   Not investing in London and Madrid has negative effects for risk and return; not investing in The Netherlands during this period did not have any effect for risk and return of the portfolios.
2.   Not investing in offices has a large negative effect on the portfolio efficiency; not investing in shops or industrial units has much less effect.
3.   Restricting the European portfolio to only the office asset class is not allowed in an efficient environment, although differences at higher return levels diminish. However, restricting investment to offices in Brussels, Paris, Amsterdam, Madrid, London and Frankfurt does not result in a different efficient frontier relative to investment in all office markets.
4.   As a result of the strong Dutch guilder, most of the local returns are higher than the return in Dutch currency, although the efficient frontier will be lower for a Japanese investor relative to the Dutch investor because of the stronger yen.

Some problems with efficient property portfolios

Rental levels are based on average market levels, deviations from which can occur because of differences in location and rental contracts attached to specific buildings. Thus property market effects can play a minor part in explaining periodic returns. Moreover, the property market is not very efficient in processing information, thus data can vary depending on the source. For instance, calculated returns for office markets sometimes differ strongly (low correlation) between two surveying firms, the consequences being that different types of information will produce different efficient portfolios and weaken the portfolio framework utilized.

Portfolios lying under, but close to, the efficient frontier and showing more or less the same risk return profile can show a substantially different composition. This can weaken the modern portfolio theory approach and render it less meaningful. In addition, and arising from the low liquidity character of property, switching between sectors as future prospects change is difficult. Furthermore, the efficient frontier is not a continuous line because of the indivisibility of property assets (large size of assets). Thus the choice of an optimum portfolio is difficult (Brown, 1991).

2.6 CONCLUSIONS

Institutional investment in property expanded widely in the post-war period; however, the property market is not homogeneous but characterized by wide variations. Location and sector influence both the expected return and associated risk. Investors normally seeking to reduce risk strive to achieve balanced portfolios with a lower volatility of return. The analysis presented in this discussion shows how the diversification of investment internationally can be used to reduce risk relative to investment within domestic markets. Hence there are attractions in international diversification into appropriate markets normally signified by low correlation coefficients between the respective countries.

With respect to the economic development of cities, property investors perceive that they can pick properties or select markets at the right time to enhance a portfolio, with rental income and the required rate of return as the two key sensitive variables. In particular the rental growth of a property is important for its investment value. Movement in rental value and market trends over time reflect the diversity of the economy, the specific quality elements of the market and the net absorption of rented space. In evaluating the investment performance of European cities the modern portfolio theory optimization programme permits the analysis of differing portfolios and combinations of investments, so allowing the modelling of scenarios ranging from conservative to aggressive. This type of approach clearly has an application in allowing investors to weight their portfolios towards specific locations or property types.

Investment decisions, subsequent wealth creation and employment growth can have major impacts on urban areas. Circumstances can and do arise where the interests of investors and government agencies overlap and are mutually supportive; however, there are other situations in which market choice is limited due to planning policy or development control activity. In a competitive environment the advantage would seem to rest with the investor who has the capability and freedom to target different city locations which fit into the desired portfolio structure.

REFERENCES

Bodewes, D.J. (1990) Beleggen in West-Europees onroerend goed, *Thesis Master Degree*, Katholieke Universiteit Nijmegen [in Dutch].

Brown, G.R. (1991) *Property Investment and the Capital Markets*, E & FN Spon, London.

Detoy, C.J. and Rabin, S.L. (1972) Office space, calculating demand, *Urban Land*, June, 4–13.

Goslings, J. and Petri, V. (1991) Beleggen in onroerend goed, *Economische en Statistiche Berichten (ESB)*, 18 September, 932–935 [in Dutch].

Jongejan, J. (1992) Cyclische fluctuaties bij het beleggen in onroerend goed, *VOGON Journal*, July, 17–21 [in Dutch].

MacIntosh, A.P.J. and Sykes, S.G. (1985) *A Guide to Institutional Property Investment*, Macmillan Press, London.

3

The Single European Market: impact on industrial property

_____ *C. Lizieri and R. Goodchild*

Business barriers within the 12 nation European Community were dismantled on 31 December 1992. European heads of government approved the move towards completion of the internal market in 1985. The Single European Act 1986 has the intention of creating:

'an area without internal frontiers in which the free movement of goods, services, persons and capital is ensured'.

The 12 nations of the Single European Market (SEM) have an estimated population of 341 million (compared with the USA's 244 million and Japan's 122 million) and a Gross Domestic Product (GDP) estimated in 1987 at $3791 billion (one billion is one thousand million here) (USA $4473 billion, Japan $1609 billion). Losses of $250 billion per year are attributed to market barriers in the community. Dismantling these barriers is likely to generate considerable economic restructuring, with inevitable geographical outcomes. Shifting patterns of supply and demand affect the property market. Growth areas generate the need for new buildings whereas property in declining areas exhibits lower real rental and capital values as functional requirements shift.

Much of the published work on the SEM has accepted the economic assumptions of the Cecchini report (Cecchini, 1988), which sees long term productive gains throughout the European Community largely due to scale economies. In this chapter it is argued that the SEM should be placed within a wider context of global industrial restructuring, encompassing changes in the organization of production, internationalization of business activity and the growing importance of scope economies. Such forces affect the design

of and demand for industrial premises and associated office/research establishments. These issues are examined and a framework provided which can
be used to assess sectoral and spatial outcomes.

These themes are considered in relation to two industrial sectors, the
brewing industry and the telecommunications industry. Although no sector
can be typical, nor represent all the changes that will occur after 1992, these
two sectors illustrate many important themes: the cost of barriers; the importance of ownership, acquisition and mergers; economies of scope across
plants; the role of public procurement policy; and the importance of
technological change.

In addition, though not directly considered in this chapter, German
unification, the upheavals in eastern Europe and the potential widening of
the European Community will obviously have a major impact, forcing the
Community to take on a new shape. It will particularly affect the hierarchy
of European cities with a major shift eastwards that may strengthen the
position of Berlin and Vienna (Hall, 1990). The shift of interest eastwards
and the opening up of the former communist economies could well further
marginalize the United Kingdom. Nonetheless, the economic forces outlined
here are still likely to shape the future demand for industrial and producer
services space.

3.1   MOVEMENT TOWARDS A SINGLE EUROPEAN MARKET

The aim of the Single European Act is to remove barriers to market access
and distortions due to national intervention. A common starting point for
the analysis of change after 1992 is Lord Cockfield's distinction between
three types of barrier: physical barriers – mainly frontier controls on goods,
service and labour movements; fiscal barriers – different rates and incidence
of VAT, excise duty, personal and corporate taxation; and technical barriers
– public procurement policy, restrictions on capital movements, technical
and regulative standards. The Cecchini report (Cecchini, 1988) uses this
classification to identify and, in part, cost the impact of these barriers. Table
3.1 shows the Cecchini estimates of border barriers to business.

Perhaps a better starting point is the matrix of impacts provided by
Pelkmans and Winters (1988) which subdivides markets into products,
services, capital and labour and examines four sets of measures: market
access; competitive conditions; market functioning; and sectoral policy.
Although interactions between and within markets must always be considered, it is possible to use this classification of measures as a framework for
assessing sectoral impacts.

Measures to ensure free market access include the abolition or reduction
of frontier controls, approximation of technical regulations, convergence of

Table 3.1 Cost of European Community border barriers. Reproduced with permission from Cecchini (1988)

Reason	Cost (10^6 ECU)
Administration	7500
Delays	415–830
Business foregone	4500–15 000
Government spending	500–1000
Total	12 915–24 330

tax rates, removal of licensing restrictions and quotas, abolition of exchange controls and capital flow restrictions, and securing rights of establishment. The European Economy (1988) report estimated initial gains of 2.2–2.7% of the GDP from improved market access.

Improvements in competitive conditions result from measures to eliminate or harmonize state aid to industry, liberalization of public procurement policies, ending price-fixing cartels and unified regulations controlling monopolies and mergers. Increased competition is assumed to increase technical efficiency, reduce factor and production costs and allow firms to enter into previously closed sectors. Liberalization of public procurement and reduction in subsidies to loss-making firms should reduce market fragmentation and lead to gains through economies of scale.

Proposals to improve market functioning tend to be sectorally specific or strategically long term – for example, through the co-ordination of research and development. Of direct relevance to the property industry are: harmonization of property law; harmonization of European company statutes; and mutual recognition of professional qualifications.

Harmonization of technical and environmental standards removes potential frictions to market access. The Commission has made a number of sector-specific policy proposals relating mainly to product and service markets such as directives on air fares and air capacity.

The official view of welfare gains from the completion of the SEM is set out in Table 3.2. However, such assessments rely heavily on conventional economic and industrial location theories. A main plank of the Cecchini arguments on growth after 1992 lies in the creation of optimally sized industrial operations following completion of the SEM. It is suggested that national barriers to trading lead to production units that are too small to benefit from economies of scale. Restructuring should thus lead to more efficient production and lower unit costs.

A second claimed source of economic benefit lies in the relocation of production to sites of optimum comparative advantage within the Community. With the removal of barriers, sectors should restructure to those site(s) providing the lowest relative costs of production. Traditional location

Table 3.2 Potential gains in economic welfare. Adapted from Cecchini (1988) and European Economy (1988)

Gain factor	Percentage of GDP
Removal of trade barriers	0.2–0.3
Removal of production barriers	2.0–2.4
Total barrier removal	2.2–2.7
Gains from economies of scale	2.1*
Gains from intensified competition	1.6*
Total market integration gains	2.1–3.7
Total gain	4.2–6.4

Value at 1988 prices: 174 billion to 258 billion ECUs.
* Upper band of estimate.

theory suggests that firms will locate at the site which minimizes factor input costs – capital, materials, labour and marketing. Distortions to optimum location would occur due to: national pricing and taxation policy; biases in public procurement; barriers to establishment and capital flow; and additional costs imposed by frontiers.

It is assumed that progress towards the SEM will progressively reduce these obstacles, leading to a European-wide restructuring of industry. Although researchers have noted a vast number of barriers, the incidence is uneven and there are few detailed studies of the effects. To counter the optimism of the European Community projections of consumer gains, a study of US-owned European manufacturers by the American Chamber of Commerce (quoted in Pelkmans and Winters, 1988) found 79% reporting no price effects from internal European trade barriers, although 25% reported difficulties due to rules of establishment and public procurement.

Nevertheless, there are likely to be sectors where the enhanced mobility of the SEM will lead to restructuring and relocation with consequent 'transitional' regional effects. Characteristics of such sectors will include: a tendency for national subsidy or preferential public procurement favouring domestic establishments; persistence of discriminatory rules of establishment preventing concentration and pan-European operation; scope for a well defined pan-European market (rather than local niche markets) currently hindered by fiscal inequalities or lack of harmonization of standards; and sectors where concentration will reap currently unrealized economies of scale. It should be noted that relocation costs may preserve 'suboptimum' operations.

The property implications of the Cecchini scenario follow from the twin forces of scale economies and relocation. Gains from scale economies imply sector shake-out as production becomes concentrated on a small number of large plants. Similarly, gains from relocation imply geographical shifts of demand. Although the theory of comparative advantage suggests that regional welfare is maximized in the long run through specialization, such a fundamental restructuring of European industry must be expected to produce 'transitional' inequalities with loser and gainer regions. Identification of gainer regions offers potential for supernormal profits, whereas the investment worth of industrial property in loser regions is likely to decrease sharply as reduced demand suppresses rents and initial yields increase in re-sponse to reduced growth potential and increased risk of voids and tenant default.

In the restructuring process, the role of transportation infrastructure will play a critical part. Britain's peripheral position in the expanded Europe and its own transport network is likely to pose a substantial barrier to the country's exploitation of the SEM. As British economic relations have historically been with the USA and the Commonwealth, Britain's transport links with mainland Europe are still underdeveloped. Furthermore, road and rail networks were developed with London as a focus; the need to fully integrate regional road and rail networks and refocus on the South Coast and East Anglian ports is acute. There are worries that commitment to upgrading transport networks may be insufficient to maintain a competitive position within the Community (Gerald Eve, 1990).

In mainland Europe there has been considerable activity in upgrading mainline railtracks and developing high speed train links such as France's TGV or MAGLEV systems (Nijkamp and Perrels, 1991). Developing rail links may determine the success of 'sunbelt' cities in the core triangle bounded by Munich, Milan and Toulouse, particularly as enhanced mobility may encourage the location of producer services in smaller cities (Conway and Bibby, 1991). Not all commentators agree: Bendixson (1989) suggests that locations along high speed routes are less affected by better rail links than anticipated (although the terminals at either end have an enhanced importance, strengthening the existing urban hierarchy), whereas Peschel (1990) and her co-workers produce evidence that there is at best a tenuous link between economic growth and economic potential (measured in terms of accessibility weighted by regional GDP).

3.2   ECONOMIC CHANGE: ALTERNATIVE PERSPECTIVES

The Cecchini model of scale economies arising from completion of the SEM is called into question by recent work on industrial organization. Changes within an industrial sector take a number of forms. At the highest level, growth and contraction of sectors as a whole may be identified. Owing to technological change, alterations in the pattern of demand or product innovation, new sectors spring up while others decline. This has led European industrial economists to use the idea of a staged product life cycle, further developing American industrial research (Vernon, 1979; Markusen, 1985). Products (and sectors) pass through innovatory and early growth phases with slow, followed by rapidly rising, sales volume before reaching maturity and, as sales fall away, obsolescence.

Technological and product innovation may trigger the growth phase. As growth proceeds, increasing economies of scale are available. Competition between producers lowers unit costs and may result in larger plants and concentration within the sector, with smaller plant closure. After product saturation occurs, economies of scale are unable to compensate for decreasing sales volumes and contraction sets in; substitution effects may accelerate the decline. There will be temporal and spatial variation in the contraction process as the least efficient (or the least protected) operations close first. The ability to create new products to replace those that are in maturity or decline may slow contraction.

Thus the SEM does not automatically open up the possibility of economies of scale and lower unit costs. A sector in late maturity or obsolescence, with near saturation of products, is unlikely to benefit merely through improvements to market access. Indeed, the removal of barriers to a substitute product may hasten the decline of that sector. In turn these sectoral changes have geographical impacts.

Recent industrial location research has focused on the mode of organization, ownership and linkages between firms, sometimes known as the 'markets and hierarchies' approach (Scott, 1986; Williamson, 1975). This standpoint concentrates on the dynamics of the internal organization, vertical and horizontal integration (and, more recently, disintegration) of firms and the locational outcomes of such dynamics. Developments in the automobile industry illustrate the value of such a framework. In particular, there is a changing relationship between assembly operations and components supply with the growth of 'just in time' delivery systems resulting in consequent diversion of inventory holding risks on to the suppliers and moves away from vertically integrated production. A geographical consequence of 'just in time' delivery systems is that component suppliers must locate near the assembly plant (Schoenberger, 1987), as with the development of component firms in industrial parks around Nissan in Sunderland (United Kingdom).

In other sectors, a distinction between tasks and levels may lead to a widely separated location of operations. Computer production is typically cited as an example. Research and development and skilled production tend to be concentrated in 'silicon valleys' in the prosperous regions of the developed world. Meanwhile, standard assembly and component manufacture take place in the newly industrialized countries or in the peripheral regions of the developed countries where labour costs are lower (Massey, 1984; Walker, 1988).

This approach casts a different light on the impacts of the SEM proposals. Although economies of scale remain important, our analysis places stronger emphasis on the role of ownership and the technical conditions of production. Technical innovation, in conventional appraisals of the impact of 1992, is either taken as given or is assumed to result from increased competition which, in driving down costs, forces more optimal use of capital and labour inputs. This secondary role seems seriously deficient given the major effects on the spatial division of labour that new production techniques can bring. Many analyses of the European Community proposals fail, additionally, to consider the rapid changes in the international division of labour and the growing importance of transnational corporations (TNCs) (Dicken, 1992). Although TNCs are still bound by national rules of operation, their business decisions should be governed by economic rationality for the company as a whole. As such, a sector 'dominated' by multinational ownership within Europe is likely to have already restructured towards a more efficient set of locations.

The process of restructuring following the completion of the Single Market is likely to further intensify merger and acquisition activity, particularly as firms seek to benefit not from economies of scale but rather from economies of scope – economies gained across a range of products and activities via shared research and development, marketing and information/financial services. Economies of scope are a powerful force for concentration and agglomeration, but in terms of ownership rather than scale and location of production. Ownership impacts, particularly when allied to freedom of mobility of capital, may be considerable in the regional context, particularly where there is a separation of head office and production plant. Capital is likely to flow into already concentrated core head office centres, casting doubt on rapid recovery from the regional impacts of restructuring. Within the British context, this may imply a continued dominance of the South-east at the expense of more peripheral regions. The analysis by Martin (1989) of venture capital provides evidence of this: London firms controlled 83% of the available capital pool and invested about two-thirds of this capital in the South-east.

Another body of theory that appears to have been ignored in published work about 1992 concerns the possible transition from 'Fordist' to 'flexible' production systems. This seems a serious omission given the potential impacts on industrial structure and by the fact that the 'Third Italy' model has been recognized in European Community industrial and regional policy. The 'flexibility' debate involves many intermingled strands of theory and has been subject to much research and criticism (for reviews, see Lizieri, 1991; Hirst and Zeitlin, 1991; Malecki, 1986; 1991).

At the risk of oversimplifying the strands of the flexibility debate, the 'Fordist' regime is characterized by high volume standardized production based on vertical industrial integration, assembly line techniques and mass consumption of those products within a formalized labour/wage bargaining system. Although the system was highly successful in promoting growth and benefiting from scale economies, a combination of product saturation, import substitution and the spread of mass production to newly industrializing countries and structural inflation through (in part) the wage/labour bargain has eroded the advantages of Fordism (Piore and Sabel, 1984).

Meanwhile, technical innovation, particularly through the use of computer-aided design and computer numerically controlled (CNC) machine tools, has transformed the nature of production. In particular, shorter batch runs become both profitable and desirable, linked to niche marketing. The key is seen as a flexible response to a changing market-place. The large vertically integrated production unit is less able to cope with this changed environment than smaller units of production with strong horizontal linkages, sharing research and development facilities.

Such a 'disintegrated' production system would be possible within an industrial conglomerate; however, attention has focused on industrial regions with closely knit networks of independent firms. A much cited example is the textile region of Emilia-Romagna in Italy where, it is claimed, small businesses using skilled labour, shared knowledge and capital react flexibly and cost effectively to the demands of the international fashion market (Brusco, 1986). Although there is considerable controversy about the importance and extent of such changes, flexibility has become a leitmotif in many industrial sectors.

Flexible production systems and short batch niche product runs alter the locational impact of labour. To operate CNC machinery, the labour force must be skilled and adaptable, with a craft ethos. Assembly plant operations, by contrast, seek a low cost, semi-skilled pliant labour force. If the flexibility model has validity, there should be more rapid growth and greater local multiplier effects in regions dominated by flexible production, whereas regions dominated by assembly plants and Fordist production techniques are likely to experience sluggish growth and be more vulnerable to recessions, restructuring and shifts in patterns of demand. This tendency will be magnified where the region is dominated by branch plants with external ownership as capital will tend to flow away from the region and hence the vulnerability to closures.

3.3   ECONOMIC CHANGE: REGIONAL AND PROPERTY IMPLICATIONS

As with the economic forces underlying conventional analysis, the restructuring implied by these theories of location and development will lead to shifts in the pattern of demand for industrial property – an area largely ignored in published work on the SEM (although see Hsia and Green, 1991). Traditional criteria for assessing future demand may prove inadequate in the new environment. Those regions with a high skill base, flexible labour and production technologies and benefiting from agglomeration economies are likely to thrive, whereas those dominated by more traditional large scale vertically integrated production sites and branch plants are more vulnerable. As Malecki (1991) notes:

> 'a plant's "life" may be relatively short in any location, particularly if it is tied to the production of a single product or product line. Only more "flexible" plants can weather the turmoil of uncertainty'.

Depreciation will thus become a critical variable in the assessment of development and investment worth. Buildings that are insufficiently adaptable will quickly become functionally obsolescent; equally significantly, the long term rental value of property in branch plant/assembly dominated regions must be uncertain. Such impacts alter the financial viability of industrial property for developers and investors.

In maintaining functionality and ensuring the long term demand for industrial premises, buildings need to maximize adaptability. This is particularly pronounced in relation to smaller high technology firms where, it has been argued, occupiers need to be able to shift their use of space between production, research and development, and marketing functions. Henneberry (1987; in press) casts doubt on the extent to which firms do shift space. What is clear, however, is that the functional requirements of firms in growth areas are for smaller but higher specification units. It is worth noting that the United Kingdom's institutional lease sits uneasily in this climate of rapid change in production technology, but with institutional funding a significant element in the development of business and industrial parks (particularly in the south of Britain) it is difficult to obtain more flexible letting terms. This may ultimately damage Britain's competitiveness in developing, maintaining and attracting high technology production industry in the completed market (Lizieri, in press).

Completion of the SEM is likely to intensify the separation of branch plant and head office/research and development activity, through corporate mergers, acquisitions and the out-sourcing of business and producer services. As Daniels (1991) notes, business and producer services are strongly concentrated in a small number of national capitals and a few other major cities. Globalization of business, market deregulation, mergers and acquisitions in the service sector (as evidenced in international accountancy and consultancy) is likely to confirm the dominance of existing centres in the European hierarchy. Daniels (1991) also notes the influence of investors (in infrastructure and the built environment) and of inertia in preserving existing dominance.

Although improved communications and information technology allow the separation of assembly and decision-making functions, they also allow decentralization, particularly of back office and administrative functions.

This may occur from cities where urban diseconomies (environment, congestion, occupation costs and inadequate investment in infrastructure) outweigh agglomeration economies. The key locational variable for business and producer services appears to be the availability of a skilled labour pool, tending to reinforce agglomeration economies and existing core regions at the expense of peripheral regions. This, in turn, translates into demand for office space.

3.4   SECTORAL IMPACTS: TWO CASE STUDIES

Possible changes in European industry, post-1992, are explored in relation to the following sectors: the brewing industry and the telecommunications industry. Although these sectors cannot represent the whole of manufacturing industry, each possesses characteristics that serve to illustrate the forces described earlier.

The brewing industry is a sector where considerable concentration has already occurred within most European countries, a process likely to continue in the SEM. This concentration has geographical implications, with plant closures a characteristic of the process of rationalization. The pattern of demand in Europe is strongly influenced by different tax structures which should be harmonized after 1992, whereas entry barriers due to local regulations and standards should be progressively removed.

The telecommunications industry has, until recently, been dominated by the public owned postal, telegraphic and telephone agencies (PTTs) with national provision protected from competition. The SEM rules on public procurement should have a considerable effect on the structure of this sector. However, with a trend towards privatization and, in particular, with the growing convergence between telecommunications and the information technology sectors, technological factors and the growing strength of a small number of international companies may be more critical than the changes to competition policy within the European Community.

Brewing industry

The brewing industry developed as a highly fragmented activity characterized by small scale production due to brewing methods, lack of portability and high transport costs. This last constraint was removed with the development of the railway network but the sophistication of the industry followed developments in refrigeration, pasteurization and, above all, biological development of purified yeast strains. This in turn led to the rapid dominance of bottom-fermented (lager) type beers in the European market with only

Table 3.3 Import penetration in the brewing industry. Imports by volume, percentage of national consumption. Reproduced with permission from Hoare Govett (1988)

Country	Wine	Beer	Spirits
United Kingdom	90	5	25
France	1	12	30
Italy	1	16	13
Spain	2	2	10
Former West Germany	37	1	25

the United Kingdom retaining a majority consumption of top-fermented (ale) beers up to the 1960s. Even in the United Kingdom, lager beers now outsell ales. Nevertheless, the brewing industry long remained bound within national and cultural borders.

Given the existence of considerable economies of scale with increasing plant capacity and the highly capital intensive nature of industrialized brewing, there is considerable concentration in all European Community countries, with the notable exception of (the former) West Germany. Plant capacities have increased and the number of producers declined. In the United Kingdom, average plant size in 1965 was 17 700 hl with 274 plants; by 1986 there were only 119 plants, but the average capacity was 460 000 hl. Similar effects can be seen in The Netherlands (1965 – 32 plants, 169 000 hl; 1986 – 20 plants, 899 000 hl). Only the former West Germany, with 1190 plants with an average size of only 79 000 hl, bucks the trend. Economies of scale and the cyclical nature of demand have hastened closure of marginal producers.

The growing scale of operation has led to the search for non-domestic markets (Table 3.3). This, however, has been achieved not through direct export but through acquisition and licensing arrangements. The European market leader, Heineken, acquired market share through takeovers of Dreher in Italy and Albra in France to complement its dominance of Dutch and Greek markets, whereas Whitbread produce Heineken under licence in the United Kingdom. Similarly Skol, based in The Netherlands but owned by Allied, expanded in The Netherlands by acquiring D'Oranjeboom and Breda. Domestic markets still tend to be dominated by locally produced beers: BSN in France, Heineken in The Netherlands and Stella Artois in Belgium.

Competition, concentration and the destruction of local markets has not led to increased product variety for consumers. There now exists a homogeneous product and a highly standardized market where 80% of European sales are of lager. One strategy has been the sale of 'premium' lagers alongside standard domestic products. This strongly relies, however, on image differentiation rather than product differentiation, which in turn requires

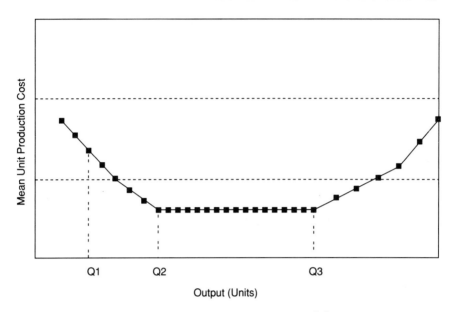

Figure 3.1   Long term average cost curve. Average cost falls as output increases until Q2. The curve is horizontal until Q3 when diseconomies of scale set in

considerable marketing and advertising expenditure. The L-shaped cost curve (Figure 3.1) means that economies of scale occur not at plant level over a certain point, but at firm level with economies of scope through marketing, research and development. It is these economies that act as a barrier to market entry for differentiated niche products.

One characteristic of the brewing industry in Europe is the considerable extent of forward vertical integration into distribution through the tied-house and brewery contract systems. The direct linkages between brewer and bar/café vary considerably across Europe. In The Netherlands virtually all cafés are contracted to breweries; in Belgium about 80% are tied. In the late 1960s about 75% of British outlets were tied but this has declined considerably; in 1985 the figure stood at 58%. Here European Community harmonization and competition policy could be significant as the brewery contract system represents a formidable market entry barrier. The Monopolies and Mergers Commission report on the United Kingdom brewing industry, recommending a separation of production and outlet operations, has led to considerable upheavals in the industry with marked property implications.

In summary, the European brewing industry can be characterized by three trends: growing concentration of ownership both within nations and across the Community; a growing dominance of economies of scale and scope at firm rather than plant level; and vertical integration providing a barrier to market entry.

Table 3.4 Estimated gains in telecommunications from the Single European Market. Reproduced with permission from Cecchini (1988)

Product	Standardization	Liberalization	
		Partial	Full
Central switching	0.45–0.07	0.8	1.3
Transmission	0.2	0.4	0.5
Terminal equipment	0.1	0.4	1.0
Other	0.1	0.4	0.9
Total	0.85–1.1	2.0	3.7

The major developments after 1992 are thus likely to be at a firm level through merger and acquisition. There are only limited gains to be made in terms of scale of operation at a plant level with constraints on the distance that bulk beers can be transported. Thus, although there is likely to be further rationalization of production within national markets, the major Community impacts are likely to be corporate and to affect office markets both for head offices and for associated business services.

Telecommunications industry

For about 100 years, the telecommunications industry was stable. Manufacturers were largely dependent on investment plans of publicly owned PTTs who tended to purchase within domestic markets. Since the mid-1970s there have been profound changes driven by technology and deregulation. Increasing convergence of computing, electronics and telecommunications has led to rapid product innovation and a shift towards the business market. Digitalization of switching and transmission forms and indeed new transmission techniques increase the number of functions performed outside the PTT network.

With respect to output, 90% of telecommunications equipment is manufactured in OECD countries. The market is dominated by switching and transmission equipment (56 and 18%, respectively, by market share according to Dang Nguyen, 1985). It is this area that has been most highly protected in European markets, with public procurement policies and fragmented national standards providing severe entry barriers. The completion of the Single Market aims to reduce these barriers through the imposition of common standards and competition rules. New regulations on procurement, harmonization of tariffs and ending restrictions on the use of leased lines should further remove market rigidities and lead to restructuring (Table 3.4).

With respect to switching and transmission, the key factor is the high research and development costs required to produce a new public exchange system. Roobeck (in deJong, 1988) suggests that the research and development costs of digital exchanges range from $500 million to $1 billion and for optic fibre exchanges from $2 to $3 billion. For example, the development of GEC/Plessey/BT's System X cost $1400 million. Given these costs and the limited scale economies obtainable, there is likely to be a considerable shake-out in telecommunications. Bjorn Svedberg, president of Ericsons, has predicted that only seven firms will survive: AT&T, Northern Telecom, two Japanese firms and just three European companies.

The need to share development costs on products with relatively short life spans has led to joint ventures, mergers and acquisitions throughout Europe as exemplified by Siemens' purchase of GTE and the absorption of the computer manufacturer Nixdorf. This merger points to another trend, the corporate convergence of computing and telecommunications producers, often crossing the boundaries of economic blocs (AT&T with Olivetti, IBM and Ericcson, for example). The completion of the SEM should see an acceleration of the trend towards concentration.

In diversifying risk and uncertainty, many major producers out-source research and development and the supply of specialized components and software. This activity is focused in regions with existing concentrations of high tech industry where skilled labour and knowledge pools allow the interface between research and small batch production. These same areas are likely to dominate the growing market for telecommunication services Value Added Networks and end-user equipment made possible by the more competitive environment resulting from the erosion of the PTTs' monopoly positions. The labour skills and techniques used accord closely with the flexible production model outlined here and the occupational requirements are again for high specification, small, flexible properties.

In the competitive market for end-user products and services, Britain and France have an initial advantage. The latter benefited from the early commitment of France Telecom to provide digital services for customers, whereas the early privatization of BT and language advantages (giving ready access to US software) aids the British position. The benefits of growth would initially accrue to the existing high tech areas of South-east England (the M4 corridor) and East Anglia, further exacerbating regional inequalities. Once again, the institutional leaseform is an inertial force that may harm competitiveness and hinder the development of suitable buildings.

Thus in telecommunications, gains are likely to occur through greater market access for end-user equipment and information service suppliers. Given the high value of these products, transport costs and a peripheral position are not major locational factors. However, agglomeration economies and the existence of a highly skilled and adaptable labour force are critical, tending to reinforce existing concentrations of high technology activity.

The United Kingdom's current comparative advantage could be eroded if institutional inertia limits the provision of suitable flexible space. With respect to switching and transmission, the high research and development costs will lead to shake-out, further concentration through mergers, acquisitions and joint ventures, with corporate moves crossing the boundary between communications and computing industries. In the major production sector only a limited number of sales are possible, precluding major scale economies at plant level, while in the end-user market a rapidly changing set of niche markets requires maximum flexibility in industrial organization and occupational space.

3.5   CONCLUSIONS

Completion of the Single Market is likely to result in the restructuring of industry across Europe. Conventional analyses have emphasized economies of scale and plant level rationalization. Such approaches have tended to underplay the corporate role in restructuring and changes in production technology. The sector studies outlined in this discussion cast doubt on many of the assumptions about economic welfare gains after 1992. This is not to suggest that there will be no relocation of industrial activity in Europe over and above mergers and acquisitions. Furthermore, the restructuring of industry, given the uneven pattern of economic activity, will produce regional effects, transitional or otherwise. However, a more realistic focus on production technologies, locational forces and corporate activity provides a stronger framework for analysis of property impacts. The importance of economies of scope and corporate activity suggests that industrial change is likely to provoke shifts in demand in the office sector as much as for industrial premises.

Economies of scope and agglomeration economies will tend to reinforce existing concentration in and around high order urban centres, although improved transport networks may boost smaller cities with favoured locations. Further vertical and horizontal disintegration and the out-sourcing of business and producer services seems probable.

Industrial growth sectors are likely to emphasize skilled labour and flexible production systems; such sectors will show close links between research, development and production activities. The built form to accommodate these industries must also emphasize flexibility, both in physical and functional configuration and institutional arrangements. Buildings that are not adaptable are likely to rapidly become functionally obsolete and consequently suffer depreciation of capital and rental values. Traditional production techniques based on standardized batch production, specialization and vertical integration look vulnerable in a rapidly innovating market-place.

Thus developers of, and investors in, industrial property must consider both the functional flexibility of the built form and regional/sectoral growth prospects. It is difficult to identify regions which might benefit from relocations, new operations or growth as realization of locational advantage is complex. It is possible, however, to identify a set of characteristics that can influence locational decisions and which may be used to classify regional potential. These include: labour force characteristics; land and building availability; resource endowment; market access; transport infrastructure; availability of capital; business environment; agglomeration economies; and regional and local incentives.

Firms faced with a locational decision must balance these factors. However, individual decisions interact. Thus in South-east England, the advantages of highly skilled labour, availability of capital, agglomeration economies, highly developed business environments and favourable transport links with mainland Europe must be set against limited land availability and high occupancy costs, housing shortages, high wages and congestion costs, which are a consequence of those locational advantages.

The importance of ownership patterns and the segmented nature of production adds a further economic complexity in that an industrial sector, even though it has growth potential, does not necessarily bestow benefit on a region containing that industry. The growing internationalization of ownership is likely to lead to flows and concentrations of capital that are not related to productive activity. Capital flows are likely to be towards the financial markets and away from peripheral regions.

Real estate investment and development has also internationalized in recent years and, with the advent of the SEM, many commercial agents in the United Kingdom have established operations and joint ventures across Europe and other non-European centres. However, larger institutional investors have tended to limit investment in industrial property, partly due to the perceived high risk and partly due to the small lot size in relation to management costs. Where the industrial building requirement is for small flexible units with flexible lease terms international investment seems unlikely; instead this provides more scope for the corporate sector and local investors/developers to become involved in provision. However, inertia and inflexibility in development, funding and financing may act as a brake to efficient industrial reorganization, limiting gains from market completion.

The role of industrial property as a facilitator of change is a neglected area. Many of the gains in economic activity that should accrue from the SEM could be frustrated if suitable business premises are not available in the right places. However, concentration on rationalization and scale economies within the European Community rather than on global forces, corporate activity, scope economies and industrial linkages may send the wrong signals to developers and investors and frustrate the aims of European economic integration.

REFERENCES

Bendixson, T. (1989) *Transport in the Nineties: The Shaping of Europe*, RICS, London.

Brusco, S. (1986) Small firms and industrial districts: the experience of Italy. In: *New Firms and Regional Development in Europe* (Eds D. Keeble and E. Wever), Croom Helm, London.

Cecchini, P. (1988) *The European Challenge, 1992*, Gower, Aldershot.

Conway, K. and Bibby, P. (1991) European transportation systems. In: *Cambridge Econometrics, European Regional Prospects*, Cambridge Econometrics, Cambridge, pp. 15–23.

Dang Nguyen, G. (1985) Telecommunications: a challenge to the old order. In: *Europe and the New Technologies* (Ed. M. Sharp), Frances Pinter, London.

Daniels, P. (1991) Business services and the European urban hierarchy. In: *Cambridge Econometrics, European Regional Prospects*, Cambridge Econometrics, Cambridge, pp. 39–48.

de Jong, H.W. (Ed.) (1988) *The Structure of European Industry*, Kluwer, Dordrecht.

Dicken, P. (1992) *Global Shift*, Paul Chapman Publishing, London.

European Economy (1988) *The Economics of 1992*, Vol. 35, Office for Official Publications of the EC, Luxembourg.

Gerald Eve (1990) *Road Transport in England*, Gerald Eve, London.

Hall, P. (1990) Remapping urban Europe, *The Planner*, **76**(8), 9.

Henneberry, J. (1987) Occupiers and their use of accommodation on science parks and high technology developments, *Land Development Studies*, **4**(2), 109–144.

Henneberry, J. High technology firms and the property market. In: *Property and Industrial Development: Towards a New Research Agenda* (Eds A. Pratt and R. Ball), Routledge, London, in press.

Hoare Govett (1988) In: *Nineteen Ninety-two: An Unworkable Utopia* (Eds M. Cusack and L. Harte), Hoare Govett, London.

Hirst, P. and Zeitlin, J. (1991) Flexible specialisation versus post-Fordism: theory, evidence and policy implications, *Economy and Society*, **20**(1), 1–56.

Hsia, M. and Green, M. (1991) European industrial property location, *Property Management*, **9**(1), 51–65.

Lizieri, C. (1991) The property market in a changing world economy, *Journal of Property Valuation and Investment*, **9**(3), 201–214.

Lizieri, C. Property ownership, leasehold forms and industrial change. In: *Property and Industrial Development: Towards a New Research Agenda* (Eds A. Pratt and R. Ball), Routledge, London, in press.

Malecki, E. (1986) Technological imperatives and modern corporate strategy. In: *Work, Production, Territory* (Eds A. Scott and M. Storper), Allen & Unwin, Boston.

Malecki, E. (1991) *Technology and Economic Development*, Longmans, Harlow.

Markusen, A. (1985) *Profit Cycles, Oligopoly and Regional Development*, MIT Press, Cambridge MA.

Martin, R. (1989) The growth and geographical anatomy of venture capitalism in the UK, *Regional Studies*, **23**(5), 389–404.

Massey, D. (1984) *Spatial Divisions of Labour*, Macmillan, Basingstoke.

Nijkamp, P. and Perrels, A. (1991) New transport systems in Europe. In: *Cities of the 21st Century* (Eds J. Brotchie, M. Batty, P. Hall and P. Newton), Longmans, Harlow.

Pelkmans, J. and Winters, A. (1988) *Europe's Domestic Market, Chatham House Papers 43*, Royal Institute of International Affairs, Routledge, London.

Peschel, K. (1990) Spatial effects of the completion of the European Single Market, *Built Environment*, **16**(1), 11–29.

Piore, M. and Sabel, C. (1984) *The Second Industrial Divide*, Basic Books, New York.

Schoenberger, E. (1987) Technical and organization change in automobile production: spatial implications, *Regional Studies*, **21**(3), 199–214.

Scott, A.J. (1986) Industrial organisation and locations, *Economic Geography*, **62**(3), 215–231.

Vernon, R. (1979) The product cycle in a new international environment, *Oxford Bulletin of Economics and Statistics*, **41**, 255–267.

Walker, R. (1988) The geographical organisation of production systems, *Society and Space*, **6**(4), 377–408.

Williamson, O.E. (1975) *Markets and Hierarchies*, The Free Press, New York.

4

Financing of property development

A. Adair

Currently a wide range of sources and techniques are available for the financing of property development and investment. Property and finance have always been linked, but over the past two decades financing instruments have expanded significantly in the United Kingdom in terms of their sophistication and complexity and they now encompass the international financial markets. The markets for finance capital are extensively globalized and property development has been stimulated by their increased deregulation and liberalization. Indeed, current property financing practices are characterized by innovation, dynamic competition among financiers and the potential for harnessing short, medium and long term finance (Pugh, 1991; 1992). The type and cost of property finance has a major impact on development schemes. Cadman (1984) uses the analogy that 'he who pays the piper calls the tune' to indicate the importance and power of both finance and financiers. The collapse of a major property company (Mountleigh) and the single largest development begun in the 1980s (Canary Wharf) as a result of cash flow problems reinforces this point.

The various financing techniques which have evolved to fund property development and investment activities are outlined in this chapter. The economic context of financing is presented and the influence of economic conditions is analysed through a brief examination of the history of property financing from 1945 to the present. Debt and equity sources of finance are the principal methods of funding development and investment in the private sector. The role of tax based methods, grants and incentives are also discussed, particularly in relation to urban regeneration. Unlike town centre, suburban or greenfield sites most inner urban regenerated areas have not seen the same scale of investment or development activity (Howes, 1988). The funding of development projects is limited and lenders are more cautious about financing schemes in such economically disadvantaged locations.

4.1   ECONOMICS OF PROPERTY FINANCING

Property financing generally involves three main participants. The developer or borrower creates the property asset normally using short term finance from a commercial or merchant bank, whereas long term finance is usually provided by an institution (Asson, 1991). For the borrower the optimum form of financing represents, *ceteris paribus*, the most preferred way of raising capital, whereas for both short and long term investors it is the best way of using capital (Harvey, 1992).

Short and long term finance reflect the two main stages in the development process. The two stages display different degrees of risk and therefore require different types of finance (Newell, 1977). The construction stage is relatively short, generally lasting from two to five years. Short term finance is required for the construction period and is generally available for a maximum of three years. The limited security of the incomplete building means that such finance may be relatively expensive, although the actual rate of interest depends on the financial status of the developer and the quality of the scheme. The developer will try to minimize the construction period to reduce interest charges. At the end of the development period the property may be sold and a profit realized, or it may be refinanced on a long term basis if the developer wishes to retain it as an investment. A successful developer will wish to retain some of the better developments as collateral and income against future borrowing. The main sources of short term finance are the commercial banks, merchant banks and United Kingdom subsidiaries of foreign banks (Balchin and Kieve, 1982; Harvey, 1992).

The second stage comprises the sale or letting of the property over the long term period of the economic or physical life of the building. Long term finance is secured on the completed building and is therefore less risky. Traditionally, the margin between interest payable and rental income provides an indication of the security of the loan (Harvey, 1992). Long term funding is therefore normally less expensive than short term finance. The main providers are the pension funds and life insurance companies who have long term liabilities and have come to dominate the property investment market since the 1950s.

The short and long term financing scenarios are also found in those sectors of the market characterized by owner-occupation; for example, residential property (Bourke, 1992). The developer, on the basis of a short term loan, usually from a bank, builds the houses which are then sold to occupiers who finance their purchase by taking out a mortgage, usually from a building society. Although building societies are not allowed to be house builders, they have promoted development in inner city areas, e.g. the Nationwide Housing Trust (Cadman, 1984).

The revolution in property financing has produced financial mechanisms which have bridged the gap between short and long term capital markets, for example, revolving short term credit, banker's guarantees in underwriting facilities and securitization (Pugh, 1992). However, there are dangers in utilizing short term credit over the longer term. Problems of illiquidity or cash flow difficulties may result in the stopping of short term credit, so leaving the developer with the problem of repayment. Such difficulties were encountered by a number of developers in the 1970s and again in the early 1990s.

4.2 HISTORICAL PERSPECTIVE OF FINANCING

Property development is cyclical in nature and is integrally linked to the performance of the underlying economy, in particular to the financial and investment markets on which it depends for its capital funding. The evolutionary growth of property development, finance and investment is covered extensively in published work (Cadman, 1984; Brett, 1986; 1990; Darlow, 1988; 1989; Cadman *et al.*, 1991). A brief history of property financing covering the four distinct phases of expansion since 1950 is outlined in this section. Particular attention is paid to the impact of inflation, the evolution of financing techniques and the shift from equity to debt during the 1980s.

The post-war building boom began in 1954, primarily to satisfy the pent-up demand for commercial property. Developers identified opportunities and assembled sites while short term finance was provided by the clearing banks, usually against a pre-arranged fixed interest mortgage from an insurance company. Initially, bank loans were expensive and difficult to obtain, so long term funding was provided by the insurance companies on approximately 65% of the value of the completed development. The developer had to ensure that this value threshold was at least equal to the development costs and that the rent roll achieved from the development covered the interest and capital repayments of the mortgage. Some developers retained developments rather than selling to an institution and so acquired property company functions.

Traditionally, the insurance companies took no part in development risk, being only bound to acquire the development on completion and when fully let. In the later part of the 1950s the institutions began to move from a traditionally passive to a more active financing role. They began to seek a larger share of development profit by entering sale and leaseback transactions with developers and by forging closer links with property companies, including the acquisition of ordinary shares in such companies.

The development boom of the late 1950s was concentrated on office development, primarily in the south-east of England. However, over-supply and recession caused a slump in demand in the early 1960s. This decade is characterized by the advent of inflation as an important influence in the general economy. As a result of inflation insurance companies granted fewer fixed interest mortgages and became more interested in participating in rental growth. Indeed, the arrival of the 'reverse yield gap', the initial short-fall of rental income over mortgage interest and capital repayments, rein-forced the desire of insurance companies to become property owners to benefit from rental growth. Fiscal measures further reinforced this trend. The corporation tax and capital gains tax provisions of the 1965 Finance Act introduced a system of double taxation on property company profits which was especially disadvantageous for tax-favoured institutions holding property company shares. The later 1960s saw insurance companies increasing their investment in property and the arrival of pension funds and other invest-ment media (Cadman *et al.*, 1991).

Political, fiscal and economic factors in the late 1960s created the condi-tions for the next property boom. The introduction of planning restrictions, particularly office development permits, led to a reduced supply of new offices and a corresponding increase in rental values for available space. Property was also being increasingly viewed as a secure investment and a superior long term hedge against inflation. The institutions began to compete for the best investments by providing short term finance to developers. Thus the traditional boundaries between short and long term finance began to blur. Furthermore, some institutions took on the role of developer, either on a project basis or by acquisition of property companies, to secure the best property investments.

Such conditions produced the second post-war property boom in 1970. The Conservative government, wishing to expand the economy, increased the money supply to stimulate investment in manufacturing industry. Much of this new money found its way into the property market. Indeed, the removal of credit controls, low interest rates and high inflation attracted money into the property sector (Reid, 1983). Bank lending to property companies increased dramatically, particularly among the secondary banks. However, the economic boom was short lived and the ensuing recession with resultant increases in interest rates had a crippling effect on the property industry. The combination of a rent freeze on commercial property, high interest rates, proposals for a first-lettings tax and other deflationary policies resulted in the collapse of the property market in early 1974.

Nevertheless, by 1976 the property market had begun to revive and the reduction in short term interest rates and stable rental values encouraged the institutions to return. Indeed, by the end of 1977 the market for prime investments had been re-established and yields were returning to low levels comparable with 1971. However, such low yields meant that mortgage

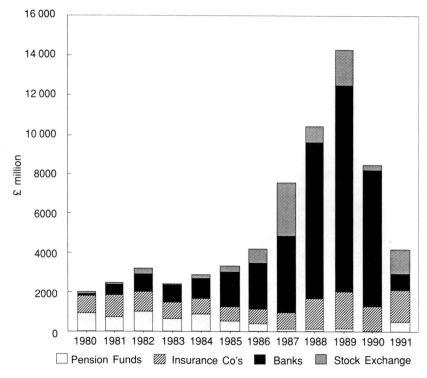

Figure 4.1 Sources of property finance. Reproduced with permission from Debenham Tewson & Chinnocks

finance for development became restricted. Sale and leasebacks were available from the institutions and forward sales were popular. The late 1970s saw the banks returning to the market.

At the beginning of the 1980s the institutions were the prime investors in commercial and industrial property, accounting for approximately 83% of the £2168 million invested in 1982 (Cadman *et al.*, 1991). However, as the decade progressed a major change occurred with a significant shift from institutional to bank finance. The institutional criteria for investing in property became very narrow and institutions began to disinvest in industrial and to a lesser extent in office property from the mid-1980s (Morley, 1989).

From 1980 to 1985 the flow of money into property remained fairly consistent, but then increased dramatically, reaching a peak in 1989 (Figure 4.1). The demand-led property boom of 1987–8 saw the banks as the main providers of development finance, reflecting in part the greater entrepreneurship and competition associated with deregulation and the globalization of capital markets. Indeed, the change in market structure has been radical, with the annual level of lending at its peak in 1989 being ten times the

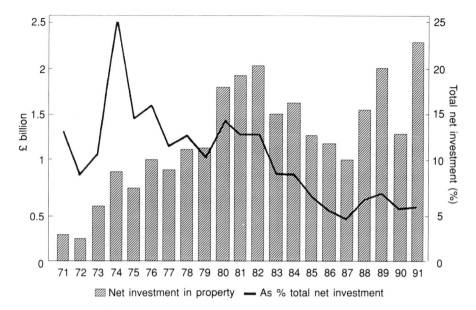

Figure 4.2   Net United Kingdom institutional investment in property in the United Kingdom as a percentage of total net investment. Reproduced with permission from Savills Commercial Research – Financing Property 1992

average in the first half of the decade (Debenham Tewson & Chinnocks, 1991). Although there has been a significant decline in lending since 1989, loans outstanding to property companies reached £39 billion (one billion is one thousand million) at the end of February 1992, which even after allowing for inflation is three times the peak reached in 1974 (Savills, 1992).

In fact, there has been a decline in net direct investment by institutions in the United Kingdom since 1971 (Figure 4.2). In 1980 the percentage of total investment in the property sector was 13%, whereas at the end of 1991 property accounted for 5.8% of the total investment (£2.2 billion). Apart from an upsurge in 1988–9 following the worldwide stock-market crash, the decade has witnessed a consistent decline in institutional investment. Schiller (1990) regards this movement as the restoration of the long term trend, with debt being the principal form of property investment before 1974. Reasons for the decline include poor investment performance when compared with the United Kingdom and overseas equity markets and government policy of maintaining relatively low levels of inflation. The traditional view of property as a hedge against inflation is ineffectual in such circumstances.

A significant aspect of bank lending in the 1980s is the increasing involvement of foreign banks in property development in the United Kingdom

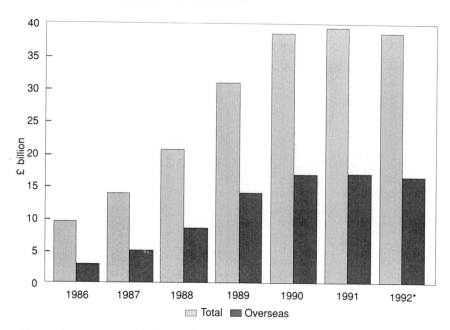

Figure 4.3 Overseas lending to the United Kingdom property sector. Reproduced with permission from Savills Commercial Research – Financing Property 1992. *To end February 1992

(Figure 4.3). Over the decade their share of the market has more than doubled, from 18% of outstanding loans in 1980 to 43% in 1992. Total lending by overseas banks reached £16.7 billion at the end of February 1992. Over this period the proportion of loans attributable to American banks has remained stable (approximately 7%), whereas European (primarily Swedish) and Japanese lenders have been increasingly active (Debenham Tewson & Chinnocks, 1989). Indeed, Swedish and Japanese investors have largely invested in the London market and together account for approximately 75% of the overseas investment (Debenham Tewson & Chinnocks, 1991) (Figure 4.4).

Stimulated by the approach of the Single European Market in 1992 and a favourable investment climate in the United Kingdom, foreign investors have provided both equity and debt finance to property companies in the United Kingdom. Furthermore, both Japanese and Scandinavian banks have become involved in direct development. However, after four years of considerable growth, recent evidence indicates a levelling off in the inflow of overseas capital (Debenham Tewson & Chinnocks, 1991).

Another significant aspect of property financing in the 1980s is the increasing globalization of international capital markets, producing a wider range of innovative debt and equity finance instruments for property

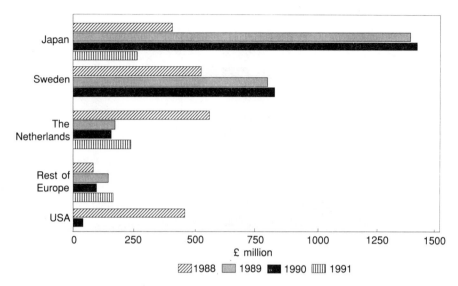

Figure 4.4 Main overseas investors. Reproduced with permission from Debenham Tewson & Chinnocks

companies (Figure 4.5). However, since 1986 hybrid financial instruments and structured finance have become less attractive. The use of revolving credit has fluctuated with movements in interest rates. Rights issues have replaced term loans as the most popular form of financing in 1991. In the first nine months of the year property companies raised just over £2 billion via the stock-market, most of which was used to repay short term debt (Savills, 1992).

The problems of repaying large amounts of short term debt have been reinforced by the collapse of Mountleigh and Canary Wharf. Mountleigh had a meteoric rise in the 1980s, beginning the decade as a small textile firm and growing to a £400 million plus property company by 1989. Despite raising £96 million in a controversial rights issue in 1991 the company found itself with cash flow problems when it failed to sell a retail scheme in the West Midlands for £125 million. With repayment deadlines due on £70 million in bonds, the company ran out of alternative funding sources. Mountleigh was placed in receivership with debts of £550 million to banks and bond holders. The two main loan facilities consist of £329 million lent by Barclays and a £38 million syndicated loan led by Citibank. There are two overdrafts and bond holders are owed £144 million.

The Olympia and York development at Canary Wharf in London's Dock-lands began in 1987 and the construction of the planned one million m² of office space was expected to take seven to ten years to complete. By 1992

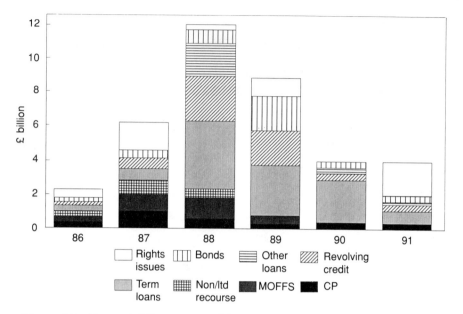

Figure 4.5   Usage of different types of finance. Reproduced with permission from Savills Commercial Research – Financing Property 1992

only 450 000 m² of space had been built and of this only 11% was occupied. The Canadian based property company required a further £300 million advance to complete the project and to pay interest on existing bank loans. However, the banks would not provide the extra finance and the company was placed in administration. Olympia and York have bank borrowings totalling approximately £1.2 billion. There are two main facilities, a £570 million loan from 11 international banks which is secured on the project and a £400 million loan from four Canadian banks. Unsecured creditors, including building contractors, are owed £50 million. The decision by the major international banks not to continue funding for Canary Wharf may mean the loss of half of the £1.2 billion loans made on the development. The collapse of this huge development, the largest undertaken in the United Kingdom, will have major repercussions for the property sector and is likely to encourage a re-assessment of the banks' role as property lenders.

This review of the evolution of financing techniques shows that the property development sector has been influenced by fiscal and monetary measures operating in the general economy as well as by specific property measures such as the taxation of development values, rent controls, building and planning controls. Not all such measures have had an adverse effect on development activity. On the contrary, in areas where urban renewal is being promoted, government has set in place a number of financial incentives to encourage development. Such incentives are outlined in the following.

4.3   SOURCES AND TECHNIQUES OF FINANCING

The historical review of property financing indicates that sources and types of finance have evolved to meet changing economic conditions. Deregulation and the globalization of the capital markets have made new sources of finance accessible. Furthermore, tax and grant incentives have been utilized to attract tax-favoured investors and new investment methods have been adapted from the world of corporate finance. Indeed, developers have proved to be remarkably resourceful in adapting a variety of financing techniques to the development industry.

A wide range of factors influence the type of financing instruments which are utilized. Briefly these can be summarized as follows: (1) the general state of the economy, in particular current trends in interest rates and inflation; (2) the geographical location of the development, with London and the south-east being preferred by both institutional investors (Riley and Isaac, 1991) and bank lenders (Evans and Jarrett, 1988); (3) the type of property whether institutionally prime or secondary (Cadman, 1984); and (4) the type of developer (Morley *et al.*, 1989).

The final factor is particularly important. Developers are not a single genre but encompass a wide range of organizations with varying economies of scale and differing objectives across the public and private sectors (Healey, 1991). For example, the sources of finance utilized by property companies will depend on whether the company is an investment or a development company, whether or not it has a Stock Exchange listing, its requirements in terms of project or corporate finance, the duration of the finance, whether the finance is secured or unsecured, the type of interest rate requirements, i.e. fixed or variable, and finally the level of guarantee or recourse required by the lender.

Such a variety of characteristics partly explains the myriad of financing instruments which have been used by companies of differing size and as-pirations. However, one principle is axiomatic, namely the type of finance in terms of size, duration and cost should always match the characteristics of the developer and the reasons for which it is raised.

There are a number of ways in which the sources and techniques of property finance may be classified. The most basic distinction is between debt and equity (Gibbs, 1987; Mallinson, 1988). Equity financing provides the investor with a claim to capital gains, but the holder is exposed to risk if failure occurs. In contrast, debt gives the lender rights to repayment but normally no share in the possible capital gain (Pugh, 1991). Savills (1989) distinguishes traditional from current methods. Project specific finance may be distinguished from non-project specific or corporate finance. Although this distinction is often blurred, it is useful in differentiating developers who have the financial muscle to raise corporate finance from those who rely solely on project specific finance. Currently nine broad groups of finance encompassing approximately 60 individual techniques can be identified. Darlow (1989) provides a useful framework which is used as the basis for Table 4.1. The main financing techniques are discussed in the following sections, which also consider the hedging methods used to minimize risk.

Tax/grant incentives

Private sector finance, like water, flows downhill in search of the best re- turn. It will only flow uphill, or against the normal trend, when it is artificially pumped by fiscal concession or government subsidy (Bourke, 1992). Concessions and subsidies are provided by government to encourage de- velopment in areas which the private sector would normally ignore. A number of tax based methods of finance are available covering capital allowances, development in Enterprise Zones, superannuation funds, finance leases, business expansion schemes and property unit trusts (Table 4.1). However, it must always be borne in mind that public sector sources play a com- paratively minor role in financing property development (Harvey, 1992).

The reduction in corporation tax from 52 to 35%, industrial buildings allowance and plant and machinery allowance were considerable taxation incentives in the early 1980s. In Enterprise Zones 100% of capital expenditure was allowed against corporation and income tax until 1992. Investments in such areas for wealthy individuals paying higher tax rates were very beneficial, although the reduction in the higher rate tax band to 40% in 1988 has reduced the benefit (Morley *et al.*, 1989). Fiscal incentives have been used extensively in the Custom House Docks scheme in Dublin. The principal measure is a 10% rate of corporation tax to 2005 for companies *in situ* by 1995. On the basis of a modest public sector input of IR £10 million it is estimated that a total capital investment of IR £350 million is likely to be achieved (Berry *et al.*, 1991a).

Finance leases are particularly applicable in Enterprise Zones to take advantage of large tax allowances. The Metro Centre at Gateshead was financed in this way. Essentially a finance lease is a long term 'loan' in the form of a sale and leaseback, which in practice works like a capital repayment mortgage. The owner of the scheme sells his interest for a capital sum to an investor who then leases it back to the vendor. The leaseback takes into account the tax or capital allowances (100% of plant, machinery, fixtures and fittings, or 100% of the price of the building in Enterprise Zones). The rent is set so that over 25–35 years the investor is repaid the capital plus a return on it. One major bank leasing company equates such an allowance to a reduction by as much as 3% in the interest rate.

A number of grant incentives (Table 4.1) devised by government to en- courage private investment in industrial and commercial property develop- ment are outlined by Howes (1988). In addition, financing techniques used

Table 4.1 Sources and techniques of finance. After Darlow (1989)

Tax/grant incentives	Debt based methods	Equity based methods
Tax based methods	Bank loans	Disposals
Capital allowances	Overdrafts	Forward funding
Enterprise Zones	Bridging loans	Forward commitment
Superannuation funds	Term loans	Project management
Finance leases	Non/ltd/recourse loans	Outright sale
Business Expansion Schemes	Syndication	
Property unit trusts	Revolving credit	Joint ventures
	Mezzanine finance	Partnerships
Grants and subsidies	Multi-option finance	Joint venture company
City Grant		Tenants in common
Urban Programme	Mortgages	Venture capital
City Challenge	Interest only	
EC grants	Bullet payment	Sale/lease and leaseback
Industrial Development	Annuity certain	Top slice (horizontal leases)
Act grants	Balloon	Side by side (vertical leases)
Historic building,	Endowment policy linked	Reverse leaseback
conservation and	Full pay back	Finance lease
repair grants	Equity participating	
		Corporate paper
	Corporate paper	Ordinary shares
	Debentures	Preference shares
	Corporate bonds	Rights issues
	Deep discount bonds	Convertibles
	Eurobonds	Warrant issues
	Commercial paper	Retained earnings
	Loan stock	
		Securitization and unitization
		Billingsgate model
		PINC
		SAPCO

by local authorities to fund small unit industrial projects (Morley, 1989; Berry *et al.*, 1991b) and loan guarantee schemes (Morley *et al.*, 1989) are considered elsewhere.

City Grant is currently the principal vehicle for stimulating development. It is available to private sector projects over £200 000 which seek to make a capital investment in deemed priority areas. The grant is designed to bridge the gap between the cost of a development and its value on completion, being the minimum necessary to make the project commercially viable. City Grant is an amalgamation of the earlier Urban Development Grant, Urban Regeneration Grant and Derelict Land Grant, although the predecessors were administered through the local authorities. A potential disincentive to the uptake of grant aid is the formality of assessing the need for each project. As a result of poorly targeted incentives in the past this assessment, undertaken by the Department of the Environment, is most thorough but requires considerable time and bureaucracy (Morley, 1989).

In July 1991 City Challenge was announced with a budget of £82.5 million per annum for five years, awarded to 11 local authorities. The finance for City Challenge comes from the existing urban block allocation which may eventually have a detrimental effect on other initiatives. The most recent initiative is the Urban Regeneration Agency which is due to become operational in mid-1993 and aims to provide more effective targeting of its proposed annual budget of £250 million.

A tangible example of partnership between the public and private sectors is Inner City Enterprises (ICE), set up in 1983 to tackle urban regeneration in areas in which the institutions would not normally lend. Formed by a group of London based financial institutions, its original remit was to act as a development agent devising financially viable regeneration projects for implementation by institutional developers. Inner City Enterprises relies heavily on the uptake of City Grant to support its development activity, which comprises high quality workshop units, apartments, retail units and restaurants for sale to owner-occupiers in a number of provincial cities (ICE, 1992). Inner City Enterprises' total equity capital amounted to £13 million in 1991.

Debt based methods

Bank loans

The dramatic growth in bank lending to the property sector in the 1980s has been outlined earlier. The sources and types of bank lending are covered extensively in published work. Wolfe (1988) compares the characteristics of lending in the 1980s with those of a decade earlier. Darlow (1989) describes how banks have developed complex funding 'cocktails' providing different layers of finance. In addition, a number of workers provide examples of bank lending illustrating funding options open to developers (Orchard-Lisle,

1987; Darlow, 1988). Furthermore, the bank's perspective on property lending and the analyses which they undertake to assess risk are described by Wright (1985), Wolfe (1988), Geddes (1989) and Morley *et al.* (1989). The principal bank financing techniques outlined in Table 4.1 are discussed in the following sections.

Term loans.   A term loan allows a property company to borrow a certain amount immediately or in stages from a bank or a syndicate of banks. The loan is for a fixed term and cannot be called in before the repayment date, which is a major advantage over overdraft facilities. The rate of interest charged reflects prevailing market rates. In London and other centres of high demand margins are so competitive that rates are expressed in basis points (100 basis points equal 1%) (Darlow, 1989). Term loan rates are usually expressed as 100–150 basis points above LIBOR, the London Interbank Offered Rate. In other regions interest rates may be quoted as base plus 1.5–2%. Alternatively, the banks may offer a marginally lower fixed rate if the borrower uses a commercial mortgage indemnity insurance or some other hedge against upward movements in interest rates.

Normally a term loan is limited to approximately 70–75% of cost or valuation. The loan amounts typically range from less than £100 million to £300 million with maturities of two to five years. Sometimes they can be converted into limited recourse loans (Pugh, 1992). Currently loan criteria for new speculative developments have tightened significantly, with many lenders requiring a pre-let before entering a transaction (Riley and Issac, 1991).

Recourse/limited/non-recourse loans.   Recourse loans allow the lender complete recourse to the finances of the borrower so that in the event of default the lender has a prior claim for interest payments on the assets of the borrower. In contrast, the non-recourse or 'off balance sheet' loan is related solely to the specific scheme. If the development fails the recourse is to the property, not to the assets of the company. Therefore they are normally only available on investment properties with an adequate and secure rental income flow. The advantage of a non-recourse loan to the borrower is that the company can benefit from the profitability of a scheme without showing the related liabilities on the parent company balance sheet. The parent company therefore maintains a low gearing status which is attractive to potential investors.

In reality, very few non-recourse loans were made to property companies (Morley *et al.*, 1989). Rather limited recourse loans were issued whereby the bank loaned a hard core of the total development costs without recourse to the developer but committing the borrower to contribute all other costs. Most of these loans are arranged using a single purpose company, thus allowing the lender recourse to the specific project and through limited guarantees to the assets of the parent company. Both non- and limited recourse loans usually carry a higher rate of interest than term loans, reflecting the additional risk to the lending banks. Typical limited recourse loans are advanced to £70 million with maturities between two and seven years.

Syndication. The growing sophistication of bank finance in the 1980s witnessed a switch in role by some banks from lender to loan manager, co-ordinating the activities of a syndicate of lending banks. Loan-earning capacity was therefore increased by combining fees with margins income (Evans and Jarrett, 1988). Syndicated loans, normally for amounts greater than £20 million, have been used to finance a number of large developments. They offer increased flexibility not only to the lenders, but also to the borrower in terms of currencies and interest rates.

Wolfe (1988) outlines the mechanics of syndicated project finance in detail. A syndication is managed by a lead bank which assesses the viability of the scheme and the developer, and normally underwrites a major proportion of the project. The other banks which wish to become involved need to assess their own risks and have no recourse to the lead bank once a commitment is given. During the development the lead bank will monitor and service the lending. Problems may arise in co-ordinating the decision-making of all syndicate members and determining the recourse which each lender has to the borrower for outstanding repayments (Beveridge, 1991).

Mezzanine finance. Normal bank lending to property companies is usually restricted to approximately 75% of the development cost, leaving the developer to provide the balance of 25%. The developer may provide all the equity to fill this gap or may borrow part of the balance as mezzanine finance. Normally mezzanine finance is limited to 15% of the development cost but developers have combined it with commercial mortgage indemnity insurance to yield a total loan of approximately 95% of cost (Asson, 1991). It is usually provided by merchant and investment banks and is normally available for a maximum of three years.

Mezzanine finance is a form of structured financing arrangement which is at an intermediate level between pure debt and pure equity. It is always junior to the bank debt but ranks above true equity for the purposes of liquidation. There is a higher risk attached to mezzanine finance which is reflected in the required return, normally 500 basis points above LIBOR plus a share in the profits of the project. Such a high return is required as the lender is contributing a substitute for equity funding which necessitates an equity remuneration. Darlow (1989) provides a worked example of mezzanine finance illustrating differing risk/reward ratios for the lender.

Multi-option financing facilities. These are packages and composites of various types of short and long term finance consisting of bankers' guarantees in underwriting loans, syndicated loans, multi-currency arrangements, Sterling and Euro commercial paper and access to Eurobond markets. Normally it is an unsecured facility with a duration of two to ten years which is only available to the largest property companies. Loan size ranges from £50 million to £300 million with £120 million being the average.

The multi-option financing facility (MOFF) is organized by a lead bank and normally consists of two parts. The first part is the guaranteed or committed facility which ensures that a syndicate of banks will provide the sum of money at a set number of basis points over LIBOR. The second part is the uncommitted facility consisting of a syndicate of uncommitted tender panel banks which may bid to provide short term funding at an interest rate below that of the committed facility. The lower rate of interest reflects the absence of a commitment to guarantee the supply of finance. If the uncommitted tender panel fails to bid the required loan or interest rate then the company can resort to the committed facility. The advantage of the MOFF is that the borrower can avail of a variety of different finance instruments, some of which may provide preferential short term borrowing while retaining the committed term facility.

Mortgages

Mortgages are a major category of debt finance. The conventional long term mortgage with a maturity of approximately 20 years was traditionally provided by the institutions, especially life insurance companies. They were normally arranged against approximately 66–75% of the value of the completed development. The fixed interest rate was set at 1.75–2.25% above the gross redemption yield of a comparable gilt edged security. The relatively high return reflects the riskiness of the investment, the lack of liquidity and the institution's lack of participation in capital appreciation and rental growth. There are a variety of repayment methods ranging from annual equal instalments of capital and interest to differing combinations of capital and interest, or interest only with capital repaid at the termination of the loan with an endowment.

Currently there is much greater flexibility in mortgage financing through the provision of variable or floating interest rates and instruments such as a bullet mortgage. In the latter the rental income from the scheme covers the interest costs and capital is repaid at some future date, either on sale or when the scheme is refinanced. Interest holidays are also possible where the rental income does not cover the servicing of the loan, say in the early years of the scheme, and a balloon payment is added at the end of the loan to recoup the lost interest.

Equity participation for the lender is also possible through convertible and participating mortgages which allow conversion to a share in the equity of the development at some future date. The advantage to the developer is in the scheduling of interest payments to reflect income growth, thus lowering interest charges during the early years of the mortgage.

Since 1986, building societies have been allowed to lend up to 10% of their loan portfolio on non-residential opportunities. Although such lending is currently restricted, societies have supplied commercial mortgages up to 90% of value and on repayment terms up to 30 years. Interest rates were charged at 1–3% above building society base rate (Dilworth, 1989). The Abbey National was the first major lender from this sector, with their £40 million loan for the Bishopsbridge development in Paddington (Evans and Jarrett, 1988).

Corporate paper (debt)

Corporate paper encompasses both debt and equity financing instruments. Corporate financing generally relates to the generation of funds from within the corporate structure, which requires the property company to have certain assets and to be a certain size. The sale of existing developments will realize profit, which provides equity for future development. Alternatively, the existing development which is retained as an investment may act as security and the income flow will service the debt for future projects. Currently a number of financing instruments are available.

Debentures and bonds.   A wide variety of debentures and bonds are available on the property finance market (Morley *et al.*, 1989). Traditionally, the institutions have purchased the corporate debt of quoted property companies, thus acquiring assets to match their liabilities. Technically a debenture is a written acknowledgement for a debt which is secured against a property, usually for 60–65% of the value, or on other assets. A variety of bonds are found, for example, mortgage debentures secured by a mortgage over a specified property (Beveridge, 1991).

Debentures are long term loans, often with a life of 15–35 years and paying a fixed rate of interest. They are comparable to gilt edged securities or bonds, a fact reflected by their description as corporate bonds. Gilt edged stocks are therefore used as a bench-mark to measure the return from debentures. A higher return is required as debentures are regarded as less secure and less liquid on the market. However, the effect of inflation, which erodes the value of long term fixed interest borrowing, reduces the attractiveness of debentures. Consequently they lost their popularity in the 1970s, a time of high inflation, whereas the 1980s saw their return as long term interest rates were low compared with short term rates. Morley *et al.* (1989) outline examples of debenture issues raised by such companies as Land Securities and Slough Estates.

In recent years a number of property companies have raised finance through the issue of debentures referred to as deep discount bonds. The investor not only earns interest on the stock but also receives an additional capital payment at the redemption date, reflecting the shortfall on interest payments from a full open market rate. The advantage to the borrower is that the instrument matches the cash flow from the property to the payment of interest on the debt. Shayle (1991a; 1991b) outlines the cash flow, accounting and taxation advantages of such hybrid financial instruments. The main advantage is that the company can raise finance based on the value of the properties without actually selling the assets.

These methods have addressed the issue of raising corporate finance in the domestic market. Currently large property companies may also raise long term finance such as Eurobonds on the international markets. Funds are raised outside the country of origin in a specified denomination, for example, Eurodollars, Swiss francs, Sterling or Deutschmarks. The popularity of a particular currency varies with changes in the exchange rate and interest rate trends. The impact of Eurobonds on property investment is covered extensively elsewhere (Schiller, 1990; Pugh, 1992). The linking of Eurobonds to interest rate swaps to achieve the type of finance required is discussed by Beveridge (1991). Eurobond borrowing is normally unsecured, therefore only the largest property companies have the necessary credit rating required to raise finance in this way. Eurobond issues range from £25 million to £100 million, with maturity dates between five and 20 years.

Commercial paper.   During the latter part of the 1980s a number of property companies raised finance by issuing Sterling commercial paper in the United Kingdom. Alternatively it may be issued in US dollars via a Euro commercial paper offering or a domestic American paper programme (Beveridge, 1991). The Sterling commercial paper market was launched in 1986 to provide an alternative method for companies to raise short term finance. It is a form of short term IOU note issued by the borrowing company and sold to investors looking for a short term home for surplus cash without a bank intermediary. The company is issuing a short term security instead of taking up a loan. A Euro commercial paper market was established in 1985. It is cheaper than Sterling commercial paper as it offers rates below LIBOR.

Commercial paper is sold at a discount as opposed to paying interest on redemption. The discount or interest earned is usually expressed as a number of basis points above LIBOR. Commercial paper is an attractive short term investment for banks, institutions and other property companies wishing to gain a return in excess of the yield on bank deposit rates. It has a maturity of between seven days and one year; however, since 1989 this has been extended to five years. However, the average life of commercial paper is more like 40 days. These short term periods are rolled over to provide medium term finance; at the end of a three month paper issue another one is started. The rolling over technique is a common feature in the money markets as it allows short term money from investors to be transmitted into long term finance for borrowers.

There are a number of restrictions on becoming established in the commercial paper market. Only companies or parent companies with a listing on the Stock Exchange can issue Sterling commercial paper. Each issue must be for a minimum of £500 000. Credit ratings are important to gain investor confidence because loans are unsecured but are very expensive.

Equity based methods

Disposals

Normally it is not possible to raise 100% debt finance for property development, therefore property companies have to increase their equity base if they wish to expand their operations. The realization of profit from the sale of completed developments provides a source of equity finance for the developer. A number of mechanisms for disposing of property are available; for example, forward funding, forward commitment, project management and outright sale. In the case of forward funding the institution provides finance for site purchase and construction and takes control of the project on completion. Excess profits may be shared with the developer. The advantage to the developer is that the rate of return on interim finance is usually lower than the bank interest rate. However, the institution may require a higher capitalization yield, reflecting the institution's greater exposure to risk, and resulting in a lower sale price. Schiller (1990) questions the future role of forward funding in an environment of continuing institutional disinvestment from property. In contrast, forward commitment involves the institution signing an undertaking to purchase when the building is let. The developer will receive the purchase price less the total development cost and rolled-up interest. In the case of project management the institution provides all finance whereas the developer obtains a management fee and percentage profit in undertaking the development. The project management fee may include a bonus reflecting any increase in profitability of the scheme.

Joint ventures

There are a number of joint venture mechanisms involving two or more public or private sector parties combining, normally on an equal basis, to undertake development (Francis, 1992). The two basic forms are partnerships and joint venture companies.

The statutory basis of a partnership is contained in the Partnership Act 1890. The partnership deed creates the framework within which the duration, capital liabilities, distribution of profits and sharing of losses in the partnership are agreed. There are taxation advantages in undertaking property development in partnership. Tax is borne by the partners on an individual basis rather than the partnership, thus avoiding double taxation.

Investors who wish to go into partnership with a property company may either enter into a tenure arrangement or form a joint venture company. The latter is a common vehicle for raising debt and equity capital as well as issuing shares in the development of a specific project (Burston and Milne, 1992; Linehan, 1992). The major advantage is that shareholders can limit their liability to the amount of capital they have invested in the project even if it is not successful. However, such a company is liable to taxation on its income and profits before any distribution to shareholders, who then may be liable to taxation themselves. A joint venture company also provides a vehicle for using venture capital. This is a type of funding which brings together an entrepreneur and sources of finance from institutions, banks and private investors to support the business venture.

Sale/lease and leasebacks

Sale and leaseback and to a lesser extent lease and leaseback arrangements have been used extensively since the 1950s for sharing the equity in individual development schemes. They refer to a financial–development–ownership relationship, originating in a context of rising interest rates and financier motivation to obtain a share in capital and rental growth. In the classic model the developer disposes of the freehold or long leasehold interest to an institution in return for a long lease on completion of the scheme. The sale proceeds are used by the developer to finance construction. The rental income from the scheme services the rent paid to the institution and provides the developer with a profit margin. The institution therefore acquires an equity interest and the developer retains an investment interest in the scheme.

Sale and leasebacks have evolved to become sophisticated and complex financing arrangements covering all possible development scenarios involving the sharing of equity (Pugh, 1992). The legal documentation for most arrangements provides options whereby the developer or institution can sell an interest to the other party. The most common arrangements consist of top slice, side by side, geared and reverse leaseback (Darlow, 1988).

Corporate paper (equity)

A wide range of equity financing instruments are available to the market; for example, placing of shares, rights issues, convertible stocks and equity warrant issues (Beveridge, 1988).

Ordinary and preference shares.   Property companies which have a full listing on the Stock Exchange can offer for sale both ordinary and preference shares. Ordinary shares are the 'equity' within a company as they participate in the profits earned after all priority interests have been met and sufficient earnings have been retained to finance further developments.

In contrast, preference shares are 'equity' capital but have characteristics similar to debt finance, paying a fixed dividend similar to that of a fixed interest loan. Investment in property company shares is not directly comparable with other forms of property investment as the share price and performance is determined not only by the underlying assets but also equity market sentiment. The speculative nature of property shares means that they can be very volatile.

Rights issues.   A rights issue is a means of raising finance for a company by the issue of new shares to existing shareholders so enabling them to extend their shareholding at preferential rates. They have been used extensively by property companies, particularly in the construction and retailing sectors (Morley *et al.*, 1989; Moss, 1991). The success of the issue is dependent on the efficiency of the company, the state of the shares and of the equity market.

Convertibles.   Convertible loan stock and preference shares are securities issued with a fixed interest payment and redemption date in the case of the former, but having the option to convert at a certain date to a stated number of ordinary shares in the company. Property companies often regard them as a cheaper source of finance than a straight loan. In reality they are a form of financing midway between equity and debt.

Securitization and unitization

The 1980s witnessed the advent of the mega development requiring a number of institutional or other investors to provide the necessary development finance. In recent years few institutional investors have been prepared to fund schemes worth more than £50 million (Morley *et al.*, 1989). The difficulties of funding and selling such large developments have produced new investment vehicles. Such vehicles have had additional advantages of making property assets more liquid, so attracting a larger number of smaller investors.

Securitization is the conversion of assets into tradeable paper securities. In relation to property investment it is the creation of a number of holdings or layers of interest within a single building. Securitization facilitates the application of the capital markets to single properties and has major implications for the future of property financing (Barter, 1988). Authorized property unit trusts, the issue of property company shares and debentures, and the application of the Business Expansion Scheme to residential property are all examples of securitization (Rodney and Rydin, 1989). One of the most celebrated and often quoted examples of securitization in the United Kingdom is the Billingsgate office development in London (valued at £79 million), which was financed using three layers of a deep discount bond, preferred equity stock and ordinary shares (Orchard-Lisle, 1987).

Related to securitization is the concept of unitization, which is a method of selling or sharing the rent that the development produces. Large or 'lumpy' assets are traded in smaller amounts in the securities market, so facilitating liquidity and marketability. The two main vehicles developed in the 1980s were the property income certificate (PINC) and the single asset property company (SAPCO). The latter is a property company whose only asset is a single development. A PINC is a composite security comprising a SAPCO with the addition of a financial intermediary to achieve tax transparency. The development of these vehicles and an evaluation of their effectiveness in the late 1980s is covered elsewhere (Gibbs, 1987; Orchard-Lisle, 1987; Barter and Sinclair, 1988; Rodney and Rydin, 1989). Such instruments have had a limited impact on property financing in Britain owing to impediments created by land law, taxation practices and market acceptance (Pugh, 1992).

Interest rate management (hedging techniques)

Property development, like any other commercial venture, is dependent on cash flow to ensure profitability. A major risk for short to medium term borrowers (and investors) is an adverse movement in interest rates. If the loan is issued in a foreign currency, then adverse movements in both interest rates and exchange rates may be critical. The property industry uses a higher proportion of borrowed money than most businesses, therefore in recent years interest rate management or hedging techniques have played an increasing part in the structure of property and development loans (Pugh, 1991). The market for hedging products in the United Kingdom is the London International Financial Futures Exchange (LIFFE), which has been in operation since 1982.

Interest rate management can cover many different financial instruments, for example, caps, floors, collars, swaps, forward rate agreements, foreign currency loans and commercial mortgage indemnity insurance. Each instrument performs a different function, therefore the chosen hedging method will reflect the developer's degree of interest rate risk; for example, is interest rate protection required over a narrow band, or will a decrease in rates be offset against a rise, or is a 'long stop' required, i.e. protection against a high jump in rates rather than a reasonable rise?

The cap. The cap is the most common hedging instrument. It places a limit on the maximum interest rate which will be paid over the duration of the loan. It is purchased from a bank and like an insurance premium it is paid at the start of the loan. If interest rates do not rise above the cap or ceiling then the premium is forfeited. The cap does not have to be purchased from the same bank as the loan is obtained. The cost will vary with the degree of protection; for example, to protect against a narrow rise from 10 to 10.5% will be more expensive than a long stop from 10 to 14%. The cap provides good protection against upward movements while taking advantage of declining interest rates.

The floor and collar.   The developer can reduce the cost of a cap by fore-going some of the benefits of an interest rate reduction. A minimum (floor) rate of interest will be specified and the instrument is sold by the developer to the bank. The collar is a combination of cap and floor whereby interest rates are set within a predetermined range. Movements in interest rates outside this range will neither benefit nor damage the developer's cash flow.

Forward rate agreement.   Such a hedging mechanism is beneficial where interest rates are likely to rise before the loan is drawn down. A forward rate agreement protects the borrower against adverse movements in interest rates or currency exchange rates. In advance of taking out the loan the borrower will purchase the agreement from a bank, thus fixing the interest rate at so many basis points over LIBOR. If interest or exchange rates rise the bank will compensate the developer and if they fall below the pre-set limit the borrower must compensate the bank.

Drop lock.   The drop lock is a mechanism within a long term floating rate facility which allows the developer to opt out and lock into a prevailing fixed interest rate for the remainder of the loan period. It is normally triggered by a reduction in long term interest rates below a pre-set level.

Swaps.   Swaps are trading facilities which allow companies to exchange variable and fixed debt arrangements in a manner which suits their cash flow requirements (Beveridge, 1991). At any point in time either fixed or variable interest may be more suitable for the developer's corporate strat-egy. It is a hedging technique that matches two parties who have a mutual interest in exchanging their interest obligations to increase efficiency and save costs. The two companies to the swap will not deal with each other, rather the whole arrangement will be conducted by an intermediary bank which will receive a fee for this transaction. The swap is totally separate from the underlying loan which it is hedging (Pugh, 1992).

Foreign currency loans.   Foreign currency loans not only enable the de-veloper to work in a country of the currency of the loan but also to hedge against interest rate and exchange rate movements. Borrowing in one of the major world currencies normally has the advantage of lower interest rates than would be available on a loan in Sterling. The ideal situation is to be able to borrow at a lower rate of interest than Sterling while the amount of debt is reducing because of favourable movements in interest rates.

Commercial mortgage indemnity insurance. Commercial mortgage indemnity insurance has already been discussed in relation to term loans. A bank may provide a larger loan (thus reducing the developer's equity) subject to the borrower taking out indemnity insurance. In the case of mezzanine finance the cost of the insurance premium is likely to be between 5 and 10% of the additional amount of loan which is insured (Riley and Isaac, 1991). If the indemnity insurance is provided for the total loan a lower interest rate is likely to be obtained from the bank.

4.4 CONCLUSIONS

The state of property financing in the early 1990s indicates an over-geared market. Currently property companies are indebted to the bank sector to approximately £39 billion (Savills, 1992). A large proportion of this debt is represented by short and medium term loans which are likely to decrease due to repayment, or rescheduling, within the next three to eight years. In addition, corporate debt instruments issued by property companies will also be maturing in due course and will have to be replaced by new issues, disposals, or through refinancing.

Disinvestment by institutions over the 1980s has produced a widening gap between traditional investors and bank debt. The dramatic growth of capital and rental values in the latter part of the decade and the need for property companies to increase their asset base due to stock-market conditions meant that developers were retaining a larger number of property assets. Consequently developers have been taking out medium term loans or refinancing initial loans over a longer period, so contributing to high levels of property debt. The crucial question is, who is going to refinance this bank debt on a long term basis?

It is unlikely that the institutions will enter the market with the same effect as they did in the period 1974 to 1980. Uncertainty regarding long term investment prospects coupled with an oversupply of space and the continuing depressed economic outlook, even though interest rates have fallen, means that developers will have to continue servicing short term debt repayments. One solution to the debt problem is the refinancing of existing loans. Listed property companies will be able to avail of the capital markets to swap debt for equity and convert short term loans into long term securities. The non-listed companies with properties offering good rental income servicing loan repayments will be able to have loans extended while a purchaser is sought for the investment. In the case of properties which are underperforming but which are in good locations and are fundamentally sound, the banks may restructure loans so as to enable them to participate in future equity or capital gain. For other underperforming properties, unless a buyer can be found, then the risk of corporate failure looms large.

Currently both developers and financiers are adopting a cautious attitude. Recent evidence suggests that bank lending ratios have declined to 60% of development cost. A rethink of bank lending policies may be an inevitable outcome of the Olympia and York crisis at Canary Wharf. It is also likely that there will be a move back to traditional forms of finance with fixed rate mortgages and possibly construction companies financing building costs. The institutions may wait for yields to rise before again investing in property in a major way. Also in the short term it is likely that there will be growth in risk limitation devices.

Investment in property in the 1990s is likely to be marked by increasing diversification and internationalization (Debenham Tewson & Chinnocks, 1991). It is also likely that environmental issues will play an increasingly important role (Beattie-Jones, 1992). Furthermore, there may be greater use of securitization and unitization vehicles to make available a wider pool of investors, given that so much interim funding is secured through loans and corporate debt securities. Such vehicles would introduce much needed liquidity to the market and the transfer of short term financed projects to long term investors.

There is a continuing need for pump priming initiatives to encourage private sector financing of urban regeneration. Present government policies envisage a continuing but contracting role for local authorities with increasing emphasis on the Urban Regeneration Agency to overcome site assembly and infrastructure problems, and on private sector developers or public development agencies to undertake the development role. Indeed, there is an argument for extending Enterprise Zone capital allowances which have been a major success in many urban regeneration schemes.

One ray of hope is that because people will always require buildings in which to live, work or spend their leisure time then the surplus space will eventually be absorbed, so creating an impetus for further development.

REFERENCES

Asson, T. (1991) Bank lending on property. A surveyor's view, *Estates Gazette*, **9106**, 113–114.

Balchin, P.N. and Kieve, J.L. (1982) *Urban Land Economics*, 2nd edn, Macmillan, London.

Barter, S.L. (Ed.) (1988) *Real Estate Finance*, Butterworths, London.

Barter, S.L. and Sinclair, N. (1988) Securitisation. In: *Real Estate Finance* (Ed. S.L. Barter), Butterworths, London, pp. 213–253.

Beattie-Jones, V. (1992) Green loans arrive, *Journal of Property Finance*, **2**(3), 318–320.

Berry, J.N., Deddis, W.G. and McGreal, W.S. (1991a) Waterfront regeneration in Ireland: public and private sector partnerships, *Journal of Property Finance*, **2**(2), 179–184.

Berry, J.N., McCluskey, W.J., McGreal, W.S. and Beamish, T. (1991b) Public and private initiatives in the 'small' industrial sector: Northern Ireland, *Journal of Property Finance*, **2**(1), 69–73.

Beveridge, J.A. (1988) The needs of the property company. In: *Real Estate Finance* (Ed. S.L. Barter), Butterworths, London, pp. 156–167.

Beveridge, J.A. (1991) New methods of financing. In: *Investment, Procurement and Performance in Construction* (Eds P. Venmore-Rowland, P. Brandon and T. Mole), E & FN Spon, RICS, London, pp. 12–21.

Bourke, J. (1992) Housing and financial markets. In: *Housing the Community – 2000* (Ed. G. Sweeney), Dublin Institute of Technology, pp. 34–41.

Brett, M. (1986) Development finance. In: *The London Property Market in AD 2000* (Ed. C. Darlow), E & FN Spon, London, pp. 115–122.

Brett, M. (1990) *Property and Money*, Estates Gazette, London.

Burston, R.J. and Milne, D.D. (1992) U.S. investment in European commercial property, *Journal of Property Finance*, **2**(3), 305–311.

Cadman, D. (1984) Property finance in the U.K. in the post-war period, *Land Development Studies*, **1**(2), 61–82.

Cadman, D., Austin-Crowe, L., Topping, R. and Avis, M. (1991) *Property Development*, 2nd edn, E & FN Spon, London.

Darlow, C. (Ed.) (1988) *Valuation and Development Appraisal*, 2nd edn, Estates Gazette, London.

Darlow, C. (1989) Property development and funding. In: *Land and Property Development New Directions* (Ed. R. Grover), E & FN Spon, London, pp. 69–80.

Debenham Tewson & Chinnocks (1989) *Banking on Property,* Debenham Tewson Research, London.

Debenham Tewson & Chinnocks (1991) *Money into Property*, Debenham Tewson Research, London.

Dilworth, S. (1989) Building societies enter the market, *Estate Gazette*, **8924**, 20–21.

Evans, P. and Jarrett, D. (1988) Non-institutional funding, *Estates Gazette*, **8823**, 20–21.

Francis, R. (1992) Financing joint ventures between the public and private sectors, *Journal of Property Finance*, **2**(4), 455–463.

Geddes, J. (1989) Arranging bank finance for U.K. property development, *Journal of Valuation*, **7**(2), 110–122.

Gibbs, R. (1987) Raising finance for new development, *Journal of Valuation*, **5**(4), 343–353.

Harvey, J. (1992) *Urban Land Economics*, 3rd edn, Macmillan, London.

Healey, P. (1991) Models of the development process: a review, *Journal of Property Research*, **8**(3), 219–238.

Howes, C. (1988) Urban regeneration initiatives in England, *Land Development Studies*, **5**(1), 57–65.

ICE (1992) *Report and Accounts 1991*, Inner City Enterprises plc, London.

Linehan, G. (1992) Institutionally acceptable properties, *Journal of Property Finance*, **2**(3), 313–317.

Mallinson, M. (1988) Equity finance. In: *Real Estate Finance* (Ed. S.L. Barter), Butterworths, London, pp. 34–80.

Morley, S. (1989) Funding of small-unit industrial schemes, *Estates Gazette*, **8940**, 28, 30, 32.

Morley, S., Marsh, C., McIntosh, A. and Harris, M. (1989) *Industrial and Business Space Development*, E & FN Spon, London.

Moss, A. (1991) Rights issues in the property sector, *Journal of Property Finance*, **2**(2), 185–193.

Newell, M. (1977) *An Introduction to the Economics of Urban Land Use*, Estates Gazette, London.

Orchard-Lisle, P. (1987) Financing property development, *Journal of Valuation*, **5**(4), 354–368.

Pugh, C. (1991) The globalisation of finance capital and the changing relationships between property and finance – 1, *Journal of Property Finance*, **2**(2), 211–215.

Pugh, C. (1992) The globalisation of finance capital and the changing relationships between property and finance – 2, *Journal of Property Finance*, **2**(3), 369–379.

Reid, M. (1983) *The Secondary Banking Crisis*, Macmillan, London.

Riley, M. and Isaac, D. (1991) Property lending survey 1991, *Journal of Property Finance*, **2**(1), 74–77.

Rodney, W. and Rydin, Y. (1989) Trends towards unitization and securitization in property markets. In: *Land and Property Development New Directions* (Ed. R. Grover), E & FN Spon, London, pp. 81–94.

Savills (1989) *Financing Property*, Savills Commercial Research, London.

Savills (1992) *Financing Property*, Savills Commercial Research, London.

Schiller, R. (1990) The importance of debt, *Estates Gazette*, **9008**, 22, 24, 58.

Shayle, A. (1991a) The use of deep discount and zero coupon bonds in the U.K. property market – 1, *Journal of Property Finance*, **2**(1), 11–17.

Shayle, A. (1991b) The use of deep discount and zero coupon bonds in the U.K. property market – 2, *Journal of Property Finance*, **2**(2), 157–163.

Wolfe, R. (1988) Debt finance. In: *Real Estate Finance* (Ed. S.L. Barter), Butterworths, London, pp. 81–112.

Wright, N.J. (1985) Bank finance for property developers, *Property Management*, **3**(2), 9–17.

5

Scope for and funding of urban regeneration in eastern Europe

_____ P. Hudson

The fall of the Iron Curtain has revealed the back-stage reality of eastern Europe in all its grim detail: corruption, inefficiency, appalling building standards, mis-allocations, and gross housing and retail shortages. The reforms have left ordinary citizens materially worse off. The need for urban renewal in eastern Europe is beyond doubt, the question is: how can it be paid for?

In this chapter the capability of commercial real estate to provide resources for social and investment needs is considered (East 8, 1991). Following an initial outline of general policy trends, property in eastern Europe is discussed in the context of the international market, the commercial scope in eastern Europe is examined and funding sources are identified. The pitfalls of investing are highlighted along with a discussion of the applicability of experience in the United Kingdom of development competitions. Finally, the chapter refers to a model urban renewal approach proposed by East 8 and taken up by the Polish Government for implementation in Warsaw.

5.1 POLICY TRENDS

From inside eastern Europe political, economic and social change appears muddled and fraught with indecision. A casual view from the west presents a similar picture, but a considered study of the metamorphosis underway in the east reveals breathtaking change and an assured direction. Even within the stirring giant of the former Soviet Union the consensus for democracy and free markets is remarkable. To understand this vast new market, its development and investment prospects, it is necessary to keep in mind the general strategy for recovery. Government legitimacy requires free elections; market economies depend on free prices, sound money and privatization. For political stability a welfare safety net is needed to protect the most vulnerable.

In the former Soviet Union there is serious doubt about the ability to secure democracy and a market economy. This is not due to a lack of political commitment, but rather the sheer inertia of a country the size of a continent which has been saddled for three-quarters of a century with communism. Stability in the former Soviet bloc is imperative not only for its 290 million citizens but also for the economic well-being of the whole of Europe.

5.2   INTERNATIONAL PROPERTY PERSPECTIVES

The property sector in the mature markets of the world is currently (early 1990s) in a poor state; the United Kingdom, western Europe, Japan and the USA are all suffering and the signs are that recovery is likely to be slow. Property tends to be seen as a high risk and low return investment and the institutions have accordingly reduced their exposure to property to almost a third of what it was in the mid-1970s.

The contrast with eastern Europe could not be greater, as rents plummet in the west they are racing ahead in the east. However, it is clearly wrong to infer that eastern Europe is a low risk market. Political, currency and title risks understandably figure highly in investors' concerns. Nevertheless, eastern Europe is currently a high return market with commercial property booming since 1989.

Hotels

In Prague, occupancy levels in four and five star hotels are over 90% and single room rates have reached US$250 per night; in Moscow the top suite in the newly refurbished Metropole will be US$1300 per night; in the Warsaw Marriott a single room is US$220 per night and Budapest is achieving US$200 per night. Tourism is also thriving, visitor numbers are increasing by 50% per year and at a time when hotel capacity is already under strain. The scope for long term growth in hotel bed spaces in the capital cities is therefore considerable (Figure 5.1).

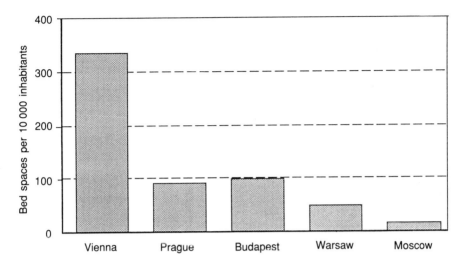

Figure 5.1 Hotel bed spaces per 10 000 inhabitants. Source: East 8

Offices

The shortfall in good quality office space in eastern Europe combined with the high demand from western businessmen has created a boom market. Typically rents for good offices are US$400/m^2, which outstrips the top rents of many west European capitals (Figure 5.2). Good quality offices are in very short supply, whereas major multinationals have recognized the market potential and the need to have a presence.

Retail

The latent market in the east is enormous; starved of access to consumer goods, east Europeans visiting the west are well known for their purchasing drive. When the Hungarians were first allowed to travel to Austria, regulations soon followed limiting currency allowances on spending. Although east Europeans have very constrained purchasing power, there is a tendency to overlook the fact that people are prepared to pay a high premium for quality, packaging and 'cache'. Clearly there is potential for long term growth in the retail sector (Figure 5.3).

Residential

Low cost housing is perhaps eastern Europe's greatest consumer need, but unfortunately there is little scope for profit in spite of the low construction costs. Housing for western clients, on the other hand, is different, with the

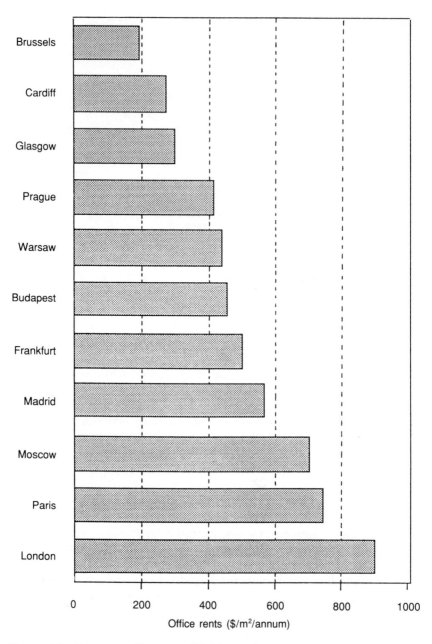

Figure 5.2 European office rents ($/m²/annum). Source: East 8

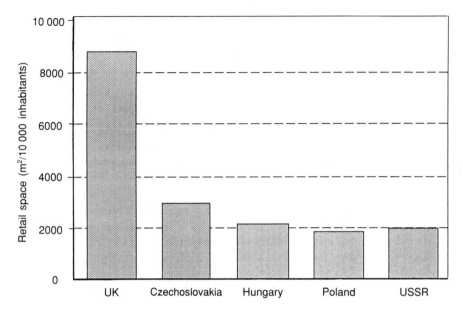

Figure 5.3 Amount of retail space (m²) per 10 000 inhabitants. Source: East 8

luxury end of the market extremely profitable. In the mature residential market of Budapest a 250 m² property can fetch US$300 000. Similar price levels at this end of the market are evident in Poland, Czechoslovakia and the former Soviet Union.

The operation of a two-tier market in the east (one tier for the general public and the other for westerners and the new entrepreneurs) is nowhere more clearly seen than in Moscow. In 1991, a Muscovite would expect to pay 30 roubles per month for a 50 m² apartment. At an exchange rate of 30 roubles to the US dollar, rent for an apartment is equivalent to US$1 per month. At the same time apartments were being advertised for rent in hard currency at $800 per month. The average monthly salary of a Muscovite is approximately 350 roubles or US$12 per month. Thus if a resident can let his flat for one month he need not work for over five years! This example illustrates the explosive nature of the market.

Infrastructure

Infrastructure in terms of road and rail is not booming and is unlikely to in the near future according to experts from the World Bank. It is their opinion that transport prices should reflect the market more closely and that central European countries are among those which can least afford subsidized transport. The main problem is that mobility has simply been too cheap. Subsidies have obscured the real costs, which should include not only capital and running costs but also congestion, environmental and accident costs.

Construction industry

Dependent on a steady stream of government work for decades, the construction industry is now having to compete for contracts within the private sector, raising the scope for low cost construction work. Legitimate concerns about the quality and reliability of construction do exist, yet it should be recognized that some eastern European concerns, particularly from Poland, have an established reputation internationally in the Middle East. Currently west European contractors are identifying and working with reliable east European partners in consortia which enable them to offer the benefits of quality, reliability, project management and low cost construction. The combination of low construction costs and high returns are the essential ingredients for profitable development and a booming market.

Attractions and concerns

The attractions of eastern Europe to potential investors are fairly clear: on the doorstep of the European Community and the largest consumer market in the world is a well educated population, with a wide range of skills available at low cost. In real estate terms market demand is high and supply is low. From an east European perspective the attractions of western investment are equally apparent. There is a need for hard currency to pay for national necessities; a need to upgrade production facilities to increase output and make products more competitive on the world markets; a need for technical, managerial and commercial expertise; and a need to provide perceived material improvements superior to the old system before political disillusion sets in. On the other hand, however, there is a concern of exploitation, which is understandable given the lack of confidence in the business acumen of eastern European countries. This is especially acute in the field of real estate where property is often an asset which can be readily converted into hard currency.

Local demand

One of the most remarkable facets of the east European real estate market, or for that matter most other business activity, is the oversight when it comes to anticipating local demand. Although it is understandable that western developers and financial institutions gravitate to hard currency, the capacity of the local entrepreneurs, especially traders, to pay substantial sums for their needs is often overlooked. To illustrate the capability of local markets, in Warsaw 300 cars were sold within one week of the opening of the new Mercedes outlet. Similarly, statistics quoted earlier clearly show the potential scope for investment in offices, hotels and housing, although perhaps the sectors which are most interesting are the retail and leisure sectors where the pent-up demand is tremendous. Throughout eastern Europe, housing estates with populations of 150 000 have been built with little or no retail or leisure facilities. With currencies which are at least internally convertible there is considerable scope in these markets.

However, the question remains: who is going to pay the higher prices of western-style goods? East Europeans are like consumers everywhere, they neither know nor follow the canon of simplistic economics. When the Berlin wall came down in Germany a remarkable phenomenon occurred. Nobody wanted perfectly good but unwashed and unpackaged East German potatoes. The reason was that washed, packaged and more expensive West German potatoes became available. Although many east Europeans will not be able to afford new cars, houses or foreign holidays, they will allow themselves some of the luxuries of the west. Clearly local east Europeans are already paying, and increasingly will be able to pay, for such goods.

Returns on profit do not have to be taken out, at least in the short term, but can be reinvested locally to build up a chain or brand. The application of western management expertise, perhaps through franchising arrangements, offers great potential at low risk as the success of a pilot project leads to greater confidence and willingness to reinvest. Retail and leisure chains have the capacity to be developed at very low cost and will be encouraged by both residents and local authorities alike.

Brakes on investment

There are two brakes which impinge on the development process, one western and one eastern. The western brake takes the form of caution stemming from the sheer newness of the market, together with assimilating technical matters such as procedures, taxation, currency and title risks. The second brake which may well prove to be the more intractable should not be underestimated. Thirty-five years or more of being told 'profit is crime' is likely to have a lasting effect. The lack of expertise is perhaps the most serious single problem; it hampers both the development of coherent government and company policies. Essential technical training is not the problem; it is the financial, managerial and professional skills which are most needed. The professional skills, particularly knowledge of commercial practice, duties and liabilities, are those most often overlooked. Fortunately it is these very skills which westerners can provide in abundance.

The brakes are being progressively released as an understanding of the market grows. Aid was the first stage, followed by politically backed financing from the European Bank for Reconstruction and Development, the World Bank, the International Finance Corporation, the International Monetary Fund and credit agreement by individual countries. Large scale private investment is the next stage and this is now well underway, most notably with Volkswagen's US$5.5 billion investment in Czechoslovakia's Skoda.

5.3   RISK FACTORS

In eastern Europe there are certain risks involved but they need to be seen in perspective. The commitment to democracy and the market economy in Hungary, Poland and the former Czechoslovakia is not seriously in doubt, and although it is still too early to make such a statement about Russia the signs are reasonably encouraging. However, international consensus is crucial to political and economic success. The west cannot afford to allow eastern Europe to fail. This factor marks out eastern Europe as a unique and attractive developing market. Consequently, political transformation in the east needs to be bolstered by economic change, otherwise those standing for promarket and democratic politics will be outvoted. Political disillusionment and instability will set in with perceived risks of militarism and mass immigration into western Europe. Although there are very sound reasons for the west to assist with political and economic development of the east, the support is not being given without strings. In exchange, tough economic policies must be adhered to in each country which will act as a key source of assurance to potential investors.

From a commercial perspective there are a lot of potential risk factors concerning the operation of the market, such as the spending power of local economies, infrastructural standards, currency convertibility, profit repatriation and land rights. Although these issues cannot be casually set aside there are equally strong counter-arguments. It is certainly the case that spending power in the local economy is low in relation to the more prosperous western countries. Eastern Europe is nevertheless developed and with the transition to the market economy there is an increasingly important entrepreneurial class with prodigious spending power. In Budapest, in particular, top specification houses and the best retail and office accommodation are being acquired by Hungarians.

With respect to infrastructure, it is certainly true that telephones, roads, pollution control and so on are some way behind the standards of western Europe, America and Japan, but what seems to be consistently overlooked is that by world standards eastern European countries are among the most advanced countries. The upgrading of the infrastructure and transformation to western standards can be expected to happen quickly as eastern Europe will be able to leap-frog several technological generations. This is most clearly so in the field of telecommunications.

The question of non-convertible currencies is being addressed. Internal convertibility has been achieved in all central European countries, although full convertibility is still some way off and requirements to convert proportions of hard currency earnings into the local currencies also remain. The requirements can be problematical, with pre-conditions on converting local currencies back into hard currency. There are also restrictions on the repatriation of profits. These complications tend to polarize investment prospects. On one hand, developments can be set up to work purely in local currency terms with little or no intention to convert into hard currency and repatriate profits. This strategy will involve long term investment in the country with profits being ploughed back to generate further indigenous economic growth. On the other hand, developments can be established to operate in hard currency terms with revenues from rentals not entering the country. International tenants are prepared to pay for high quality accommodation in hard currency and are not particular if they pay locally or by credit card into accounts in Austria. The strategy here is more opportunistic with limited exposure to the longer term. The essence of the currency issue is that there are strategies to address the concerns by taking either short term or long term views.

The rights to land can be problematical, but a careful approach can produce results. The clearest example of the exaggeration of the land rights problem in the east is perhaps the Polish 'perpetual usufruct' which is prevalent in Warsaw. Often held in scorn by western commentators, but is it different to the 999 year lease which is common in the City of London? There are, however, additional problems in the east, particularly with respect to title legitimacy since the Second World War. Property was often confiscated, sometimes illegally, even by the terms of the regimes which prevailed at the time. Poland, Czechoslovakia and Hungary have all developed their own approaches to the issue, but all the countries do have forms of land register and if the 'lineage' of title can be traced back to the war, which in most instances it can, there is scope for distinguishing problematical titles from those which are 'clean'.

From an investor's perspective, these issues, even though they are not insurmountable, can nevertheless act as a constraint, with similarities often drawn with South America. However, arguably eastern Europe is distinguishable from South America in the following ways: higher education and skill levels; better infrastructure; higher population densities; close proximity to major markets; popular democratic governments; mass tourism potential; larger capital base; and common cultural heritage with western Europe.

The current political, economic and commercial transformations taking place in eastern European countries can be compared with Europe after the war, or, more recently, Spain after Franco with respect to periods of growth and prosperity. Spain emerged from the oppressive Franco regime and was for many years on the periphery of the European Community before eventually becoming a member state. Foreign investment in Spain grew from US$2 billion in 1984 to US$15 billion in 1987. Public debt and the debt service ratio were halved over the same period and this economic resurgence was matched by a boom in the real estate market.

5.4   DEVELOPER'S ROLE

A surprising facet of developments to date in eastern Europe is the paucity of developers. The reality is that consultants are often making the running and deals are struck by introducing contractors to eastern state companies or to the local authorities who control the land. On reflection it is not surprising; work in the west is drying up for consultants while developers are struggling to survive in the depressed market.

The developer is the specialist who normally brings the keen sense of opportunity, the team of consultants and the financial arguments to convince the funders. However, developers to date have been so sceptical about the likelihood of selling on a scheme that they have seldom gone in search of projects, with the result that there are perhaps more funds available than there are developers who can make convincing proposals. The ethos of most developers in the United Kingdom and USA is to trade the development. Currently there is scope for this in eastern Europe by selling to tenants. This can work with individual houses, but in the case of hotels, owners tend to make their own joint ventures or go for management contracts, whereas offices are rarely let to one tenant alone. Consequently, developers may need to consider holding the property for longer than would normally be the case, which can act as a disincentive.

Joint ventures

The increasing use of joint venture developments is due to a potent mix of tax incentives, profit repatriation and land rights. Land can be offered by the eastern partner as the basis of his share in a joint venture. A typical arrangement might be for the land to be valued at about 10–20% of the total development value, although an eastern partner may well wish to increase its stake through the provision of local currency, consultancy, materials, infrastructure, substructure or superstructure works. In some circumstances, it has been known for a land stake to be valued as high as 50% of the equity of the joint venture depending on the timing of the contribution. At the crucial early stage of a development it could be the most significant asset by giving security to the providers of finance. However, the effect of this arrangement could leave a western partner to raise finance for 85% of the project's costs with only 50% of the equity to show for it.

Land valuation

Land valuation and the eastern partner's profit share tend to be at the core of negotiations. In the absence of a mature land market the residual land valuation method assumes greater importance than is normally the case in western Europe. It provides a mechanism for valuing the land from projected rents and approximations of the rate of return on investment. The residual land valuation establishes the gross value of a project from rents and yields, it deducts all the project's costs from the gross value and the balance represents the value of the land. Valuations require consistency on two factors; the going cost of building plots and the ratio of land value to gross development value (10–20% is a generally accepted range).

Yields

Yields in eastern Europe have to be set against returns on the relatively secure savings and equities in the west. A significant factor is clearly needed to take account of the added risk of operating in eastern Europe. Currently, with bank interest rates at about 10% in western Europe and less in the USA, a yield of 20% on hard currency investments is fairly usual for central Europe, whereas in Moscow, the Soviet/American joint venture Perestroika is working on the basis of about 33%.

5.5 FUNDING

The opportunities in eastern Europe are dependent on an adequate provision of funds. There are a variety of ways in which an investor can seek to raise funds for projects which almost certainly involve one of the following organizations.

World Bank

The International Bank for Reconstruction and Development (IBRD) is part of the World Bank and has provided loans to Hungary since 1983. It is moving away from massive infrastructure investments and more towards operational studies followed by well-proven, pragmatic investments. For example, it currently (1992) is launching an investment programme for Polish housing aimed at implementing new technical, managerial and financial solutions with an emphasis placed on mortgage credits. These may extend to 85% of the total costs.

International Finance Corporation

The International Finance Corporation (IFC) is affiliated to the World Bank and offers a variety of financing packages tailored to meet the needs of an individual project. Among the financial instruments offered are loans, subordinated and convertible loans, income notes or equity. The IFC also provides stand-by financing and organizes the syndication of loans. International Finance Corporation loan and equity investments are usually limited to no more than 25% of the project cost, up to US$100 million. For equity investments, up to 35% of the share capital for the investment can be supplied.

The IFC has been active in Hungary, Poland and Czechoslovakia and up to the summer of 1990 had invested over US$290 million in Hungary alone. In addition, the IFC has taken a surprisingly positive line on real estate projects in Poland; for example, it is putting US$9 million into Trusthouse Forte's Bristol Hotel project in Warsaw and is understood to be helping with the funding of an office project in the same city. Although not contrary to its constitution it is unusual for the IFC to be involved in what appears to be straightforward commercial projects. Arguably its involvement may work as a stimulant to the more conventional sources of real estate finance. Certainly the IFC can be a catalyst in building the credibility of a project; it can provide funds, participate in the equity of a venture and also help to mobilize other methods of funding.

European Investment Bank

The European Investment Bank (EIB) is an autonomous institution within the European Community. It raises money on the capital markets for investment in central Europe and by the end of 1990 had made available ECU 1 billion for investment in Poland. Loans are project linked and orientated to the financing of the fixed asset components of an investment. The EIB finances both public and private sector projects in infrastructure, agriculture, tourism and industry.

European Bank for Reconstruction and Development

As yet the role of the emerging European Bank for Reconstruction and Development (EBRD) is still not clear. However, it considers itself as the first international financial institution of the post-Cold War period, its aim being to foster the transition towards market economies and to promote private and entrepreneurial initiatives. Some observers see the EBRD in the mould of the old World Bank, providing funding at preferential rates for infrastructure schemes, whereas others, particularly the United Kingdom and the USA, consider that it should be more involved with private projects. The latter view is increasingly holding sway, with suggestions that 60% of its lending will be to the private sector. Various western governments have given assurances on funding and specific projects are already being considered. Total capital is likely to be US$13 billion; currently US$1.7 billion has been earmarked for Poland and the same for Hungary. Regarding real estate the bank made its first investment in eastern Europe in early 1992, this involved the US$120 million National Bank of Poland office building in Warsaw.

Institutional investors

Although institutional investors are gathering information, only a few are considering investment. Their lack of activity constrains the secondary real estate market. The difficulty is often not finding the money, but matching the project to the onerous conditions of the particular fund. In 1990 alone around 25 country funds with interests or potential interests in eastern Europe were set up; two years later not one of these funds is fully invested and, in fact, most are less than 50% invested. There are also a large number of development funds and venture capital operations established by banks, governments or groups of investors (Table 5.1). These funds will generally provide project financing at commercial rates and may wish to take up equity in a venture.

Private banks and project finance

Clearing banks can provide funds for investment in eastern Europe but they tend to be conservative and often require stringent security. The current downturn in the United Kingdom and USA economies, and real estate markets in particular, has not helped.

Financial sector's perspective

It would be short-sighted of financial institutions to consider eastern Europe as simply a real estate development opportunity. The prize is much greater. Although eastern Europe languished under the communist yoke for almost

Table 5.1   Selected funds with east European projects. Investment given as millions of US dollars

Fund	Sponsor(s)	Investment
E. Europe Development	Invesco MIM, Dalwa Europe	40
Austro-Hungary Fund	Merrill Lynch	49
Hungarian Investment Company	Kleinwort Benson	100
First Hungary Fund	National Bank of Hungary/ Andrew Sarios & Associates	80
Emerging Eastern Europe Fund	Bear Stearns & Co., George Soros, IFC	15
East German Investment Trust	County NatWest, Word Mackenzie, Berliner Bank	40
Deutschland Investment Corporation	Robert Fleming	55
Creditanstait Hungary/Fund	Creditanstait, Bank Verein	50
Polish American Enterprise	US Government	240

half a century the ubiquitous service industries seen in the west have been stunted in the east. It is hardly surprisingly to find that the financial sector is perhaps the most stunted of all. Mortgages, insurance, pensions, banks and the stock-exchange can best be described as vestigial. Yet there is a market of 400 million consumers who have a tremendous desire for western comforts, both tangible and intangible.

Real estate investments in eastern Europe have the capacity to provide handsome returns and are entirely justifiable in their own right. However, possibly a more exciting perspective still for the institutions is that fairly modest commitments now provide scope for developing comprehensive relations with eastern institutions. Indeed, it is even conceivable that joint ventures can be forged by provisions of management alone and in so doing western institutions can position themselves to take full advantage of the enormous growth in the new financial services sector that will surely come.

5.6   URBAN REGENERATION: APPLICATION OF EXPERIENCE IN THE UNITED KINGDOM

Throughout the capital cities of eastern Europe great offices and hotels are rising out of the ground with precious little tangible benefit for the local population. Meanwhile shortages in the housing stock, and towns and cities in desperate need of refurbishment and inadequate infrastructure highlight the need for urban renewal. In some respects it can be argued that eastern Europe has similar conditions to those prevailing in the United Kingdom in the early 1980s, but of course on an altogether more comprehensive scale. Local authorities are left to provide for enormous needs with few resources. State companies are devoid of cash to provide for their investment needs. In this scenario real estate assets may offer part of the answer.

Under the Thatcher-led Conservative administration of the 1980s, local authorities and state companies in Britain had their budgets slashed as privatization became the creed. Starved of funds these bodies looked to their assets, particularly their real estate assets, to raise funds for investment needs. The offering of land for sale with development potential, the 'development competition', is in reality more of a commercial process than a design competition. Although the latter plays a significant part, it is the commercial dimension which is most often decisive and which makes the approach distinctive. However, the advent of the 'development competition' followed a remarkable rise in the real estate market, so making this approach feasible. The subsequent fall in the property market (in the early 1990s) has been predictably matched by a decline in development competitions. This contrasts with eastern Europe where the property cycle certainly augers well for the next few years, as shown earlier in this chapter (Figures 5.1 and 5.3).

Early development competitions in the United Kingdom tended to be small infill sites with simple commercial elements. The projects would simply raise money for the local authority or state company and the money would be transferred to the appropriate part of the local authority budget. British Rail, for instance, developed relatively straightforward 'air right' developments over the tracks of certain mainline stations in London, namely Charing Cross, Cannon Street and Victoria. In time, larger sites were considered and this brought the local authorities and state companies into contact with local pressure groups who had ideas of their own. Invariably such groups would not be satisfied by vague assurances that the money raised by development competitions would be put to good use elsewhere in the borough; instead, they wanted to see the benefits immediately and on the site to be developed. Typically housing, shopping and employment opportunities were perceived as key priorities. In the development process these pressure groups could not be ignored and their interventions promoted change. Instead of cash being generated by land disposal the development competition became an enabling mechanism for development, not only of commercial facilities but also of social facilities as the revenues raised from the commercial elements can be transferred directly into social facilities on the same site.

Local authorities and state companies responded creatively to the evolving situation and, recognizing that local support was a key element to the success of a project, schemes started to take on an all-embracing nature. A project could involve the provision of housing, a park, road improvements, railway lines and stations. For example, in London at Liverpool Street station land was provided by British Rail for commercial development in exchange for a comprehensive upgrade of the station. Subsequently at King's Cross massive new facilities to serve the new channel tunnel traffic, housing and an enormous park were proposed. At the Bishopsgate Goodsyard project, in addition to commercial uses (namely offices, shops and hotel provision), an extension of the underground line, housing, small business units, a park and various other community provisions were agreed.

Benefits to the local authority/state company

The first and most obvious benefit is a capital sum in exchange for the sale of the land. However, benefits can be far more extensive. It is important to appreciate that the cash benefits do not have to involve the outright sale of land; rather, the site may be leased to the developer. Alternatively, the developer may enter into a joint venture with the local authority/state company and the lease may be granted to the joint venture on the basis of a ground rent. In the case of a local authority it will, of course, have the additional benefit of the extra local tax revenue stemming from the occupiers of the scheme. At the same time a derelict site is put to good use, employment is created and local needs are directly addressed. Furthermore, and arising from the developer's involvement, the use mix in the scheme is more likely to relate to the demand in the locality. In addition, the local authority benefits from the entrepreneurial skills of the private sector, the use of the professional team to give credibility to a development and, in doing so, to access diverse funding sources. Close to the heart of local politicians is the fact that a built project is a tangible manifestation of their contribution to the locality.

This kind of approach can have direct application in eastern Europe; however, it requires developers with a broad vision. Competitions demand a greater range of skills and place an emphasis on management, thus within the development company sub-management groups are formed around particular provisions. For instance, the team which deals with the housing element of the project requires different skills from that working on the commercial elements. Also, the developer may be dealing with a dozen sources of finance ranging from short term commercial funds from banks to long term institutional investors and public sources of finance.

Problems and abuses

In identifying this approach as appropriate for eastern Europe it is also important to draw attention to likely shortcomings.

Firstly, the two sides of the development competition can behave equally badly. With respect to the developer, a 'promise the earth, win the competition and then renegotiate' attitude may prevail. Undoubtedly winning a competition without payment of ground rent or a capital sum is an excellent way of increasing a development company's assets. It builds a 'land bank' for the developer for when the time is right to develop. Another tendency on the part of the developer is to evaluate the offer as high as possible but leaving actual payment qualified by market conditions. The manipulation of phasing is another area open to abuse. This entails developing the commercial elements as quickly as possible and being slow on those elements which are not commercially worthwhile. The developer will seek to incorporate as much commercial content as possible.

On the local authority/state company side abuses include a tendency to use the competitions as idea generators with little serious intent to actually develop the project. Competition rules can be badly drafted, leading to poor responses and an arbitrary selection of winners. Also, where the local authority is seeking to dispose of land, special issues can arise. Furthermore, the temptation of local politicians to interfere in the process is difficult to resist as they very readily see the political benefit of projects. Perhaps the most worrying area of abuse by the local authority is joint interest with the developer to incorporate as much commercial content as possible. Simply put, what is to stop the local authority from over-developing? When the treasury department of a local authority is set against the architectural department, the arguments of raising finance to meet the needs of the electorate tend to hold sway. This can lead to the abuse of its planning control procedures and support of local authority sponsored schemes at the expense of other private developments.

Case example: East 8's initiative in Poland

The experience of the United Kingdom in the 1980s can and is being applied to eastern Europe. Clearly fundamental conditions exist, but there is the need to stimulate the commercial real estate sector and the macro-economy in general. The development competition approach will not solve all of the local authority or state company investment needs, but it can offer some assistance in the difficult circumstances which prevail. Also the problems and abuses of the mechanism can, with care, be addressed.

A practical application of this approach comes from the work of East 8 in Poland where the government, acting on the advice of East 8, applied to the European Community for technical assistance for a model urban renewal project using the principles expressed in this chapter. The proposal involves the creation of mirror teams of western and Polish consultants to appraise a number of potential development sites submitted by Warsaw district authorities. The most attractive site will be selected and a tender document prepared, complete with funding statement, including a statement by the World Bank Housing Finance Project Office. Although there is still some way to go to bring this project to fruition, it at least offers the prospect of fitting the provision of low cost housing into the overall real estate context.

5.7   CONCLUSIONS

In eastern Europe the early years of the 1990s have been remarkable not only for the resolution of the newly elected governments to take the tough measures necessary to set their economies on a sound footing, but also the readiness by the public to accept a lowering of living standards on the understanding that the benefits of reform will eventually materialize. As the mature markets of the west stagnate, new horizons are emerging in the east, currently in real estate and almost certainly across the whole financial sector in the near future. However, while the commercial real estate sector is booming in eastern Europe, the conditions of most of its people are deteriorating. Resulting disenchantment with the virtues of the market will follow swiftly unless tangible benefits can be produced.

The property sector has some scope to generate such benefits from the proceeds of commercial real estate elements. The example of the model urban renewal project using development competition techniques can be replicated, but its impact on the overall social and housing needs will be limited. It would be wrong to suggest that the development competition approach is much more than a first step in addressing the fundamental needs of eastern Europe. Nevertheless, realized projects cannot only provide benefits for the locality but also impart vital commercial skills to the local authorities, state companies and local consultants with the prospect that they will themselves be able to optimize at least some of their dormant assets.

REFERENCE

East 8 (1991) *Real Estate Development in Eastern Europe*, 2nd edn, East 8, London, 240pp.

6

Fiscal measures in promoting urban regeneration: Custom House Docks, Dublin

_____ *J. Gahan*

Urban development in Ireland has been characterized by periods of wide-spread expansion, interspersed with years of stagnation and decline. In terms of expansion the past three decades have seen the translation of rapid economic and population growth into extensive physical development in urban areas. Over the period 1960–80 population, gross national product and investment in building and construction grew at an annual compound rate of 1, 4 and 6.3%, respectively. This resulted in a 20% increase in population, a two-fold increase in the production of goods and services, and more than a three-fold increase in the output of the building and construction sector.

In the period 1980–90, following Ireland's decision to join the European Monetary System, which links the Irish pound to the exchange rate mechanism, monetary discipline was introduced into the fiscal equation. This resulted in periods of real growth in the economy with levels of inflation over the last seven years averaging between 2 and 3.5% per year. This low level of inflation linked to the low cost of money, together with real growth, has resulted in a huge increase in the provision of goods and services. These factors, taken in conjunction with the significant transfer of resources through the European Regional and Social Fund, has meant that a level of confidence in terms of business activity has been established in Ireland. Growth has resulted in significant property development opportunities, particularly in terms of urban regeneration.

During the last decade, running parallel with these positive economic features, the Irish Government took a policy decision to promote the re-development of cities throughout Ireland by means of special taxation incentives within designated areas. The linkage of these two factors has brought about a fundamental and radical alteration to the core of urban areas within Ireland. The Custom House Docks Development Project in Dublin is one of the areas included in the Irish Government's strategy.

6.1 THE DEVELOPMENT PROCESS

The process of development takes place where land and buildings can be used for a new purpose or where an existing use can be carried out more intensively or efficiently. However, development activity is complex and lengthy, accordingly promoters must look ahead and project into the future. In essence there is the need to prepare a phased programme which projects forward over the expected duration of the development process and possibly beyond. Economic factors, including monetary trends, building costs over the development period, the level of rental likely to be achieved, the general state of the letting market and investment conditions should be considered, analysed and studied before a decision to proceed in principle is made.

Additional to economic and viability considerations, an issue fundamental to the decision to promote a particular development is the level of difficulty which may arise in terms of the planning process. This may cause delay, restrictions on the type and form of development, or the likelihood of third party appeals which can frustrate and ultimately prolong the development process. Also, for development to begin there must be a promoter. This may be a private individual, a government agency, a local authority, a bank/financial institution, a special purpose development agency, or any combination of these.

Potentially, several other factors are influential in the development process. Firstly, consumer demand must exist for the finished product, both in the letting and capital investment market. This may be either demand in commercial terms or indeed demand from a social perspective. Secondly, the development must be physically capable of being implemented. In this respect a number of issues are important.

1. The possession of the land must be unencumbered and freely available for development.
2. There must be an unencumbered legal title to the land with planning permission immediately available.
3. The promoter must have the skill and expertise to organize the entire operation from the pre-development phase, through the development phase and to the marketing phase.

Furthermore, the promoters of the project must have sufficient resources either in their own possession or be capable of raising the necessary finances to fund the project from start to completion. In the case of large schemes, such as the Custom House Docks, where the development period extends beyond two years, the economics of the project must be robust enough to withstand significant changes in market conditions throughout the construction phase.

Once these criteria have been satisfied, in particular the economic rationale of the development, the promoter must then consider the concept of the development balance sheet. This effectively involves preparing a detailed financial calculation to establish the viability or otherwise of the specific components within the project. Initial calculations using valuation techniques, namely the residual valuation method, are used as a basis for more sophisticated appraisal, including sensitivity analysis, discounted cash flow, timing and critical path analysis. These techniques are discussed elsewhere (Darlow, 1988). Such analysis is used to show whether, on the basis of a given set of circumstances, the various inputs into the project are less than or at least equal to the capital value of the completed development.

6.2   FUNDING OF DEVELOPMENT

In considering the funding of any urban renewal development scheme, it is necessary to clearly differentiate between short term and long term finance. In the case of short term finance this usually takes the form of a straightforward loan facility either by way of a term loan or overdraft. These are normally secured by way of a fixed or floating charge on the development site and possibly on other property owned by the promoters. It is common for short term finance to be linked with long term finance and for a moratorium on interest repayments to be allowed, up to the time the project becomes income producing – a concept known as capitalization of interest charges. Such an arrangement usually provides for the financial institution to either purchase the completed investment at a slight discount on current investment yields or, alternatively, the institution may obtain a share in the equity of the development.

The prime sources of short term finance are normally the major banking groups or their investment offshoots, the major insurance companies, the pension funds, the merchant banks or, to a lesser extent, private sources of venture capital, as well as state or regional funds. However, it should be stressed that it is extremely difficult to raise short term finance on any project without strict financial criteria being met, both in terms of the method of securing the money advanced and the viability of the project from conception to completion.

The degree of difficulty in raising such finance will depend on the status of the promoter, whether it is a private individual, a private company, a public company or a public authority. The track record of the promoter in terms of ability to complete the project successfully is also important. In most urban development schemes in Ireland over the last ten years a combination of public and private sector finance of one kind or another has normally been used.

Short term finance is usually drawn down as required during the development period. In general, the actual amount of funds drawn down will be approximately half the total amount committed in terms of interest charges. On substantial and long term projects, such as Custom House Docks, the general cost of short term funding would be variable to reflect the change in the money market over the development period. In property development terms, five years would be regarded as being extremely long and, therefore, short term funds are committed at a variable rate of interest depending on market conditions.

Long term finance on the other hand arises basically in three situations. Firstly, in circumstances where a promoter proposes to retain the investment on completion, long term finance will be raised to pay off short term finance. Secondly, where major developments, because of their size, are able to arrange finance for the development programme on a long term basis either as an overall financial package or as an equity sharing/ discounted investment sale. The third scenario arises where the promoter is a financial institution or a pension fund. In these circumstances, the project can be funded by the internal cash flow arrangements of the institution or pension fund. Several different forms of long term finance are available (Brett, 1990), including secured loans, mortgage finance, sale and leaseback, equity funds and various equity sharing arrangements.

6.3 DEVELOPMENT SENSITIVITY

In any property development situation the success or otherwise of a particular project depends on the financial viability of the proposed scheme. Development proposals are prepared on the basis of known costs and values. However, if these costs or values move out of synchronization the effect on the overall development equation can be dramatic. This is particularly true in large scale projects where the time frame for the development is of the order of three to five years. Consequently, optimum use must be made of the prevailing market forces in a 'bull' situation. Alternatively, a retrenchment must be available in a 'bear' market where circumstances prevail against the development. On large scale projects, such as the Custom House Docks Development with a time-scale of five years, at least one downturn in the market can be expected over that period. Indeed, as discussed by Nabarro and Key (1992) the turning points in the economic cycle can be painful for those involved in large scale development schemes.

The preparation and use of cash flow techniques linked to sensitivity analysis is, therefore, vital to ensure that as the development scheme moves through from the planning to the completion stage the elements in the project are not adversely affected by a downturn in market conditions. This tumble effect, where rental levels fall and at the same time investment yields rise, can make the project literally uneconomic and unviable in a very short period of time.

A good example of this tumbledown effect is the Olympia and York Development in London Docklands at Canary Wharf. It is, therefore, vital in terms of securing a large scale project that every effort is made at the financial planning stage to avoid the effects of tumbledown. This can be achieved by the early placement of long term funding linked to the proper and planned phasing/timing of the construction programme.

Many international projects such as Canary Wharf would have progressed successfully through the planning and development phase were it not for the bad timing built into the sensitivity analysis and the over-ambitious targets set. In controlling tumbledown effects it is necessary to incorporate within the development process a sensitivity barometer which will signal immediately the implications of falling rents and increasing yields and, furthermore, within the development agreement to have the ability to match the delivery of the completed development with the market-place. In the context of urban development it is better to survive and live to fight another day than to keep on building regardless, only to find that the project ends up going into liquidation or receivership.

6.4   CUSTOM HOUSE DOCKS DEVELOPMENT PROJECT

The Custom House Docks Development Project consists of approximately 11 ha of dockland adjoining the north central business district of Dublin. It is located about 500 m from Dublin city centre (Berry *et al.*, 1991). Within the site there are two interlinked dock basins consisting of approximately 3 ha of water, which are being retained as a feature within the development.

The site at the Custom House Docks has for the previous 200 years been part of Dublin's dockland area. However, with the introduction of containerization and roll-on/roll-off (ro/ro) freight in the 1960s the port of Dublin developed eastwards of the existing dockland area. Continuing development in port technology over the last 30 years rendered a large area of the north docklands, from Custom House Quay to the Eastlink Bridge, redundant and hence available for urban renewal purposes.

Strategic planning of project

The long time-scale of waterfront schemes is highlighted by the fact that for about ten years before the actual project began debate had taken place at both central and local government level to decide on the best method of regenerating this important and valuable city centre site. Discussions mainly centred not on the actual content of the scheme that might be proposed, but more on the macro-structure that would be necessary to achieve an orderly and efficient execution of the development. The Irish Government at the time was conscious of the controversy that had arisen in relation to planning issues in the London Docklands and the consequent effect that such delays and controversy had on the completion of parts of the development programme.

To ensure that a proper exercise in terms of strategic planning was carried out a special team was established by the Department of the Environment to examine and report on the experiences of other similar developments world-wide. Stemming from this examination it was apparent that a number of fundamental issues had to be addressed, namely: the land would have to be in one single ownership; the agency charged with development responsibility would have to be single-purpose; the planning control function would have to be vested in the development agency; a range of urban renewal and other tax incentives would have to be put in place to ensure, as far as possible, the economic viability of the entire project at a macro-level; and a mixed form of development should be contemplated, i.e. commercial, quasi-commercial and social uses to ensure a substantial positive impact in terms of its linkage with the existing central business district of the city.

Custom House Docks Development Authority

In October 1985, the Irish Government agreed in principle to establish a special agency to enable the 11 ha site to be redeveloped in a substantial and co-ordinated form over a five year period. To bring the development programme forward as rapidly as possible the Irish Government introduced the Urban Renewal Act 1986, which provided for the establishment of the Custom House Docks Development Authority. The Authority was given power under the Urban Renewal Act to acquire, hold and manage land in the Custom House Docks area for redevelopment by itself or others, or to dispose of land. Hence the existing and facilitating legislation meant that the Authority was able to approach the development with a large degree of certainty. For example, under the legislation, ownership of the site was immediately transferred from the Dublin Port and Docks Board to the Authority by means of a single transfer order signed by the Minister for Finance. Indeed, within four months of this transfer order being effected, the Authority was able to register freehold title on the entire site free from all encumbrances.

The Authority's remit was specific: its *raison d'être* was to regenerate and improve the area under its control, so as to rebuild confidence and encourage investment. In so doing the Authority would contribute to the diversification of the city's employment base, to the development of local enterprise and to the mobilization of skills from within the metropolitan area of Dublin.

The legislation also provided for a system of exempted development under the Planning and Development Acts. The Authority, having received ministerial approval for its development plan, was allowed to certify development which complied with the approved plan. This system of exemption allowed the pre-development phase of the project to be shortened, which in turn facilitated speedy commencement of development on the site. Furthermore, the Urban Renewal Act 1986, taken in conjunction with the Finance Act 1986, put in place a wide range of urban renewal incentives which has helped to underpin the economic viability of the development.

Regarding the pre-development marketing of the project, potential investors/developers were given a degree of certainty in terms of land ownership, planning and economic viability. Consequently this structured approach helped to market the project as an attractive and lucrative proposition which would embrace both the public and private sectors (Benson, 1989). This was particularly beneficial in an international arena, the market which the Authority was targeting in terms of securing a joint venture partner.

Under the Urban Renewal Act 1986 the Authority was to receive grant in aid for two years up to the end of 1989, and thereafter was expected to be self-financing. The non-availability of substantial grant in aid from the Irish Government meant that the Authority had to find a method of developing the site which would in essence be a joint venture between the public sector and private enterprise. However, the legislation allowed the Authority, with the relevant approval, to borrow up to £10 million for capital purposes (all amounts of money quoted in this chapter are in Irish pounds, not Sterling).

In accordance with its statutory obligations, the Authority published its planning scheme in June 1987, which formed the basis for inviting international developer groups to submit proposals for joint venture development of the site (Custom House Dock Development Authority, 1987a). It was considered essential that an integrated planning, design and development approach was adopted. The general response to the planning scheme underlined the tremendous development potential offered by the site. Consequently, eight proposals for the development of the entire site were received, together with eight submissions for individual elements within the scheme. The eight submissions made to the Authority were for the design, finance and construction of the entire project.

The Authority put in place rigorous procedures for assessing the various submissions. This assessment was a critically important part of the evolving process for the redevelopment of the site. It helped to establish and crystallize more clearly the Authority's development objectives, which are summarized as follows (Custom House Dock Development Authority, 1987b):

1. To have the Custom House Docks site completely developed and functioning within a period of five years from the date of the initial commencement of development work on site.
2. To reunite the Custom House Docks site with the city centre to achieve the revitalization of the central business district of Dublin.
3. To act as a catalyst to stimulate the redevelopment and regeneration of other quayside and obsolete areas in Dublin.
4. To create a wide range of new investment and job opportunities reflecting the hopes and aspirations of the citizens of Dublin.
5. To promote the development of a high standard of design and accommodation of which Dublin would be proud and in which its people would want to live, work and spend leisure time.
6. To provide private residential development within the site, which would help to secure a better balance in the social mix of housing in the inner city area.
7. To promote a partnership based on the concept of leverage by which public sector investment would lever a significant multiplier of private sector investment.

The Authority's evaluation framework for selecting the preferred developer contained three key elements against which the proposals were tested: quality of design, financial capacity and deliverability. In accordance with these criteria the project was awarded to the Custom House Docks Development Company Limited, which consisted of a joint venture between Hardwicke Limited, McInerney Properties plc and the British Land Company plc. A master project agreement between the Authority and the development company was signed in January 1988 (Custom House Dock Development Authority, 1988). This constituted a legally binding agreement, which specified the requirements for the build out of the development in accordance with an agreed master plan and building programme. It defined the relationships, rights and obligations of the parties to the agreement, including matters relating to the capitalization of the joint venture company, covenants and guarantees by the sureties, project monitoring procedures, financial provisions, transfer of lands, and the management regime for the completed development. The intended purpose of the agreement was to minimize the implicit risks which can arise from partnership involving the public and private sectors. Consequently, its role was to strike the right balance between the normal risk associated with the commercial realities of the market-place and the desirability of securing the redevelopment of the site in accordance with the approved planning scheme.

The development components for the site include an International Financial Services Centre (45 000 m^2), commercial offices (55 000 m^2), 200 residential units, a 200 bedroom hotel, a museum (15 000 m^2) and a retail leisure area (20 000 m^2). The total size of the proposed development will be approximately 200 000 m^2, representing a capital investment of £350 million.

Financial incentives

The legislation allows participants, either purchasers of buildings or occupiers, to avail of various incentives. With respect to capital allowances, all development expenditure within the Custom House Docks site qualifies for 100% capital write-down against profit. Where the building is purchased for owner occupation, it is possible under the taxation regime to write down the full 100% in the first year, provided there is sufficient profit to write it against. In circumstances where the building is purchased for investment purposes, the capital provisions provide for 54% write-down in the first year and 4% per year until the full 100% allowance is used up. If the building is subsequently disposed of within 25 years there is a pro rata claw-back provision.

Regarding occupiers, it is permissible to set off two times the rent reserved against profit for taxation purposes for a period of ten years from the date of occupation. This provision has the effect, depending on the taxation rate of the taxpayer involved, to considerably reduce the net cost of the rent reserved. To qualify for this allowance all lettings must be bona fide third party lettings and not contrived lettings made by the owners of buildings. Furthermore, there are no local property taxes payable for a period of ten years from the date of occupation. Within the current Dublin office market, the cost of local property tax per year is roughly equivalent to £3/m^2 per month in occupation costs.

The residential component in the development also receives special incentives. For example, investors in residential units, for letting to third parties, qualify for 100% capital allowance against other rental income in Ireland. For owner-occupiers of residential accommodation, 50% capital allowance is available against earned income in addition to the normal mortgage interest relief.

6.5   INTERNATIONAL FINANCIAL SERVICES CENTRE

In addition to these urban renewal incentives, which are site-specific, the Irish Government, with the approval of the European Community, designated the Custom House Docks Area as the location for the Dublin International Financial Services Centre (IFSC). The inclusion of a prestigious financial centre has undoubtedly enhanced the overall viability of the development. Essentially a company licensed by the Irish Minister for Finance to carry on international financial services within the centre, in accordance with the provisions of the Finance Act 1987, will pay a rate of corporation tax of 10%

until 31 December 2005. In terms of international financial services the only restriction on financial activity is that all dealings must be in currencies other than Irish pounds. Arguably, the IFSC is regarded as the flagship element within the overall development scheme (Berry *et al.*, 1991), and by mid-1992 over 220 special financial service companies were licensed to trade from the centre.

Once the decision was taken to establish the IFSC in Dublin, a number of promotional initiatives were put in place. The most important of these was the setting up of an International Financial Services Centre Committee by the Prime Minister to provide a forum and a clearing house for ideas which would advance the implementation of the project and monitor its progress. The marketing function for the development of the Docks Area Project, as a whole, was assigned to the consortium engaged in the development. The Custom House Docks Authority has joint responsibility with the developer for facilitating, monitoring and promoting the overall development, while the Irish Industrial Development Authority is responsible for the direct marketing of the centre, through its overseas representatives (Industrial Development Authority, 1990). The marketing of the IFSC also involves a powerful combination from both the public and private sectors (the Financial Services Industry Association, leading bankers, accountants, stockbrokers and solicitors), all participating actively in a vigorous programme in partnership with the IFSC Committee, the Irish Government's marketing group and the Department of Finance. A considerable level of success has been achieved over the three year programme, which clearly demonstrates the benefits that good marketing can make within a major development programme.

Throughout the marketing campaign strong emphasis was placed on detail, particularly with regard to the special features which will appeal from an international financial services point of view. These key issues can be identified as follows:

1. All office buildings in Phase 1 provide fully raised floors and large ceiling voids, variable air volume, air conditioning, and information technology networking throughout (Custom House Dock Development Authority, 1987b). The buildings are being finished to the highest possible standard to reflect the image of an international financial services centre.
2. Within the development a special purpose telecommunications centre linked to two separate telephone exchanges by double-loop fibre optic cables has been installed. This guarantees the operating financial services companies round the clock access to international telecommunications both on a voice and data basis.
3. The Irish telecommunications system has been rebuilt over the last ten years, involving capital investment of approximately £1.4 thousand million. The main trunk system within the country is now over 20%

fibre optic cable and the international access out of Ireland is by way of fibre optic cables from the south coast of Ireland to either the USA or directly into France and Holland. A second system of access to international telecommunications is in place by means of three separate land stations accessing directly to three separate satellite systems worldwide. In addition, a third route exists by means of a new fibre optic cable from Dublin directly to the United Kingdom, via the British Telecom system. The Irish telecommunications system is now generally accepted as being one of the best systems existing within the European Community, thus allowing the concept of the IFSC to become a reality.

6.6 CURRENT STAGE OF DEVELOPMENT

In the three years since construction began on the project in June 1988, five buildings have been completed comprising in gross terms 350 000 m², or approximately 40% of the planned development in the original concept plan. All of these buildings have been sold and, in gross terms, the sales to date have aggregated approximately £130 million. More importantly, all of the buildings are occupied and over 2000 people are employed in financial services and other related activities in the IFSC.

The current plans will provide two more financial service office buildings, both of which are scheduled to begin construction towards the end of 1992. Additionally, the residential element is scheduled to begin construction, together with the retail element, in the third quarter of 1993. It is anticipated that the entire development will be completed by the end of 1996. On completion, approximately 5000–6000 people will be permanently employed within the development.

It should be stated that, based on the original five year plan from mid-1988, there has been some slippage in the development programme. This slippage has mainly been linked to a change in the conditions prevailing in the Dublin property market over the last two years and, as a result, a revised development programme has now been put in place. Based on the present conditions in the market, it appears that the revised time frame is a realistically attainable objective.

6.7 CONCLUSIONS

The Custom House Docks Development Project, despite the apparent slippage in the building programme over the last few years, has been extremely successful. In retrospect, the original time programme set for the project was highly ambitious and did not fully reflect the likelihood of changing circumstances arising in the Dublin property market and the international economy generally.

An analysis of the project to date indicates a number of positive features:

1. The organizational structure of a special purpose development agency was the correct decision; the project would not have advanced as rapidly had the agency not been in place.
2. The concept of transferring the ownership of all land to the development agency facilitated the early delivery of the site for development.
3. The transfer of planning control to the development agency was an essential prerequisite to securing a joint venture partnership to undertake the project, and ensuring the successful international marketing of the development.
4. The inclusion of an IFSC flagship element within the scheme has enabled the project to progress in spite of the downturn in the Dublin property market in the early 1990s. Essentially, the Custom House Docks Development Project has generated its own demand for accommodation on the basis that all of the licensed financial service companies are new, both to the Irish economy and to the Dublin property market. It was clear, even at the pre-development stage, that the success of the project would be judged on the number of international companies locating in Dublin.
5. The public sector support for the project was, and still is, vital and without such support driving the flagship element it would not be possible to complete the full development, which is currently planned.

On the negative side it is disappointing that it has not as yet been possible to bring forward construction of the less remunerative elements within the scheme such as retail, leisure and housing units. It is appreciated that these are currently being planned over the next few years, but with tighter control it should have been possible to parallel some of these less remunerative elements with the more rewarding financial services component.

However, on balance, there is no doubt that the Custom House Docks Development Project to date has been a resounding success, and the current feeling within the Dublin property market is that the development will be successfully completed by 1996. What has been achieved to date is a testament to the workings of a strong public–private sector partnership where a less than desirable redundant dockland area has now been reborn to become part of the north central business district of Dublin and, indeed, on completion may become its heart.

REFERENCES

Benson, F. (1989) The roles of the public and private sector. Paper presented at the *13th International New Towns Association Conference, September 1989, Paris* (unpublished).

Berry, J.N., Deddis, W.G. and McGreal, W.S. (1991) Waterfront regeneration in Ireland: public and private sector partnerships, *Journal of Property Finance*, **2**(2), 179–184.

Brett, M. (1990) *Property and Money*, Estates Gazette, London.

Custom House Docks Development Authority (1987a) *Planning Scheme Information Supplement*, The Authority, Dublin.

Custom House Docks Development Authority (1987b) *Annual Report and Accounts*, The Authority, Dublin.

Custom House Docks Development Authority (1988) *Annual Report and Accounts*, The Authority, Dublin.

Darlow, C. (Ed.) (1988) *Valuation and Development Appraisal*, 2nd edn, Estates Gazette, London.

Industrial Development Authority (1990) *Dublin International Financial Centre*, The Authority, Dublin.

Nabarro, R. and Key, T. (1992) Current trends in commercial property investment and development: an overview. In: *Rebuilding the City, Property-led Urban Regeneration* (Eds P. Healey, S. Davoudi, M. O'Toole, S. Tavsanoglu and D. Usher), E & FN Spon, London, pp. 45–59.

PART TWO

REGENERATION POLICY AND PRACTICE

Editorial

Urban agglomerations are dynamic economic and social entities, acting as centres of population, production and consumption. At best the city embodies all the positive advantages of economies of scale, concentration of resources and the associated spin-off benefits, while at worst cities can show negative externalities, namely congestion, environmental pollution and a negative image. The challenge facing many cities in consequence necessitates the formulation of a proactive policy approach and the involvement of public sector agencies. This may embody inputs across European, national and local perspectives.

Emphasis in the second part of the book is thus placed on the integration of regeneration policy and local economic development, specifically focusing upon the role of the public sector. Key issues include the impact of policy directions, and the ability of governments to lever private sector monies and to act as facilitators of regeneration by creating the opportunity for development. Furthermore the public sector is a consumer of property resources, goods and other services and in this respect can be a major contributor to the stimulation and sustainability of economic performance.

Grover, in considering the European Community's public procurement directives, discusses the policy implications for central and local government, and for private bodies in receipt of public finances for urban regeneration programmes. The procurement of construction works by public bodies and utility undertakings, together with the purchase of architectural and town planning services, are considered within the context of urban regeneration programmes. The reform of the European Community's structural funds has enabled a source of finance to be made available for urban regeneration projects, as well as the deployment of regional assistance to the least favourable areas. Another major aspect of European Community legislation which Grover considers is the impact environmental assessment procedures will have on certain urban regeneration schemes.

In considering European cities, Hanley comments on how changed patterns in development and redevelopment have led to the abandonment of large tracts of inner city land with the decentralization of population and activities to the city fringe. The inadequacies of planning systems to effectively respond to this problem is discussed and in certain circumstances is considered to have contributed to the process. Hanley argues for the need to focus on sustainable development with environmental strategies to the forefront. Consequently, a new agenda for renewal should consider the environmental performance of the area, namely buildings, mix of uses and travel demand either within individual sites or as part of an overall city strategy. It is considered by Hanley that the economic performance and well-being of cities is increasingly interlinked with environmental performance.

The targeting of finance for development, together with the growing environmental awareness of the impact of projects within European

Community countries, can be contrasted with the structural, organizational and strategic problems in an eastern European country. Diamant and Matouskova, with specific reference to the Republics of the former Czechoslovakia, discuss the effects of institutionalization, centralization and bureaucracy on the development process. In transferring to a market economy, consideration is given to those areas where change is deemed necessary, such as physical planning concepts, sources of funding, methods of construction, project management and legislative reform. Economic development programmes in the Republics are evidently depend on more public–private partnerships, together with greater subsidization and an influx of international capital to supplement internal investment.

Lloyd and Black, in the British context, acknowledge the importance of land and property to the national economy, both as a component of investment and as a collateral for loans to companies to finance investment. The main thrust of their argument examines the contribution which property-led strategies make in terms of local economic development, particularly the regeneration of inner city areas. Within the context of current political ideology, three strands to the urban regeneration process are identified. Firstly, the locality approach incorporating Urban Development Corporations and Enterprise Zones; secondly, the agency approach as epitomized by the Scottish Development Agency and its successor body, Scottish Enterprise; and, thirdly, a proactive policy approach which seeks to liberalize the processes of development by a relaxation of public sector land use controls. The vulnerability of the property-led approach to urban regeneration and economic development is considered in the context of the slump which characterized the British economy in the early 1990s. Lloyd and Black conclude that the emphasis on land and property as the basis of urban policy must therefore undergo further refinements to achieve the effective management of urban and economic change.

Falk, in reassessing the goals of urban regeneration, argues that it is naive to judge success in terms of physical development and the level of investment alone without measuring the opportunities provided for the fulfilment of social objectives. In considering the principles on which to judge successful regeneration, recognition is given to social justice, natural balance and the minimization of waste. The nature of urban problems demands 'balanced incremental development' by proceeding in stages in which new uses are attracted, rather than the 'big bang' approach resulting in the provision of large amounts of space saturating the market. In this context, Falk makes reference to the successful achievement of regeneration objectives in Birmingham's Jewellery Quarter and Bradford's Little Germany. Both examples show that is possible for old areas, through a combination of pilot projects and flagship schemes, to attract new uses into previously redundant space.

One of the major successes of urban regeneration policy in Britain in the 1980s and a frequently quoted example is the revival of Glasgow. In

Chapter 12 Cowan and Lindsay examine the role of public sector bodies and agencies in this process. The contribution of wider strategic policy and need for the public sector to stimulate the development process are seen as key influences at a global level and also in terms of specific land use sectors, namely, offices, retail, housing, transportation, environmental improvement and cultural activities. It is stressed that the overall environment in which the revival of the city centre took place was highly favourable in terms of the structure of local government, the planning context, the enhancement of the transportation system and housing trends. However, Cowan and Lindsay point to a number of potential factors which may, throughout the 1990s, reduce the competitive advantage of Glasgow's city centre and lead to greater decentralization of uses. In this context the authors express particular concern over proposals for a single tier local authority structure, which they argue is an inappropriate method of meeting the need for strategic planning in a metropolitan area.

The role of the public sector in promoting urban regeneration is further emphasized by the Belfast example. In the final chapter of Part Two, Berry and McGreal contend that Belfast throughout the 1970s experienced a period of decline characterized by the decanting of population, decentralization of functions and a consequent loss of commercial viability. The regeneration of the city throughout the 1980s meant that urban policy had to focus on economic, social and political objectives in an environment where, initially at least, development and investment opportunities were weak due to peripherality and a negative image. Thus the public sector had by necessity to be to the forefront in creating an environment conducive to private enterprise. In this context planning policy increasingly favoured the city centre for retail and office uses; furthermore, an array of regeneration mechanisms were introduced, some paralleling those used in other British cities, whereas others were specifically designed to meet the special needs of Belfast. As Berry and McGreal point out, the convergence of favourable market conditions with the regeneration strategy being pursued by the public sector promoted an exceptional period of development activity in Belfast's city centre in the latter half of the 1980s. This, in turn, was translated into a strong performance of the commercial market with rental growth and returns in retail and office property exceeding comparable cities elsewhere in the United Kingdom.

7

Public procurement policies in the European Communities: implications for urban regeneration

—————————————— *R. Grover*

A central feature of government policy in the United Kingdom towards urban regeneration in the 1980s has been its attempts to secure investment by private capital in urban regeneration schemes. A variety of policies have been used in the attempt to achieve this aim, including Enterprise Zones, Urban Development Corporations and Simplified Planning Zones. Although these policies may have altered the balance between public and private funding in urban regeneration, it should not be overlooked that there is an important part to be played by public finance. This includes the provision of infrastructure, the preparation of derelict land for development and the provision of social housing. Governments may provide these directly through their own efforts or indirectly by means of grants and subsidies to private bodies. Public procurement, including that for urban regeneration, is subject to regulation by the European Communities. This is principally concerned with ensuring that public procurement is not used in a discriminatory fashion to favour domestic industry at the expense of firms located elsewhere in the European Communities. The rules apply to publicly funded projects, including those funded by the European Communities, as well as to projects undertaken by central or local government. This chapter examines how the European Communities' regulatory framework for public procurement affects urban regeneration programmes and discusses its implications for central and local government and for private bodies in receipt of public finance for urban regeneration programmes. It also considers other policies of the European Communities that affect urban regeneration, principally regional and environmental policies.

7.1   PUBLIC PROCUREMENT POLICY

The European Communities have regulated public procurement since the 1970s to avoid discriminatory behaviour by public bodies. The Public Works Directive of 1971 (Council Directive, 26 July 1971) set out a framework for the regulation of construction contracts, and the Public Supplies Directive of 1977 (Council Directive, 21 December 1976) one for the purchase of goods. The directives sought to open up public works and supplies contracts to firms throughout the European Communities. This was achieved by providing for contracts that exceed a minimum value to be advertised in the European Community's *Official Journal*, prescribing the methods of tendering that can be used, restricting the circumstances in which it is permissible to negotiate contracts with a single firm, and setting down the criteria to be used in the selection of tenders. However, during the 1980s evidence accumulated to suggest that these two directives were not proving effective and that their rules were not always being followed. Alleged abuses include the failure to advertise all appropriate contracts, the wrongful exclusion of qualified bidders, the use of discriminatory technical specifications that favour domestic producers, and the wrongful use of negotiated contracts rather than open tendering (Economic and Social Committee, 1987).

A series of public procurement directives has been adopted or proposed since 1988 to overcome the perceived deficiencies in the earlier legislation. These have closed loopholes and extended and clarified the 1970s directives as well as applying the public procurement principles to previously exempted areas, notably to utilities undertakings and to services. The principal measures are: the revised Public Supplies Directive of 1988 (Council Directive, 22 March 1988); the revised Public Works Directive of 1989 (Council Directive, 18 July 1989); a Utilities Directive which extends the public procurement principles to supplies and construction works by entities operating in the water, energy, transport and telecommunications sectors (Council Directive, 17 September 1990); a Public Services Directive (Council Directive, 18 June 1992) and a proposed Utilities Services Directive (proposal for Council Directive, 31 December 1991) which are intended to extend the principles of public procurement to the purchase of certain services; and a family of compliance or remedies directives which are intended to provide more effective means of redress for suppliers who have been wrongfully excluded from the award of a contract (Council Directive, 21 December 1989).

The measures which are likely to be of most significance in urban regeneration are the Public Works Directive, which is concerned with the procurement of construction works by public bodies, the Utilities Directive, which covers the procurement of construction works by utility undertakings, and the Public Services Directive and the proposed Utilities Services Directive, which include within their scope the purchase of architectural and town planning services.

The Public Works Directive came into force in the United Kingdom in July 1990. It was initially brought into effect by administrative action but, subsequently, the Award of Public Works Contracts Regulations were adopted in December 1991 (The Public Works Contracts Regulations, 1991). The Directive applies to public works contracts, including design, building and civil engineering work, and the installation of fittings and fixtures (Grover and Lavers, in press). The contracts affected are those that have an estimated value net of VAT of at least 5 million ECU (£3.5 million). Contracting authorities are not to split up contracts with the aim of avoiding the provisions of the Directive. Certain types of contract are excluded, for example those that affect national security. The contracting authorities to whom the Directive applies are central, local and regional government and bodies regulated by public law. The latter are bodies which draw most of their finance from public sources or are controlled by public bodies. They include Urban Development Corporations, the Northern Ireland Housing Executive, Scottish Homes and English Industrial Estates Corporation. The Directive also applies to private projects where public bodies provide more than 50% of the finance for civil engineering works and the building of hospitals, sports and leisure facilities and educational buildings. As discussed later, it applies to projects which draw finance from the European Communities' Structural Funds or loans from bodies such as the European Investment Bank. It should not be assumed that the Directive just applies to construction projects undertaken by central or local government. Other bodies, including private organizations, that derive finance from public or European Communities sources may also be affected. The Directive also applies to public works concessions. These are public works contracts in which the contractor is paid by receiving the right to exploit the works constructed. For example, a contractor could be paid for building a road by being given the right to receive tolls.

Three types of procedure are set out for the award of contracts: open procedures, whereby all interested contractors may submit tenders; restricted procedures, whereby only invited contractors submit tenders; and negotiated procedures, whereby the contracting authority negotiates terms with the contractors of their choice.

Restricted procedures include situations in which contractors must pre-qualify before being allowed to bid. Negotiated procedures may be used only in specific limited circumstances. These include where open or restricted procedures have failed to produce appropriate tenders, for reasons of extreme urgency as a result of unforeseeable events, or where a particular contractor has to carry out the work for artistic or technical reasons. In addition to these three procedures, there is a special award procedure for certain public housing schemes. These are schemes that, as a result of their size, complexity and duration, require the contractor to be a part of the team, together with the contracting authority and its advisors. The procedure is intended to enable the selection of the contractor who is most suitable for integration into the team. The Directive lays down the forms of advertising contracts, what information the notices must contain and the minimum time periods that must be allowed to elapse between the publication of the notice and the last date for the receipt of bids.

There is evidence that technical specifications have been used in the past to discriminate against foreign contractors. The Directive therefore sets out the specifications that are to be used in order of priority. The rules on technical specifications appear to apply to all public works contracts and not merely to those in excess of the threshold for the advertising rules. Preference is to be given to European standards where possible. Where these do not exist, the Directive lays down a hierarchy of alternative specifications. The use of trademarks is prohibited unless the product cannot be specified with sufficient precision by other means, when they must be qualified by the words 'or equivalent'. The Directive lays down the economic and technical references that can be sought from contractors. The economic and financial references include extracts from accounts, bankers' statements and the turnover from construction work. The technical references include the contractor's educational and professional qualifications, the works carried out over the past five years, the tools, plant and technical equipment, and the technical support available from inside and outside the firm. Contractors can be excluded from participation under certain circumstances, such as insolvency, misrepresentation and failure to pay taxes. Contracts can be awarded on the basis of either the lowest price or the most economically advantageous tender. If the latter is to be used, the contract notice or documents are to identify the criteria by which this is to be determined. In other words, it is not possible to opt for the selection of the most economically advantageous tender after the bids have been received using criteria not previously disclosed.

The Public Works and Supplies Compliance Directive (Council Directive, 21 December 1989) requires Member States to set up review procedures so that infringements of Community law can be rapidly corrected and to compensate those contractors who have suffered. Only contractors from within the European Communities can benefit from these provisions. An aggrieved contractor in the United Kingdom must take action in the High Court. The court has the power to suspend the contract procedure, set aside an award decision and to award damages. The European Commission is also empowered to intervene where it thinks that there has been a breach of European Community requirements.

The Utilities Directive (Council Directive, 17 September 1990) has many similar provisions to the Public Works Directive. It applies to contracting entities in the water, energy, transport and telecommunications industries irrespective of whether they are in public or private ownership. Thus, it applies to publicly owned bodies such as British Rail, but also to private companies such as BAA. Many of these bodies, such as British Gas, are significant property owners in areas affected by urban regeneration schemes. However, the Directive only applies to utility operations of these bodies and not to any other activities they may undertake. This indicates that the Directive may apply to certain work they may undertake as part of an urban regeneration scheme, for example, the building of a railway, but not to others, such as the redevelopment of surplus land.

The Public Services Directive is to apply to the same bodies as the Public Works Directive and the proposed Utilities Services Directive will apply to utility bodies. Certain services are excluded from their provisions, including contracts for the purchase, lease or rental of real property. The services covered by the proposals are divided into two groups, one of which is subject to the full public procurement rules and the other to only partial application. The former group includes property management services and design services, such as architectural, engineering, urban planning and landscape architectural services. There is nothing in the proposals that obliges Member States to put public services out to competitive tender. However, if they do so, the Directive will set the framework within which this will take place. The rules for advertising, the award of a contract, contractors' references and the exclusion of contractors are similar to those discussed for the Public Works Directive. There are different thresholds that determine whether the proposals will apply. In most instances, the threshold is 200 000 ECU (£140 000). For architectural services the threshold is that the construction works, for which they are to be used, must have an estimated value of at least 5 million ECU. The Directive will also lay down rules for the conduct of design contests in areas of architecture, town and area planning and civil engineering, where there is a prize of at least 200 000 ECU. The rules include how the contests are to be advertised and how the jury is to operate.

7.2   EUROPEAN COMMUNITY FUNDING FOR URBAN REGENERATION

The European Communities can be a source of funding for certain types of urban regeneration project. The present funding arrangements largely stem from the reform of the European Communities' Structural Funds that took place in 1988 (Commission of the European Communities, 1989). The reform is intended to result in a substantial increase in the resources made available for regional development. The Structural Funds consist of the European Regional Development Fund, the European Social Fund and the European Agricultural Guidance and Guarantee Fund Guidance Section. In addition, the European Communities' sources of loans, such as the European Investment Bank and the European Steel and Coal Community, are also used to support the objectives set out in the reform. The reform came about partly as a result of the enlargement of the European Economic Community with the admission of Spain, Portugal and Greece, which increased the proportion of the population who live in the least favoured regions. Closer economic union as a result of the development of the Internal Market and European Monetary Union could work to the disadvantage of the least favoured regions. Trade barriers that have protected their industries are being removed and the regulations that limited investment flows from them to more developed areas are being dismantled. There is also evidence that regional disparities widened during the 1980s (Emerson and Huhne, 1991). The principal aim of the reform is to promote the development of the least favoured regions.

In 1988 a Council Regulation set out the five objectives to be achieved by the Structural Funds, supported by the European Investment Bank (Council Regulation (EEC) No. 2052/88, 24 June 1988): Objective 1, promoting the development and structural adjustment of the regions whose development is lagging behind; Objective 2, converting regions or parts of regions seriously affected by industrial decline; Objective 3, combating long term unemployment; Objective 4, facilitating the occupational integration of young people; and Objective 5, the speeding up of the adjustment of agricultural structures and promoting the development of rural areas.

Objective 1 is of limited importance to the United Kingdom as a whole as the only area designated for assistance is Northern Ireland. Only 7% of the European Regional Development Fund commitment for the United Kingdom in 1990 was under Objective 1 (Commission of the European Communities, 1991). The principal beneficiaries of funds under this objective are Spain, Portugal, Ireland, Greece and southern Italy. Finance for projects can be obtained from the European Regional Development Fund, European Social Fund and European Agricultural Guidance and Guarantee Fund Guidance Section and loans from the European Investment Bank and European Steel and Coal Community. About 80% of European Regional Development Fund resources are devoted to this objective. The Structural Funds can contribute up to 75% of the total cost and at least 50% of public expenditure for projects in areas eligible for assistance under Objective 1.

In contrast, 79% of the commitment to the United Kingdom was under Objective 2. Qualifying areas under this objective must satisfy three criteria. They must have had: an average rate of unemployment over the last five years that has been above the European Community average; a percentage share of industrial employment in total employment that equalled or exceeded the European Community average in any reference year from 1975 onwards; and an observable fall in industrial employment compared with the reference year.

Expenditure can also be undertaken under certain conditions in areas adjacent to the qualifying ones, in urban communities with an unemployment rate at least 50% above the European Community average where there has been a substantial fall in industrial employment, and areas threatened with substantial job losses. The parts of the United Kingdom that are eligible for funding include South Wales, part of the West Midlands, Merseyside and north-east England. Finance can come from the European Social Fund or European Regional Development Fund and loans from the European Investment Bank and European Coal and Steel Community. The Structural Funds can contribute up to 50% of the total cost of projects and at least 25% of public expenditure.

The European Social Fund finances training programmes and subsidies for job creation (Council Regulation (EEC) No. 4255/88, 19 December 1988) and so is aimed more towards people than property. European Social Fund finance is available for projects under each of the five objectives. The European Regional Development Fund can finance productive investment for the creation or maintenance of permanent jobs and investment in infrastructure (Council Regulation (EEC) No. 4254/88, 31 December 1988). The latter can include investment in inner cities and in urban areas 'whose modernization or laying out provides the basis for the creation or development of economic activity'. Thus, the European Regional Development fund can be a source of finance for property projects for urban regeneration. The fund provides finance for projects under Objectives 1, 2 and 5. Other programmes to provide finance for urban regeneration projects may be available from other European Communities sources. For example, there is the Rechar programme for economic conversion of coal mining areas, the Resider programme for the conversion of steel areas and the Renaval programme for the conversion of shipbuilding areas.

It should be noted that projects and programmes financed by the Structural Funds, or which receive loans from institutions such as the European Investment Bank, are subject to the public procurement rules discussed earlier (Notice C(88)2510, 28 January 1989). Failure to follow them can result in the suspension of payments and the recovery of assistance already paid as well as the possibility of prosecution before the European Court. The Structural Funds contribute only part of the finance for projects so that there must be additional finance from the Member State.

7.3   ENVIRONMENTAL ASSESSMENT

The European Communities' Environmental Assessment Directive which came into force in 1988 has implications for certain types of urban regeneration project (Council Directive, 27 June 1985). The Directive has been brought into force in the United Kingdom by a number of regulations such as the

Town and Country Planning (Assessment of Environmental Effects) Regulations 1988, SI No. 1199. Guidance on environment assessment has been produced by the Department of the Environment and the Welsh Office (1991). This booklet reproduces the text of the Directive and identifies the regulations that have brought it into force in the United Kingdom and the guidance documents published by official bodies. The impact of the Directive on the United Kingdom planning system is discussed by Lichfield (1990).

The Directive requires that an environmental assessment is carried out before consent for development is granted for projects that are likely to have significant environmental effects. The projects include construction works and interventions in the natural surroundings and landscape, such as mineral extraction. Article 4 of the Directive identifies two classes of project: those listed in Annex I, for which an environmental assessment is required in each instance; and those listed in Annex II, for which an environmental assessment is to be carried out 'where Member States consider that their characteristics so require'.

The types of project listed in Annex I include oil refineries, power stations, integrated steel works, chemical installations, ports, aerodromes and waste disposal installations for dangerous wastes. Of particular relevance to urban regeneration, they also include the construction of motorways, express roads and lines for long distance railway traffic.

The projects listed in Annex II include: certain types of agricultural installations; extractive industry; certain types of manufacturing installations concerned with metal processing, glass making and the chemical, food, textile, leather, wood, rubber and paper industries; certain projects concerning the energy industries, such as overhead electrical transmission lines; infrastructure projects; and a range of miscellaneous projects, such as holiday complexes and waste water treatment plants. Infrastructure projects include a number of categories that may form part of urban regeneration projects, such as industrial estates, urban development projects, roads that do not fall within the scope of Annex I, and elevated or underground passenger railways. However, such projects do not automatically require environmental assessment but may do so under some circumstances.

Article 4 allows Member States to specify the types of project that are to be subject to environmental assessment and to establish the criteria or thresholds to be used in determining whether environmental assessment is to be undertaken. The thresholds and criteria adopted by a Member State therefore play a key part in determining whether environmental assessment needs to be undertaken for an Annex II project. These may vary between Member States. Indicative criteria and thresholds have been given to local planning authorities by the Department of the Environment (Department of the Environment, 1988). The criteria are indicative and the key test is whether a project is likely to have significant effects on the environment by virtue, for example, of its size, nature or location. A developer can apply to the local planning authority for an opinion on the need for environmental assessment and can appeal to the Secretary of State against the opinion given. Thus, a developer can be given a clear ruling as to whether there needs to be an environmental assessment well before a formal planning application has to be lodged. Examples of the thresholds and criteria include: for new manufacturing plants, having a site in the range 20–30 ha; for industrial estates in excess of 20 ha or having significant numbers of dwellings in close proximity; an urban development scheme in a historic town centre; and for new urban roads or major improvements to existing roads with more than 1500 dwellings lying within 100 m of the centre line.

The guidance indicates that the redevelopment of previously developed land is unlikely to require environmental assessment unless the proposed use is a category of Annex II other than an industrial estate development or an urban development project, or the project is on a very much greater scale than the previous use of the land. Although the Directive sets out the situations in which environmental assessment is mandatory, there is nothing to prevent a developer from carrying out such an assessment voluntarily in circumstances in which there is no obligation to do so.

The developer is responsible for preparing the environmental statement and this must be submitted with the planning application. There is no prescribed form that this is to take but it must contain certain specified information: a description of the proposed development, including the site and the design and scale of the development; the data necessary to identify and assess the effect of the development on the environment; a description of the measures envisaged to avoid, reduce and remedy significant adverse effects; the identification and assessment of the direct and indirect effects on human beings, flora, fauna, soil, water, air, climate and landscape, the interaction between these factors, material assets and the cultural heritage; and a summary in non-technical language.

The planning authority is to have regard to the environmental statement in determining the planning application. It can request additional information where it considers the environmental statement to be inadequate. There is a requirement to consult certain statutory consultees and encouragement to developers to consult with non-statutory bodies with particular expertise.

The Directive has implications for one of the policies for urban regeneration used in the United Kingdom, namely, simplified planning zones. Annex I projects must be excluded from the scope of simplified planning zones as they require environmental assessment before consent can be given. A way must also be found to ensure that environmental assessment of Annex II projects takes place where appropriate. This could be achieved by requiring planning consent to be sought in such situations. Alternatively, the developers could be required to notify the planning authority where they intend to carry out such developments so that it has the opportunity to consider the environmental effects. An example of how this may be achieved is Derby City Council's Sir Francis Ley Industrial Park (Derby City Council, 1988). The conditions for planning consent within the zone include the requirement that no Annex I development shall take place. The conditions for permitted developments are defined so as to preclude Annex II for which environmental assessment is required. These include setting out road access, limiting the scale of developments, designating landscaping zones and limiting the developments that can take place within 'sensitive boundary subzones' close to housing.

7.4   CONCLUSIONS

The public procurement directives can affect publicly undertaken or publicly funded urban regeneration schemes, including those for which part of the funds come from a European Communities source. They can apply to private bodies as well as to public bodies; for example, to private utility companies and private companies receiving public subsidies. They lay down a set of rules governing the advertising of contracts, their award, the references that may be sought from contractors, the exclusion of contractors and the technical specifications to be used. The Public Works and Utilities Directives deal with the purchase of construction works. The directives on the purchase of services will affect the procurement of architectural and town planning services and the conduct of design contests.

The reform of the European Communities' Structural Funds in 1988 should lead to substantially greater resources being deployed for regional assistance. However, most of this will be spent in Greece, Portugal, Spain, Ireland and Italy. The only area of the United Kingdom to be designated for expenditure under Objective 1 is Northern Ireland. There are other areas designated for spending under Objective 2. Funds from the European Regional Development Fund are available for Objectives 1 and 2 projects and these can include those requiring investment in urban infrastructure. Projects in receipt of finance from the European Communities' Structural Funds or loans from bodies such as the European Investment Bank are subject to the public procurement rules.

The requirement for particular types of project to have an environmental assessment is likely to affect certain urban regeneration schemes. In particular, there are implications for those affecting historical town centres, for those involving large scale manufacturing or industrial development, especially where these are in proximity to housing areas or involve an increase in the scale of development, and for those that involve the building or improvement of roads and railways.

REFERENCES

Commission of the European Communities (CEC) (1989) *Guide to the Reform of the Community's Structural Funds*, CEC, Luxembourg.

Commission of the European Communities (CEC) (1991) *24th General Report of the EC 1990*, CEC, Luxembourg.

Council Directive of 26 July 1971 concerning the co-ordination of procedures for the award of public works contracts (71/305/EEC), *Official Journal*, **L 185**, 16 August 1971.

Council Directive of 21 December 1976 co-ordinating procedures for the award of public supply contracts (77/62/EEC), *Official Journal*, **L 13**, 15 January 1977, pp. 1–14.

Council Directive of 27 June 1985 on the assessment of the effects of certain public and private projects on the environment (85/337/EEC), *Official Journal*, **L 175**, 5 July 1985.

Council Directive of 22 March 1988 amending the Directive 77/62/EEC relating to the co-ordination of procedures on the award of public supply contracts and repealing certain provisions of Directive 80/767/EEC (88/295/EEC), *Official Journal*, **L 127**, 20 May 1988, pp. 1–14.

Council Regulation (EEC) No. 2052/88 of 24 June 1988 on the tasks of the Structural Funds and their effectiveness and on co-ordination of their activities between themselves and with the operations of the European Investment Bank and the other existing financial instruments, *Official Journal*, **L 185**, 15 July 1988, pp. 9–20.

Council Regulation (EEC) No. 4254/88 laying down provisions for implementing Regulation (EEC) No. 2052/88 as regards the European Regional Development Fund, *Official Journal*, **L 374**, 31 December 1988, pp. 15–20.

Council Regulation (EEC) No. 4255/88 of 19 December 1988 laying down provisions for implementing Regulation (EEC) No. 2052/88 as regards the European Social Fund, *Official Journal*, **L 374**, 31 December 1988, pp. 21–24.

Council Directive of 18 July 1989 amending Directive 71/305/EEC concerning co-ordination of procedures for the award of public works contracts (89/440/EEC), *Official Journal*, **L 210**, 21 July 1989, pp. 1–21.

Council Directive of 21 December 1989 on the co-ordination of the laws, regulations and administrative provisions relating to the application of review procedures to the award of public supply and public works contracts (89/665/EEC), *Official Journal*, **L 395**, 30 December 1989, pp. 33–35.

Council Directive of 17 September 1990 on the procurement procedures of entities operating in the water, energy, transport, and telecommunications sectors (90/531/EEC), *Official Journal*, **L 297**, 29 October 1990, pp. 1–47.

Council Directive of 18 June 1992 on the co-ordination of procedures on the award of public service contracts (92/50/EEC), *Official Journal*, **L 209**, 24 July 1992.

Department of the Environment (1988) *Environmental Assessment, Circular 15/88*, 12 July 1988.

Department of the Environment and the Welsh Office (1991) *Environmental Assessment: A Guide to Procedures*, DoE and Welsh Office.

Derby City Council (1988) *Sir Francis Ley Industrial Park Simplified Planning Zone Scheme Written Statement*, City Council, Derby.

Economic and Social Committee, Opinion of the proposal for a Council Directive amending Directive 77/62/EEC relating to the co-ordination of procedures on the award of public supply contracts and deleting provisions of Directive 80/767/EEC, *Official Journal*, **C 68**, 16 March 1987, pp. 7–9.

Emerson, M. and Huhne, C. (1991) *The ECU Report: The Single European Currency – and What it Means to You*, Pan Books, London, pp. 149–151.

Grover, R.J. and Lavers, A. *Quality Management in Construction: The Impact of European Communities' Policy*, Construction Industry Research and Information Association, London, sections 6–8, in press.

Lichfield, N. (1990) Environmental assessment, *Journal of Planning and Environmental Law, Occasional Papers No. 16*.

Notice C(88) 2510 to the Member States on monitoring compliance with public procurement rules in the case of projects and programmes financed by the Structural Funds and financial instruments (89/C 22/03), *Official Journal*, **C 22**, 28 January 1989, pp. 3–6.

Proposal for a Council Directive on service procurement procedures of entities operating in the water, energy, transport and telecommunications sectors, *Official Journal*, **C 337**, 31 December 1991.

The Public Works Contracts Regulations 1991, SI 1991 No. 2680.

8

Urban renewal and environmental quality: improving performance

N. Hanley

The need for constant change and renewal of the fabric of cities is a manifestation of their response to the economic and social pressures placed on them. Archaeologists delight in plotting the evolution of a city in its layers of artifacts and remains of older buildings beneath development sites in the centres of our present day cities illustrating, in a historical context, that urban renewal is not a new issue. However, until recent decades the limitations and high cost of transport strongly influenced the city development process. Land use theory and neoclassical urban economic models focus on the traditional pattern of high land values in the centre of urban areas and the rapid fall-off in prices with increasing distance from the core (Harvey, 1992). Consequently, apart from periods of decline in particular cities, the land market process encouraged the retention of compact and mixed use cities, which in theory should mitigate against long term dereliction and the abandonment of land in or near central city areas.

An appreciation of the centre of many European cities indicates that this process is no longer functioning as efficiently. Substantial areas of land abandoned for many years can often be identified, in addition to the gradual dereliction of whole areas of inner city housing. Whether in the historical time frame such dereliction is momentary or represents some major changes in the factors which influence the development and redevelopment process of cities is yet to be resolved.

8.1 PROCESS OF DERELICTION

The occurrence of substantial areas of derelict land in older industrial cities is perhaps inevitable as the pace of decline and closures in steel, ship-building and other traditional industries has taken place at a rate which could not be matched by even the most active regional/urban development policies. Additionally, the contamination of land left behind by some of these activities poses very real problems and high costs for new uses. Although the United Kingdom has operated a major derelict land reclamation programme in these areas, the progress in preparing such sites for new uses has been less marked. In those regions struggling to attract 'mobile industry' to replace job losses in traditional industries, the reclamation of derelict land has often been a second priority; instead, easily developable green-field sites have been made available to capture investment. The situation in Belgium highlights this issue where, for example, little attention has been paid to the reclamation of derelict land until recently. However, around most of the industrial centres a new outer ring of industrial development on greenfield sites has been established beyond the derelict land of the inner city.

The changing patterns of urban development have not, however, restricted this process of dereliction to declining industrial centres. It is also a feature of cities with buoyant economies where the 'market' has directed growth and new economic activity increasingly into suburban and satellite areas. In seeking to understand the reason for these changes it is necessary to consider the various factors influencing city development.

Clearly one factor which has significantly changed the city development process has been accessibility to transport. The expansion of public trans-portation networks began the process of dispersion of cities away from their traditional dense and mixed use centres to the development of more expensive suburbs located around rail and underground stations. Furthermore the growth of car ownership over the last few decades removed the last remaining constraints on urban form, making the city centre even more accessible to distant suburbs. Although lower land prices can be seen as part of the attraction of the suburbs, the increasing congestion, noise and poor environment of central districts undoubtedly also contributed to the process of decentralization.

As the city expanded in residential terms other uses followed. Greenfield sites provided attractive opportunities for new industrial estates, office loca-tions and commercial activities. Likewise the suburbs matured, allowing many householders to live an increasingly suburban lifestyle with less reliance on the older city core. Furthermore, as requirements for a central location for many activities disappeared it can be argued that the conditions for dereliction and abandonment were set in place.

Despite the loss of activities from the centre, land values still remain high, fuelled by hopes of profitable office or commercial redevelopment. Combined with substantial redevelopment costs, this meant that only those relatively high value land uses could be 'justified' in the centre even if the availability of sites for these exceeded the realistic needs of such uses.

The process of dereliction in cities has not solely been limited to the abandonment of sites by commercial uses, either through displacement or discontinuation of business activities. In addition, the fabric of inner city housing has seen a progressive decline. Furthermore, the old, poor and immigrant populations in such areas do not possess the resources to 'escape' to the suburbs or to adequately maintain this older housing stock. Although in some instances this has been countered by a reverse process of gentrification, in many European cities there remains very substantial areas of inner city housing where dereliction by lack of upkeep continues. However, the linkage between poverty and dereliction in housing areas is not restricted to inner city areas. Certain cities, in good faith, sought to 'solve' poor housing standards by redevelopment, but as a consequence have often transposed the problem to different localities. Lack of maintenance, which is often linked to poor original design concepts, often leads to the deterioration of housing conditions in new developments. Furthermore, physical separation from the city core, problems of isolation and lack of urban facilities add to the housing difficulties of occupants.

8.2   ROLE OF PLANNING

As the greater part of this process has occurred in the post-war years and is coincident with the growth of statutory town planning, it is therefore logical to access the contribution of the land use planning system. As one of the key objectives of planning is to ensure the integrated development of cities, making effective use of land resources should be the expected outcome. However, it is possible to argue that the planning system has actually aggravated the problem by encouraging the decentralization of population and activities into new and expanding towns, or at best has reinforced trends already in place. The development of new cities such as Milton Keynes (United Kingdom) competes economically with traditional cities and also, perhaps more importantly, is incurring major costs to the public purse which could perhaps have been better utilized in inner city renewal initiatives.

The generous availability of land for development has meant that attention has failed to focus on overcoming the considerable difficulty in reusing derelict land within cities. Failure to do so is in part due to a lack of effective planning for the city region and also a lack of commitment to the restructuring of the inner city. A permissive planning framework tends to encourage land speculation with the anticipation of utilizing city centre sites for commercial development. Ultimately this process pushes residential use out of central area locations and gradually imposes on cities the concept of functional division which originally stemmed from the Garden City and New Town movements. However, the trend is not without its opponents. For example, controversy about the Coin Street area in central London indicates the conflicting opinions regarding the societal objectives of urban renewal.

Nevertheless, although it is only a matter of speculation, it is possible that tighter planning policies in, for example, the 1960s and 1970s may have succeeded in encouraging inner city renewal. However, in the absence of positive action to make abandoned land genuinely available, more restrictive policies may well have been counter-productive in forcing up land and property prices, thereby placing further restraints on economic development.

Throughout the 1980s greater attention has been given to inner city re-generation programmes. The success of urban renewal in this period has generally required significant public sector support or subsidy for land acquisition, reclamation and infrastructure to prepare the way for private sector investment. This has essentially been one of the key roles of Urban Development Corporations, which have been charged with encouraging the renewal of large tracts of land within central areas of many British cities. Despite the much publicized and perceived success of the private sector in the renewal of the London Docklands, it is becoming increasingly apparent that this was achieved by the substantial preparation investments of the London Docklands Development Corporation and also on the part of the local authorities having responsibility before the establishment of the London Docklands Development Corporation. Setting aside the rhetoric of political ideologies, the development achieved by Urban Development Corporations does nevertheless reflect the success of public–private partnerships in city renewal.

8.3   URBAN RENEWAL AND ENVIRONMENTAL PERFORMANCE

Most of the recent initiatives on urban renewal in the United Kingdom and Europe have placed a high priority on environmental aspects. The use of materials, design and landscaping are of increasingly high quality, creating a visually attractive environment. However, important as these matters may be in providing a pleasant environment, both for those who use and market such developments, they only partially meet the current environmental agenda. The latter is instead being set by concern for wider environmental issues within the city, for example, air quality, congestion, noise and, in addition, the city's contribution to the solution of wider global issues such as the greenhouse effect and acid rain.

With respect to buildings, energy efficiency has been a concern for many years. A wide range of design and technological options are now available allowing the construction of buildings with low energy consumption. The European Community's commitment to stabilize carbon dioxide emissions by the year 2000 is providing the impetus for further attention. European Commission proposals, under the Specific Action for Vigorous Energy efficiency (SAVE) programme, requests member states to review thermal insulation requirements for new buildings and also to introduce energy certification schemes. The latter is intended to apply initially to newly constructed property for sale, but will also eventually include the rented sector. Energy is, however, only one of a number of factors to be considered. The design of buildings to encourage water and waste recycling and the use of environmentally sound material are also issues which are receiving increasing attention in the 'green buildings' movement (Construction Industry Conference Centre, 1992). In this context the Building Research Establishment in the United Kingdom has introduced an innovatory scheme of environment assessment of buildings which includes consideration of global, local and indoor environmental factors (BREEAM: Building Research Establishment Environmental Assessment Method).

Concern for the environmental performance of buildings is not restricted to new developments. Pioneering schemes, particularly in Germany and Denmark, have shown how such principles can be applied to the renovation of existing buildings. The major renovation programme in the Kreuzberg district of Berlin is one of the best examples in terms of the variety of approaches, techniques used and the involvement of the existing community in the improvement of their own area.

The performance of a redevelopment area as a whole needs to be addressed; in this respect the introduction of environmental impact appraisal allows the assessment of the potential effects of development on the surrounding area. Aspects such as emissions, noise, generation of traffic and visual disturbance are key factors in such an analysis. Although effective treatment of such issues can ensure a successful integration of the development into the city, at a strategic level it does not necessarily address the question as to whether the development is improving the environmental performance of the city as a whole or simply reinforcing existing trends. In the aftermath of the 1992 United Nations Rio conference on Environment and Development, a renewal of international commitment has emerged which seeks to create more sustainable patterns of development. This will have implications for the future planning and development of cities and the need to integrate sustainability.

8.4   URBAN RENEWAL AND THE SUSTAINABLE CITY

In purely conceptual terms the achievement of the sustainable city is debatable because cities, by their very nature, rely on a constant stream of resources from surrounding areas. Although sustainability is perhaps a more valid concept at a regional scale, for the city to move towards a more sustainable form of development attention must be paid to the various cycles of resources which it uses by minimizing waste, encouraging recycling and using renewable resources wherever possible. This kind of thinking is being actively promoted in a number of European countries; Sweden, in particular, has made good progress in implementing such issues (Environmental Advisory Council, 1992).

In considering the implications of sustainability for city planning and urban renewal, energy issues are undoubtedly of central concern. Energy use is the fundamental source of carbon dioxide, the main greenhouse gas, and is also closely related to many of the other environmental impacts causing concern within the city, namely, air pollution, noise and traffic congestion. Policies which are aimed at reducing the use of fossil fuels are therefore likely to bring relief to global and local environmental problems, thus making a significant contribution to sustainability. However, the dispersed city form which has evolved over the last few decades, based heavily on the use of the private motor car, has and continues to generate increasing demands for transport.

There is a growing consensus in the western world that the environmental consequences of the unfettered expansion of the car can no longer be afforded. Development based on its use is certainly not sustainable. In seeking to break this trend attention focuses initially on the prospects of improving public transportation and an integration of such systems with land use developments. Although the problems affecting the Canary Wharf development in London Docklands are partly due to the economic recession of the early 1990s, there can be little doubt that the absence of a significant public transport access has been a major contribution.

Policies to encourage public transportation have implications for planning in terms of the density and location of development, particularly as public transport is not an economic reality in areas of low density housing on the fringe of the city. Consideration must also be given to the link between employment location and public transport – a policy to this effect is now being actively pursued in The Netherlands, restricting office developments to locations well serviced by public transport.

In addition, attention is focusing on the question of the contribution that different patterns of land development can make in reducing the demand for transport. The European Commission (1990) in its *Green Paper on the Urban Environment* argued the case for breaking with the planning theory of functional division which has so influenced urban development in the post-war years and a return to the concept of mixity. The case for this is not based on some romantic attachment to historic city patterns but to reducing transport needs and providing people with the accessibility they need by proximity rather than mobility. Similar conclusions are being reached by a number of other organizations exploring the issue; for example, the World

Resources Institute (1992) argues the case for a reform of land use planning, placing an accent on fairly high residential densities combined with mixed zoning and integrated public transportation. The issue of sustainability and cities is also receiving attention in the OECD's Urban Affairs Group, where initial discussions and studies are considering the need for a planning contribution to reduce transport and energy demands.

The idea of 'replanning' our cities is certainly a bold one which will take time, require a new vision and will certainly influence the lifestyles of city dwellers. Although sceptics will question the willingness of people to change, it must be recognized that the scale of the problem is such that it is virtually inconceivable that it can be solved without some lifestyle adjustments. Some interesting ideas as to how this could be achieved in practice have been presented in the Urban Villages Group (1992) report, which proposes the development or redevelopment of mixed use communities of populations of 3000–5000 with all facilities needed for daily life within walking distance of each other, ideally on a site of approximately 40 ha. Although its authors recognize that the 'ideal' conditions are rare, the general principles are considered applicable at any scale. Indeed, many of the ideas presented are not new but are drawn from existing experience of renewal both in the United Kingdom and abroad.

8.5 CONCLUSIONS

The implications of such thinking for urban renewal are important. A sustainability strategy for cities should place a high priority on renewal with the redevelopment of abandoned sites being given active preference over the development of greenfield areas on the city edge and beyond. It is also suggested that the sites which are available should be used to promote new patterns of development which offer more sustainable lifestyles to their inhabitants. Already proposals for such mixed used developments are emerging on major sites in European cities – the proposed waterfront development in Amsterdam and the early ideas for a major railway site in Copenhagen are examples – but as yet such ambitious plans for a major redevelopment in the United Kingdom are still to emerge. The London Docklands development has to date concentrated on large schemes and with correspondingly less emphasis on mixed housing and office developments. However, the remaining areas to be developed within docklands and many other possible locations offer the option for a different, arguably more sustainable, approach.

REFERENCES

Commission of the European Communities (CEC) (1990) *Green Paper on the Urban Environment, EUR 12902*, CEC, Brussels.

Construction Industry Conference Centre Limited (CICS) (1992) *Green Buildings – Design Construction Services*, CICS, Welwyn.

Environmental Advisory Council (EAC) (1992) *Ecocycles – The Basis of Sustainable Urban Development*, EAC, Stockholm.

Harvey, J. (1992) *Urban Land Economics: The Economics of Real Property*, Macmillan, London.

Urban Villages Group (1992) *Urban Villages – A Concept for Creating Mixed-use Urban Developments on a Sustainable Scale*, Urban Villages Group, London.

World Resources Institute (1992) *The Going Rate: What it Really Costs to Drive*, World Resources Institute, Washington DC.

The views in this chapter are those of the author and not of the European Commission.

9

Structural, organizational and strategic problems of urban regeneration in the Republics of the former federation of Czechoslovakia

———— *A. Diamant and K. Matouskova*

Since 1971 the settlement pattern in the former Czechoslovakia has been organized in 'settlement centres' involving the concentration of population, housing, production, technical facilities and civic amenities. Such centralization tendencies were based on a hierarchical distribution ranging from the capitals of the republics and the regions, down to the capitals of the districts and selected settlements at the subdistrict level. In terms of population size, settlements were classified into five groups, namely over 100 000, 50 000–100 000, 20 000–50 000, 5000–20 000 and less than 5000. The classification also took into account geographical position, socioeconomic characteristics and politico-strategic criteria. A commitment to develop these centres has resulted in the decline and, in some instances, the physical extinction of smaller villages. The principles of urbanization were subordinated to dirigist principles based on centralization and the hierarchical distribution of settlements.

9.1 ORGANIZATION AND INSTITUTIONALIZATION OF URBAN DEVELOPMENT

Planning and development of urban activities has been based on three distinct types of plan: a long term plan covering a 15–20 year period; a medium term plan of five years' duration; and a short term annual plan. The organization of urban development gradually evolved into bureaucratic formations with divided authority and was often characterized by an unwillingness to co-operate. Furthermore, decision-making from the centre was primarily concerned with immediate and partial goals irrespective of what was considered desirable for the comprehensive development of the territory.

Thus, territorial planning became an instrument of central control. Comprehensive planning based on the real needs of the population, the town, or the region was forced into the background, while the bureaucratic complexities of the system and the institutions, particularly with regard to the process of discussion, negotiation and approval, became increasingly moribund. This automatically weakened control of and the overall effectiveness of territorial planning, with the result that 'Party Palaces' were constructed on development sites for which the master plan had envisaged entirely different uses.

In illustrating the harmful nature and impact of such manipulation of and interference in the planning system, a simplified analysis of the territorial and functional definition of urban planning, together with the specification of the prevailing character of an area and the failure to observe the basic rules is considered. Territorial borders were set with disregard to the natural dividing elements, primarily because with state ownership of property the basic rules of territorial planning were often ignored and little attention was given to environmental principles. Water courses were re-directed, forests removed, ground configuration disregarded and construction projects undertaken which resulted in enormous soil and material displacements. Technical elements such as transportation routes and utility corridors were mostly determined by political and often military objectives of the state. All this resulted in enormous ecological losses.

It has not, therefore, been possible to create a balanced unit operating to definitive economic or social objectives. Instead, development was consistently subordinated to the edicts of monopolistic state construction industry with its meaningless, useless and almost perverted tendency to maximize prefabrication and mechanization regardless of quality and price. In a sense the residential zones of monofunctional character were deprived of individuality and human scale. Within the settlements this lack of identity caused alienation together with a sense of hopelessness and frustration, which manifested itself in household instability, increasing divorce rates and high levels of criminality. In the case of production and technical zones, these were often formed as non-functional colossi within the urban system consisting of heavy industry which was inefficient and unable to compete even with third world countries. Such zones contradicted all principles of urban planning by devastating the environment and frequently failing to adhere to the fundamental requirements of hygiene and working conditions.

Haphazard development in the area between the monofunctional resid-ential and production zones often resulted in the belated construction of civic amenities, usually on a scale which was insufficient to satisfy needs. In the mixed use zones the situation was better, especially in those repre-senting the historical parts of the urban structure, where traditional building structures have remained intact. However, the historical and architectural quality is suffering from prolonged general neglect and failure to carry out basic maintenance and reconstruction work.

9.2   STRUCTURAL CHANGES CONDITIONING FUTURE DEVELOPMENT

The principal prerequisites to future development in the Czech Republic and Slovakia depend on rectifying previous errors and fostering the regenera-tion of settlements by encouraging harmony with the environment. This will involve the restoration of desirable relations between the various elements of housing, open space and leisure/recreation on the one hand, and trans-portation, agriculture and industry on the other. Profound changes in the structure and organization of society are required and will occur; agriculture and industry need to be transformed; property rights and associated tenure arrangements must substantially change. The mutual relationships between individual functional units and the links which originated in the course of historical development are in the process of being revived. Likewise the function of labour requires restructuring and although a number of integrating processes will emerge, the disintegration of other processes will take place.

Living standards and habits among the greater part of the population will be affected by the transition to decentralization. New social group rela-tionships and structures will result from the increased participation of the population in decision-making on public matters such as the development of settlements. This will undoubtedly require a creative response from local authorities, working within the new political structures and with the local community in their area.

Political transformation in the Republics will in the short term, at least, result in budgetary constraints on state expenditure at all levels. The short-age of public funds together with a slow influx of capital investment will affect the development process. Other key factors such as the unclear rela-tionships to property and the uncertainty of ensuing litigation will further influence the rate and extent of development activity. It is imperative that the new political structures and legislatures encourage universal and perma-nent development. In this respect, the territorial planning approach as pre-viously used needs to be transformed into comprehensive spatial planning systems similar to that in western European countries. Events are gradually beginning to move in this direction with architects from the socialist era being challenged and superseded by foreign professionals entering the field. However, a potential challenge will be in educating the public on the respective merits of the design, quality and functional convenience of the new architecture.

9.3 ORGANIZATIONAL PROBLEMS AND REMEDIAL PHASES

In the Republics, a number of construction projects have been suspended due to the obsolete design concepts on which the proposed development was based or, alternatively, because of a shortage of funding, or a combination of both. With respect to the problems impeding on the development process, several remedial phases are now being followed. The first phase involves reassessing previous territorial planning concepts and establishing the necessity, scope and method for continuing with proposed development schemes. At stage two, the phasing and funding of development projects, the degree of conformity with proper urban planning principles and the resulting effect on the environment will be considered to avoid an unnecessary burden being imposed on the state or the amenity of an area.

The third phase embodies changes in the method of construction, the organization of construction companies and the introduction of project management, by reducing the negative impacts, improving the quality of development, shortening construction periods and raising the architectural and planning standards of building projects. This particularly applies in the field of housing construction and provision of civic amenity.

The fourth phase will involve gradually transforming legislation, introducing changes which define more explicitly the principles of spatial planning, and formalizing the rights and duties of the various levels of state administration. Moreover, it is considered necessary to simplify the methods of drafting and discussing the planning and design documents for construction projects, to accelerate the process of approval and to generally create a more flexible administrative procedure. This will involve giving legal protection to the status and rights of the individual in relation to the state.

9.4 TRANSFORMATION OF CONDITIONS FOR DEVELOPMENT

The first condition is to recognize the historical development of settlements and to assess the cultural and architectural heritage of the Republics in a European context. Most urban settlements have historical cores containing quality buildings worthy of preservation which are protected by designated conservation zones. Protection status extends to include the natural environment and its elements. However, it will be necessary to establish technical information regarding the condition and the functional use of all such buildings. The acquisition of the information through survey analysis, although constituting a major long term task, should be facilitated by the development of information systems within urban areas.

As a second condition, it will be necessary to formulate a rational programme for area development and to establish a system of financing which will assist long term economic restructuring. Consequently, a development and financing programme is required to link up with the new taxation system which is due to be introduced in 1993. This represents an endeavour to create a system, within a re-emerging modern European state, reflecting the period between the two world wars and the progress of the last two decades of the 20th century.

The third condition involves defining a specific role for the larger cities within a unified Europe and their promotion beyond state boundaries. In this context, it is imperative that European Community countries, together with other developed countries, particularly the USA, are persuaded by the benefits of investing in the Republics, namely its traditions, skilled workforce and the geographical position of the country.

9.5 STRATEGY FOR THE TRANSITION STAGE

The transition period is characterized by several distinctive features. The political scene needs to stabilize following the separation of the Republics and the formation of the two new nation states on 1 January 1993. Differences of opinion are hindering the adoption of laws and legal norms and in some instances the concealed influence of the old communist structures still prevail. Consequently, the restitution of confiscated property is not yet fully complete, particularly in the case of church property and other entitled groups.

The transition period is also characterized by a shortage of domestic capital and restrictions on the influx of foreign investment. The transformation to a market economy is not yet complete; indeed, the privatization of the larger and more important enterprises is still at a preparatory stage. In a period of transition, there is a tendency to aim development towards activities promising a speedy economic return such as banks, hotels and commercial facilities. However, the proper functioning of even these priority activities necessitates an innovative solution to the problems of transportation, primarily those of air and rail. The latter mode is the least developed of all the transportation networks. Similarly, development of the telecommunications network is seen as an essential requirement to both society and to economic growth.

The transition phase highlights the necessity to formulate and establish a number of fundamental principles.

1. The creation of the necessary prerequisites for the influx of capital and international assistance in the form of sponsorship with the minimum involvement of domestic capital.

2. The prevention of uncontrolled construction in areas where it would cause further deterioration by using internal resources together with the participation of various world organizations, universities and the leading centres of urban and physical planning.
3. Use of all available knowledge from workshops and seminars such as Workshop Prague 91, and drawing on the expertise of planners, conservationists and property professionals from other countries.
4. Investment of internal resources and funding in the infrastructure to ultimately create the necessary requirements for future development.

Already it is becoming apparent that the major cities of the former Czechoslovakia are a source of interest to architects and planners around the world. Prague, for example, as a major centre in Europe with strong cultural values and an impressive heritage was the subject of consideration at Workshop Prague 91, which involved the participation of eight foreign groups including such names as Ricardo Bofill, Vittorio Gregotti and Jean Nouvelle. The task for the workshop was to consider possible solutions to the problems of Prague. However, the enormity of the challenge is made more problematic by the inadequacy of legislation, the vagueness of property relations and the deficiency of information on land costs. The Prague Municipality expected the workshop to solve the development problems of the urban area, yet the authorities themselves had no clear concept or plan for the city. They have been unable to fill the gap vacated by the previous decision-makers and lack the means of ascertaining the needs of the community.

One of the designs presented at the workshop proposed a system of two large green communication belts across the historical core of the city. Another proposed a linear development consisting of hotel and commercial complexes on the edge of the Prague basin. Those schemes which were potentially more valuable either proposed to establish green enclosures within the city or to form a green ecological corridor. Overall the aesthetic approach predominated within the various schemes, followed by ecological and commercial approaches. None of the participants proposed more broadly based schemes for economic, social or cultural development. Consequently, the workshop, which initially sparkled, ultimately fizzled out. However, from a positive perspective the workshop did bring together expertise, ideas and contacts from which Prague can learn and build upon.

Over the past 40 years, the building stock in Czechoslovakia suffered from neglect largely because the finance for upgrading and maintenance purposes has not been available to either the municipalities or to individual owners. With the market system not yet developed, communal budgets are based on subsidies received from the state. The costs of construction continue to increase with the result that practically every town and city is experiencing a disproportionate balance between the availability of and the need for resources. It appears unlikely that this situation will improve with the introduction of the new taxation system. According to recent estimates, the quota of taxes in city budgets will not be large enough to cover their respective needs. It may therefore be necessary to create a state subsidy policy for towns and regions, similar to neighbouring countries, to finance the needs of cities and to fund urban regeneration and property development.

Although there is an absolute shortage of funds at all levels, the privatization of state and municipal property is generating considerable cash flow. Privatization brings monies into central government funds and, in the case of auctions of municipal property, into the budgets of cities. In some cities these funds are deposited in accounts held under the City Development or City Regeneration Fund. As the name suggests, the intended purpose of the fund is to grant monies to those proprietors investing in reconstruction or the upgrading of their properties. The work must be performed speedily and to a high quality. Cities can use various mechanisms of returnable or non-returnable contributions and provide loans with advantageous conditions. An illustrative example is the sale of real estate for one-third of the auction price with the remainder waived, provided the new owner repairs or redevelops the property within a two year period. The funds being acquired from privatization represent only a short term supply of capital for financing urban regeneration. Over the longer term, once the current transition phase has passed and the privatization process is complete, this source of funding will weaken. It is therefore imperative that all available funds from this source are invested to yield capital growth, even though it is likely that profits will only increase slowly.

9.6   STRATEGY FOR THE POST-TRANSITION STAGE

Legislation

The pragmatism with which the new social order is being considered reflects a desire for the individual freedom of citizens and democracy in decision-making. In the field of urban development several pieces of legislation are under consideration. The act relating to the Territorial Planning and Building Code of 1976 is undergoing revision, and may well be superseded in the Republics by legislation to link up with the European Charter on Spatial Planning. The Building Code will, as in neighbouring European countries, become much more comprehensive. Amendments will incorporate regulations for the implementation framework for development in urban areas, environmental impact assessments and public participation procedures. Furthermore the planning and implementation of development in historical city centres will constitute separate sections within the legislation.

Legislation for the conservation of monuments and the cultural heritage is being prepared. This will deal with the recording and documentation of historic property as well as compensation for owners whose businesses may be restricted by conservation designation. Some responsibility for the cultural heritage is likely to be transferred from the two Ministries of Culture to the planning and building authorities. Additionally, the legislation governing the Chambers of Architects defines the role of architects within society and specifies the ethics of the profession. Consequently, public interest is given protection in relation to architectural and planned works through regulations at both individual and institutional levels; ultimately these will have to come into line with standards in other European countries.

Education and professional development

A high quality educational system is required with emphasis placed on special training schools. The strategic educational programme envisages schools with specialities, together with the organization of international conferences and seminars, the exchange of students and opportunities for study periods abroad. For example, specialists trained in areas such as urban development could help improve the professionalism of municipal authorities. It is essential that staff have the capabilities to work at the local political level, to have a clear grasp of the problems and to determine priorities. The Municipal Board, consisting of members of the general public and representatives from the commercial sector, is the body which is primarily concerned with the management of urban development, whereas the Municipal Authority, as an arm of state administration, is responsible for co-ordinating and moulding the future development of cities.

Market economy

The transition from the old socialist system to a new economic structure depends on putting in place the principles of a market economy and private ownership as a means of production. Over the longer term this will be followed by changes in the structure of enterprises and a transformation in production programmes and property relations. This transitional phase may be characterized by imbalances which may require intervention by the Republics, for example, through a policy of subsidization. However, once tax revenues begin to stabilize, cities will then be in a better position to use their own resources more effectively by providing for the development of facilities such as education and public health. In this context the co-operation of the public and private sectors will be essential in developing the urban economy. Good design standards, proper aesthetic criteria and a healthy environment are crucial to the development of enterprise programmes and to the needs of the population.

The policy of the state supporting the budgets of cities and regions through subsidization will have to continue on lines similar to those of western European countries. However, the allocation of funds may have a different application to that formerly used. Determining criteria will include the objectives/initiatives of cities, regions or individual owners, the utilization of their own funds and the efficiency of the organizational structure. The financial institutions will have an enhanced role in the allocation and monitoring of investment capital.

The amount of funds accruing as a result of the privatization of property will gradually reduce; the new social and economic structures should in turn begin to provide resources for regeneration and urban development purposes. For example, taxation law will allow a small percentage of income tax to be used for reconstruction and repairs of real property while the banks are in the process of encouraging a 'housing savings' plan. The introduction of the market economy will benefit the commercial sector, particularly the owners and users of real estate. Consequently, the state, regions and cities should facilitate those activities which are in the public interest. With respect to the historical city centres, economic motivation is being seen as a trigger to their regeneration, and the need to be able to compensate any businesses suffering loss as a result of conservation policies is seen as a natural corollary. Tourism and the influx of foreign capital should also emerge as an important source of additional revenue and further assist in development and economic growth.

9.7   ECONOMIC DEVELOPMENT PROGRAMMES

The governments of both republics are establishing economic development programmes for their territories. The programmes are classified into several groups.

1. General Purpose Programmes for the development and privatization of small and medium sized enterprises, supported by environmental funds for ecologically orientated projects or the cultural funds for the regeneration and reconstruction of protected monuments.
2. Single Purpose Programmes, which support the conversion of the armament factories in Slovakia.
3. Local Programmes, which support the development of neglected border regions including the towns situated within these areas.
4. Focal Programmes, which entail the regeneration of villages and urban reserves/urban protected zones.

In the case of the village regeneration programme which began in 1991, the purpose is to stimulate environmental awareness and to plan for future development by providing the necessary infrastructure and regenerating the housing stock in accordance with proper planning and design principles.

In March 1992 the Government of the former Czechoslovakian Federation introduced a programme for the regeneration of urban protected territories. Within this programme, assistance was given to facilitate cities (urban reserves and urban protected zones) in making a smooth transition to a democratic system with a market based economy. Hence, by commitment, the government showed its political will to preserve the cultural heritage in addition to creating the conditions for the regeneration of potentially the most valuable parts of urban areas.

The programme embodied the activities of the Ministries of Culture, the Environment, and Economic Policy and Development. The concept was based on the state's duty of care for valuable buildings as determined by the Act No. 20/1987 on State Conservation of Monuments. However, being aware of the restricted possibilities of the state, the programme emphasized the use of extra fiscal resources to be connected with privatization. Given the shortage of capital resources the programme also envisaged an important role for public–private initiatives and joint ventures, and from the benefits of exploiting the positive advantages offered within historical city centres for the benefit of regeneration projects.

According to the principles on which the programme is based, the success of regeneration depends on the active support and financial commitment of the owners and users of real estate, together with the necessary co-operation of the cities in implementing municipal programmes. Over the next few years, with the ongoing transformation to the market economy, the availability of finance is likely to remain low. For this reason, it is necessary to guarantee financial support from the Czech and Slovakian Governments for conservation and regeneration. Cities which apply for funding under the development programmes will be expected to show professionalism in the preparation of regeneration schemes as well as active participation of the general public. Necessary prerequisites for the successful development and implementation of these programmes include a professional input from staff, an advisory and information service, public promotion and the publicity arising from good quality results.

9.8 CONCLUSIONS

With the Czech and Slovakian states now responsible for their own affairs, the strategy for city development depends on professional decision-making and the effective functioning of its institutions. The consequence of communist rule created centralization and bureaucracy which stultified the planning and development process. However, the transformation to a market economy has necessitated changes in territorial planning concepts, funding, methods of construction, project management and legislation. The regeneration of urban areas ultimately may depend on the influx of international capital to supplement the internal investment currently being directed into infrastruc-tural improvement and developments. Economic development programmes will require public and private sector participation as well as state subsidies for the budgets of the cities and regions operating along lines similar to those in Western Europe. However, both emergent states will need to convince outside investors of their economic credentials and political stability. The irony being that as barriers are being removed in western Europe new borders are emerging with former eastern bloc countries.

10

Property-led urban regeneration and local economic development

G. Lloyd and S. Black

Land and property is a generic term that encompasses both developed and undeveloped land resources. The former may also be categorized by use and includes residential, office retail and industrial development sectors. The importance of land and property to the economy is now acknowledged by government, politicians and policy makers. The contribution of commercial property to the national economy, for example, is significant both as a component of investment, but also as the main collateral for loans to companies to finance investment. It has been estimated that the commercial property development and construction sector was worth £250 thousand million to the United Kingdom economy in 1989 and its direct contribution was equivalent to almost 6% of the Gross Domestic Product (GDP). This is comparable with the contribution of the energy sector (including North Sea oil and gas) to the national economy (Currie and Scott, 1991).

The land and property development sector also has an effect on the scale and location of economic activity within the macroeconomy. The residential development sector, for example, can constrain or enhance labour availability and mobility with an impact on regional economic development. Similarly, the design, layout or location of industrial property can affect the scale and location of individual firms by constraining their ability to respond to changing circumstances and opportunities (Fothergill _et al._, 1987). Thus land and property development has an important contribution to make in terms of regional and local economic prosperity. Development for residential, commercial and industrial purposes can facilitate inward investment, create employment and other opportunities for local builders and suppliers and increase the supply of space for economic activity.

The role of land and property in the process of economic development has been relatively neglected by policy makers. It was conventionally assumed that land and property development was relatively problem free (Healey, 1990; 1991a). In practice, however, land and property development is far more complex in terms of the interrelationships between the resource, the agents and the institutions involved (Healey, 1991b). Notwithstanding this, the potential of land and property development as a policy instrument in its own right has been increasingly recognized by government. This is particularly the case in the context of policies targeted at the regeneration of metropolitan regions and inner city areas. The history of inner city policy in Britain, for example, shows a changing emphasis of positive discrimination for the inner cities from an enhanced provision of social and educational services to local regeneration through economic and industrial development (Lawless, 1989). In the 1980s, however, property-led policies increasingly assumed a more central role to the extent that policy innovations such as science parks embrace a property element (Henneberry, 1992). Indeed, at the present time, it has been suggested that land and property development has become synonymous with urban regeneration and economic development itself (Solesbury, 1990).

An important characteristic of property-led urban economic regeneration is the embedded emphasis on the private sector in the lead role of policy implementation (Healey, 1991b). This generally takes the form of partnerships between the public and private sectors with the former involved in the co-ordination of local infrastructure and site provision, capital formation and investment and the development of effective local institutional arrangements (Carley, 1991). The emphasis on the private sector does not, however, preclude schemes designed, financed and executed by business interests alone (Lloyd and Newlands, 1990). The combination of property-led measures and private sector interests is reflected in prevailing urban policies. In England and Wales, for example, Action for Cities (HMSO, 1988) sets in place a policy framework with a marked emphasis on the development of land and property. This is achieved through central government assuming the lead role via its development powers, the relative downgrading of local authorities and the emphasis on private sector initiatives (Lawless, 1988). Similarly, in Scotland, New Life for Urban Scotland (Scottish Office, 1988) emphasizes the same critical areas of policy action. In particular, attention is drawn to the problems of the large, peripheral public sector housing estates which are to be addressed through private action, including self-help on the part of residents, the private sector and partnership arrangements designed to secure self-employment, small business development and the creation of community enterprises. In Northern Ireland, British policy and practice is often adopted and the principal focus of urban initiatives is in Belfast (Deddis and McGreal, 1989). The market and property based principles of the government were reflected in the Belfast Urban Area Plan (Department of the Environment for Northern Ireland, 1990), which attempted to identify and satisfy the land requirements of defined economic sectors in the city (Gaffikin and Morrissey, 1990).

Throughout the 1980s, the emphasis on land and property-led urban regeneration characterized urban policy in Britain. The property slump of the early 1990s, however, has called into question the validity of such an attempt to secure the physical, social and economic renaissance of urban areas. This chapter examines the nature of property-led urban regeneration strategies in Britain. It sets out the ideology of a property-led approach to urban economic development and identifies the perceived advantages of such a strategy. The chapter then considers three broad approaches to urban economic redevelopment through land and property. Firstly, the locality based regeneration strategies which are associated with Urban Development Corporations and Enterprise Zones. Secondly, the agency-led approaches typified by the work of the Scottish Development Agency and Scottish Enterprise are discussed as an alternative to urban property re-generation. Thirdly, attention is drawn to the government's attempts to liberalize the development of land and property in general. The conclu-sion draws together the advantages and disadvantages of the property-led approach.

10.1   IDEOLOGY AND LAND DEVELOPMENT

The adoption of a land and property-led development approach to urban economic regeneration was not an accident. It was a consequence of a deliberate shift in policy by the Conservative government to address the perceived problems of the inner cities and metropolitan areas. Why should such an emphasis be given to the development of land and property re-sources in the context of the inner cities? It is possible to gain an insight into this question by examining the ideology of the present government.

Ideology may be taken as the sets of political ideas which are held by identifiable groups in society, including those exercised by government. The political ideas essentially serve a dual function: on the one hand, to explain, justify or contest the prevailing political arrangements within a community and, on the other hand, to provide plans for action for public political institutions (Freeden, 1990). As a consequence, in terms of gov-ernment action there is likely to be a strong connection between ideology and public policy. This was particularly evident in 1979, for example, when the then newly elected Conservative government introduced a powerful market-led ideology which challenged the political consensus that had prevailed throughout the earlier post-war period. This had resulted in an unwritten cross-party political agreement regarding the balance of interests between the public and private sectors (Wapshott and Brock, 1983). The new ideology also challenged established Conservative ideas about the legitimate and politically acceptable nature of state intervention and economic management itself (Loney, 1986). The Conservative government's ideology stressed the need to ensure the freedom of market forces and the traditional Conservative values of hierarchy and allegiance to authority (Thornley, 1990). These radical facets to the new Conservative philosophy had a marked effect on its subsequent public policy agenda. They were particularly apparent in the private sector, market-led property- based urban regeneration strategies of the 1980s.

In practice, the relationship between ideology and policy is constrained, however, by a number of established political and institutional factors (Freeden, 1990). There are potential economic and political costs likely to be associated with policies solely, or even primarily, based on doctrinal grounds (Cox, 1980a). The resulting restraint has been evident, for example, with respect to fiscal policies for land values (Cox 1980b; 1983). Similarly, the abolition of land use planning controls may result in considerable uncertainty for the property development sector (Evans, 1990). Thus, the present government's fierce commitment to a free market doctrine is tempered by the political economy of land and property. The government has not, for example, removed public controls from the land and property development process. Notwithstanding such constraints, the government has modified established mechanisms and policy instruments and introduced its own market based initiatives. This is an important point because although certain policy instruments may appear familiar, the ideology driving them is markedly different.

10.2   ADVANTAGES OF A PROPERTY DEVELOPMENT STRATEGY

There are a number of reasons for the interest in property-led urban regeneration initiatives as the basis of the present government's urban and inner city policy. Firstly, there was an expressed dissatisfaction with the then existing urban policy measures which were deemed to be conventional. Conventional may be expressed in terms of being overtly interventionist and perceived by government as 'crowding-out' private sector investment and initiatives in inner urban areas. The Enterprise Zone experiment, for example, illustrates this point. Enterprise Zones were introduced as an alternative form of urban policy, being intended for 'areas of economic and physical decay where conventional economic policies have not succeeded in regenerating self-sustaining economic activity' (Department of the Environment, 1980). Furthermore, Enterprise Zones were located in different parts of the country and comprised different types of site with the intention of testing the effectiveness of the approach in different circumstances. It was argued that the establishment of Enterprise Zones was not part of established regional policy nor other policies such as those concerned with inner cities, rural development or derelict land. It is clear, therefore, that Enterprise Zones were intended to be effected independently from the more conventional, interventionist policies which had developed through the latter part of the post-war period.

Secondly, there were a number of perceived political advantages to a property-led urban regeneration strategy. It was clear that such an approach would enable specific geographical areas to be targeted for positive discrimination. Furthermore, a property development strategy would involve the physical transformation of the designated areas with a visible and tangible effect. In short, a property-led development strategy offered a demonstration that the government's free market ideology was superior to conventional policy measures. The political arguments gained the support of various groups with a vested interest in market-led solutions to economic problems. Although the Conservative government appeared to repudiate formal neo-corporatist links with major economic interest groups (Wilson, 1990), it did maintain informal links with lobby groups on the margins of the public policy agenda. These included bodies that advocated greater freedom for landowners and property developers and supported the political lobby for the liberalization of the land and property development sector (Lloyd, 1989).

Finally, there were a number of perceived economic advantages of property based strategies for local urban regeneration (Turok, 1992). These include, for example, the direct and induced effect of increased construction activity in a specific locality; the stimulus to indigenous growth in an area through the development of property via the provision of adequate supplies of commercial and industrial floorspace to enable the expansion of existing enterprises; the provision of premises for inward investment, as demonstrated by the effects of relocations over relatively short distances in the Enterprise Zones (Department of the Environment, 1987); facilitating local economic recovery through a process of neighbourhood revitalization, as with the Glasgow Eastern Area Renewal Project (Wannop, 1991); and the promotion of massive local economic restructuring via property development such as the 'mega-projects' undertaken in American cities where formerly derelict land is developed into integrated office, retail and conference facilities (Turok, 1992).

The present government has implemented its property-led economic regeneration strategy for urban areas in a number of ways. These include locality initiatives based on the designation of specific areas, development agency-led measures which initiated property-led schemes and through a process of liberalizing the development of land and property by landowners and developers. These measures are not mutually exclusive. The Urban Development Corporations, for example, are specific bodies established for the purposes of economic and physical regeneration in designated localities. Indeed, the idea of a development agency with executive development powers over land and property is an established one in Britain. It has been argued, for example, that the legislative basis of Urban Development Corporations was modelled on the 1959 New Towns Act (Brownhill, 1990).

10.3   URBAN REGENERATION: THE LOCALITY APPROACH

Property-led urban regeneration initiatives have been used in specific geographically defined localities. This section examines two examples of this approach: Urban Development Corporations and Enterprise Zones.

Firstly, Urban Development Corporations have been described as the flagship of urban policy in Britain in the 1980s and epitomize the idea of property-led urban regeneration (Imrie, 1992). The Local Government and Planning Act 1980 introduced Urban Development Corporations for specific localities to bring land and buildings into effective use, to encourage the development of existing and new industry, to create an attractive environment, and to ensure the provision of housing and social facilities to encourage people to live and work in the area. This approach was to be achieved by acquiring, reclaiming and disposing of land, carrying out building works, providing infrastructure, providing financial assistance to developers and generally doing anything necessary or expedient leading to regeneration (Brayshaw, 1990; Brownhill, 1990). In other words, the regeneration of the localities in question was to be secured through the development of land and property.

The relationship of the Urban Development Corporations to the private sector was fundamental to the initiative. It was intended that they would act as catalysts for private property development by providing a framework through the provision of the necessary land and infrastructure resources. This was deemed essential as an incentive to the private sector, which was perceived as the principal agency for securing the required regeneration (Lawless, 1989). Thus, to this end, the Urban Development Corporations were given substantial planning powers which were far greater, for example, than those originally given to the New Town Corporations. As a consequence, Urban Development Corporations have powers to grant planning permission and thereby replace local authorities in their areas as the relevant development control authorities. Furthermore, they also have special development powers to grant planning permission for land development without the need for consultation or the holding of planning inquiries. In addition, Urban Development Corporations are granted an area of land by

Parliament without appeal and are accountable only to that body. The Urban Development Corporations are run by a board appointed by the Secretary of State rather than elected representatives (Brownhill, 1990). Paradoxically, however, they are not plan-making bodies and must take account of local authority plans, although, crucially, they are not bound by them. These powers have enabled Urban Development Corporations to implement market-led regeneration strategies almost wholly based on private sector property development.

The Urban Development Corporations have been introduced in two phases. The first two, set up in 1981, were the London Docklands Development Corporation and the Merseyside Development Corporation. The next phase came in 1986 with four more in England, in the Black Country, Teesside, Tyne and Wear and Trafford Park, Greater Manchester. An additional Urban Development Corporation was set up in Wales for the Cardiff Bay area. In 1987, three further small Urban Development Corporations were announced for Bristol, Leeds and central Manchester. In 1988, the policy statement Action for Cities announced that the Lower Don Valley in Sheffield was to become an Urban Development Corporation, while the Merseyside Corporation was doubled in size. No further Urban Development Corporations were envisaged at this time (Lawless, 1989).

The second locality based measure, that of Enterprise Zones, was also introduced in the Local Government, Planning and Land Act 1980. Enterprise Zones were initially established on an experimental basis for a ten year period and were specifically intended 'to test how far industrial and commercial activity can be encouraged by the removal or streamlined administration of certain statutory or administrative controls' (Department of the Environment, 1980). Subsequent to the enabling legislation, the government embarked on three successive rounds of Enterprise Zone designation, in 1981, 1983 and more recently in 1989. As a consequence, over 25 Enterprise Zones are now operational, albeit at varying stages of maturity, in Britain.

The concept introduced a simplified planning regime, providing 'deemed' consent for many developments if certain standards of height, access and land use were met. More crucially, however, Enterprise Zones provided two important financial incentives. Firstly, firms locating in the zones did not have to pay rates for ten years. Secondly, 100% capital allowances against tax were provided for industrial and commercial buildings. This proved particularly attractive for developers. Further fiscal incentives included exemption from training levies.

In 1986, the Department of the Environment commissioned an economic evaluation of the Enterprise Zone experiment. This assessed the contribution of Enterprise Zones to economic and physical change in the localities in which the zones were located and measured the associated public costs and benefits. The study concluded that the Enterprise Zones 'in operating on both the demand side and the supply side of property markets have simultaneously encouraged the development of new premises in hitherto derelict or neglected sites and attracted firms into those premises. In this respect the experiment was well designed' (Department of the Environment, 1987). In addition, the study suggested that Enterprise Zones had involved the removal of physical dereliction and secured the improvement of the environment in the designated areas. With respect to the physical development of the designated Enterprise Zones the key indicators are the improvement to the stock of land and property and the availability of floorspace for subsequent productive use. By October 1988, for example, about 72% of the total land area of the Enterprise Zones (3513 ha) had been developed, 45% since designation. Of the available floorspace in the Enterprise Zones, 80% was located in the English Enterprise Zones and 70% in the first round designations. Furthermore, 42% of the available floorspace was in industrial use and 42% in warehousing, including open land storage. Office activities were restricted to 6% and retailing to 5.9% of the total floorspace.

10.4   URBAN REGENERATION: THE AGENCY APPROACH

An alternative and complementary approach to urban regeneration adopted by the government is the agency approach. This involves the execution of property-led redevelopment strategies through the specific institutional arrangement of a Development Agency. This is the approach adopted for the development, financing and implementation of urban policy in Scotland. Since the mid-1970s the principal agent in the execution and control of urban policy in Scotland has been the Scottish Development Agency. The Agency established in 1975 was charged with the responsibility for securing economic development in the whole of Scotland, apart from the area covered by the Highlands and Islands Development Board. More specifically, it was made responsible for providing, maintaining and safeguarding employment, promoting industrial efficiency and international competitiveness, and furthering the improvement of the environment in Scotland (Scottish Development Agency, 1976).

Initially, the Scottish Development Agency exercised its economic functions and addressed the problems associated with industrial restructuring in the Scottish economy (Keating and Boyle, 1986). In the later 1970s, however, it developed an interest in urban regeneration. This followed its involvement in the management and co-ordination of the GEAR project in which the agency assumed a central role (Boyle and Wannop, 1982). The interest in locality-specific economic regeneration was subsequently confirmed in the light of a critical review of its development activities by government. This resulted in the Scottish Development Agency adopting a 'modified market' approach to local economic regeneration within Scotland, an approach which stressed the development of competitive and efficient business, the leverage of private investment and property-led initiatives (Moore and Booth, 1986). This resulted in the proliferation of area-specific schemes based on property development through the mechanism of private sector involvement. In 1990–1, for example, expenditure by the Scottish Development Agency was allocated primarily to its area-specific schemes as follows: inward investment (5%), investment (7%), industry (29%), property (22%) and environmental improvement (37%) (Scottish Development Agency, 1991).

The Scottish Development Agency introduced a range of area-specific schemes (Gulliver, 1984; Boyle, 1988). These included its active managerial involvement in large scale comprehensive urban renewal initiatives, such as GEAR; specific programmes of economic and environmental regeneration targeted at areas suffering from concentrated economic decline and industrial collapse; and, latterly, an emphasis on 'self-help' schemes which resulted in the proliferation of private sector backed enterprise trusts in Scotland. The nature of the projects' approaches changed over time as a consequence of experience and the increasing commercialization of the Scottish Development Agency, which emphasized the role of the private sector interests in executing the public agenda for urban regeneration. It was argued, for example, that 'there has been a significant change of direction over the four generations of area approaches. In general, this shift has been characterised by a movement from a strategic long term, redistributive and community based approach to a tactical, short term, market and business oriented approach' (Moore and Booth, 1986). This drift also involved greater reliance on local property based strategies to attract the private sector to assume greater responsibility for urban change (Boyle, 1988).

Notwithstanding the government's modification of the objectives and remit of the Scottish Development Agency, the body was replaced by Scottish Enterprise in April 1991. This transformation of the institutional arrangements for economic development in Scotland was not an isolated incident, but formed part of a broader ideological drift to reorganizing the delivery of training and business development in Britain (Danson *et al.*, 1990). Scottish Enterprise was a different type of development body and was created from the merger of the Scottish Development Agency and the work of the Training Agency (formerly the Manpower Services Commission, now the Employment Department) as it had operated in Scotland. In formal terms, Scottish Enterprise was charged with the responsibility of stimulating self-sustaining economic development and the growth of enterprise, securing the improvement of the environment, encouraging the creation of viable jobs, reducing unemployment and improving the skills of the Scottish workforce. The evidence of the government's ideology is clearly illustrated in the degree to which the private sector is involved in the administration and policy formulation of the body. Thus, although Scottish Enterprise is a central strategic policy making, monitoring and enforcement agency, its board of ten members incorporates that at least six of whom have a business background.

A distinguishing feature of the Scottish Enterprise arrangements involves the mechanisms for the delivery of business development, training and environmental improvement services. This is to be facilitated by Local Enterprise Companies (LECs), which are local business-led interest groups. The 12 Local Enterprise Companies in the Scottish Enterprise network are responsible for a range of functions: assessing the circumstances and requirements of local labour markets in Scotland; arranging for the delivery of national training programmes; developing training initiatives for specific local needs; and designing business development services and raising private sector monies – leverage – to supplement the public sector resources being made available to them. The Local Enterprise Companies are based loosely on local authority boundaries and are bound by a contractual arrangement to Scottish Enterprise to deliver the national training programmes and business development measures. Individual projects over a certain financial threshold are referred back to the parent bodies for approval. Although the Scottish Local Enterprise Companies and the Training and Enterprise Councils in England and Wales are both concerned with the provision of national and local training programmes, the Scottish Local Enterprise Companies also have a substantially wider range of economic and environmental improvement responsibilities to discharge at the outset than is the case for the Training and Enterprise Councils (Danson *et al.*, 1989). As a consequence of their responsibilities, Scottish Enterprise and the Local Enterprise Companies will consider land and property development as a means of encouraging indigenous economic activity within their local strategic plans for their respective localities.

10.5 LAND DEREGULATION AND ECONOMIC DEVELOPMENT

The creation of property-led urban regeneration through locality based initiatives and the use of agency mechanisms has been accompanied by a general relaxation of public sector controls over private land development. Indeed, a number of land use policy statements have sought to encourage land development by redefining the nature and extent of public sector land use controls – in short, to ensure that planning does not inhibit the driving force of private sector led property development (Thornley, 1990). The government's general principles regarding land use policy and planning have been stated as follows: 'the system should be efficient, effective and simple in conception and operation, to facilitate much needed development and to strike the right balance between that development and the interests of conservation. It should not be regarded simply as a means of preventing change. Properly used it can help to secure economy, efficiency and amenity in the development and use of land' (Department of the Environment, 1988).

The land use planning system has been used not in its traditional controlling format but as an enabling function, as a means of allowing or encouraging private enterprise to undertake development in circumstances that would be otherwise difficult or unattractive.

In seeking to achieve this specific role of planning, the government has used a number of ways of defining the correct balance of interests in the land development process (Rowan-Robinson and Lloyd, 1986). Thus, for example, a number of primary legislative measures have included the Local Government, Planning and Land Act 1980, the Housing and Planning Act 1986 and the Planning and Compensation Act 1991. An example of this approach is that of Simplified Planning Zones, which were introduced in the Housing and Planning Act 1986. Indeed, Simplified Planning Zones (SPZs) are a direct result of the Enterprise Zone experiment. The government drew attention to the perceived success of the streamlined planning agreements involved in Enterprise Zones stating that they 'provide a real stimulus to the development or redevelopment of areas in need of regeneration, without leading to a decline in design standards or deterioration in the local environment' (Department of the Environment, 1988).

The Housing and Planning Act 1986 imposed on local planning authorities a duty to consider, as soon as was practicable, whether it would be desirable to establish Simplified Planning Zones and, where it was considered desirable, to draw up schemes establishing such zones. Simplified Planning Zones are intended to act as an incentive to property developers by relieving the perceived burden of conventional land use planning regulations and procedures on land and property development. In Scotland, the Scottish Development Department issued practical advice to local planning authorities on the form and content of such zones (Scottish Development Department, 1987). Crucially, it was suggested that in defining a Simplified Planning Zone 'there should be a demonstrable need to redress physical or economic problems through regeneration. SPZ designation should therefore be seen as part of a positive programme for the promotion of investment and improvement in targeted areas and not simply as the lifting of controls'. In addition, it was suggested that 'land in local authority ownership is not a pre-requisite: SPZs can help clear a path for development without the need for site acquisition or assembly. There must, however, be an adequate supply of immediately available land capable of sustaining early development'.

10.6 VALIDITY OF PROPERTY-LED URBAN REGENERATION

The validity of a property-led approach to urban regeneration and economic development is questionable at the present time with the prevailing slump in the property sector and in individual markets. The uncertainty in the land and property sector has been evident in the problems of individual property development companies, the difficulties associated with specific flagship projects, such as Canary Wharf, the implications of a stagnant housing market and the loss of confidence in the construction industry. These matters have called into question land and property development as central urban policy instruments. Thus, for example, the contribution and achievements of individual Urban Development Corporations have increasingly come under attack, particularly as the property slump has undermined their property-led development strategies. The collapse of Canary Wharf has undoubtedly heightened criticism of the London Docklands Development Corporation, which has already been subject to the scrutiny of two parliamentary committees and was criticized for focusing too narrowly on physical regeneration and failing to benefit the local community (Turok, 1992). Against this backcloth of criticism and uncertainty we may identify a number of key issues.

Firstly, a reliance on the land and property development sector as the mainstay of urban regeneration is vulnerable to the uncertainties of that sector. This may be illustrated by the poor takeup of the Simplified Planning Zone initiative. Subsequent to the enabling legislation in 1986, only a very small number of such zones have been proposed and designated. In England and Wales, for example, three Simplified Planning Zones have been designated at Corby, Nottingham and Derby. In Scotland, there is one adopted zone, at Dingwall, and two in the process of designation, at Coatbridge and Grangemouth. There are a number of arguments that may be considered for this poor rate of adoption of what promised to be a radical idea for the purposes of simplified planning. The government's view is that the idea requires further simplification (Lloyd, 1990).

Secondly, a key element of a property-led approach is the role played by the private sector. This participation has been extended to policy formulation, financing and implementation. The Scottish Enterprise arrangements illustrate the nature of this corporate involvement and raise a number of questions in relation to the nature of economic development and land use planning controls. Although planning controls have remained with local authorities there are two broad possible sets of relations between Scottish Enterprise and the land use planning system. On the one hand, the economic and business development strategies of Scottish Enterprise and the Local Enterprise Companies may ignore local authority planning (and their responsibilities for the provision of infrastructure). This is likely to lead to conflict as and when the respective modes of decision-making clash over local development issues, particularly where assumptions are made about the availability of land, its servicing and its phased release by planning authorities. On the other hand, there may be a convergence of ideas between the two forms of planning. This possibility raises the question of which institution sets the agenda for the consensual approach to planning in specific areas. It has been suggested, for example, that as planning authorities adopt district-wide local plans and update the content of the plans to a more strategic level (away from a focus on development control matters alone), then there is a possibility that some influence will be brought to bear on the behaviour of the Local Enterprise Companies in the devising of their business development plans (Hayton, 1991). It is possible, however, that the local development agenda may then be set or directed by the Local Enterprise Companies rather more forcibly than this. Furthermore, a completely different relationship may be possible whereby the Local Enterprise Companies set the agenda for local planning matters.

An indication of this possibility can be gleaned from the draft *National Planning Policy Guideline 2: Land for Business and Industry* (Scottish Office Environment Department, 1991). This discusses the strategic relationship between land policies for business and industry, but stated that Scottish Enterprise and the Local Enterprise Companies will 'operate within the context of the planning system, particularly where they are involved in urban renewal, property development, land renewal and environmental improvements. Each year the LECs will prepare three year Business Plans incorporating one year detailed operating plans. Where these have land use and development implications, close co-operation between the planning authority and the LEC will be essential. Development plans will continue to set the context but may need alteration in consultation with the LEC, especially where they were prepared before the LEC was in operation'. This suggests the possibility that undue influence may be exercised by unelected local business groups over the preparation of development plans by democratically elected and accountable local planning authorities. Clearly this raises a number of worrying implications for the accountability and the future execution of land use planning policies in Scotland (Lloyd and Black, 1992).

Simplified Planning Zones, for example, also demonstrate the extent to which private interests are being encouraged into the land development process. Indeed, these zones have been described as a form of 'trend planning' which seeks 'to facilitate private sector development rather than control it. The resulting economic activity and change in the built environment is regarded as the evidence of successful planning. This style considers that the public interest is best served by the actual development itself rather than by any planning gain that may be secured from the developers. The preferred pattern of land uses in an area is that identified by market actors rather than professional planners, and the latter are urged to be responsive to market pressures' (Brindley *et al.*, 1989). This emphasis raises questions as to the accountability and control of property based and private sector-led arrangements (Salmon, 1992). Thus, concern has been expressed as to the extent to which Urban Development Corporations represent an attack on local democracy (Lawless, 1989). To a certain extent the overriding of local democratic processes was a deliberate part of the thinking behind Urban Development Corporations as the bodies aimed to cut through the red tape of bureaucracy to achieve private sector development in areas where it had previously been perceived as lacking. In the London Docklands Development

Corporation area this has resulted in conflict between the Corporation, the local councils and the community. Subsequent Urban Development Corporation designations have attempted to secure greater local participation in decision-making, but it has been argued that they look increasingly dated as urban policy moves into a new era of partnership and community involvement (Imrie, 1992). The notion, however, of community involvement in the context of local property-led initiatives is questionable given the incompatibility of such ideas within a market-led decision-making environment (Robinson and Shaw, 1991).

Finally, concern must be expressed as to the costs of property-led urban development schemes. This is an important point because an implicit notion in involving the private sector was the redistribution of cost-bearing from the public to the private developers. Yet the evidence shows that the public costs of the property-led schemes was considerable. It has been estimated, for example, that the Canary Wharf development received a hidden subsidy of £470 million in capital allowances (Brownhill, 1990). Similarly, in terms of the costs of the Enterprise Zone experiment for the period 1981–8 public sector expenditure was £472 million (at 1987–8 prices). Of this estimate, capital allowances accounted for 65% and rates revenue foregone for 35%. In addition, there was an estimated public sector land acquisition cost of £41 million and £188 million for infrastructure investment by the public sector. The role of the public sector in financing private sector schemes is an important one in many projects (Vickerman, 1989). In this context also, attention must be drawn to the opportunity costs of the property-led measures. There is a problem that by concentrating public resources and private investment on specifically designated areas a 'honey-pot' may be created. This may then have the effect of displacing activity, investment and jobs from elsewhere with a redistributive rather than a stimulative impact on the local economy. In the context of the London Docklands Development Corporation, for example, in the period 1981–7, 77% of new employment in the area was through transfers of existing jobs. Surveys also showed that between 2 and 24% of new jobs went to locals (Brownhill, 1990). This was also evident with Enterprise Zones in terms of the origins of jobs and establishments. In 1986, for example, although about 23% of all firms were in the zones at designation, transfers into the zones comprised 37% of the total (Department of the Environment, 1987).

10.7   CONCLUSIONS

In a thoughtful discussion of the forces shaping urban change and the role of urban policy in easing the adjustment costs of that change, Cheshire (1988) asserted that 'this cannot be done by means of economic policy instruments or traditional instruments of development alone. It is necessary to assist the whole process of urban adaptation including strengthening those factors which contribute to the quality of urban life and culture, to the physical fabric of the city and the urban environment'. The reliance on property-led measures and policy instruments to secure urban regeneration shows that such an approach in isolation cannot address the multitude of problems that characterize such areas. Although land and property development is a necessary input, it is not a sufficient element of urban policy for economic regeneration. Thus, the emphasis on land and property as the basis of urban policy must undergo further refinements to form a consistent and integrated policy context to managing urban change.

REFERENCES

Boyle, R. (1988) The price of private planning: a review of urban planning policy in Scotland. In: *The Scottish Government Yearbook 1988* (Eds D. McCrone and A. Brown), Edinburgh University Press, Edinburgh, pp. 183–199.

Boyle, R. and Wannop, U. (1982) Area initiatives and the SDA: the rise of the urban project, *Frazer of Allander Quarterly Economic Commentary*, **8**(1), 45–57.

Brayshaw, P. (1990) Urban Development Corporations and Enterprise Boards revisited: a survey of current policies and practice, *Local Economy*, **5**(3), 214–224.

Brindley, T., Rydin, Y. and Stoker, G. (1989) *Remaking Planning. The Politics of Urban Change in the Thatcher Years*, Unwin Hyman, London.

Brownhill, S. (1990) *Developing London's Docklands*, Paul Chapman Publishing, London.

Carley, M. (1991) Business in urban regeneration: a case study in Birmingham, *Local Economy*, **6**(2), 100–115.

Cheshire, P. (1988) Urban revival in sight: the end is where we start from? *Local Economy*, **3**(2), 96–108.

Cox, A.W. (1980a) Adversary politics and land policy: explaining and analysing British land values policy making since 1947, *Political Studies*, **24**(1), 16–34.

Cox, A.W. (1980b) The limits of central government intervention in the land and development market: the case of the land commission, *Policy and Politics*, **8**(3), 267–284.

Cox, A.W. (1983) The unintended consequences of policy initiation: a study of the British Conservative Government's property policy in the 1970s, *Environment and Planning C: Government and Policy*, **1**, 347–356.

Currie, D. and Scott, A. (1991) *The Place of Commercial Property in the UK Economy*, London Business School, London.

Danson, M., Lloyd, M.G. and Newlands, D. (1989) Scottish Enterprise: towards a model agency or a flawed initiative? *Regional Studies*, **23**(6), 557–564.

Danson, M., Fairley, J., Lloyd, M.G. and Newlands, D. (1990) Scottish Enterprise: an evolving approach to integrated economic development in

Scotland. In: *The Scottish Government Yearbook 1990* (Eds A. Brown and R. Parry), University of Edinburgh, Edinburgh, pp. 168–194.

Deddis, W.G. and McGreal, W.S. (1989) Urban regeneration: a comparative assessment in Great Britain and Northern Ireland. In: *Land and Property Development. New Directions* (Ed. R. Grover), E & FN Spon, London, pp. 199–207.

Department of the Environment (1980) *Enterprise Zones. A Consultation Document*, HMSO, London.

Department of the Environment (1987) *An Evaluation of the Enterprise Zone Experiment*, HMSO, London.

Department of the Environment (1988) *General Policy and Principles of Planning. Planning Practice Guidance No. 1*, HMSO, London.

Department of the Environment for Northern Ireland (1990) *Belfast Urban Area Plan, 2001*, HMSO, Belfast.

Evans, A.W. (1990) No room! No room! The costs of the British town and country planning system, *Institute of Economic Affairs, Occasional Paper No. 79*.

Fothergill, S., Monk, S. and Perry, M. (1987) *Property and Industrial Development*, Hutchinson, London.

Freeden, M. (1990) The stranger at the feast: ideology in twentieth century Britain, *Twentieth Century British History*, **1**(1), 9–34.

Gaffikin, F. and Morrissey, M. (1990) *Northern Ireland. The Thatcher Years*, Zed Books, London.

Gulliver, S. (1984) The area projects of the Scottish Development Agency, *Town Planning Review*, **55**(3), 322–334.

Hayton, K. (1991) Planning and Scottish Enterprise, *Scottish Planning Law and Practice*, **34**, 69–70.

Healey, P. (1990) Structure and agency in the land and property development process: some ideas for research, *Urban Studies*, **27**(1), 89–104.

Healey, P. (1991a) Urban regeneration and the development industry, *Regional Studies*, **25**(2), 97–110.

Healey, P. (1991b) Models of the development process: a review, *Journal of Property Research*, **8**(3), 219–238.

Henneberry, J. (1992) Science parks: a property based initiative for urban regeneration, *Local Economy*, **6**(4), 326–335.

HMSO (1988) *Action for Cities*, HMSO, London.

Imrie, R. (1992) Beyond the Urban Development Corporations, *Local Economy*, **6**(4), 351–353.

Keating, M. and Boyle, R. (1986) *The Making of Urban Scotland*, Edinburgh University Press, Edinburgh.

Lawless, P. (1988) British inner urban policy: a review, *Regional Studies*, **22**(6), 531–541.

Lawless, P. (1989) *Britain's Inner Cities*, Paul Chapman Publishing, London.

Lloyd, M.G. (1989) Land development and the free market lobby, *Scottish Planning Law and Practice*, **26**, 8–10.

Lloyd, M.G. (1990) Simplified planning zones in Scotland: government failure or the failure of government? *Planning Outlook*, **33**(2), 128–132.

Lloyd, M.G. and Black, J.S. (1992) Scottish Enterprise – casting a shadow over continuity and accountability? *Town and Country Planning*, **61**(4), 109–111.

Lloyd, M.G. and Newlands, D. (1990) Business interests and planning initiatives: a case study of Aberdeen. In: *Radical Planning Initiatives: New Directions for Urban Planning in the 1990s* (Eds J. Montgomery and A. Thornley), Gower, Aldershot, pp. 49–58.

Loney, M. (1986) *The Politics of Greed*, Pluto Press, London.

Moore, C. and Booth, S. (1986) From comprehensive regeneration to privatisation: the search for efficient area strategies. In: *The City in Transition* (Eds W. Lever and C. Moore), Clarendon Press, Oxford, pp. 76–91.

Robinson, F. and Shaw, K. (1991) Urban regeneration and community development, *Local Economy*, **6**(1), 61–72.

Rowan-Robinson, J. and Lloyd, M.G. (1986) Lifting the burden of planning – a means or an end? *Local Government Studies*, **12**(3), 51–64.

Salmon, H. (1992) Urban regeneration and the community: Birmingham heartlands – mid-term report, *Local Economy*, **7**(1), 26–38.

Scottish Development Agency (1976) *Annual Report*, SDA, Glasgow.

Scottish Development Agency (1991) *Annual Report*, SDA, Glasgow.

Scottish Development Department (1987) Simplified planning zones, *Planning Advice Note 31*, SDD, Edinburgh.

Scottish Office (1988) *New Life for Urban Scotland*, Scottish Office, Edinburgh.

Scottish Office Environment Department (1991) *Draft National Planning Policy Guideline 2: Land for Business and Industry*, SOEnD, Edinburgh.

Solesbury, W. (1990) Property development and urban regeneration. In *Land and Property Development in a Changing Context* (Eds P. Healey and R. Nabarro), Gower, Aldershot, pp. 186–195.

Thornley, A. (1990) Thatcherism and the erosion of the planning system. In: *Radical Planning Initiatives* (Eds J. Montgomery and A. Thornley), Gower, Aldershot, pp. 34–47.

Turok, I. (1992) Property led urban regeneration: panacea or placebo? *Environment and Planning A*, **24**, 361–379.

Vickerman, R. (1989) The private provision of infrastructure: the Channel Tunnel project, *Local Economy*, **4**(2), 132–142.

Wannop, U. (1991) The Glasgow Eastern Area Renewal (GEAR) Project: a perspective on the management of urban regeneration, *Town Planning Review*, **61**(4), 455–474.

Wapshott, N. and Brock, G. (1983) *Thatcher*, Futura, London.

Wilson, G.K. (1990) *Interest Groups*, Basil Blackwell, Oxford.

11

Regeneration and sustainable development

N. Falk

For several decades Britain's major towns and cities have been struggling with the challenges of urban regeneration brought on by the decline of traditional industry. The closure of docks, factories and warehouses as a result of technological change and manufacturing contraction has created some exceptional opportunities for remaking cities and introducing new uses. However, it has also left behind a legacy of physical, economic and social problems, which have often outstripped the capacity of local communities to adapt and respond.

Now that many parts of Europe, particularly the former Eastern bloc, are going through a similar transition, it is becoming important to bring together lessons from areas that have undergone a transition, so that there is a better understanding of the process of regeneration and how it is best promoted. One particular concern is how to make the most of an area's existing resources, including not only a heritage of waterfronts and historic buildings, but also small enterprises and the skills of its community, to secure development that is sustainable and in the wider public interest.

This chapter draws on the experience that the Urban and Economic Development Group (URBED) has gained since 1976 (when we started in London's Covent Garden, at the time a redundant fruit and vegetable market) to reassess the goals of regeneration, in the light of lessons from Birmingham's Jewellery Quarter and Bradford's Little Germany, before suggesting what are the key factors for success.

11.1   GOALS OF REGENERATION

In the early 1970s, the prevailing idea was that once an industry was in decline, it should be assisted to move into modern premises, while the site was comprehensively redeveloped for socially relevant uses. Thus the large areas of water in London's Surrey Docks were filled in at public expense. When buildings burned down, as they did frequently, few showed concern.

During the 1970s, however, a transition in thinking, a kind of 'paradigm shift', began to take place. First came the disillusionment with comprehensive development. Even before the bulldozers had finished, concern was being expressed about the loss of community, the lack of character in large scale new developments, such as the Barbican or the Aylesbury Estate in Southwark, and the waste of resources. At the same time people started to become aware of a different approach, based on the 'adaptive reuse' of buildings, and inspired by pioneering examples in the USA. The shift can be seen clearly in Cantacuzino's work; his early published work, *New Uses for Old Buildings* (Cantacuzino, 1975), largely dealt with the conversion of old buildings into publicly funded art centres and museums, whereas his later book is full of more commercial examples (Cantacuzino, 1989).

Two examples were of particular influence to Britain, although these will not be dealt with at length as they have been well covered elsewhere (Falk, 1992). The first was Baltimore Inner Harbour, where a succession of visitor attractions, which included a 'festival market place' inspired by prototypes in Boston (Quincey Market) and San Francisco (Ghirardelli Square and the Cannery) transformed the city's fortunes and put it on the map as a place to visit. Although successive Conservative politicians drew inspiration from the level of private investment, the reality was that the whole process had been organized as a series of public–private partnerships led by the City, who then let others take the credit, through an organization set up to promote the area's overall regeneration. The second example, which was even more relevant, was Lowell, a former mill town on the edge of Boston, which was turned from a dying city into one of the main centres for the electronics industry, symbolized by the conversion of one of the many mills into the headquarters of Digital. Here the designation of the whole city as a National Park, but one whose attraction came from its industrial buildings rather than wildlife, inspired many visitors to see whether the model could be transferred to Britain.

Twenty years later, there are now plenty of successful examples of British towns and cities which have found new uses for their industrial heritage, and which have lessons for the rest of Europe. However, in the process it is easy to lose sight of the aims and also the factors that lead to success. Thus regeneration is often treated as though it is simply about property development, and as if success can be measured by the level of investment, or even worse by the leverage ratio, the proportion of private to public investment. Such a view can lead to seduction by grand schemes, such as can be seen in much of London's Docklands or in a project such as Birmingham's new International Convention Centre, while the little projects are forgotten about. Yet because cities constitute far more than just the buildings in them, or the investment that these represent, it is naive to measure and judge regeneration in physical terms alone. Rather there is a need to think of cities in a more organic or holistic way, where success can be measured in the opportunities they give for the growth and fulfilment of human beings, and for both commercial and social enterprises.

In looking for ways of judging plans and planning that would win widespread support, three principles suggest themselves as the key to successful regeneration, as well as the fundamental reasons why our industrial heritage is worth conserving. The principles are those of social justice, natural balance and the minimization of waste. They need to be understood before considering strategies for area regeneration (Falk, 1984).

Social justice, the first aim, is concerned with responding to the needs of the least well-off and ensuring that they are not hurt in the process of change. Unfortunately, many development schemes have paid little or no regard to the existing community, and it is not surprising as a consequence that the process of reaching agreement on major projects can end up being long-drawn out and extremely painful. However, by conserving existing buildings and adapting them to new uses it is often possible to satisfy pressing local concerns and, in the best examples, provide the community with something it can own and control.

The idea of natural balance is derived from ecology, and is concerned with preserving diversity and the capacity to adapt to change. Old buildings often provide a ladder of opportunity, and a kind of ecological niche in which the new enterprises so crucial to an area's long term sustainability will make a start. This idea came originally from projects in Rotherhithe in London's Docklands, which involved converting Brunel's engine house for the Thames Tunnel into a small museum, and warehouses into craft workshops, through the vehicle of a development trust (Falk, 1992). This in turn attracted in uses such as Dartington College's Community Arts Programme, while a major film-maker took over several of the warehouses. Though the conversions may not have won architectural prizes, the enterprises that have taken root have enriched the surrounding area, providing inspiration as well as employment. They have also helped to conserve something timeless, providing an important link between the past and the future which no modern building could ever achieve.

The third, and perhaps the most convincing argument of all for conserving old buildings, is the idea of the minimization of waste. Old buildings represent past energy stored up in a usable form. If they are left to rot or go up in flames we are wasting our inheritance. Although the costs of reuse can easily become uneconomic, if buildings are properly maintained and gradually converted to appropriate uses, then conservation can also make economic sense. Indeed, the significant number of people who have become very rich as a result of low grade conversions of industrial buildings into small business units is telling proof of this.

11.2   CHALLENGE OF SUSTAINABLE DEVELOPMENT

Despite the basic appeal of these three principles, and the hundreds of successful examples of adaptive reuse, it is still common to find good buildings decaying for lack of use, or overelaborate conversions that fail to recover their costs. Over the years URBED had not only undertaken a considerable programme of research, reflected, for example, in *Reusing Redundant Buildings*, a guide produced for the Department of the Environment (URBED, 1986a) but has also undertaken the project management of a number of pioneering schemes.

Experience has shown that because regeneration is often seen as just being about designing an exciting building or attracting private investment, projects fail to turn visions into successful results. Common mistakes are to try to rely on planning controls alone, which are of little influence and can even be counter-productive in a weak market. Listing a building or including it in a conservation area does not stop it being bought by a speculator, nor do feasibility studies by themselves lead to action unless there is the right driving force.

The nature of these problems suggest the answer is neither leaving it to the market nor the public sector trying to do it all itself. Rather it involves creating a partnership, and promoting regeneration over a period of years (and it is best to think in terms of several decades rather than the short lives of the latest generation of Development Corporations). The key to the process is that of balanced incremental development, to proceed in stages in which new uses are gradually attracted, rather than going for the 'big bang' approach, in which a large amount of space suddenly comes on to the market.

A host of pioneering projects have been launched with the aim of finding the catalyst which would put areas that were being abandoned to good use again. Some projects were successful in changing attitudes away from simply abandoning older areas and building on the periphery. They have attracted new uses, such as housing, leisure and retail into areas that once were only used for industry, as well as mobilizing a variety of sources of finance. Where they have been less successful is in enabling existing activities to survive and grow, which, together with the pioneers, have been squeezed out by demand for space and rising property values.

The process of commercial 'gentrification' is little different from what previously took place in areas like Islington (London) which formed the battlegrounds for community action in the 1970s. Once again it has been encouraged by a mixture of financial incentives to private property owners to undertake improvements, an upswing in the property market and relaxations in planning controls. These have included not only changes in the Planning Use Classes Order aimed at 'lifting the burden' of bureaucracy, which have effectively eliminated the distinction between light industry and offices, but also cuts in the powers and resources of local authorities.

Although there have been many individual projects worth celebrating, the overall results have been disturbing, particularly for the havoc that uncontrolled property development had on vulnerable business and community networks, as well as for the damage done to the public realm. Some examples from London will illustrate what has happened.

In Covent Garden, virtually all the creative firms that acted as pioneers in the 1970s have left the area, community gardens have given way to faceless office blocks and the market buildings, which had been developed by the Greater London Council as a specialist shopping centre with independent traders, have been sold to an insurance company which is driving up the rents and 'squeezing out' the character.

In Clerkenwell, one of the pioneering examples of managed workspace, developed with the help of the Greater London Council to house some of the many craft businesses which have made the area distinctive, has been bought by a developer because it was expected to be profitable to terminate the licences and replace the occupants with office users who can pay more.

In north Southwark, a historic materials testing works renovated by a building preservation trust and occupied by small firms, was sold to a development company. However, instead of occupying the vacant space the building was sold on to another developer, who cleared out the small firms which occupied the space and then sold it to yet a third developer. They made some modest improvements and eventually only let the building in its entirety to a single firm after it had stood empty for several years.

These are just a few of the examples of what happens when a development boom gets underway and there is no way of keeping a balance between developers' objectives and environmental and community concerns. Yet most people would agree that the goals of regeneration are far wider than buying and selling property with money borrowed from the banks, particularly when improvements to the environment, on which increased values depend, are publicly funded. The 'boom' or 'big bang' mentality leads to excessive prices being paid for property, which after the crash still stands idle because of the paper values which have been generated. It can also contribute to 'private affluence and public squalor'. There is a paradoxical situation when the very people needed to occupy the space go elsewhere because the quality of life is poor as a result of insufficient investment in the public realm, including public transport and clean streets.

The successful regeneration of a historic industrial area is made up of many projects, both big and small. The idea of designating a place as an 'industrial heritage area' has been promoted by Nottingham in connection with the Lace Market, which is one of the leading examples. In some instances the original industry has all but died out, whereas in others it is what makes the area special. There are also major differences in size and whether the buildings are large or small. Here, to illustrate how the process of regeneration can work over time, two contrasting places with which URBED has been involved over a period of years are considered, that is, Birmingham's Jewellery Quarter and Bradford's Little Germany, to see if there are some common lessons to be learned.

11.3   BIRMINGHAM'S JEWELLERY QUARTER

The Jewellery Quarter is an area of roughly 40 ha on the edge of Birmingham's city centre. It originally belonged to the Colmore Estate and was developed as housing in the middle of the 18th century. Many buckle, jewellery and 'toy' makers took over houses, toys being the cheap trinkets for which Birmingham became famous. The buildings in the quarter include former houses, particularly in the northern section which has come to be known as the 'golden triangle', and where there are now over 100 shops selling jewellery, purpose-built workshops with the front acting as an office and showroom, and a few large factories, such as Argent Works, now the Argent Centre, where pens were once made.

Although industrial processes caused some works to expand, such as electroplating (which started in the old Elkington's Works in 1840, where the Museum of Science and Industry now is), on the whole the jewellery industry is made up of small workshops where specialized functions are carried out, and where the streets form the production line. Birmingham, which accounts for most of the manufactured jewellery made in Britain, that is, jewellery for the mass market, is still a place where the craft skills that made Britain the 'workshop of the world' in the 19th century are still carried on.

The industry has always gone through ups and downs, and so it has been essential to have a supply of cheap premises that could be occupied readily in response to demand. Businesses were and still are started by people who have learned the trade working for someone else, and there are real economies in working close together. Indeed, in the 19th century it became the densest industrial area in Britain. The remaining houses were slums with appalling poverty, vividly recalled in Kathleen Dayus's various autobiographies.

'Many people with large families who once lived in these hovels had no prospects, just living from hand to mouth, and many who could not afford their rent let off their living room to people wanted to start a small business . . . there are still the back yards, brew houses, and even old brick sheds where people used to keep pigeons and did their washing ready for the pawnshops, yet people still ply their trades there.' (Dayus, 1982)

After the Second World War there were grandiose proposals to clear away the old workshops and modernize the area. However, when Birmingham City Council redeveloped part of an area it owned as the Hockley Centre in 1971, displacing 150 businesses for a multistorey block of flatted factories, almost none of the units were taken by jewellery firms, and other businesses moved in instead. Apart from this development most of the other new buildings have been relatively small scale, and so the area retains its Victorian character, with an astonishing diversity of buildings.

The area was insulated from development pressures by several factors. First, many of the buildings formed part of large estates: the King Edward's Estate (which is used to support education) and the Vyse Estate, which was bought by the City Council. Second, it is cut off from the city by the ring road, which forms a 'concrete collar' round the centre. Third, the rent levels were insufficient to justify much in the way of redevelopment, except close to the ring road, where some large blocks of offices were developed in the 1960s, including what is now the Telecom Tower.

By the 1970s attitudes were beginning to change, with the potential of Birmingham's Jewellery Quarter being increasingly recognized. Indeed, much of it was included within conservation areas. These may restrict development pressures, but designation by itself does not necessarily restore buildings which have fallen into neglect. The initiative to start regenerating the area came largely from the West Midlands County Council, under their chief planner, whose background in Norwich made him particularly aware of the scope for conservation. The area was designated as an Industrial Improvement Area in 1980, which provided grants under the Inner Urban Areas Act towards refurbishment. However, even more significant was the County's scheme for 'enveloping' buildings, in which the visible exterior was improved, by relaying the brick pavements, cleaning the walls and repairing the roofs and other external features.

As the buildings began to 'sparkle', and some of the manufacturers turned part of their premises into shops, so the area's potential for regeneration became more obvious. Several flagship schemes led the way. A former factory making gold pens was turned into the Argent Centre, one of the pioneering managed workspace schemes, by the Midlands Industrial Association (URBED, 1986b). In St Paul's Square one of the houses was converted into offices on the initiative of a firm of architects, backed up by a scheme developed by Inner City Enterprises and financed by Guardian Royal Exchange. At the same time the first of what is now a colony of restaurants opened up, and significantly it was a Chinese restaurant, Wong's, that probably led the way by providing something really special.

In 1987, the city, concerned about reconciling the need to promote tourism and making the most of its Victorian heritage while sustaining an important source of employment, commissioned studies by Segal Quince Wickstead on the industry and from URBED on the area. These were put together as a strategy, with projects ranging from the improvement of the main corridors into the area and the creation of a Discovery Centre for visitors to proposals for assisting the industry to adapt, through technical assistance and a trade centre to rival those in Germany and Italy. The recommendations of the report were accepted and gradually implemented (apart from the trade centre). However, following the City Centre Challenge Symposium, organized by URBED, which was later christened the Highbury Initiative, it became clear that if the area was to be transformed in time for the opening of the Convention Centre, a greater impetus was needed, with co-ordination on the ground to involve both the industry and all the different agencies and departments. Proposals were therefore prepared at the invitation of the government's City Action Team, and funding provided to set up an 'action team' under a steering group that included the City Council and the Chamber of Commerce. Support was given early on for the formation of an Improvement Association to represent the businesses in the area.

Although Jewellery Quarter Action was limited in what it could do itself, a strategy was agreed covering environmental improvements, tourism initiatives and enterprise development. The project team's role included working up ideas, bringing different interests together through topic groups, publicizing plans and achievements and organizing events, such as the Going for Gold exhibition, which helped the Quarter to achieve a higher profile and sense of identity.

Environmental achievements include proposals for overcoming the known shortfall in parking provision, resulting in the refurbishment of the existing multistorey Vyse Street car park and creation of new pay and display sites on formerly derelict sites in the area; the introduction of street furniture, bollards, waste bins and street lights, in keeping with the backdrop of Victorian buildings; and preparation of a shopfront design guide that is acting as a basis for shopfront improvement schemes. Other environmental improvement initiatives included a range of reports and studies on specific sites or topics, which made recommendations on, for instance, the cemeteries, housing and the need for a Jewellery Quarter Trades Centre. Unfortunately, planned schemes for an arcade and 'gateways' at key entrance points into the area had to be abandoned on financial grounds.

Tourism initiatives were aimed at increasing the general public's awareness of the Quarter's location. One way was to contribute to a vast range of publications, from local and national newspapers to specialized magazines, such as British European Airways' own *Airtime* magazine. Articles were tailored to the prospective readership and covered a brief history of the Quarter's unique development, what it has to offer, how to get there and how it fitted in with the city's emerging international profile.

A singularly successful promotional tool was the leaflet produced in association with the Regional Passenger Transport Executive-Centro, called *How to find the Jewellery Quarter.* Subsequently revised and reprinted, about 200 000 copies were distributed through a range of outlets where the public were likely to ask for basic information about the area; for example, how to get there by public transport, foot, rail or private car, where the 'golden triangle' is in relation to the district and city, and what to see while there. Other tourism orientated projects included the printing of a 'discovery trail' leaflet that starts at the Jewellery Quarter Discovery Centre on Vyse Street. Taking people through the heart of the area, this self-guided trail, produced and funded by the city, points out key buildings and places of historical interest to its readers.

Meanwhile manufacturers were approached to allow members of the public into their premises and actually see the skills of jewellery making at close quarters while on their benches. An introductory 'factory tours' pack covered all aspects of initiating factory tours, such as security. Retailers were asked to support the production of a prestigious shopping guide, co-sponsored by the World Gold Council, which may go to a one million print run and potentially world-wide distribution.

The final area of concentrated effort was in enterprise development. Supported by funding from British Telecom, local training initiatives included a one-day seminar dedicated to explaining the emerging role of the Quarter to local businesses, and a series of training courses for retail staff showing them how to improve their presentation and sales techniques to prospective purchasers. In association with Birmingham Training & Enterprise Council, URBED, through Jewellery Quarter Action, was able to deliver a series of 'business health checks'. Also, assistance in the establishment of the 'Jewellery Sector compact' and Jewellery Quarter Business Club was provided, often tailored to meet the different promotional needs of well or newly established businesses by setting long term goals, specialized training schemes and providing a relaxed forum in which to meet and do business.

Particularly valuable techniques pioneered by Jewellery Quarter Action were the issue of regular newsletters and the use of 'topic' groups. These brought together representatives of the private and public sectors to discuss common issues and a ginger group acted as a means of communication. Use was also made of festivals and events to generate interest and enthusiasm.

11.4   BRADFORD'S LITTLE GERMANY

'We don't want Little Germany to become Bradford's Covent Garden'. This is a common remark made by local businesses to Little Germany Action, a

locally based action team working to regenerate Bradford's historic merchants' quarter.

Little Germany is a unique area. Standing on the edge of Bradford city centre, it is one of the finest collections of Victorian warehouses in the United Kingdom. Of the 85 buildings, 55 are listed and the area was designated as a conservation area in 1973. It was built in a frenetic period of construction between 1855 and 1875 by German and east European merchants and was once the distribution hub of Bradford's textile trade. However, by the early 1980s half of the floorspace was vacant and many of the buildings were derelict. Today, Little Germany has been transformed. Just ten of the buildings remain vacant, 147 companies are located in the area employing almost 3750 people, the buildings are no longer blackened by soot and more than £15 million of public and private investment has been attracted.

The process started with the City Council funding stone-cleaning. Then in 1986 URBED were commissioned by the Council and the English Tourist Board to draw up a strategy for Little Germany's revival. Confidence was built through the early development of Festival Square as a much needed public open space in the heart of the area (Figure 11.1). This was used for a festival in 1986 which attracted over 10 000 people and which has since grown into the Bradford Festival, the largest community festival in the country.

A vision was set out for Little Germany's future which highlighted its potential for recreation, a base for innovative companies and designers, and also as a place to live. The City Council has promoted two important flagship schemes, Merchant's House, providing managed workspace, and the Bradford Design Exchange, completed in April 1992 with 27 studios and 400 m² of exhibition space. This in turn has attracted private investment in refurbishing a further 14 buildings.

The initial project also sought to overcome the barriers to regeneration such as the poor environment and parking problems. The City Council have since undertaken extensive improvements, installing new street lighting and relaying York stone paving, creating a landscaped 141 space car park and introducing a business permit system for on-street parking.

Four years after the original study, as many of these projects were nearing completion, it was felt that the time was right to take a fresh look at the area. Recovery had not yet become self-sustaining and a number of large vacant buildings were still idle. A 'local action' team was therefore set up by URBED in July 1990, with funding from the Leeds/Bradford City Action Team and British Telecom, building on the experience of Jewellery Quarter Action. The idea was to put full-time project staff into the area for two or three years who had the time and commitment to develop and implement projects rather than just making recommendations.

Business uses, both traditional firms and office uses, continue to form the

Figure 11.1   Festival Square and the Design Exchange, Bradford

backbone of the area. However, in addition, the team aims to develop new roles to broaden the area's economic base and increase activity, particularly outside office hours. Three uses have been identified: a regional cultural and creative centre; an exciting place to visit; and a desirable place to live.

Initially the team is building on the improvements which have taken place. Little Germany Action has designed a family of signboards, including a map, to strengthen the area's identity. Cast iron litter bins have been commissioned along with benches and signs for Festival Square. These are being financed by the project team and sponsorship has been raised for further signboards, bins and benches. Postcards have been produced with photographs from the award-winning photographer Ian Beesley and tourist trails are being developed. A very successful 'clean sweep' day was organized with local businesses and the Little Germany Improvement Association has been re-established. The team has updated the property register and produced a vacant property sheet to market space. Business support initiatives have been established, including advice sheets and holding a business open day which attracted 60 businesses, as well as the Little Germany Business Watch crime prevention scheme which involves 140 companies.

In addition to this the most important short term proposal was the organization of the Little Germany summer season. This builds on the success of the 1986 festival in changing perceptions of the area, but unlike the festival will not shine brightly for just one weekend but will generate activity and publicity for the whole summer. Urban Programme funding of £25 000 was secured for the season and sponsorship totalling over £60 000. The season opened with a carnival followed by a series of themed weekends such as an American car rally, a jazz festival, a Victorian weekend, children's weekends and radio roadshows. Aimed at transforming people's attitude towards Little Germany and to establish the area as a thriving cultural quarter on a permanent basis, the season drew 24 000 visitors. This was recognized in being shortlisted for the Arts Council/British Gas Working for Cities award.

In the longer term the aim is to develop a number of flagship schemes. The team is working with building owners to develop artists' studios, gallery space, a residential scheme and cultural uses. One major scheme is the development of Chapel Street as the main cultural axis for the area with environmental works and traffic calming measures. This is being developed as an urban sculpture trail and a competition was held to commission a £5000 sculpture for the trail.

However, major problems remain with property speculation. A number of important buildings were bought up when property prices were very low and have been left vacant as values have risen with the recovery of the area. This is a difficult issue and Little Germany Action have explored the possibility of establishing a development trust with the City Council and English Heritage which could take a more proactive approach to such properties.

11.5   KEY FACTORS FOR SUCCESS

Birmingham's Jewellery Quarter and Bradford's Little Germany, along with other places such as Nottingham's Lace Market and London's Covent Garden, show that it is possible for old areas to find new roles which conserve their fundamental character. However, regeneration is not a fast process and therefore cannot be left to conventional property developers, although the investment required is too much for local authorities to bear on their own. Instead successful regeneration seems to involve a process of balanced incremental development, in which a combination of pilot projects and flagship schemes are used to attract and establish new uses for redundant space. Such a process can be greatly assisted by the right kind of planning, which needs to be active rather than passive, and concerned with economic rather than just physical development. Although each place is unique and must find its own role, there are four or five key ingredients needed, whether the area is an industrial heritage area, a town centre or an urban waterfront.

The first is a shared vision. It is important that there is a plan for the area that provides a sense of direction. In part this needs to protect the fabric through the designation of conservation areas and industrial or commercial improvement areas, thus enabling grants to be used as incentives for owners to restore their buildings. However, just as important is the need to focus efforts on key routes and gateways and on problem sites or buildings. Thus significantly the basic strategy for Little Germany was only a few pages long, but it focused attention on the creation of Festival Square, which in turn provided a visible symbol of the area's transition to a new role as a creative centre.

A second requirement is to respond to potential demand, which tends to go in waves. The first new users are pioneers, including artists and voluntary organizations attracted by cheap space and the romance of the area. Later come the settlers, and early uses include restaurants and bars if they can serve both a lunchtime and evening trade. Undoubtedly areas like St Paul's Square in the Jewellery Quarter benefited by being on the fringe of the city centre, and by developing an image as being a 'smart place' to visit. It is only as the area improves in terms of both its environment and image that it becomes possible to attract housing for sale, and care is needed to avoid speculation driving out traditional uses.

A third requirement is to strike a balance between social or environmental goals and benefits and the commercial need to make a profit from investment. It is therefore important early on to tackle the main problems that are perceived by the existing community to ensure their collaboration. Typically this involves measures to assist parking and to make the environment better for staff, for example, through improved street lighting or cleaning.

Fourthly, there have to be people with the confidence to take the plunge in establishing new enterprises and activities. Ultimately the question of whether a historic building is brought back to use successfully depends on there being the right driving force. As the process is essentially entrepreneurial, it often depends on people already in the locality who see the opportunities, and are prepared to stick at a particular venture. Often the pioneers go under to be replaced by others who build on what has been achieved. During the process there is a danger that funds are sucked out of the area by 'traders' rather than reinvested. The public sector has a key part to play in setting an example and by creating a sense of partnership, so that the key interests see themselves as working for the long term good of the area and not just their own private gain. Where the returns from renovating buildings do not pay off, either because rents are too low or the buildings are in too poor a condition, then it is also important to have an organization with the remit and backing to take on the more complex projects and put schemes together. Here the model of the Development Trust is becoming increasingly fashionable, as such a body can be used to package finance and to secure a mix of uses that contribute to the ongoing vitality of the area.

The experience of the Jewellery Quarter and Little Germany, along with many other locally based regeneration projects, shows that there is an alternative to the conventional wisdom of relying on privately-led property development to secure the goals of regeneration. Furthermore, the idea of what we call balanced incremental development has now been proved in situations ranging from London's Covent Garden to the provinces. Although each area requires a unique strategy, the general principles of starting with a shared vision, promoting early results, striking a balance between public and private interests and establishing the right driving force seem fairly universal.

Nevertheless, despite the apparent successes there are still some major worries. First is the problem of avoiding speculation leading to buildings lying vacant and existing businesses being squeezed out. This is a problem that requires a national solution. Second is the problem of packaging finance for the kind of complex schemes that are required, and which can take years to put together. Finally, there is the most fundamental problem of all which is funding the long term process of managing urban change, which includes a large element of maintenance or 'gardening' work, when political priorities shift so frequently, and resources are so hard to come by. It will be in the area of public–private partnerships and new funding mechanisms that progress towards more sustainable forms of development will need to be fashioned during the 1990s.

REFERENCES

Cantacuzino, S. (1975) *New Uses for Old Buildings*, Architectural Press, London.
Cantacuzino, S. (1989) *Re-architecture: Old Buildings/New Uses*, Thames and Hudson, London.
Dayus, K. (1982) *Her People*, Virago, London.
Falk, N. (1984) Our industrial heritage: a resource for the future? *Journal of the Royal Society of Arts, Proceedings*, December.
Falk, N. (1992) Turning the tide: British experience in regenerating urban docklands. In: *European Port Cities in Transition* (Eds B.S. Hoyle and D.A. Pinder), Butterworth, London, pp. 116–136.
URBED (1986a) *Re-using Redundant Buildings*, HMSO, London.
URBED (1986b) Argent Centre case study. In: *Re-using Redundant Buildings*, HMSO, London, pp. 27–31.

12

City centre regeneration in a regional context: the Glasgow experience in the 1980s

_____ M. Cowan and C. Lindsay

In any review of urban regeneration activity it is unusual not to read of Glasgow's revival in the 1980s. The change in fortune was part of the wider process of urban regeneration which occurred throughout the Clydeside Conurbation, the metropolitan area centred on Glasgow. This analysis, however, is confined to an examination of the regeneration process within Glasgow city centre (Figure 12.1), which has traditionally been the focus of private sector development activity in the Clydeside Conurbation. The chapter specifically examines the contribution of wider strategic policy to the regeneration of the city centre and considers the effects of public sector intervention within the most favourable microenvironment for private sector development throughout the whole Clydeside Conurbation. Before 1970, development activity in Glasgow city centre, with few exceptions, was promoted by private interests. However, one of the effects of the social, economic and environmental decline experienced on Clydeside between 1945 and 1970 was a need for public sector bodies to stimulate the development process. Despite continuing private sector interest, this need was also apparent in Glasgow city centre, both in respect of certain types of development and particular locations of a rundown nature.

Figure 12.1 Map of Glasgow city centre

Retail Core

Office Core

Rail Line and Station

Underground and Station

250m

GARNETHILL

Sauchiehall Street

Queen Street Station

STRATHCLYDE UNIVERSITY CAMPUS

MERCHANT CITY

Argyle Street

ST. ENOCH

Central Station

BROOMIELAW

River Clyde

River Clyde

12.1 ADMINISTRATION

The Clydeside Conurbation is the urban core of west central Scotland and is currently administered on a two-tier basis by Strathclyde Regional Council and a number of district authorities. Strategic planning policy is determined by the Regional Council, which also provides major services such as education, roads, water and drainage. The responsibility for local planning and the control of development in Glasgow city centre lies with the City of Glasgow District Council, the largest district council in the Clydeside Conurbation.

Various central government agencies have contributed to the regeneration of the Clydeside Conurbation and one of the most influential has been the Scottish Development Agency. Established at the end of 1975, one of the initial purposes of this agency was to further the improvement of the environment. Within a few years the Scottish Development Agency had also become involved in the promotion of urban renewal projects. Its budget reflected the need to fund these activities. Glasgow, including the city centre, was a beneficiary of this funding. In 1983 the government introduced the 'LEG-UP' scheme (Local Enterprise Grants for Urban Projects), which was administered by the Scottish Development Agency. The purpose of the scheme was to encourage private investment in urban areas through the provision of financial subsidies. Assistance took various forms, including low interest loans, participating mortgages and equity grants. The scheme acted as an incentive to help overcome difficult site conditions, land assembly problems and extraordinary costs. LEG-UP finance was awarded on a competitive basis and several projects in the city centre benefited.

In 1991, the Scottish Development Agency was merged with the Training Agency in Scotland to form a new body called Scottish Enterprise. This was accompanied by the establishment of a network of subsidiary local enterprise companies. One of these companies, the Glasgow Development Agency, is currently the funding body for urban renewal and environmental improvement projects within Glasgow, including the city centre. The LEG-UP scheme continues to be administered by the local enterprise companies and two areas in the city centre, Garnethill and the Merchant City (see Figure 12.1), are priority areas for LEG-UP funding. Currently, the Glasgow Development Agency expects the leverage ratio of a project to be at least 3:1 in favour of private funding.

12.2 PLANNING POLICY

Since its inception in 1975, Strathclyde Regional Council has encouraged development on vacant and derelict land, the refurbishment of unused buildings within the urban fabric and has pursued complementary policies to limit the development of greenfield land on the periphery of the Clydeside Conurbation. This policy was the basis of the first Structure Plan, approved by the Secretary of State for Scotland in 1981, and of successive reviews and updates (Strathclyde Regional Council, 1991). When necessary, the Regional Council has used its statutory power to call in development applications (submitted to district councils) for determination. These powers are exercised infrequently (less than 15 occasions per year) and only in circumstances involving a perceived threat to the development strategy. In support of the strategy there are Structure Plan policies to control speculative office development outwith Glasgow city centre and retail development outwith centres in the shopping hierarchy. The development strategy and supporting policies have been applied positively to encourage regeneration throughout the Conurbation. This has been to the particular benefit of the city centre in the 1980s when this was the only location in the Conurbation where major (over 2000 m^2) speculative office development proposals were in accord with Structure Plan policy.

Responsibility for local planning in the city centre lies with the City of Glasgow District Council. A first attempt at a draft local plan was prepared in the early 1980s, followed by two further drafts in 1987 and 1990. Currently there is no adopted local plan for the city centre, but the draft plans of the 1980s have been used as reference points in the consideration of development proposals. The draft plans have been treated in effect as adopted plans and most of the development which has taken place in the city centre in the 1980s has been in accordance with the requirements of the draft plans, particularly in relation to plot ratio controls, parking requirements and the massing of buildings. In the 1987 draft of the Central Area Local Plan, special project areas were identified to provide a focus for investment opportunities. Three of the four areas – Broomielaw, St Enoch and the Merchant City – are areas of mixed uses and have experienced significant change following private sector interest in their regeneration (City of Glasgow District Council, 1987).

The Merchant City, lying to the east and north of the main shopping area, was identified as having residential potential by the District Council (City of Glasgow District Council, 1992). This area was originally built in the 18th century and consisted of town houses for Glasgow's merchants with associated commercial and public buildings. During the 19th century the area evolved into a primarily commercial centre dominated by the warehousing/wholesale distribution industry, a role which continued until the mid-1960s. However, the area fell into decline because it could not adapt to the demands of modern warehousing and distribution methods. Furthermore, it was blighted by road proposals and the proposed expansion of the University of Strathclyde, neither of which materialized. The effect was an increase in vacancy levels and decay of buildings, leading in many instances to demolition. Some sites and buildings came into public (i.e. District Council) ownership, although the most significant feature of the Merchant City, the original street pattern, remained intact. In deciding to pursue the regeneration of the area the District Council was able to overcome the complexities of development through a combination of roles as landowner (site ownerships), planning authority (modification of standards) and housing authority (provision of finance).

12.3   ACHIEVEMENTS IN THE 1980S

This section reviews the major changes in the city centre in the 1980s; describes the involvement of various public sector bodies; and illustrates by example situations where public sector funding has helped to stimulate private investment. In the city centre, the changes which have helped to raise the awareness of Glasgow's revival embrace a wide range of development activity in the office, retail, residential, cultural and leisure sectors. This activity has been supported by environmental improvements and the enhancement of parts of the transportation infrastructure.

Glasgow city centre is the principal office location in the Clydeside Conurbation. The core area for office use is bounded by the retail core on the east and the inner ring road on the west (Figure 12.1). Before 1985, most new office development projects were located in this area. During the 1980s, development activity has been supported by the public and private sectors in various ways. Regarding the former, purpose built buildings were completed to house the headquarters of Britoil (when in public ownership) and jobs transferred from the Ministry of Defence in London. In the latter half of the decade, the city centre experienced the effects of private sector-led growth in office building which was occurring throughout the United Kingdom. A study of office development (Debenham, Tewson and Chinnocks, 1988) observed that in 1988 Glasgow had possibly the largest office development pipeline of any city centre outside central London. In 1980 around 14 100 m^2 of office floorspace was completed in the city centre, the equivalent figure for 1990 was 89 900 m^2. Between 1981 and 1989 the total area of office floorspace increased from 778 000 to 1 163 000 m^2 (+49%). The scale of change is also shown by the fact that almost 28% of the 1989 floorspace had been completed in the previous nine years. These statistics illustrate the most significant physical change in the city centre in the 1980s. The additional floorspace was sourced from the redevelopment or refurbishment of obsolete office buildings, changes from other uses and by the development of sites which had been vacant since the 1970s.

With the exception of the bespoke accommodation for the Ministry of Defence and Britoil (subsequently occupied by British Petroleum), most of the office activity in the 1980s was funded in the normal way by the private sector. However, one interesting example of public and private sector involvement occurred in a mixed use development on a river front site in the Broomielaw area. Glasgow and Oriental Developments brought forward a proposal which included 100 000 m² of high quality office floorspace. The Scottish Development Agency assisted with the planning of the development and subsequently contributed 7% of the £75 million required to complete the first phase of the project (Scottish Development Agency, 1991). This involvement was justified by the potential benefits of upgrading a part of the city centre that had not been considered previously as a prime location for office development.

In terms of public awareness, regeneration activity based on retail development has a high profile. Glasgow city centre has been one of the principal shopping centres in the United Kingdom for many years. There are two prime shopping areas – Sauchiehall Street to the north and Argyle Street to the south (Figure 12.1). The two areas are linked by Buchanan Street and Renfield Street, which also have important retail frontages. In 1980 there were approximately 469 000 m² (gross) of occupied floorspace and by 1989 the equivalent total was 491 000 m², an increase of 4.7%. This modest increase conceals a number of significant qualitative changes. Aside from a number of redevelopment projects to upgrade floorspace on the existing shopping streets, two enclosed shopping centres were opened in the late 1980s. The St Enoch Centre (24 500 m²) was developed on the site of a former railway station, immediately to the south of Argyle Street, and the Prince's Square Centre (7500 m²) is located at the southern end of Buchanan Street. The latter development was funded privately by Guardian Royal Exchange, but the St Enoch Centre is an excellent example of co-operation between the public and private sectors.

The site of the St Enoch Centre was originally acquired by the Scottish Development Agency to assist in the relocation of civil service jobs from London. After a decision was taken to develop elsewhere in the city centre for this purpose, the Scottish Development Agency promoted the site for the development of an enclosed shopping centre. In 1986, the participation of property developers, the Church Commissioners for England and Sears Properties (Glasgow) was secured. The developers constructed and let the centre which includes an ice rink and a multistorey car park as well as modern retail floorspace. Strathclyde Regional Council funded the multistorey car park as part of a programme to increase the numbers of car-parking spaces in the city centre. The Scottish Development Agency also stimulated activity in the retail property sector by investment through the LEG-UP scheme.

The 1980s represented a watershed for the role of housing in Glasgow city centre. For the first time in over 100 years significant additions to the owner-occupied stock were achieved through the completion of 1127 dwellings in the ten years to March 1991. A further 88 housing association dwellings for rent were also completed in this period. In total, 33 schemes were completed, mainly in the Merchant City and, to a lesser extent, in Garnethill. Conversion of existing buildings amounted to 41% of total completions.

Glasgow District Council was the prime mover in this process. The District Council undertook feasibility studies on property which it owned in the Merchant City and established that conversion for housing use was physically possible (City of Glasgow District Council, 1992). Previously, it had been more difficult to establish an economic case until the Local Government (Miscellaneous Provisions) (Scotland) Act, 1981 gave local authorities discretionary powers to offer grants to developers for the conversion of buildings to housing. The District Council used these powers to offer buildings in their ownership to developers at attractive prices, along with flexibility in the application of planning standards and conversion grants at an average level of £5100 per dwelling.

Three schemes in the Merchant City were initially promoted by the District Council following feasibility studies. The first scheme began in 1982 and in each instance the District Council gifted the building and provided grants from existing housing department budgets up to the level allowed by the legislation. In one of these pilot schemes, District Council grants were augmented by a grant from the Scottish Development Agency. The public sector contribution to these three developments amounted to 39% of total development costs, plus the value of the buildings. In one of the schemes the District Council retained ownership of six new shops for letting, thus obtaining some return.

The initial schemes promoted by the District Council achieved their objective of establishing developer interest and by the mid-1980s several schemes were underway in Merchant City, taking advantage of District Council or Scottish Development Agency funding, or both. The largest development to date, Ingram Square, moved from the single building approach of earlier schemes to the renewal of a complete street block by conversion of three warehouses, a department store and new building on vacant gap sites, involving 239 dwellings in total. In this scheme the District Council and the Scottish Development Agency were involved as formal development partners, each having a 25% share in the investment via grant and buildings (District Council) and grant and loans (Scottish Development Agency). Other schemes have involved mixed use developments such as the Italian Centre, which combines housing, offices, flats and licensed premises, again partly funded by the two public bodies. To date only one new building scheme in the Merchant City has been completed without public subsidy. The regeneration of the area has been acknowledged by the award of the Silver Medal of Honour by Europa Nostra, an international federation of associations for the protection of Europe's heritage, in 1988.

Glasgow city centre is bordered to the north and west by the main arterial motorway in the Clydeside Conurbation, the M8. The city centre is also the focus of the region's public transport system: it has two mainline rail termini, the most extensive suburban rail network in the United Kingdom outside London, a circular underground railway route and 290 bus services terminate in or traverse the area. Transportation matters are the responsibility of Strathclyde Regional Council and Strathclyde Passenger Transport Executive. During the 1980s the major thrust of the Council's revenue and capital expenditure on transport was the improvement and integration of the public transport network. The underground railway was completely rebuilt and between its reopening in 1980 and 1991 annual patronage increased from 9.8 to 13.7 million passengers (Strathclyde Passenger Transport Authority and Executive, 1981–91). The suburban rail network was extensively modernized with additional electrification and provision of new railway stock for services to Lanarkshire and Ayrshire in 1979 and 1986–7, respectively, and new diesel rolling stock was introduced on other lines. Between 1980 and 1992 a total of £150 million was invested (actual spend), utilizing a mix of European Commission and central government grants and loans, as well as Regional Council funding. Bus services, which represent the majority of all public transport trips to the city centre, were supported from revenue budgets.

Public transport investment was complemented by parking policies in the city centre which restricted parking for new developments to that required for operational needs and deterred long stay commuter parking through control of parking charges. However, this comprehensive approach was undermined by bus deregulation arising from the Transport Act 1985, and resulted in an even greater concentration of bus journeys in the peak hour with a consequent increase in traffic congestion. A major traffic management scheme was subsequently introduced in 1987 in an attempt to ameliorate these difficulties.

The character of Glasgow city centre is derived from a grid iron street pattern with several large squares, all bounded by tall stone-fronted buildings, principally built in the Victorian era. The planning policy of the District Council (City of Glasgow District Council, 1990) is to retain and enhance the character of the city centre through retention of the street pattern and building lines and containment of views, along with tight controls on building form and detailing. Plot ratios on non-residential buildings are restricted to a maximum of 3.5:1. In the 1980s action was taken on three specific measures (pedestrianization, floodlighting and stone cleaning) to enhance the city centre environment, with the image of the city very much in mind. Pedestrianization of two of the three principal shopping streets, Buchanan Street (1972) and Argyle Street (1978) had been carried out earlier, but it was not until 1988 that the third, Sauchiehall Street, was completed. This scheme was seen to be important for the image of the city because the National Garden Festival was held in Glasgow in that year and many visitors were anticipated. The Sauchiehall Street scheme cost £650 000, to which the retail traders contributed £50 000, with the balance split between the Scottish

Development Agency, the promoters of the Garden Festival (50%) and Glasgow District and Strathclyde Regional Councils (25% each). Unlike floodlighting and stone cleaning projects, pedestrianization schemes convey functional benefits to shoppers, retailers and those living and working in the city centre, as well as visual enhancement.

The Garden Festival also provided an incentive to floodlight buildings which was seen as further means of enhancing the image of the city that would be immediately effective, and involved relatively little outlay. Initially the District Council promoted a programme of lighting key bridges, private buildings and 20 District Council owned properties. This was funded by the Scottish Development Agency through Glasgow Action. Since then the Scottish Development Agency has continued to fund projects for privately owned buildings, initially through Glasgow Action and now by the Glasgow Development Agency in a scheme entitled 'City Lights'. Glasgow District Council currently funds smaller scale schemes for buildings or monuments in its ownership and privately owned buildings in non-commercial use. Over 100 floodlighting projects have now been completed, most of which are in the city centre or its approaches. Current grant levels are for a proportion of the capital costs up to £6000–7000. Maintenance and electricity costs are the responsibility of building owners.

Stone cleaning has also been used as a means of environmental improvement in the city centre. Rehabilitation schemes for residential tenement buildings throughout the city during the 1970s and early 1980s usually involved stone cleaning. This simple cosmetic treatment has created such a strong image of a 'new' Glasgow that its extension to non-residential buildings in the city centre was inevitable. Schemes are funded in the same way as the floodlighting project and there is a similar gain in environmental terms for limited cost. In this instance grants are the lesser of £25 000 or 30% of capital costs.

The city centre is the focus of cultural and leisure activity in the west of Scotland, a role it has held for many years. Significant developments in these sectors took place in the latter half of the 1980s. The stimulus of receiving the European Commission nomination as City of Culture in 1990 led to the completion of a longstanding commitment to build a concert hall (2500 seats) which would attract international orchestras. Financed by the District Council, the available funds were augmented by the sale of a lease for land adjoining the hall. In contrast with other development projects, this arrangement resulted in an indirect private sector contribution to a public sector proposal. The District Council, as part of the City of Culture programme, also refurbished the McLellan Galleries in Sauchiehall Street as a modern venue for visual art exhibitions. In addition, a new building, including auditoria for public performances, for the Royal Scottish Academy of Music and Drama was opened in 1987. Clearly development activity for cultural purposes has been largely supported by public sector funding.

Facilities in the catering and accommodation sectors have also improved dramatically in the 1980s, particularly in terms of the quality of public houses, cafes and restaurants. Although these improvements have paralleled the other changes in the city centre, the initial impetus was most probably derived from the introduction of new licensing laws in 1976. Similar improvements have occurred in the provision of hotel accommodation. National and multinational operators have opened two new hotels and a third is under construction. Some existing hotels have been refurbished or extended, in one instance with the assistance of a LEG UP grant.

12.4 EVALUATION OF CHANGES

One of the principal benefits accruing from office building in the 1980s was the provision of modern floorspace attractive to prestige white collar employers. Britoil (now British Petroleum) and the Ministry of Defence occupied bespoke buildings, but the quality of speculative floorspace was such as to secure lettings from new employers such as the Department of Social Security, British Telecom, the Student Loan Company and British Airways. Glasgow Action, an initiative organized by a group of prominent local businessmen and supported by the Scottish Development Agency, had as one of its overall aims the attraction of more company headquarters activity to Glasgow (Scottish Development Agency, 1985). Regeneration of the office sector in the city centre has helped to realize this aim. Office building in the 1980s has done more for the city centre than simply extend the provision of modern floorspace. Other benefits such as the refurbishment of listed buildings, retention of listed facades, take up of vacant sites and the regeneration of run-down areas have cumulatively helped to improve the appearance of the city centre as well as acting as a stimulus to further development activity.

Data collected by Debenham, Tewson and Chinnocks over the period 1981–8 for prime quality office floorspace in Glasgow city centre indicates that rental growth in the city centre was 9% less than in London (City), Edinburgh and Manchester, 10% higher than Leeds and 16% higher than Birmingham. These figures suggest that rental growth in Glasgow city centre was approximately in the middle of the range for the larger office centres in the United Kingdom. Consequently, it is apparent that city centre office building in the 1980s does not appear to have generated excessive rental growth relative to comparable centres. To this extent, the competitiveness of the city centre as an office location has remained unimpaired, but this situation is less favourable if local authority rates are taken into consideration.

Full understanding of the benefits of the recent changes in retail provision in the city centre follows from consideration of the situation in the 1970s. During the decade, only one fairly modest shopping development (approximately 17 000 m^2 gross) offering an enclosed and traffic free environment was completed. By comparison with other metropolitan shopping centres in the United Kingdom such as Manchester, Newcastle and Nottingham, Glasgow city centre was deficient in enclosed retail floorspace. The completion of Prince's Square and the St Enoch Centre in the late 1980s significantly extended the provision of enclosed floorspace. St Enoch proved attractive to multiple retailers whereas Prince's Square was designed for up-market and specialist retailers. Both centres helped to attract retailers who had not previously been represented in Glasgow city centre and from the consumer's viewpoint the attractiveness of the city centre was enhanced. By the end of the 1980s almost 50% of the retail and service floorspace was either accessible from pedestrianized streets or enclosed centres.

Development activity in this sector does not appear to have had a significant impact on the vacancy rates of retail units. Vacancy in city centre retail floorspace increased marginally from 8% in 1986 (before the opening of the two centres) to 11% in 1989. In other city centres the development of new enclosed centres has sometimes led to the demise of some streets as principal shopping areas, for example, Oldham Street in Manchester (Davies, 1984). Whereas in Glasgow other environmental benefits have been achieved in that the St Enoch Centre has taken up 5 ha of vacant land in a prominent location and Prince's Square incorporates previously under-used buildings.

The urban renewal policies of the Strathclyde Structure Plan, complemented by restrictions on greenfield development, took effect in Clydeside Conurbation from the early 1980s with a rapid increase in development of infill or 'brownfield' sites for housing. In the city centre this process took rather longer, notwithstanding the emphasis placed by Glasgow District Council on the role of housing in the regeneration of the city centre. The reason for this is not difficult to find. Most of the early brownfield completions elsewhere in the Conurbation were on substantial, cleared sites on which development was relatively straightforward. In the city centre sites were more likely to involve conversion of existing buildings, or a mix of conversions and new buildings making it difficult to meet planning standards. Thus significant completions were not achieved in the city centre until the mid-1980s.

Substantial investment in public transport infrastructure took place in the 1980s, following major road investment which created the urban motorway network in the 1960s and 1970s. However, a substantial reservation of land remained to the south and east of the city centre for public road construction to complete a motorway 'box'. A major transportation review was carried out for the 1988 update of the Strathclyde Structure Plan, starting from the premise that quality of access should be maintained for both private and public transport users (Strathclyde Regional Council, 1988). So far as public transport was concerned new investment increased the number of suburban rail stations to six and 80% of the city centre is now within five minutes' walking distance of a station. This level of accessibility is good compared with other British cities.

Despite the substantial investment in public transport, problems of road congestion remain but, compared with other British cities, road access to Glasgow city centre is good. In fact, survey information showed that many trips to the city centre were actually through trips which were not using the existing M8 motorway and were adding to congestion in the city centre. A major objective of the review was to consider ways of taking these trips out of the city centre. The outcome was the retention of a reservation for a west–east motorway route south of the River Clyde on a modified line, with new bridges adjacent to the existing Kingston Bridge to improve access to the city centre. However, these scaled down proposals were not without controversy and were unsuccessfully challenged in the courts by a pressure group. Nevertheless, implementation is unlikely before the year 2000.

Improvements to the environment of the city centre have been an important element both through the development process and specific schemes; for example, floodlighting and stone cleaning have helped to raise the image of the city. This is especially so for visitors, most of whom stay in the city centre hotels or pass through the city centre after arriving at railway termini or from the airport. The existing pedestrianization schemes have been less successful in these terms because of initial poor quality, unsatisfactory maintenance of finishes and street furniture, and difficulties in controlling the activities of underground service providers.

Improvements in the cultural and leisure sectors are less obvious in terms of physical change, but are very significant in helping to change the city's image in a positive way. The quality of life has been improved for the existing population and Glasgow and the Clydeside Conurbation have become more attractive locations for in-comers, whether they be companies or individuals. Improved cultural and leisure facilities also increase the city's attractiveness as a tourist centre.

The city centre is the major employment location within the Glasgow District Council area. In 1981, 31% of jobs in the District were within the city centre and any evaluation of development activity must be accompanied by a review of employment changes. It is often assumed that the changes of the 1980s have resulted in employment growth. However, this is not the case and the city centre has shared in the general decline in employment throughout the Clydeside Conurbation, albeit less severely. Although most of the jobs in the city centre are in the service sector, a growth area in the late 1980s, the Department of Employment's census returns indicate that there were 98 316 full-time and part-time jobs in this sector in 1981 and by 1989 the equivalent figure was 90 473, a decrease of 8%. The decline does not appear to have been continuous and there may have been some growth in the latter years of the decade. Although the banking, finance, insurance and business service categories have recorded an increase of 17%, there has been a decline of 22% in retail employment, 19% in hotels and catering and 54% in transport. Factors such as the loss of companies, relocations within the rest of Glasgow and the Clydeside Conurbation and productivity improvements derived from lower staffing levels appear to have more than offset additional employment created by companies moving into the city centre and from the expansion of existing companies.

12.5   PROSPECTS FOR A CONTINUING REGENERATION PROGRAMME

The overall environment in which the revival of the city centre has taken place since 1980 has been favourable in many respects – the structure of local government, the planning context, the enhancement of the transportation system and trends in housing demand. A number of recent and prospective changes are likely to affect the circumstances in which the regeneration of the city centre can continue. These changes are reviewed chronologically and thereafter other changes which have been influential throughout the 1980s and are likely to remain significant in the 1990s are considered.

In March 1989, the Town and Country Planning (Use Classes) (Scotland) Order came into force. This order changed the relationship between the office, light industry and research and development classes of use. A new 'business' use (Class 4) allows the three uses to be freely interchanged without the need to obtain planning permission. Consent for buildings to be used for 'business' use could be implemented in the form of office floorspace. Previously a policy in the Strathclyde Structure Plan identified Glasgow city centre as the preferred location for speculative office development of more than 2000 m². The policy was successfully implemented and very little development of this type occurred outwith the city centre. An immediate consequence of the amended Use Class Order was an upsurge in planning applications for business use developments in the rest of the Glasgow district and the other districts of the Clydeside Conurbation. Between 1989 and 1991 490 554 m² of office and business floorspace was granted planning permission compared with an equivalent figure for the city centre of 290 400 m² over the same period.

It is too early to assess the impact of this change, but it is evident that the city centre, as an office location, has been placed in a more competitive market. Sites for 'business' use outwith the city centre are largely intended to be accessed by car, the on-site parking provision is much higher than in the city centre and many of the locations are not well served by the public transport system. In total, the supply of floorspace with planning provision both within and beyond the city centre exceeds potential demand considerably and there is now the possibility of land being blighted for the development of other uses. The changes embodied in the Use Classes Order are part of a wider pressure to decentralize employment to peripheral locations. In the 1990s the contribution of office development projects to the continuing regeneration of the city centre will depend on the perception of its traditional attractions, namely good accessibility by public and private transport and the immediate availability of a wide range of supporting commercial and leisure services.

Although there is an identified capacity for a further 1500 dwellings in Glasgow city centre, and Structure Plan policies continue to emphasize the role of renewal, the prospects for the continuation of housing development at significant levels are uncertain. After reaching a peak of 331 in 1985–6, completions declined thereafter to only 22 in 1990–1. This may in part reflect the recent national downturn in housing completions, but there are also indications of circumstances which are unique to the city centre. In the Merchant City the District Council's further involvement in housing provision is limited because only two properties remain in their ownership and funding from the council's housing budget is no longer available. Whilst the Glasgow Development Agency is financially committed to the Merchant City, the remaining opportunities involve high development costs related to poor ground conditions, complex structures and conservation issues. Although the District Council is prepared to be flexible on the application of the 60% residential floorspace policy to overcome problems of viability, three mixed use schemes, with significant housing components, are currently languishing. It may be that the property market will need to strengthen before the continued viability of this area can be proved at low levels of subsidy or none at all.

In June 1991, the Government issued a consultation paper on the future structure of local government in Scotland (The Scottish Office, 1991). The proposals favour a system based on single tier authorities. However, such a system would be an inappropriate method of meeting the need for strategic planning in a metropolitan area such as the Clydeside Conurbation (Strathclyde Regional Council, 1991). At present it is unclear whether special arrangements will be made to allow for the proper planning of Clydeside Conurbation once it is administered by unitary local authorities. In the absence of a strategic planning authority the favourable planning context for the city centre could deteriorate with the pressure for decentralization of various activities and uses ceasing to be controlled by policy.

Notwithstanding the considerable environmental improvements which have taken place in the city centre, there is an awareness that, in comparison with other similar European cities, Glasgow city centre has shortcomings and in particular lacks a focal point or feature synonymous with the city. In an attempt to remedy this, the Glasgow Development Agency is promoting 'The Great Street' project with the intention of upgrading the existing pedestrianized area of Buchanan Street and three contiguous squares, and creating an additional feature at the southern end with the working title of 'The Glasgow Tower'. There are several key features of this scheme, all of which are designed to avoid the shortcomings of earlier pedestrianization schemes. These are ducting of services, use of good quality natural materials, prior arrangements with statutory authorities over maintenance and improved management. The anticipated cost of this scheme is £17 million over ten years. Agreement with other parties about the funding of the whole project has not yet been completed, but the Glasgow Development Agency is funding the first phase, involving the three squares, as a demonstration project. This will cost £1.9 million and, subject to Scottish Office approval for the expenditure, is due to begin in 1993.

One of the continuous influences affecting further regeneration of the city centre is growth in car ownership and traffic levels. By the standards of other parts of Great Britain and western Europe, the Clydeside Conurbation has a low level of car ownership. However, the rate of growth in ownership level is higher than the British average and it is clear that a catching up process is underway. Increasing levels of car ownership have stimulated the decentralization of economic activity in other British conurbations and a similar effect is likely in the Clydeside Conurbation. Depending on the effects of all other influences, there are risks to the well-being of city centres from the forces of decentralization, and Glasgow is unlikely to be an exception in this respect.

The issue of maintaining quality of access to the city centre for users of public and private transport remains under consideration by the Regional Council. Projected growth in car ownership and road traffic is rising, while 68% of peak hour journeys to the city centre are made by public transport, a higher proportion than in any British city outside London. Faced with this dichotomy the Regional Council published in February 1992 a consultation document on the Integrated Transportation Strategy, which incorporated the roads proposals in the 1988 Structure Plan Update and Recommendations from a Public Transport Development Study in 1990 (Strathclyde Regional Council, 1992). The public transport options include further upgrading of the suburban rail network and a series of light rail routes. The strategy also proposes a major review of traffic management in the city centre, involving further pedestrianization and vehicular movement restrictions.

The second continuous influence running through the 1980s into the 1990s is the pressure for out of centre retailing, deriving in part from the growth in car ownership. This pressure has manifested itself in different ways. The development of food stores in suburban centres and off-centre locations has had little effect on the city centre because floorspace vacated by food retailers in the core shopping area has been taken up by non-food retailers. Equally, the movement of so-called 'bulky goods' retailers to retail warehouses has not resulted in any major problems of increased vacancy levels. Consumers, on the other hand, have been disadvantaged to the extent that the ability to buy certain types of goods (do-it-yourself products, for example) in the city centre has been considerably impaired and if the range of goods sold in retail warehouses were to extend beyond the bulky category, the threat to city centre retailing could increase. At present, a policy in the Strathclyde Structure Plan restricts new retail warehouse parks to the sale of bulky goods. Without this restriction, the ability to operate from cheap floorspace in retail warehouse parks might prove irresistible to some non-food retailers.

On the basis of experience in the USA, the main threat to the city centre's retailing function is the out of town megacentre. Such developments are usually in the form of enclosed malls, adjoining a motorway standard road, with between 75 000 and 200 000 m^2 of retail floorspace, largely selling non-food items. The configuration may also include a large food superstore (around 9000 m^2) and various leisure uses. A number of centres of this type are trading in the principal conurbations of England. Proposals of this type in various locations around the Clydeside Conurbation have been resisted by Strathclyde Regional Council, Glasgow District Council and the other district councils.

Despite this, the Secretary of State for Scotland granted planning permission, after a public inquiry, for a megacentre on a site west of the city centre on the motorway network. At the public inquiry, it was acknowledged that a development of the size proposed (50 000 m^2 within a mall and a retail warehouse park of 35 000 m^2) would not, by itself, affect the vitality and viability of retailing in Glasgow city centre. However, without the benefit of a strategic overview, it is possible that the pressure to develop further megacentres could result in their proliferation around the periphery of the conurbation, thereby weakening the city centre as a retailing centre.

12.6   CONCLUSIONS

It would be inappropriate to complete this assessment without reference to the economic recession of the early 1990s. The most obvious effect of the recession is the lack of interest in new projects by developers. It is increasingly apparent that the pace of development activity in the early 1990s will be less than that experienced in the 1980s. The rate of progress is also likely to be hindered by a residue of difficult projects which require higher levels of subsidy and are particularly unattractive to developers during a recession. Some of the inward movement of employment attracted in the 1980s is likely to be lost. In 1992, British Petroleum closed their exploration headquarters in the city centre and there is likely to be a reduction in the number of people employed by the Ministry of Defence. Current indications suggest that it cannot be assumed that progress will be continuous in the 1990s.

The city centre is also facing new challenges resulting from other locations competing, in particular, for office and retail development. This is one feature of the general trend towards decentralization of economic activity that has affected urban Britain since 1945. The two-tier structure of local government in the Clydeside Conurbation has played an important part in maintaining the city centre by means of strategic planning policies and investment in the transportation system. Without an effective regional planning regime, the ability to control pressure for further decentralization and encourage investment in the city centre will be lost and the efforts and achievements of the 1980s will be devalued.

On the positive side there are two other considerations which may help to sustain the regeneration programme. European cities are now competing with each other to attract commercial and industrial activity, the associated employment, as well as leisure and tourist business. Cities and their central areas are becoming more frequently recognized as gateways to their hinterlands and support for enhancement is more evident. The improvement of Glasgow's competitive position in Europe is one of the Glasgow Development Agency's principal objectives. Secondly, both central government and the European Commission are advocating more sustainable patterns of development, reflecting the need to curb the demand for travel by car. Such an approach will require the location of development at nodal points in the public transport system as well as the reuse of land and buildings. If these principles are pursued vigorously by public sector bodies, the city centre can only benefit from the outcome and private sector interests would continue to regard Glasgow city centre as a major opportunity for investment and development.

ACKNOWLEDGEMENTS

The authors thank staff at the following organizations for assistance in preparing this chapter: the Glasgow Development Agency, City of Glasgow District Council (Departments of Finance, Housing and Planning), Strathclyde Passenger Transport Executive and Strathclyde Regional Council (Chief Executive's Department and Departments of Physical Planning and Roads).

REFERENCES

City of Glasgow District Council (1987) *Central Area Local Plan – Draft Written Statement*, District Council, Glasgow.
City of Glasgow District Council (1990) *Central Area Local Plan – Draft Written Statement (Revised)*, District Council, Glasgow.
City of Glasgow District Council (1992) *The Renewal of Glasgow's Merchant City*, District Council, Glasgow.

Davies, R.L. (1984) *Retail and Commercial Planning*, Croom Helm, London.

Debenham, Tewson and Chinnocks (1988) *Office Rent and Rates*, Debenham Tewson Research, London.

Department of Physical Planning, Strathclyde Regional Council (1991) *The Case for Maintaining the Function of Strategic Planning in the West of Scotland*, Regional Council, Glasgow.

Scottish Development Agency (SDA) (1985) *Annual Report*, SDA, Glasgow.

Scottish Development Agency (SDA) (1991) *Annual Report*, SDA, Glasgow.

Scottish Office (1992) *The Structure of Local Government in Scotland – the Case for Change*, Scottish Office, Edinburgh.

Strathclyde Passenger Transport Authority and Executive (1981–91) *Annual Reports and Accounts*, the Authority, Glasgow.

Strathclyde Regional Council (1988) *Strathclyde Structure Plan, Update Written Statement*, Regional Council, Glasgow.

Strathclyde Regional Council (1991) *Strathclyde Structure Plan, Consolidated Written Statement*, Regional Council, Glasgow.

Strathclyde Regional Council (1992) *Travelling in Strathclyde*, Regional Council, Glasgow.

13

Public sector initiatives in the regeneration of Belfast

J. Berry and S. McGreal

Urban regeneration intrinsically implies a cyclical process of growth followed by decline and then subsequent renaissance. Considering Belfast these phases of urban evolution are sharply focused in a temporal dimension as highlighted by the developmental path of the city, in particular its central business core, over the last three decades. In this context the 1960s represented the growth phase while the 1970s and early 1980s constitute the second phase, a period of stagnation characterized by physical and economic decay. The principal factors contributing to this decline arise from an amalgam of influences, namely macroeconomic conditions, decentralization tendencies and additional problems of a political nature specific, though not entirely unique, to Belfast.

Examining these factors either individually or collectively an array of negative growth influences are apparent. Firstly, macroeconomic conditions including the property crash of the mid-1970s in the United Kingdom, and tight monetary and fiscal policies ensuing from budgetary deficits, made property development opportunities less attractive. Additionally, when integrated with a declining regional economy in Northern Ireland, in particular a diminishing manufacturing sector, problems became increasingly acute. Furthermore economic decline and ensuing social problems within inner cities tend to be most apparent in those formerly reliant on manufacturing industry (Lawless, 1989; Crouch, 1990). Belfast as an industrial city peripheral to the core economy of the United Kingdom arguably experienced decline comparable with that of any other British city during this period of substantial economic restructuring.

Likewise the decay of the inner core of Belfast was influenced by the same decentralization tendencies operating within other urban areas in the United Kingdom. However, this process was accentuated by planning policies operative in the 1970s which placed emphasis on the development of district towns outside Belfast. Brown (1987) observes how, in the absence of developer interest in the city centre, the planning authorities were willing to grant permission for shopping development in out of town locations. In what Brown considered to be 'laissez-faire retail planning', a policy whereby planners were not overly restrictive on development opportunities emerged. The consequences were that such locations became increasingly attractive as the central core of Belfast declined in prestige. The latter, arising from the process of urban decline, was also influenced by a major terrorist campaign designed to effectively weaken the business heart of Belfast. Although destruction in physical terms was significant, resulting in the loss of almost one-quarter of the retail floorspace, arguably the negative image projected to investors or developers was equally damaging and potentially longer term (Deddis and McGreal, 1989). Hence the legacy of the 1970s on the urban structure of Belfast was one of economic and physical decay with outward movement of business, retailing, population and housing.

The third phase, the regeneration of the central core of Belfast in the 1980s, saw urban policy focus on economic, social and political objectives in an environment where development and investment opportunities were weak due to peripherality and a negative image. The scenario in essence was distinctly unattractive to the private sector. Thus to instigate and achieve effective regeneration the public sector had by necessity to be to the forefront in creating an environment conducive to the property industry and into which the private sector would follow. In evaluating the regeneration model as applied in Belfast it is thus critical, as a starting point, to appreciate the distinctive political and administrative structures within Northern Ireland, how they relate to the city of Belfast and the key part played by public sector agencies.

13.1   ADMINISTRATION

Within the United Kingdom context, Northern Ireland has historically possessed a distinctive legal and administrative structure. The 1920 Government of Ireland Act provided a form of regional government for the province (Birrell and Murie, 1980) with powers devolved from Westminster including education, health, personal and social services, law and order, planning, housing and economic development (Connolly, 1990). However, the effectiveness of regional government was hampered to some extent by inadequate powers, especially of finance, and by the key role assigned to local authorities (Buckland, 1981). As Murray (1991) points out, political tensions operated on two distinct levels – outwards to the Westminster exchequer and downwards to the mosaic of local government institutions. Devolved government in Northern Ireland remained in place until 1972 at which stage the United Kingdom government resumed direct responsibility for the administration of the province.

With respect to local authorities, the Local Government (NI) Act 1972 abolished the system which had been operative since 1898 and in place established district councils to administer 26 newly created local government districts. As a result of the 1972 local government reforms there has been a considerable increase in the centralization of decision-making in Northern Ireland and a reduction in the responsibilities of elected local authorities (House of Commons Environment Committee Report, 1990). One consequence of this has been the increased use of public agencies for various types of administration namely centralized boards for housing and economic development, and area boards for education, and health and social services.

Since 1972 various attempts have been made to re-establish a devolved government in Northern Ireland. However, with all such attempts having failed to win cross-party support the province has continued to be governed directly under the provisions of the Northern Ireland Act 1974. The Act permits the Westminster parliament to legislate for the province and places the Departments of the Northern Ireland Civil Service under the direction and control of the Secretary of State for Northern Ireland and a team of ministers. Those departments most directly concerned with development and investment in Northern Ireland are the Department of the Environment NI (DoE) and the Department of Economic Development (DED). Two main functions relevant to regeneration and shared to varying degrees between these departments are firstly establishing the principle of how land is to be used and secondly activating land into use.

The DoE has overall responsibility for formulating and co-ordinating development policy in Northern Ireland, with the Town and Country Planning Service providing the framework within which development can take place. Policy matters are considered for the province as a whole at headquarters level, whereas responsibility for development plan and development control procedures are handled by six divisional and two subdivisional planning offices, each of which cover a number of district council areas. Local authorities are consulted in an advisory capacity only on planning matters. Thus the DoE occupies a unique role. Although exercising executive control over planning, the department at the same time actively seeks to promote development and investment opportunities in the property sector through the operation of various mechanisms under the direction of differing sections and branches within the DoE (Figure 13.1).

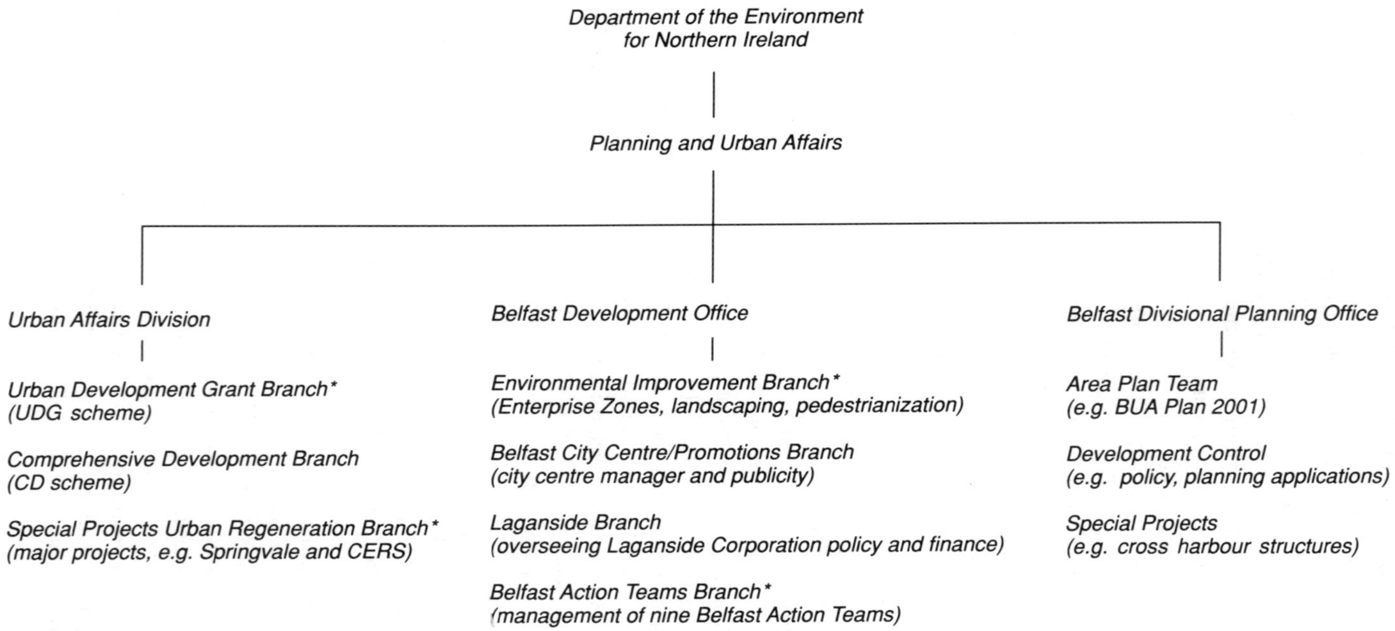

Department of the Environment
for Northern Ireland

Planning and Urban Affairs

Urban Affairs Division

Belfast Development Office

Belfast Divisional Planning Office

Urban Development Grant Branch*
(UDG scheme)

Comprehensive Development Branch
(CD scheme)

Special Projects Urban Regeneration Branch*
(major projects, e.g. Springvale and CERS)

Environmental Improvement Branch*
(Enterprise Zones, landscaping, pedestrianization)

Belfast City Centre/Promotions Branch
(city centre manager and publicity)

Laganside Branch
(overseeing Laganside Corporation policy and finance)

Belfast Action Teams Branch*
(management of nine Belfast Action Teams)

Area Plan Team
(e.g. BUA Plan 2001)

Development Control
(e.g. policy, planning applications)

Special Projects
(e.g. cross harbour structures)

*Additional funding provided by Making Belfast Work for specific schemes in disadvantaged areas of the city

Figure 13.1 Administration structure for regeneration in Belfast.

There are two administrative groupings within the DoE which have specific responsibility for the regeneration of Belfast. The Belfast Development Office promotes and co-ordinates the revitalization programme within the context of the DoE's overall objective of improving the environment and quality of life throughout Northern Ireland, whereas the Urban Affairs Division operates the Urban Development Grant scheme, implements comprehensive development programmes and co-ordinates area development proposals. The demarcation between the Belfast Development Office and the Urban Affairs Division is that the former takes the lead in framing policy and dealing with the public sector whereas the latter is more involved in implementation with the private sector.

In contrast, the DED attempts to stimulate economic development and employment by strengthening the existing industrial base within the province, and by seeking to attract inward investment from abroad. The Industrial Development Board and the Local Enterprise Development Unit as DED agencies have more specific remits. The Industrial Development Board's strategic policy is to encourage the international competitiveness of Northern Ireland's economic base by providing financial assistance, strengthening management expertise, improving products and processes, developing marketing know-how and penetrating export markets. In tune with the Industrial Development Board's approach, the Local Enterprise Development Unit's responsibilities are to stimulate the potential of small businesses, promote a more enterprising culture and improve competitiveness for export markets.

13.2   PLANNING POLICY

The physical and economic base of Belfast, like many traditional industrial cities, has undergone dramatic change. Driven by the success of its industrial enterprises in engineering, shipbuilding and textiles, the extraordinary economic growth in the early part of this century began to falter after the Second World War. Inner city redevelopment came on the agenda in the late 1950s but action on the ground was slow, and it was not until the 1960s that the first major planning response was initiated (Morrison, 1990).

The unplanned growth of the Belfast Urban Area in contrast with the lack of development elsewhere in the province led to the formal preparation of a plan for the Belfast Region. Published in 1964, the Belfast Regional Survey and Plan (the Matthew Report; Matthew, 1964) was concerned principally with physical development. In particular the report claimed that the Belfast Urban Area contained too high a proportion of the province's population with impending problems of suburbanization and deterioration in the amenity value of the surrounding landscape (Boal, 1990).

The plan imposed a development stop line round the Belfast Urban Area allowing sufficient space for an estimated 600 000 people by 1981, a net population increase of approximately 40 000. In the absence of this strategy the total population would in all probability have reached 700 000 by 1981.

The proposals embodied the demagnetization of Belfast and the development of the new city of Craigavon, together with seven other growth centres within the Belfast Region. As Murray (1991) points out, the strategy was one of development concentration designed to facilitate expansion in several of the larger towns in the eastern part of the province, while at the same time curtailing the attraction of the Belfast Urban Area. Matthew recognized that both these aspects of policy were complementary in opening up the province more widely for inward economic investment and at the same time allowing inner city development at lower densities.

In essence, although the Matthew Report provided a broad framework for growth and urban development the strategy depended ultimately on the preparation of a comprehensive plan and investment programme for the Belfast Urban Area. Subsequently, in 1969 the Belfast Urban Area Plan provided for a major rebuilding and transportation programme within the city, including extensive redevelopment of densely populated inner city wards (Building Design Partnership, 1969). The plan recommended the accelerated development of the growth centre strategy, the decentralization of new government offices and the establishment of 12 district centres to service the needs of neighbourhoods within the Belfast Urban Area. In addition, the 1969 Belfast Urban Area Plan placed considerable emphasis on reducing the population of inner city Belfast so that sufficient space could be made available to facilitate the proper provision of housing and other services. Political emphasis also focused on those areas of greater need, and following a study of multiple deprivation within the city, a Belfast Area of Need Plan Team was established to co-ordinate the provision of social and community facilities (Morrison, 1990).

Although the plans produced during the 1960s were essentially growth orientated, by the mid-1970s economic circumstances had altered (Mooney and Gaffikin, 1988). A combination of factors, including the impact of housing redevelopment programmes, industrial recession, an escalation in civil disturbance, and a greater restraint in government expenditure prompted the DoE to re-assess planning policy. The Regional Physical Development Strategy 1975–95 stated that Belfast, in 1975, faced a combination of economic, social, communal and physical development problems unparalleled in any major city in Europe. The strategy recognized that between the early 1960s and the mid-1970s the inner part of the Belfast Urban Area lost about 150 000 people and projected that the population over the period 1975–95 would continue to fall from its 1975 level of 560 000 to approximately 520 000 by 1995. Although the decanting of population parallels trends within other cities in the United Kingdom, the consequences of outmigration left large parts of inner Belfast with an ageing population in small households, declining birth rates and an over-representation in the lower socioeconomic groups, the classic inner city syndrome. Despite reduced population pressure in Belfast the stopline continued to function not so much as an instrument to control population growth but rather as a boundary to limit suburban sprawl and to protect the natural setting of the city [DoE (NI), 1977].

Consequently, with the changing economic and demographic circumstances in the Belfast Urban Area, the Regional Physical Development Strategy recognized that the tempo of physical planning had to undergo a radical reorientation from the growth scenario of the 1960s to a situation of planning for a static or declining population base. This arguably provided an opportunity to start the process of regenerating the heart of the city, especially as the image presented by the centre can set the tone for the urban area as a whole.

The most recent strategic planning document, the Belfast Urban Area Plan 2001, gives specific priority for urban renewal. Unlike the Regional Physical Development Strategy the plan is based on the concept that neither the decline of the urban structure nor continuing population loss are inevitable. Instead it takes a more optimistic long term view based on population stability and a renewal of growth within the Belfast Urban Area. Key objectives of the development-led strategy include the revitalization of the city centre, waterfront development at Laganside and the renewal of inner city wards in a desire to increase the attractiveness of Belfast as a place to live, work and invest [Department by the Environment (NI), 1990].

In the case of Belfast city centre there were clear signs of a revival in the mid-1980s led by the retailing and entertainment sectors (Berry and McGreal, 1991). The shopping strategy of the Belfast Urban Area Plan is designed to strengthen the city centre's primary retailing role by supporting new investment and ensuring against excessive dispersal of large scale shopping development. Consequently major retailing developments are being concentrated in the prime shopping nucleus centred on Donegall Place and Royal Avenue. In the remainder of the city centre developments with a gross floorspace capacity of 2500 m² or less may be allowed in existing shopping locations. Furthermore, in helping to promote the economic regeneration of the city centre current planning policy encourages the concentration of office development in appropriate central locations, including the regeneration targets of Laganside and Northside. An upper limit of 200 m² gross floorspace for the rest of the Belfast Urban Area has been imposed to safeguard the economic and administrative importance of the city centre (Figure 13.2).

The plan recognizes that implementation, particularly the focusing of investment on priority areas and exploiting development opportunity, requires partnership arrangements between the public and private sectors and the participation of the community in Belfast. The regeneration thrust is public sector-led and consequently within priority areas the DoE's role is to integrate the development programmes of various bodies in a comprehensive approach to urban renewal.

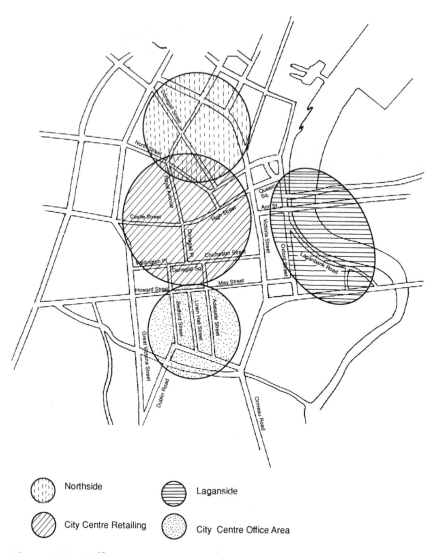

Figure 13.2   Belfast city centre: a zonal representation

13.3   MECHANISMS

In promoting regeneration the principal instruments available to government include policy initiatives, sustained public sector funding and political commitment. The regeneration model for Belfast with its strong public sector lead, provided by central government, ensures that these criteria are being met. The regeneration thrust has also been enhanced by the increasingly market orientated perspective of the relevant government departments and agencies, in particular the multifunctional role of the DoE.

Although policy formulation for Northern Ireland has distinctive characteristics, there nevertheless is a tendency to follow the broad direction given at the national level in the United Kingdom but invariably displaying some time lag. Specifically concerning regeneration several of the major instruments used to varying effect elsewhere in Britain in the 1980s have been applied within Belfast, including an Enterprise Zone, a Development Corporation, Urban Development Grant, Action Teams and Environmental Improvement schemes. These mechanisms, essentially supply-side based, rely heavily on the use of grants and other incentives to stimulate development by the private sector in the expectation that property based regeneration will accrue. Thus policy emphasis in Belfast has focused on achieving physical and economic objectives of which property development is a tangible expression.

An inherent weakness in the application of regeneration policy in England and Wales lies in its spatial connotation with boundaries demarcating the areal extent of the various initiatives. Hence the potential for blight occurs in those locations immediately surrounding designated areas. However, the package of mechanisms available within Belfast and their overlapping nature, for example, the potential availability of Urban Development Grant within the Enterprise Zone, in the area designated for the Laganside Corporation and in the Action Areas, essentially means that the greater part of the central core of the city has received public sector backed assistance in one form or another.

Belfast Enterprise Zone

Designated in October 1981 the Belfast Enterprise Zone, in common with other first round zones, expired in the autumn of 1991. Spatially the zone encompassed two substantially different sites. The north foreshore location on reclaimed land adjacent to the province's motorway system arguably represents what could be considered as a key location for warehousing and distributive uses, whereas that part of the zone located in the north-west of the city shows the characteristics of an inner area location.

Appraisal of the Belfast Enterprise Zone by PA Cambridge Economic Consultants (1988) points to the real benefit conferred on designated sites notably through job stimulation and enhanced development opportunities in the property market. In this context the local economy is considered to have gained from the supply of new premises, the removal of derelict buildings and the refurbishment of old mill accommodation in the inner city zone, in addition to improvements to the local environment. It is argued that Enterprise Zone policy has boosted the supply-side by removing constraints inherent within the local development process, in essence serving to reduce the risk factor for developers/investors.

Economic statistics available from government place the total public sector costs of the Belfast zone at about £21 million (up to March 1990), with approximately £11 million attributable to capital allowances and a further £10 million of revenue foregone in rates relief. Estimated private sector input at £50 million indicates a leverage ratio of 1:2.5. However, there has not been any substantial flow of investment monies from companies seeking a tax shelter for clients (PA Cambridge Economic Consultants, 1988) unlike the situation pertaining in Enterprise Zones in Great Britain (McDougall and Filer, 1990; Johnson, 1991). Indeed, the Belfast zone appears to provide a focus for local developers who wish to hold or retain a part interest in their own investment.

On the basis of performance indicators, namely investment, floorspace provision, change in the number of firms and employment, the Belfast Enterprise Zone is considered to have experienced growth rates below its British counterparts. However, the PA report does highlight that Enterprise Zone policy is only one instrument available to government and specifically to the DoE. Consequently more overall control concerning property development and refurbishment incentives both off-zone and on-zone is possible relative to Enterprise Zones elsewhere in Britain, so reducing the potential for adjacent stagnation and dereliction. Thus in the Belfast example planning policy and other regenerative mechanisms help to offset the lower investment profile.

Laganside Corporation

The reciprocity of mechanisms between Northern Ireland and England and Wales is mirrored in the approach used to regenerate dockland areas. The first phase of Urban Development Corporations under the Conservative administration of the 1980s found expression in major schemes such as London and Liverpool. Although Belfast still retains an important, indeed growing, port function, changing technologies meant that under-used dock facilities and land, fronting the river Lagan, were in close proximity to the city centre. Spurred on by the sweeping enthusiasm for waterfront development the DoE commissioned the consultants Shepheard, Epstein and Hunter, in association with Building Design Partnership, to prepare the Laganside Concept Plan (1987) as an input into the new statutory plan for the Belfast Urban Area. The outcome of this was the formation of a DoE company, Laganside Ltd, in 1987 as an interim measure until enabling legislation allowed the establishment of the Laganside Corporation in 1989 (Berry et al., 1991a). The designated area within Laganside covers about 120 ha (48 of which are developable) and has eight major development sites along 2.4 km of waterfront.

Laganside Corporation bears close comparison with Urban Development Corporations in England and Wales. Statutory powers include compulsory purchase, the ability to hold and retain land, and through its classification as a List 1 public company the Laganside Corporation has the right to seek funding and hold monies from different sources including the European Community. However, in the key area of planning, powers have not been devolved and remain a function of the DoE.

The Laganside Corporation is primarily a facilitator charged with the responsibility for overseeing development, marketing and encouraging investment opportunities. Laganside offers supply-side advantages by bringing forward development sites in agreement with landowners, primarily other public sector bodies, and initiating infrastructural schemes. Key components of the latter are a weir to regulate flow and improve water quality, together with other environmental improvements including riverside walkways. In addition, a major cross-harbour road and rail bridge are currently in the early stages of construction. Although the latter is not the responsibility of Laganside Corporation, such infrastructural improvement will inevitably have a significant impact on the regenerative process and environment created. These capital cost components serve to show the high public sector commitment to Laganside. Over the five year period 1991–6 Laganside Corporation alone has expenditure plans of about £60 million; anticipated leverage ratios are 1:4.

The pace of private sector development on key sites has, however, been slow. Two factors are seemingly at play. Firstly, the policy of phased release of design briefs for development sites, the process of selection of a preferred developer/scheme and the negotiation of a development agreement has obvious time implications. For example, the Abercorn Centre, Laganside's first major scheme, a £20 million complex of offices (15 000 m^2), retailing (1500 m^2), apartments (24) and multistorey parking, only began in the autumn of 1990, a time lag 15–16 months after selection of the development company. Phase one of this development was completed in the second half of 1992. Likewise the flagship Laganbank site (6 ha) for which a £100 million scheme was announced in July 1991 and consisting of 42 500 m^2 of offices, 9000 m^2 of retailing, a concert and conference hall, 200 bedroom hotel, parking and a small marina is likely to be characterized by a long development period. The sequencing of the component parts of the Laganbank scheme are crucial to the ultimate achievement of this development opportunity with the £29 million concert/conference hall being the lynch-pin around which the hotel, offices, festival retailing and other uses will follow. Laganside Corporation are unlikely to start infrastructural work on site until the final decision is made by the Belfast City Council about this major civic building (this should be confirmed in January 1993).

The second time constraint may arise from the actions of the chosen developer who, for various reasons including current market conditions, financial and property, may wish to defer the start of development activity. Although the agreement between Laganside Corporation and the developer may specify back-stop dates these are likely to be spread over several years giving the latter considerable flexibility. In consequence, due to the nature of the development process, the regeneration thrust can become diluted in a time context and from an economic property perspective the fulfilment of regeneration goals are long term. However, with infrastructure in place and environmental quality enhanced Laganside should be well placed to attract users, assuming a strengthening of the macroeconomy of the United Kingdom in the mid-1990s.

The main subsidy offered to the developer and occupier is essentially infrastructure based as Laganside lacks the financial and rating incentives of an Enterprise Zone location, though potential exists for the Corporation to offer Urban Development Grants to encourage new development as well as the refurbishment of existing properties (Laganside Corporation, 1992). Arguably some form of fiscal incentive may be useful to stimulate the pace of development in Laganside (Berry et al., 1991a) and help to remove the time lag between the selection of a developer and commencement of work on site. In this context property agents have pointed to the pace of development initially achieved at the Custom House Docks, Dublin.

With respect to land uses, mixed assemblages with a high office content characterize several of the development sites in Laganside. The marketing thrust thus seeks to complement Industrial Development Board policy with respect to capturing the 'foot-loose' back-office user, a strategy underpinned by current planning policy for Belfast. A key selling point has been the lower occupancy costs in Belfast. However with current high vacancy rates in the London market (20% vacancy in the first half of 1992) and declining rents in real terms the cost benefits of relocating within Belfast, or more specifically Laganside, are becoming more marginalized.

Urban Development Grant

Analogous to the Urban Development Action Grant used in the USA, the Urban Development Grant was introduced to stimulate economic regeneration within urban areas in Great Britain and Northern Ireland. The high risk associated with speculative property development and the lower rates of return in inner cities provided the *raison d'être* for the grant. Introduced into Northern Ireland in 1982 the origins of the programme parallel the British experience (Johnson, 1988) but differ in application depending on the degree of urban dereliction (Berry and McGreal, 1992).

Concerning the application of the Urban Development Grant within Belfast, policy evolution has seen a number of distinct changes in the targeting of the grant. The low development confidence prevailing in Belfast in the early 1980s focused the initial use of the Urban Development Grant in the city centre and major arterial routes. Under the standard rate of grant up to 50% of construction costs and fees were available to owner-occupiers for re-structuring purposes and up to 30% on speculative development. However, in a major policy shift an enhanced rate of grant was made available in the designated Northside area of Belfast's inner core where, in spite of planning policy and the existing standard rate Urban Development Grant, there still remained a high proportion of unfit buildings and under-utilized floorspace. In an effort to focus more sharply and maximize developer interest the experimental programme, as well as being locationally targeted, was restricted to applications made during 1988. An enhanced Urban Development Grant made available grants of up to 50% of the total development costs for speculative development and up to 60% of construction costs and fees for owner-occupiers restructuring property, the latter rising to 75% for those who purchased property which was vacant for 12 months or more (Deddis and McGreal, 1989). More recent policy changes have seen a redirecting of the Urban Development Grant away from the centre of Belfast (though the possibility still exists for its use, particularly in Laganside) and towards Action Team Areas in disadvantaged inner city wards.

The application of the Urban Development Grant within the central core of Belfast has been primarily towards commercial uses (in 87% of instances), though other use sectors, namely social, community, industrial and housing, have been funded under the programme. Regarding work type, assisted schemes have primarily been refurbishment programmes concerned with improving the quality of existing buildings; investment projects account for only about 14% of all Urban Development Grant funded schemes. The propensity towards small scale refurbishment schemes and external works has served to skew leverage downwards, hence the Urban Development Grant has stimulated mainly low risk projects with low leverage ratios [mean leverage of 1:2.73 for central area projects (Berry and McGreal, 1992)]. Although on the basis of leverage statistics the performance of the Urban Development Grant may appear modest, the collective impact of assisted schemes together with Environmental Improvement (annual budget about £1–1.5 million for Belfast) has helped to physically regenerate many locations within the city centre. In contrast, investment projects, although relatively fewer in number, attracted significantly higher mean leverage ratios (1:4.89), but the accompanying high values of standard deviation (6.99) suggest a wide variability of outcomes highlighting the greater uncertainty with such schemes.

Total public sector input under the Urban Development Grant has been about £48 million (to December 1991). The availability of assistance under the programme served to lessen or reduce the risk component for developers, particularly in the weak market conditions prevailing in Belfast in the early

1980s. In addition, locally based financial institutions perceived the Urban Development Grant favourably as a factor helping the viability of particular schemes. Arguably, it was a key influence in kick-starting the development process in Belfast, forming the platform for a period of unprecedented development in the retail and office sectors. During the period 1985–91 many speculative schemes proceeded without recourse to the grant, reflecting the revived commercial property market in Belfast.

Inner city initiatives

The extent of inner city decay in Belfast in physical, economic and social terms necessitated specific targeting of areas particularly as the benefits of urban regeneration can be slow to trickle-down to the wider community. Using indicators of deprivation, namely housing, unemployment, health, education and the environment to establish areas of greatest need, the Belfast Action Team initiative was designated in 1987. The work of the Belfast Action Teams, of which there are currently nine teams, seven of which are in the north and west of the city, is supplemented and reinforced by Making Belfast Work. The latter initiative is interdepartmental based and takes a broader, arguably a holistic approach, towards regeneration. Introduced in 1988 the Belfast Special Action Group, drawing key personnel from relevant government departments and agencies, co-ordinates Making Belfast Work. Spending programmes are subsequently carried out by appropriate departments and agencies.

The purpose of these mutually supporting initiatives is to stimulate economic activity, promote local enterprise, improve environmental quality and enhance the employment skills of the local population. Given the need to succeed within the inner areas of Belfast the political thrust is underwritten by a substantial package of financial funding with the Making Belfast Work initiative attracting £22 million of public sector funding in 1990–1, rising to £27 million in 1991–2. In addition, the Action Team Areas are now the prime target for Urban Development Grant funding, including the availability of an enhanced rate of grant.

The need for innovative measures in highlighted by the Community Economic Regeneration Scheme jointly funded by the DoE and the International Fund for Ireland. The latter body, the International Fund for Ireland, established as an outcome of the Anglo-Irish Agreement (1985) has among other functions particular concern for disadvantaged areas. Under the Community Economic Regeneration Scheme financial assistance (100% funding with 20% claw-back potential) is available to community groups with proved ability to bring forward projects which will assist in the regeneration of local economies. The scheme is specifically designed to concentrate on those areas with high unemployment, a lack of investment activity by the private sector due to political unrest and urban decay, and where communities are playing an active part in self-help initiatives (International Fund for Ireland, 1991). Currently three major schemes are being funded under the Community Economic Regeneration Scheme in the north and west of Belfast.

The overlapping nature of many of these inner city initiatives is particularly apparent in the embryonic Springvale Project, a comprehensive development scheme in the west of the city, a location described as one of the most deprived districts in Belfast, if not in the whole of western Europe. In Springvale a plethora of initiatives and hence funding sources are available through Making Belfast Work, the Community Economic Regeneration Scheme, the Action Team programme, Urban Development Grant and the Environmental Improvement budget. However, the achievement of regeneration goals in such localities will require a differing perspective from that used in the city centre as the private sector continues to display a considerable reluctance to follow the public sector lead in inner locations. Furthermore, there is the danger that the multiplicity of initiatives may fragment the regeneration thrust and not provide the co-ordinated approach required.

13.4 PROPERTY PERFORMANCE

The evaluation of urban regeneration policy and initiatives can be considered from differing perspectives, namely physical improvement of the urban fabric, economic regeneration or social revitalization. Essentially property based schemes to a greater or lesser extent span all of these criteria, but particular attention is given by developers/investors to property performance indicators in that they provide an assessment of past and current market conditions and allow the forecasting of likely future trends. In particular emphasis is placed on rental and capital growth and property investment yields. Such indicators allow assessment of property-led schemes to be made in terms of current added value and revenue return on a sector basis. With respect to the regeneration of the central core of Belfast, retail and office use constitute key components, the performances of which are critical to the process of economic regeneration. Furthermore, in terms of fund holdings institutional investment in Belfast is heavily weighted towards these sectors.

Retail sector

Nationally this market sector was characterized by a strong growth profile during the 1980s, a trend which has been replicated and arguably surpassed in Belfast (Myles, 1992). According to an analysis by the Investment Property Databank (1990) covering the ten years from 1980 to 1989 retail investments in Belfast have shown an annualized total return of 16.9% per annum, outperforming the average return for United Kingdom retails by 2.2%. Regarding rental growth the Valuation and Lands Office index for Belfast peaked at 370 in 1990 relative to the base value of 100 in 1980. This index, which is compared against the Investor's Chronicle/Hillier Parker Shop Rent Index, again shows the Belfast market to outperform national trends in the United Kingdom. Concerning prime retailing, zone A rentals for Donegall Place doubled over the period 1985–90, rising from £750/m^2 to £1500/m^2. However, by the end of the 1980s a slowing down in the market was apparent with annual growth rates slipping back to 5.2% and by 1991 a negative growth situation was apparent (−4.4%) compared with a peak growth figure of 18% in 1987–8.

Clearly from such evidence Belfast was among the best performing regional centres in the United Kingdom, a fact confirmed by turnover evidence from major retail multiples whose reports credit Belfast stores with profitability levels per square metre greater than elsewhere within their organization. Such evidence enhanced the city's reputation as a high profit earner, ultimately attracting the interest of several major United Kingdom investment institutions. However, the pattern is often a single large investment with the tendency to retain portfolios rather than to sell on. Although those institutions which have invested into property in Belfast quote high returns, the market is nevertheless relatively small with few players, raising some concern about liquidity. In this respect it is therefore questionable whether Belfast has truly established itself as a property investment market.

In terms of development several major city centre schemes came to fruition in the mid to late 1980s. The largest, Castle Court, occupying a 3.5 ha site with frontage onto Royal Avenue, provides 40 000 m^2 retailing, 17 500 m^2 of offices and a 1600 space car-parking facility. Arguably Castle Court represented 'the jewel in the crown' regarding the commercial revitalization of Belfast. Furthermore the influence of regeneration mechanisms in pump-priming this development is particularly apparent through the provision of the Urban Development Grant (£10 million) and a high quality Environmental Improvement Scheme (Figure 13.3). New developments, including Castle Court, redressed previous imbalances, and the demand for retailing space clearly had been satisfied by 1991. Indeed, excess supply and economic recession, the effects of which were less acute in the province, have contributed to the negative rental growth reported for 1991.

Office sector

The office market in Belfast has historically operated within levels of marginal viability and has been highly dependent on public sector occupation; for example, 44% of occupied city centre office space (about 425 000 m^2) is

Figure 13.3   Belfast city centre: retail development

in use for public administration (Valuation and Lands Office, 1991). However, as in retailing, though lagging behind in a time context, Belfast has experienced considerable growth in the office sector (Berry and McGreal, 1991). The Investment Property Databank (1990) report highlights an annualized total return of 15.8% per annum for office property relative to a national average of 13.9%, with Belfast outperforming most other comparable cities in the United Kingdom. Likewise the Valuation and Lands Office (1991) report draws attention to a period of relatively high investment activity by United Kingdom based institutions in the Belfast office market.

With respect to rental values the early 1980s were largely a period of steady but unspectacular growth with rental levels reaching £55/m² by 1985. Rising demand and a perceived shortage of quality office space pushed rentals levels to £75/m² in 1987 and by 1990 to between £100 and £110/m². However, it should be noted that despite the strong rental growth over this period office rents in Belfast are still appreciably below other regional centres in the United Kingdom. In common with the retail sector, there has also been an apparent weakening in the office market during 1991–2 reflecting both national trends and the growing supply of accommodation in Belfast as development schemes conceived during the latter part of the 1980s are completed (Figure 13.4). Regarding the latter several factors, including market conditions, planning regulations, the impact of regenerative mechanisms

Figure 13.4 Belfast city centre: office development

and Industrial Development Board back-office relocation policy were instrumental in promoting what can be considered as a major phase of office construction in the city centre (Berry *et al.*, 1991b). Although the pace of development activity may have slowed down, the impact in physical terms has been significant together with appreciable employment gain.

Yields

The scale of the property market and the relatively small number of transactions annually act as a constraint on the use of yields as an indicator of performance. Nevertheless in both the retail and office sectors, rental growth led to a reduction in yields to as low as 7% (for retail property) and 8.5% (for office property) in 1989–90. The combination of rental performance and lower yields meant capital growth and an incentive for investors which was translated into an exceptional period of development activity. Thus in the latter half of the 1980s there was a convergence of favourable market conditions with the regeneration strategy being pursued by the public sector.

Since 1990, the slowdown in rental growth and general recession in the United Kingdom economy have forced yields in Belfast upwards again to over 8 and 9.5%, respectively, in the retail and office sectors. The impact that this will have on the property market and investment potential during the 1990s is difficult to predict. However, it would seem unlikely that existing funds would disinvest and indeed the sophisticated investor wishing to spread risk may be attracted to Belfast as a high yielding location. Certainly the scale of development activity now means that Belfast has a stock of good quality commercial property with secure tenants, key criteria required of any investment opportunity.

13.5 DISCUSSION

In raising some of the contextual issues impinging on urban regeneration in Belfast, it is apparent that an intermingling of economic decline, social deprivation, political conflict, demographic restructuring and financial deficiencies characterize much of what has been happening within the city. However, the speed and scale of physical, social and economic decline distinguishes Belfast from other cities. The rapid growth of Belfast dating from the latter part of the 19th century has precipitated attempts over the last two decades to counteract the massive problems of obsolescence inherited from that era. This urban pattern characterized by initial rapid growth and subsequent decline has placed enormous demands on the social, economic and managerial structures of the city. The regeneration programme started with housing redevelopment in the 1970s and has, throughout the latter part of the 1980s, concentrated resources on the commercial revitalization of the city centre and the waterfront areas of Laganside. Based largely on public–private sector initiatives, such as the enhanced Urban Development Grant programme and, more recently, Community Economic Regeneration Schemes, evidence suggests that market investment follows state expenditure.

According to Brindley *et al.* (1989) the economic recession and associated restructuring has had an uneven spatial effect within urban areas. This has been associated with a varying level of private sector interest in land and property development between areas and has resulted in a fragmentation of planning into distinct styles based on the response of market processes. Brindley *et al.* (1989) identify a three-fold typology which consists of: buoyant market areas where the private sector is willing to invest normally without public sector support or subsidy; marginal areas where the private sector could be induced to invest with appropriate support or subsidy from the public sector; and unattractive areas where no subsidy could induce the private sector to invest and instead requires large scale action involving public sector investment or private sector management.

This topology neatly fits the regeneration areas of Belfast, namely the retail and commercial core, Laganside/Northside and the inner city sectors,

Table 13.1 Regeneration typology as applied to Belfast

Regeneration areas	Reaction of market processes	Key planning components and mechanisms
Retailing and commercial core	Market viable and relatively buoyant	Private sector investment Development-led Facilitating Deregulating Place marketing
Laganside/Northside	Market potential but pockets of urban problems	Leverage Infrastructural investment Land packaging Public–private partnerships Subsidy (Urban Development Grant) Image building

Inner city sectors	Market limited with comprehensive urban problems	Public sector investment
		Community Economic
		   Regeneration Scheme
		Area based management
		   programmes

respectively. The planning response and mechanism used in each of these areas differ depending on market reaction and the nature and extent of the problems prevailing (Table 13.1).

The current regeneration mechanisms being applied in Belfast are geared to tackle problems broadly similar to those experienced in other British cities. Key criticisms stem from land ownership, land assembly, area location problems, lack of accountability and difficulties in evaluating the real costs and benefits. However, in a high risk urban economy such as Belfast public sector-led regeneration has a crucial part to play in levering private investment.

In the funding of new development projects banks will not lend unless public assistance is available, whereas the public sector agencies will not provide grant aid unless the banks are willing to be involved (Northern Ireland Economic Council, 1992). The advantages of these arrangements to both the public and private sectors are apparent. The financial institutions gain a larger measure of business at a lower risk than would be possible if no government money was available, whereas the public sector agencies secure leverage of private funds and some spreading of risk as a result. Developers also gain from having access to a range of funding sources.

The benefits of such arrangements between the public and private sectors to the urban economy and society as a whole is an extremely difficult issue to quantify. However, if there are additional benefits over and above those accruing to a private sector operator, such as additional employment, then it is legitimate to expect the public sector to bear some of the development risks in urban regeneration projects.

REFERENCES

Berry, J.N. and McGreal, W.S. (1991) Regeneration game, *Estates Gazette*, **9140**, 98–102.

Berry, J.N. and McGreal, W.S. (1992) Urban Development Grant: funding the commercial revitalisation of Belfast, *Journal of Property Finance*, **3**(1), 59–65.

Berry, J.N., Deddis, W.G. and McGreal, W.S. (1991a) Waterfront regeneration in Ireland: public and private sector partnerships, *Journal of Property Finance*, **2**(2), 179–184.

Berry, J.N., Deddis, W.G. and McGreal, W.S. (1991b) The regeneration of Belfast city centre, *Pleanail*, **10**, 81–89.

Birrell, D. and Murie, A. (1980) *Policy and Government in Northern Ireland: Lessons of Devolution*, Gill and Macmillan, Dublin.

Boal, F.W. (1990) Belfast: hindsight or foresight – planning in an unstable environment. In: *Geographical Perspectives on the Belfast Region* (Ed. P. Doherty), *Special Publication No. 5*, Geographical Society of Ireland, Dublin, pp. 4–14.

Brindley, T., Rydin, Y. and Stoker, G. (1989) *Remaking Planning: The Politics of Urban Change in the Thatcherite Years*, Unwin Hyman, London.

Brown, S. (1987) Shopping centre development in Belfast, *Land Development Studies*, **4**, 193–207.

Buckland, P. (1981) *A History of Northern Ireland*, Gill and Macmillan, Dublin.

Building Design Partnership (BDP) (1969) *Belfast Urban Area Plan*, BDP, Belfast.

Connolly, E. (1990) *Politics and Policy Making in Northern Ireland*, Philip Allan, Hemel Hempstead.

Couch, C. (1990) *Urban Renewal Theory and Practice*, Macmillan Education, London.

Deddis, W.G. and McGreal, W.S. (1989) Urban regeneration: a comparative assessment – Great Britain and Northern Ireland. In: *Land and Property Development – New Directions* (Ed. R. Grover), E & FN Spon, London, pp. 199–207.

Department of the Environment (NI) (1977) *Regional Physical Development Strategy 1975–1995*, HMSO, Belfast.

Department of the Environment (NI) (1990) *Belfast Urban Area Plan 2001*, HMSO, Belfast.

House of Commons Environment Committee (1990) *Environmental Issues in Northern Ireland First Report*, HMSO, London.

International Fund for Ireland (1991) *Annual Report.*

Investment Property Databank (1990) *IPD Special Regional Report: Northern Ireland,* IPD, London.

Johnson, D. (1988) An evaluation of the Urban Development Grant programme, *Local Economy,* **2**(4), 251–270.

Johnson, R. (1991) Enterprise Zones. To invest or not to invest? *Estates Gazette,* **9115**, 76–77.

Laganside Corporation (1992) *Corporate Plan. A Vision for the Future,* Laganside Corporation, Belfast.

Lawless, P. (1989) *Britain's Inner Cities,* 2nd edn, Paul Chapman Publishing, London.

Matthew, R. (1964) *Belfast Regional Survey and Plan,* HMSO, Belfast.

McDougall, B. and Filer, A. (1990) Enterprise Zone investment. What happens when the benefits go? *Estates Gazette,* **9015**, 20–21.

Mooney, S. and Gaffikin, F. (1988) *Reshaping Space and Society. A Critical Review of the Belfast Urban Area Plan,* Belfast Centre for the Unemployed, Belfast.

Morrison, W. (1990) Making Belfast work, *The Planner/T.C.P.S.S. Proceedings,* **76**(49), 32–35.

Murray, M. (1991) *The Politics and Pragmatism of Urban Containment,* Avebury.

Myles, D. (1992) Northern Ireland: what recession? *PIDA Newsletter,* Spring, 4–5.

Northern Ireland Economic Council (1992) *The Financial Services Industry in Northern Ireland, Report 91,* NIEC, Belfast.

PA Cambridge Economic Consultants (1988) *An Evaluation of the Enterprise Zone Experiment in N. Ireland,* HMSO, Belfast.

Shepheard, Epstein and Hunter (London) and Building Design Partnership (1987) *Laganside Concept Plan,* Belfast.

Valuation and Lands Office (1991) *The Belfast Office Market,* VLO/UU, Belfast.

PART THREE ————

REGENERATION MECHANISMS

————————————————————

Editorial

The political and economic strengths of many European cities have been weakened by structural shifts and regional changes in employment and population. At the same time as this relative decline, the roles of public and private sector agencies have been changing and local initiatives are now playing an increasingly important role in the attempts by government in coming to terms with the consequences of scientific and technical developments. The impact of initiatives on the spatial and socioeconomic structures of cities must be considered in the context of the decline in their industrial base and the high levels of long term unemployment.

In arresting this decline, the evolution of public policy has involved new forms of partnership between the public sector (central and local government and quasi government agencies) and the private sector (financial institutions, business corporations and development companies). The principal aim has been to encourage conditions under which a market in land and property can be created or stimulated by mobilizing private sector resources. Consequently, mechanisms have emerged concerning land availability, infrastructure and urban marketing with public sector financial support underpinning the market for private sector development and investment.

Throughout the 1980s, in most west European countries, private interests and market forces have been given a central role in determining the direction, shape and pace of urban regeneration with the public sector operating in a facilitating capacity. Indeed, in Britain, the most recent proposal involves the establishment of a new statutory agency to promote the reclamation and development of derelict, vacant and underused land and buildings in urban areas. The aim of the new Urban Regeneration Agency is to remove obstacles to the effective operation of the market by contributing grant aid to developers, using compulsory purchase powers to help with site assembly and providing advice on the operation of the market.

Consequently, Part Three of this book concentrates on key regeneration mechanisms, namely public–private partnerships, Enterprise Zones, Urban Development Corporations and area based initiatives. A distinguishing feature of these initiatives comes from differences in the scale of operation, areal extent, financial resources and delegated powers. However, there are also common strands in particular shared basic objectives, the creation of organizational frameworks for action and the desire to create schemes/projects which will revitalize specific urban localities.

Kohnstamm, in the opening chapter of Part Three, considers the contribution and reciprocal arrangements of public–private partnerships in The Netherlands. The growth in partnerships has arisen from the increasing budgetary problems faced by national and local authorities on one hand and the willingness of institutional investors to provide finance for development projects on the other. Local authorities provide planning and infrastructural support whereas the private sector contributes professional advice and knowledge of the market. Although research shows that urban development by means of partnership still needs to be more clearly defined, Kohnstamm argues that in several Dutch cities such arrangements have nevertheless offered a new impetus to institutional investors and project developers by providing concerted management, the spreading of risk, the attraction of risk-bearing capital and the pooling of knowledge.

Witbraad and Jorna focus specifically on the public–private partnership in the development of the IJ Embankments project in Amsterdam. The need to reduce or control risk in such a complex development scheme resulted in the establishment of the Amsterdam Waterfront Financieringsmaatschappij (AWF), a partnership involving the local authority, the NMB Postbank and the insurance group Nationale Nederlanden. The local authority, with a capital holding of 50%, has responsibility for preparing a strategic zoning plan to establish the development potential and ensure the integration of the scheme with the city core, whereas the prime task of the AWF is to prepare a business plan incorporating a financial appraisal. Outturn performance indicates that the investment level required for the project can be completely covered by revenues in spite of the high capital outlay necessary to overcome physical and substructural problems. Furthermore, Witbraad and Jorna argue that the management of the financial result can be conducted within agreed margins. In this context an important element in managing risk is considered to be the implementation of market research activities to evaluate the effects of changing social and economic circumstances.

With respect to the stimulation of investment and development activity within urban areas in Britain, Brodtman and Johnson evaluate the contribution made by Enterprise Zones. The removal of fiscal burdens and the streamlining of statutory controls within the zones have encouraged new development activity, particularly high quality office accommodation. Regarding investments, Brodtman and Johnson infer that a relatively high volume of activity has come from property companies and from individuals through Enterprise Zone Property Unit Trusts. In this respect the benefits which are available to owners of property in Enterprise Zones have also been extended to include the trusts and individual unit holders. The Doxford international case study in Sunderland demonstrates the benefits of capital allowances in attracting private investors into Enterprise Zones by providing tax shelters and lucrative returns on property investments. It is argued that such case study evidence emphasizes the need to extend the Enterprise Zone regulation as a means of promoting economic development, although it is maintained that the cost effectiveness of the scheme could be further improved by reducing the amount of deadweight on both capital allowances and rates relief.

Urban Development Corporations were also initially introduced in the early 1980s by the Conservative administration largely to bypass the perceived inflexibility of the planning system. In evaluating these single purpose agencies Bintley argues that by adopting procedures to facilitate the speedy implementation of projects and by operating to specific objectives within a clearly defined area, regeneration can be achieved quicker than by providing local authorities with the necessary resources. The profiles of the various corporations reveal a commonality of approach to urban regeneration, with development strategies building on the proposals which were adopted by the local authorities before designation. Bintley also stresses the importance of high profile flagship schemes and environmental improvements in creating confidence and enhancing the image of an area for private sector investment. Leverage of private investment within development areas has been further facilitated by the Urban Programme and City Grant. However, in terms of impact it is argued that too much emphasis has been placed on physical performance indicators with insufficient guidance given to social change. Corporate plans require a greater recognition of strategic issues and a more systematic monitoring, not only of inputs and content, but also of wider and longer term objectives. Consequently Urban Development Corporations are now recognizing that the regeneration process demands a co-ordinated programme of infrastructural development supported by investment in jobs, education and skills training.

The latter chapters in Part Three provide case study profiles of regeneration approaches at different spatial levels of the urban hierarchy. Lockwood, in Chapter 18, develops the concept of holistic regeneration. In Calderdale, West Yorkshire, the local authority, faced with the virtual collapse of textile and engineering industries, in partnership with private sector interests created a remarkably successful community based regeneration programme. The Inheritance Project under the direction of a small multidisciplinary team with support from Business in the Community adopted a proactive strategy to encourage development and attract investment. This was achieved by the development of three interlinked campaigns involving partnership, exemplar projects and promotion. Lockwood argues that the integration of these three elements within a balanced and co-ordinated strategy creates an effective tool for the management of urban change.

Lawton, in evaluating regeneration projects in small towns, argues that each locality has its own particular set of problems dictated by such influences as political persuasion, economic base, ethnic make-up and geographical position. Specifically focusing on Brigg, a traditional market town in Humberside with a rich historical legacy, the challenges included a general lack of confidence, physical deterioration, a lack of investment, loss of major retail occupiers and the occurrence of heavy through traffic. The Brigg Regeneration Project, a Civic Trust initiative involving a partnership between the local authority, business interests and the community, adopted a property-led approach to encourage practical schemes of development, environmental improvement and building repair. The various grant regimes proved invaluable in triggering private sector monies and promoting property refurbishment. Indeed, Lawton argues that in marginal investment areas, such as small towns, the proportion of grant may be the key which swings a decision whether to develop or not. Furthermore, the local authority's programme of capital expenditure is seen to be of crucial significance in priming follow-on investment by the private sector. Concerning value for money, Lawton argues that the Brigg Project provides economy, effectiveness and efficiency at a relatively low per capita cost set against the investment levered from the private sector.

However, circumstances may arise where the costs of undertaking an urban renewal project are far in excess of the reclaimed value of the land, with the result that a potentially successful regeneration project is tipped from profit into substantial loss. In developing this issue, Syms stresses the importance of gaining as much knowledge as possible about redevelopment sites, particularly in urban waterfront locations, before making a financial commitment. The process of cumulative decline, producing further obsolescence, and in turn discouraging investment, were the characteristic features which typified what is now Piccadilly Village in central Manchester. The concept plan for the redevelopment of this depressed area envisaged a high density urban development comprising a mix of uses together with an environment in which people would wish to live and invest. A joint development company, Piccadilly Village Limited, was established to carry out the urban renewal project. Syms, in examining the development process, again highlights the importance of public sector support, particularly City Grant, in securing private sector investment. Furthermore, it is of interest that the residential component has been one of the most successful elements with prices fixed at realistic levels for a quality design. This has helped to attract purchasers into a previously untested housing market area.

14

Urban renewal and public–private partnership in The Netherlands

P. Kohnstamm

The mid-1980s marked the start of a new period in the history of Dutch city planning. In the post-war years, repairing the damage was the central theme; later, the focus shifted to expansion based on rapid population growth. However, the ultimate stabilization of demographic trends and the emergence of new ideas about the function of urban centres led to a veritable rush of activities in the field of urban renewal in the 1970s. Currently, innovations which focus on the multifunctional role of the historic heart of the city are now in the spotlight. In implementing new construction projects every effort is now being made to stimulate and reinforce co-operation between the public and the private sectors.

The city can be viewed as an independent organic unit that is unceasingly undergoing metamorphoses. In some instances, these changes can be brought about by intervention on the micro-level, such as replacing specific buildings by others with either the same or perhaps a different function. In other instances there have been, and still are, large scale alterations in the very structure of the city. The significance of these changes in terms of the overall appearance of urban areas can only be effectively assessed if attention is focused on the position of the city with respect to the environment and society of which it is an integral part. The relations between the city and the national authorities, as well as those with business and capital in the private sector, shape the opportunities enabling the city to advance, develop and grow. What is more, the instruments it has at its disposal are in a state of constant flux. There is also a considerable variation in the financial, legal and organizational leeway a city has at different points in time.

The conception of space and scale held by a society also affects the way it deals with the tangible spatial and infrastructural aspects of its cities. For each period of time, varying priorities are accorded to urban planning modes, which in turn present different solutions regarding housing, work, traffic, recreation and education. The appraisal of such matters as the advisability of high rise construction or various levels of density or accessibility can also show considerable variation. The city planning option favoured at any particular moment in time depends on a number of fluctuating factors including: the particular society's point of view as to the function of the city; the significance the society attributes to one or more existing urban functions at any particular moment in time; the relation between the national and the local government authorities; the position of various commercial interests in the urban area to be developed; the relation between authorities and the private sector; the way political responsibilities are spread over several departments; and the political, organizational and economic vitality of the city.

The significance of the city for society as a whole is subject to change not only by government but also by the private sector in its appraisal of the attributes of the city. The willingness on the part of the latter to make sizeable financial investments in the quality of city centres, which fell to an all-time low in the 1970s, has been a notable feature in recent years. In instances where the disappearance of former urban functions called for the creation of new ones to take their place, private companies are now showing themselves willing to invest in the process, particularly in the context of partnership arrangements (van der Boor, 1991).

14.1   THE INTEREST OF PUBLIC–PRIVATE PARTNERSHIP

An essential characteristic of public–private partnerships is the co-operation between government and industry. Public–private partnership is not an objective in itself, but an instrument for carrying out important projects. Co-operation between government and industry is not new; in The Netherlands there has always been, without advertising, a manifestation of public–private partnerships in the housing sector. For example, through ample subsidy regulations, social housing has never been the exclusive domain of the government and local authorities. Particularly in the case of more expensive housing for rent, institutional investors have co-operated closely with local authorities, whereas building contractors and project developers played an active part providing both cheaper subsidized housing either for sale or for rental through housing associations.

Nevertheless, city planning has to a large extent been the exclusive task of government. However, the emergence of public–private partnership as a strategy for urban regeneration has served to highlight issues and demonstrate the complex problem of revitalizing urban areas. In particular, there are many functions which are connected, and it is necessary to provide a combination of remunerative and non-remunerative elements. At the same time government has been taking a decreasing role in the provision of social housing. Consequently, an important pillar in the urban renewal process was lost, and cities have become more dependent on investment by the private sector. Land prices for housing development in The Netherlands contribute little to the capacity to exploit land for large and difficult urban renewal projects. Consequently, shops and offices form the most important base, resulting in a higher exposure to the property cycle. Also high costs related to infrastructure, roads and public transport, play a dominant role. The experiences of waterfront development in Boston, Baltimore and San Francisco, and in particular those in the London Docklands are well-known, but despite the recorded problems abroad, in The Netherlands, there has remained a strong interest in PPPs.

14.2   WHY PUBLIC–PRIVATE PARTNERSHIPS?

Several factors have contributed towards the growth of public–private partnerships. A key influence is the increasing budgetary problems faced by national and local authorities, and hence their resultant interest in the funds of institutional investors, both national and international. In addition, for the realization of large urban plans, institutional investors are needed for the construction of shops, offices and expensive houses; activities which are increasingly part of plans but are outside the domain of local government. As plans must have conditions within which the private sector can operate, it is desirable to have these parties involved in the initial stages. Furthermore, in an effort to achieve quality, most importantly in public spaces, the plans could not in the first instance be subdivided into private and public segments. Also it is apparent that certain projects to be exploited on a long term basis, by the municipality or the national government, may not be suitable for public–private partnerships.

14.3   ROLE OF LOCAL AUTHORITIES IN PUBLIC–PRIVATE PARTNERSHIPS

The contribution of local authorities within partnerships is varied. In particular, a key ingredient is their expertise and knowledge in the field of physical planning, land provision, housing, infrastructural works and municipal services. In addition, they provide a channel of communication with the residents and give subsidies and guarantees for the exploitation of unprofitable projects such as museums and other cultural provisions.

14.4 ROLE OF PROJECT DEVELOPERS/INVESTORS IN PUBLIC–PRIVATE PARTNERSHIPS

In contrast, the private sector contributes a knowledge of the market and specific products, namely office and shopping centre development, and the ability to undertake feasibility studies and market research activities. Particularly significant is the risk-bearing participation, with the private sector sharing this in terms of land development and through making available professional expertise and money for external advice while plans are still in their initial stages.

A further key role is acting as an intermediary between future users and long term investors and financiers with respect to the projects to be developed. In certain instances the project developer can play an initiating role in parts of the plan and so doing set the realization of the total plan into motion; in other circumstances the institutional investor may fulfil this role.

14.5 RECIPROCAL EXPECTATIONS

The public sector expects: creativity from the side of the developer/investor; the reduction of risks for the public with respect to sustaining and upgrading the total spatial quality; a contribution of financial means by the private sector towards non-remunerative parts of the plan; and continuity of the planning process and upholding of all rights and entitlements of the local authorities and the public. In essence, the public sector is seeking an increase in the chances of the plan being implemented with a guarantee for public interests.

Likewise, the private sector has expectations which include: continuity and consistency in conduct and regulations of authorities, especially newly elected local councils keeping agreements made by their predecessors; clear and rapid decision-making, namely who takes which decisions and at what moment; and a financial contribution to risks in the non-remunerative parts of the project.

14.6 PRINCIPAL FORMS OF PUBLIC–PRIVATE PARTNERSHIPS

With respect to the involvement of government, there are two principal forms of public–private partnerships: indirect and direct. In the former the municipalities lays down the conditions, but it is for the industry to carry out the assignment. Whilst in direct partnerships the local authorities participate in carrying out the assignment whereas the private sector concentrates on the remunerative aspects, and through the operation of profit sharing arrangements the public sector share all the proceeds financing the non-remunerative aspects.

Also, with respect to legal structure, there are two further forms of public–private partnership: co-operative agreement and mutual participation. The co-operation agreement consists of three categories: agreements regarding intentions, framework agreements and detailed agreements. In contrast, the mutual participation is through a legal person (Besloten Vennootschap or Naamloze Vennootschap) or other co-operative form (Vennootschap onder Firma; partnership).

14.7 CURRENT STATE OF AFFAIRS

Public–private partnerships as a mode of urban renewal are not living up to expectations as most projects are currently experiencing stagnation. The length of time taken to make political decisions in the municipalities is often singularly considered to be the cause of problems. Furthermore, conflicts of interest between the public and private parties are not fully considered and pushed into the background. Although intensive negotiations have taken place in recent years, there is still a wide gap between the initial plans to restructure an urban area on the basis of shared risk, and the actual signing of a contract which will eventually lead to the realization of a project.

However, public–private partnership has attracted much interest with respect to urban renewal. The current government explicitly included public–private partnership in the coalition agreement when entering office for the second term in 1986, with these partnerships seen as the expected means to increase investment in urban renewal. In several cities partnerships offerred a new impetus to existing plans and municipalities dynamically entered into negotiations with institutional investors and project developers. The national government played a pioneering role by pinpointing five projects which could serve as a model and allocating resources in the form of subsidies (Kohnstamm and Uittenbogaard, 1991).

For the five renewal projects highlighted by the government in 1988, the municipalities involved and the national authorities agreed on binding contracts regarding subsidies and the objectives to be achieved. In 1990 the contracts were, under the title 'key projects', included in the Fourth Report for Planning Extra.

Other agreements were made between municipalities and private parties. In most instances these contracts referred to the initial stages of a project and did not constitute binding obligations with respect to the financing and realization of plans. This is illustrated by the financing company Amsterdam

Waterfront, which was established for a project on the River IJ in Amsterdam. The participants in this company, so far the Amsterdam City Council, Nationale Nederlanden and the INGbank Group, have an obligation to draw up a business plan. If the parties cannot agree about further co-operation after the business plan is drawn up, they will lose a part of the starting capital, but are free to waive further obligations. The next stage which requires resolution is that of plan realization and risk sharing. The same principle applies to ambitious projects in other large cities; for example, the South Point in Rotterdam, the New Centre in the Hague and the Utrecht City Project. Only the Sphinx–Céramique–Terrain contract in Maastricht included the actual realization of the plan.

14.8   STAGNATION

Research carried out by the Centre of Investment and Real Estate in Amsterdam and involving extensive interviews with parties concerned with public–private partnerships suggests that urban development by means of public–private ownership is a concept that is not sufficiently worked out. In this context reports about the stagnation of projects have credibility. Indeed, it appears to be difficult to sign contracts which proceed beyond the intention agreements. The resultant hesitation is not merely due to the conflict of interests between the parties, but arises from a variety of reasons including: large scale; insecurity with respect to future developments; the absence of clear targets; division of authority; differences of working methods and knowledge; the prolonged non-binding character of the contract; lack of management capacities; lack of experience; and third party involvement. Hence it is not surprising that reports about stagnation continue to increase.

14.9   EXAGGERATED EXPECTATIONS

The abundance of funds available to institutional investors created expectations for public–private partnerships which were highly exaggerated. Firstly, institutional investors are responsible for the management of pension and life insurance funds, and thus evade high risks. Secondly, profit margins in the Dutch property market are restricted. Current high interest rates combined with low inflation rates give a gross yield of between 7 and 8%. City projects, which usually include unprofitable elements, will never yield such margins. Although property offers protection against inflation, in the current market situation this does not weigh up against the risk of non-occupancy or receiving lower rents than expected. Thus from the viewpoint of an investor, property compares unfavourably with alternative investments in these circumstances.

14.10   DIVISION OF AUTHORITY

Contracts curtail the freedom of decision making of the parties involved; the municipalities in particular find this hard to accept. Firstly, because their influence on planning is restricted for a long period of time, they fear that their responsibility to the public will be too restricted by obligations under private law. Secondly, they are not used to dealing with the concept of exertion of public responsibility at a time when the ultimate target is still unclear. Furthermore, the municipal authorities appear to have to cross a mental barrier before they are willing to share power. On the other hand, private parties demand a certain amount of control before they commit themselves to financial risks. Investors will not invest when their public partner has the freedom to take decisions which can have a negative effect on profits. Although private parties wish to have binding obligations, they, in turn, find it difficult to give up decision-making authority. Their resistance is aimed towards obligations which restrict a flexible response to changing market circumstances.

14.11   SCALE

Scale is another recurring and complicating factor. The planning area of public–private partnership projects becomes multifunctional and includes offices, shops, housing, social and cultural provisions. Moreover, every function will consist of several concepts and levels of quality. The result of large scale is that the supply of housing and production space will impact for a considerable period of time, on the market segments, in the region where the project takes place.

14.12   THE LONG TERM

The time involved with urban restructuring leads to many insecurities. Between the first initiative and the actual completion of the last building there can be a time span of 20 years. Predictions about market circumstances, political relations, viewpoints and the economic cycle are impossible over such a period. Private parties therefore consider it irresponsible to commit to obligations as the risks cannot be estimated. The need for flexibility to changing market circumstances is an absolute condition to them. An equally important consideration is the contractual protection of each other's interests, though for both parties it seems increasingly doubtful that these contrasting aspects can be incorporated into one contract. The recent development of Canary Wharf in London is a clear example.

14.13   ORGANIZATION

Public–private partnership in urban renewal is a complex process which is difficult to control. Results from interviews show that decision making for both public and private parties is difficult as each party consists of many sections which all have their own responsibilities. The negotiators are accountable to them. A consensus made at the negotiating table is therefore only the beginning of an agreement. In this way many parties, sections and people are involved in decision-making. The consequence is a prolonged and complex process which repeats itself in every phase of the project. Hence for a long time the parties are not sure whether the results of the negotiations will actually lead to an agreement.

14.14   PUBLIC SUPPORT

It is not easy to obtain large scale public support for urban renewal. Many third party interests are involved, thus current public–private partnership projects aim for market segments in which residents of the surrounding neighbourhoods do not recognize their interests. Moreover, planning requires that construction projects fit into the character of the existing area. The accessibility of the planning area usually requires considerable adjustments. Furthermore, the interests of the people involved are not restricted to the residents of the neighbouring areas but also include residents and companies outside the centre. Formerly the municipalities were solely responsible for obtaining the public support required. However, the private parties can no longer argue that this is the task of the municipality. Scale and public sensitivity demands a clear and, more importantly, unambiguous communication.

14.15   UNCLEAR TARGETS

Parties enter into partnerships without having clear targets in mind. Even after many years of negotiation, parties still expect too much of each other in spite of a co-operation agreement being the principal point of discussion at initial meetings. The traditional confusion between goals and means are characteristic of public–private partnerships. Furthermore, the pioneering role of the national government had a detrimental effect as subsidies were linked to public–private partnership constructions. Hence discussions came to be dominated by the interpretation of plans and in consequence a careful exploration of possibilities and starting points received little attention with most projects. Also plans usually leaked out, raising public criticism about the elitist character of restructured areas before such plans had been fully developed.

14.16   RECOMMENDATIONS

Intensify starting discussion

The importance of an intensive starting discussion has been underestimated, particularly with respect to defining targets. Past experiences have also shown that a basis of trust is imperative and creativity important, as every public–private partnership project will go through times of stagnation. Setbacks have to be overcome and new solutions found to handle changing circumstances. Creativity is seen as an essential element to make complex projects economically and socially successful.

Masterplan

The problems involved with the duration and scale of a project can be managed better if the parties draw up a masterplan together and divide this into small parts at an early stage. A condition is that both parties are involved in drawing up the masterplan with respect to financing as well as the contribution of knowledge. Success depends on the pooling of information and the financial involvement of all parties. The division of the masterplan can relate to either time phases or area sections, for each of which a separate public–private partnership contract can be drawn up.

Decision-making process

Organizational problems and decision-making processes can be improved by defining limited conditions, for each phase of the public–private partnership process, in which a prominent project organization can have a certain freedom of action. The central point in the starting phase is finding a balance between conflicting interests. An independent expert or organization speaking the language of both parties and in charge of the project management can fulfil a critical role. Such external experts function as intermediaries and, together with representatives of the parties concerned, prepare a decision-making framework to focus discussion on the main issues. They have to present clearly defined targets as soon as possible to those responsible for making the final decisions. It is frustrating if, after long discussions, either local government or the investors do not agree with the starting points. However, with the advance of the public–private partnership process and the definition of limited conditions, there are more opportunities to pass down responsibilities. Founding a legal construction in which the parties concerned participate and have freedom to act, within prior conditions, can offer a solution.

Fiscal incentives

Fiscal incentives for property investments in urban areas can considerably increase the feasibility of projects. This instrument has been utilized effectively in the United Kingdom, the USA and Ireland. Examples exist of early write-offs of property investments in specific locations appointed by national governments in urban renewal areas or alternatively making parts of the profit tax deductible. A further mechanism, deductions for value increase due to inflation, may also be considered.

14.17 CONCLUSIONS

Current public–private partnership projects have been started in a climate of high expectations and a large measure of consensus about the necessity to develop high quality urban settlement environments. The impact of these may restrict the spread of office location, which is distinctive of The Netherlands, and reduce the unbalanced population mixture of inner cities.

If a co-operation agreement is dismantled at an early stage, the traditional division of roles reappears and the favourable climate created may disappear. The advantages which public–private partnerships bring are concerted management, the spreading of risk, the attraction of risk-bearing capital and the pooling of knowledge. In the absence of such valuable inputs the chances of securing schemes which exceed beyond the average in terms of quality, are considerably reduced.

The need for co-operation and the acknowledgement that public–private partnership in urban renewal is a concept which is not sufficiently worked out strongly supports the case for continued dialogue between public and private parties. The exchange of knowledge, the search for new possibilities and, above all, clarity about each other's capabilities and restrictions, are vital ingredients.

REFERENCES

Kohnstamm, P.P. and Uittenbogaard, L.B. (1991) Public–private partnerships study, *Economisch Statistische Berichten.*
van der Boor, W.S. (1991) *Stedebouw in Samenwerking, Groningen* [in Dutch, with English summary, pp. 322–323].

15

Waterfront regeneration: the IJ Embankments project in Amsterdam

_____ *F. Witbraad and P. Jorna*

The IJ Embankments project in Amsterdam ranks among the larger projects which The Netherlands expects to implement in the coming decades. The programme is based on a mixture of functions with a floor surface area of 1 000 000 m^2 and together with new infrastructure the project will mean a level of investment expenditure ranging between six and eight thousand million Dutch guilders. Thus IJ Embankments can arguably be included among those waterfront developments which are identified by Torre (1989) as having a world-wide reputation, namely Baltimore, Boston, San Francisco, Sydney and London. More specifically, the Amsterdam example contains three factors of particular relevance to the development opportunity.

1. The availability of large plots of under-utilized land in or very close to the heart of the city. Reasons for land vacancy reflect those of other European cities (such as London) and include: the development of transportation technologies; the switch from boat to air travel causing the dereliction of harbour passenger terminals and piers; the switch to container transport and the deployment of larger vessels leading to the abandonment of freight terminals and the re-positioning of harbour activities, often closer to the sea; and the development of the road network with linkages to ship–truck transportation modes resulting in disused freight rail sidings.
2. Enlargement of the service sector and increased demand for office buildings to be developed on centrally located sites.

3.   The increase in the amount of leisure time available has led to the re-
     discovery of water as a source of urban recreation.

Waterfront developments have several characteristics which require close
collaboration between the public and the private sectors if successful regeneration is to be achieved. Particularly relevant is the capital intensive nature
of the developments, the application of renewal plans, the implementation
of concepts and the large scale construction of new infrastructure. Hence
public–private partnership is providing the mechanism for the development
of the IJ Embankments, making it possible to aim for a high quality regeneration scheme.

15.1   PUBLIC–PRIVATE PARTNERSHIPS

Public–private collaboration is not new and indeed, as discussed by
Kohnstamm (1992), in The Netherlands there have always been partnership
arrangements in the housing sector. In the period following the Second
World War three distinct periods can be distinguished during which public–
private partnerships have been used within the development process.

Period of post-war reconstruction

After the Second World War successive governments positively set out to
stimulate reconstruction activities. Given that consensus existed concerning
the goals to be pursued, the public and private sectors worked with one
another in a spirit of collaboration. In the USA, this period ranged from 1945
to 1965, whereas in The Netherlands a similar, though slightly longer, time
span was apparent from 1945 to 1970.

Period of economic growth

During this period the management of public–private partnerships and their
overall impact declined. Protests against the unbridled and stimulating role
played by government were being heard from various quarters as economic
growth was accompanied by campaigns for wider social justice. This period
extended from 1965 to 1975 in the USA; in The Netherlands, it was from
1970 to 1982.

Period of urban renewal

After a period of urban decay resulting from recession it became clear that
large scale approaches were required to provide solutions to the economic

restructuring of urban areas (de Jong, 1991). The need for renewed public–private collaboration was recognized and, once again, it has proved to be a highly useful mechanism. As in earlier phases of the economic cycle time-scales differ; in the USA this period started in 1975, whereas in The Nether-lands it began in 1982.

Arising from the renewed interest in public–private partnerships in The Netherlands, in 1982 the Amsterdam city authority, seeking to generate ideas, awarded a prize for the best scheme which would provide a possible solution to the development of the waterfront on the IJ Embankments. However, it was not until February 1991 that a public–private joint venture agreement was concluded.

15.2   REVIEW OF LOCAL AUTHORITY PLANNING 1982–91

The 1982 competition had a number of specific objectives: to produce an urban development programme for the area surrounding the Oosterdok; to contribute to a new and restored relationship between Amsterdam and the IJ Embankments; and to receive ideas about how the area, starting from the head of the Oostelijke Handelskade and including the Oosterdok, could be developed in such a way that it would eventually form an integral part of the inner city.

Thus at this stage the city planning authority was seeking ideas which would incorporate a comprehensive regeneration package and a develop-ment strategy. Following this stage an advisory group was established to specifically consider the IJ Embankments. The advisory report produced in 1984 made a number of recommendations which included the following: to revitalize the central part of the IJ Embankments to form an area which would attract the public; to improve the infrastructure connections between the inner city and the IJ Embankments; to create a characteristic image of Amsterdam on the IJ and utilize the environment of the IJ Embankments; to improve accessibility with the north of Amsterdam; to maintain the IJ as a waterway; and to improve the urban environment, maintain environmental quality and provide as much public access as possible.

On the basis of these recommendations a global view of the development was available by May 1985. This further emphasized three key features: to improve the relationship between the inner city and the IJ Embankments by creating public attractions with sufficient appeal and increasing the acces-sibility between both areas; to develop, where possible, typical inner city uses which because of their scale and accessibility requirements are difficult to fit into the inner city's present morphology; and to create the linkage of the inner city to the IJ Embankments.

However, it was not until five years later (January 1990) that proposals emerged. Although adhering to the ideals of the 1985 global development perspective, the basis of the 1990 outline proposal placed much greater emphasis on the type of end-user and the marketing of Amsterdam as a business location. Thus at this stage core elements of the proposal included the following: the need to strengthen the inner city so that it would be regarded as a prime location with possibilities of expansion on the IJ Embankments; the need to develop an environment on the IJ which meets the international standards of ambiance and accessibility, whereby the IJ Embankments functionally supplement the qualities of the inner city; and the need to develop the location in a manner that generates the image of an international business centre.

While the local authority was engaged in planning activities, discussions were continuously held with the private sector about the financing of the development proposals. Initially the larger institutional investors were targeted. However, the discussions did not lead to a commitment because of the perception that development of the IJ Embankments constitutes a risky operation. Much of this risk arises from the lack of available land for development along the IJ axis, and the consequent need to reclaim land necessitates a high expenditure. The problem of reducing or controlling risk in such a complex development scheme further highlights the difficult nature of the assignment.

15.3   AMSTERDAM WATERFRONT FINANCIERINGSMAATSCHAPPIJ

During the period in which the Amsterdam local authority was formulating its land use planning, from 1988, development proposals were continuously being brought forward by project development companies to establish their acceptance and feasibility. The most active role was played by the Maatschappij voor Bedrijfsobjecten (MBO), the project development subsidiary of what was the Nederlandsche Middenstandsbank. Indeed, the activities of the MBO have also influenced the local authority's formulation of their plans and have, among other things, led to a more closely knit set of plans for the area surrounding the Central Station.

At the initiative of the MBO a proposal was detailed to establish a financing company: the Amsterdam Waterfront Financieringsmaatschappij (AWF). The prime task of the AWF was to prepare a business plan for the development and realization of the IJ Embankments incorporating the development programme from a technical, financial and social perspective. The total cost of drawing up the business plan is estimated at 13 million Dutch guilders.

The AWF contains a number of participants: the Amsterdam local authority with a capital holding of 50%, the NMB Postbank group* with a capital holding of 35% and the Nationale Nederlanden* (an insurance group) with a capital holding of 15%.

In the proposals drawn up by MBO (a development company subsidiary

---

* *The NMB Postbank group and the Nationale Nederlanden have now merged into the Internationale Nederlanden Groep (ING).*

of NMB) the legal and fiscal structures are detailed. The report also schedules the way in which the business plan is to be phased, including the working apparatus required for its implementation. In essence it embraces the establishment of a fully independent private company based on an agreement between the AWF and the Amsterdam local authority. The proposal enjoys the support of and is sufficiently well backed by the local authority and the private companies concerned. Negotiations about the form and content of the agreement were completed in 1991.

With respect to the local authority, detailed procedures were prepared to facilitate the decision-making process. These include the following:

1. The memorandum of points of departure published by the Amsterdam local authority was taken as the point of departure for the business plan.
2. The Council of the local authority decided to draw up a zoning plan at the same time the business plan was being prepared to act as a frame of reference. This zoning plan offers the private sector the security that the necessary building permits will be issued.
3. The Council decided to participate in the private enterprise. The AWF reserved an amount of 6.5 million Dutch guilders.
4. The Council decided to sign an agreement with the AWF as a private company; with this, the public–private partnership was sealed.

15.4   BUSINESS PLAN

This represents a critical stage of the process with the development of the IJ Embankments dependent on its outcome. The business plan was to be prepared within one year with completion on 1 October 1992. A period during the last quarter of 1992 was made available for negotiations and consultations, after which, in 1993, decisions are to be finalized. Regarding the bodies to the agreement, the local authority can test the business plan using the memorandum of points of departure and the zoning plan. In contrast the private sector is to primarily undertake its testing using the profitability criteria included in the agreed covenant.

The business plan is to be drawn up in a number of phases or scenarios of which the following may be distinguished: the programmatic scenario; the spatial scenario; the financial–economic scenario; and the social scenario.

Programmatic scenario

The specific attributes which Amsterdam possesses can be classified under two themes: Amsterdam as a city of knowledge and as a city of tolerance in which new trends, ideas and cultures are visible. Indeed, Amsterdam may arguably be considered as the spiritual capital of Europe, a profile which matches the character of the inner city and which should lead to the strengthening of its position. Research conducted for the programmatic content shows that distinction ought to be made between three separate clusters: the creative, the experiential and the organizational. Depending on the quality of the location and the character of the inner city behind it, the clusters have been positioned within various subareas.

Considering the use of themes the IJ Embankments demonstrate clearly their suitability for small and medium sized businesses; furthermore, entrepreneurs, due to their locational preferences, are led by and sensitive to the experiential factor of the inner city and the services already located there. Such businesses demonstrate a wide variety of dynamics concerning the amplitude of companies and their corporate activities as well as the dynamics of their behaviour in choosing a location. In this respect it is therefore important that the programme has a dynamic character.

In addition, given the long development time span required, the programme must also ensure that functions are interchangeable. Flexibility is necessary to guarantee an efficient response to ever-changing social and economic circumstances without undermining the desired programmatic, spatial and economic qualities. In ensuring the quality of the location high density needs to be supported by a degree of functional mixing. Hence the spatial scenario has been designed on the basis of the aforementioned themes and the programmatic colouring from subarea to subarea. Thus the physical development, which is composed on the basis of the programmatic as well as the spatial scenarios, incorporates dwellings (425 000 m^2), commercial functions (675 000 m^2) and public functions (150 000 m^2), producing a total planned development of 1 250 000 m^2.

Spatial scenario

The island structure along the IJ is to undergo a renaissance with each island given its own identity. With respect to construction the largest concentration is to the eastern side of Central Station where the intelligent office city of the 21st century is to be realized (Figure 15.1). The Station Island is to accommodate, on its waterfront, a raised promenade above which will be housed urban cultural functions including a library and a centre for contemporary music. Flanking this both to the east and the west will be the new residential development. Design quality is to be emphasized throughout, not only in terms of the buildings, which will be based on progressive architecture, but also in the varied atmospheres of public areas. The latter will be completed using squares, parks, piers, quaysides and harbours.

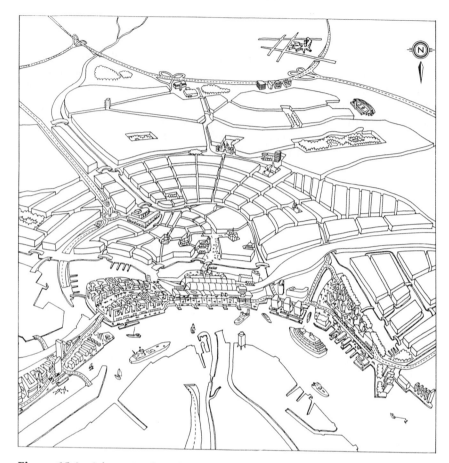

Figure 15.1   Schematic plan of IJ Embankments

The city side of Central Station is to be redesigned using squares which will be interconnected in such a way that an attractive route is created from the city to and along the IJ. This will serve to both strengthen the inner city and link it to the waterfront. The vision for the IJ Embankments of the 21st century is for an extension of the rich urban tradition reaching back to and harmonizing with the development of the Canal Zone in the 17th century, the Southern Extension Plan at the beginning of the 20th century (Amsterdam Physical Planning Department, 1983) and, rather later, the western garden suburbs laid out in accordance with the CIAM concept (van der Heiden and Wallagh, 1991).

Financial–economic scenario

Regarding the financial organizational structure of the AWF the land bank plays an important part, namely regulating the acquisition of land, making plots ready for construction and issuing leasehold agreements. This phase involves the largest financial risks for the whole project with the shares held by the public and private partners determining the degree to which the financial risks for the project as a whole are spread among the partners. Concerning the organization of the AWF, the development company acquires land for construction and realizes the various components of the programme. Following the development phase responsibility then passes to the management company.

Outturn performance accrues from the revenue derived from the buildings less the construction costs, thereby providing a valuation of the land input. However, projections need to allow for the phasing of the project over the 15 year period from 1995–2010. The financial result, subtracting state subsidies, indicates that the investment levels required can be completely covered by revenues in spite of the high outlay necessary to overcome physical/subsoil problems.

Investment levels amount to 6500 million Dutch guilders broken down as 4000 million in buildings, 500 million for land costs and a further 2000 million to cover the main infrastructural schemes. Concerning expected income the annual rental level of office space, depending on location, is within the range 250 to 450 guilders/m^2 and the purchase price of residential property between 2000 and 3500 guilders/m^2. The programmatic and spatial flexibility within the scenarios allows for financial risks to be properly managed at the earliest possible stage. Furthermore, management of the financial result is possible within the agreed margins; in this context an important tool in risk management is the implementation of market research activities to evaluate the effects of changing social and economic circumstances.

In addition, there is the wider economic impact as the investment will generate about 30 000 jobs during the realization of the project. Activities will provide Amsterdam with a positive balance of 300 million guilders, stabilizing after realization to 70 million guilders annually. The Gross National Product will through time rise by 0.6%, or 3000 million guilders annually as a consequence of the project. After realization the extra income to the state is likely to stabilize at 1000 million guilders.

Social scenario

The process of formulating the plan is continuously subject to the scrutiny of social/community organizations, namely: the Chamber of Commerce; the Amsterdam City Association, embracing retailers and community workers; house boat residents and the captains of inland waterways vessels.

Thirteen organizations, including the aforementioned, have drawn up a so-called 'programme of social demands' which was submitted to the local authority and the AWF. This programme forms the testing frame of reference by which these social organizations can assess the proposals made by AWF. The demands are both rigorous and wide ranging, including: the coherence and management of the spatial developments in the city and the region must be visibly reflected in the IJ Embankments project; the use of officially appointed plan limits should not adversely affect the flexibility of the development of the plans; the existing qualities of the location must be utilized in the development of the plans; in the construction of new infrastructure slow traffic must receive as much attention as public transport and rapid traffic; the future users of the public areas must be offered accessible and attractive places in which to sojourn; in determining the functions within the plan area, the desired present and future end users must remain points of departure; social influence on the development of the plans must be guaranteed and, for the implementation phase, ensured; decision making regarding the financing of the IJ Embankments project must be reviewable and financial yields must in part at least be deployed to realize social demands; in the business plan of the financing company, recession resistant phasing of the implementation must be included; independent committees ought to be appointed for the assessment and management of the quality of the built environment and the public areas; the creation of jobs on the IJ must, in the first instance, be undertaken by improving schooling and labour training; the negative effects of the IJ Embankments project must be signalled well in advance by periodic impact reports; and the possibility and options for repaying loan finance requires research in the short term.

15.5   CONCLUSIONS

A common feature of waterfront regeneration initiatives is the long time scale required from conception to completion. Rehabilitating and reintegrating substantial tracts of derelict and under-utilized waterfront land, or the reclamation of land, cannot be accomplished in the short term. Major waterfront schemes inevitability require extensive infrastructural works to make the area ripe for development.

In the vision of the AWF three goals are pivotal to the realization of plans for the IJ Embankments: the neglected areas which have changed functions need to be made part of the city; the need to strengthen the economic structure of the inner city; and the need to ensure for high quality development of an international standing.

The enormity of the project is dependent on public–private collaboration and partnership arrangements which are now in place. A further critical factor is the need to consult the various community groups through participation procedures at various stages in the development of this project. To achieve the regeneration objectives it is therefore necessary to manage the process in an efficient and co-ordinated manner. This calls for a strategic approach involving the preparation of a zoning plan to establish the development potential and bring about the integration of the scheme with the existing city core.

The purpose of the business plan is to undertake a financial and economic appraisal, to facilitate funding and encourage investment, and ultimately to translate the proposed scheme into reality. Projections indicate the profitability of the scheme as well as highlighting the wider economic gain to the city of Amsterdam and indeed to the economy of The Netherlands.

REFERENCES

Amsterdam Physical Planning Department (1983) *Amsterdam Planning and Development*, Amsterdam Physical Planning Department, Amsterdam.

de Jong, M.W. (1991) Diversifying a service economy – building on strong sectors in Amsterdam. In: *Urban Regeneration in a Changing Economy* (Eds J. Fox-Przeworski, J. Goddard and M.W. de Jong), Clarendon Press, Oxford, pp. 217–231.

Kohnstamm, P.P. (1992) The role of the private sector in housing. In: *Housing the Community 2000* (Ed. G. Sweeney), Built Environment Research Centre, Dublin Institute of Technology, Dublin.

Torre, L.A. (1989) *Waterfront Development*, Van Nostrand Reinhold, New York.

van der Heiden, N. and Wallagh, G. (1991) How the Republic of Amsterdam got the Kingdom of the Netherlands to play its game, *Built Environment*, **17**(1), 34–42.

16

Enterprise Zones: property development and investment

———— *M. Brodtman and R. Johnson*

Enterprise Zones first came to public attention in a speech by Sir Geoffrey Howe to the influential Bow Group in 1978 (Bruinvels and Rodrigues, 1989). In the following year the concept emerged as a key element in the policy package introduced by the then newly elected Conservative Government to rejuvenate inner city areas and other unemployment blackspots. Enterprise Zones were specifically created with the intention of providing the right environment in which free enterprise and market forces could flourish, thereby stimulating investment and development activity and leading to job creation. The 1980 consultation paper stated that 'the purpose of these zones is to test as an experiment, and on a few sites, how far industrial and commercial activity can be encouraged by the removal of certain fiscal burdens, and by the removal or streamlined administration of certain statutory or administrative controls'.

16.1 ENTERPRISE ZONE DESIGNATION

Enterprise Zones have been designated in three phases. The first and possibly the most dramatic was in 1981–2, which concentrated on the major conurbations. The intention was to offer a radical solution to areas with high unemployment and physical disrepair. This phase included London (Isle of Dogs), the West Midlands (Dudley), Manchester (Salford Quays and Trafford Park), Newcastle (Tyneside), Glasgow (Clydebank) and Belfast (North Foreshore and Inner City Zone).

The second period of designation in 1983–4 incorporated smaller urban areas which would otherwise not have attracted the interest of the private sector and included such diverse locations as Londonderry, Rotherham, Scunthorpe and Wellingborough. The third phase, spanning several years, has largely been a response to the closure of industries in towns which became over-dependent on a single source of employment. These have included three shipbuilding locations at Chatham, Inverclyde and Sunderland, and most recently the industrial steel area of Lanarkshire.

In total, 28 zones have been designated since 1981 in selected areas where the particular combination of taxation and other benefits were considered desirable to promote the restructuring of local and regional economies (Figure 16.1). Specific details on the various zones are summarized in Table 16.1.

16.2   STATUTORY BACKGROUND

Legislation enabling Enterprise Zone designation was introduced under the terms of the Local Government, Planning and Land Act 1980, Schedule 32 [for Northern Ireland, the Enterprise Zones (NI) Order 1981]. The regulations set out three stages for the creation of an Enterprise Zone. In the first stage, an invitation to prepare a scheme for an Enterprise Zone is given by the Secretary of State to specified bodies, namely district councils, London borough councils, New Town Corporations or Urban Development Corporations. The second stage involves the preparation, publicity and adoption of the scheme. Notice of adoption must be advertised by the scheme-making body and a copy of the adopted scheme sent to the Secretary of State. In stage three, the Secretary of State has a discretion by order, in the form of a statutory instrument to designate an area as an Enterprise Zone. The order must: (1) specify the date of the designation taking effect; (2) specify the period for which the area is to remain an Enterprise Zone; (3) define the boundaries of the zone by means of a plan or map; and (4) designate as the Enterprise Zone Authority the body which was invited to prepare the scheme.

16.3   BENEFITS WITHIN AN ENTERPRISE ZONE

Benefits available to both new and existing industrial and commercial enterprises operating within a designated zone have effect for a ten year period (Heap, 1991). The nature of incentives are wide-ranging and include the following: exemption from rates on industrial and commercial property; exemption from Development Land Tax before its abolition in April 1985; 100% allowances for corporation and income tax purposes for capital expenditure on new and unused industrial and commercial buildings; employers

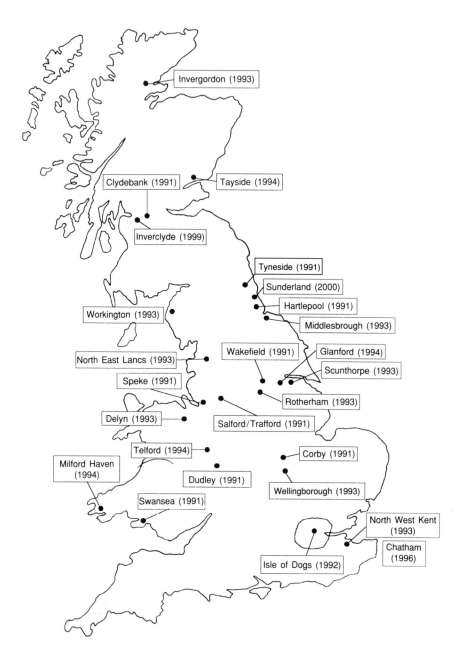

Figure 16.1 Enterprise Zones in Great Britain: location and date of expiry

Table 16.1 Designation details of Enterprise Zones

Location	No. of sites	Approx. site area (ha)	Expiry date of zone
Belfast	2	207	21 October 1991
Chatham Maritime	5	210	10 October 1996
Clydebank	1	190	1 August 1991
Corby	3	113	22 June 1991
Delyn (Flint)	1	118	21 July 1993
Derry/Londonderry	2	109	13 September 1993
Dudley	1	219	10 July 1991
Glanford (Flixborough)	1	50	30 April 1991
Hartlepool	3	109	23 October 1991
Inverclyde	11	111	5 March 1999
Invergordon	2	60	7 October 1993
Isle of Dogs (London Docklands)	1	195 (incl. water)	26 April 1992
Middlesbrough	1	79	8 November 1993
Milford Haven	13	146	23 April 1994
North-east Lancashire	7	114	7 December 1993
North-west Kent	7	152	3 October 1993
Rotherham	1	105	16 August 1993
Salford/Trafford	5	352	12 August 1993
Scunthorpe	2	105	23 September 1993
Speke (Liverpool)	2	138	25 August 1991
Sunderland	3	34	28 April 2000
Swansea	1	298	11 June 1991
Tayside	7	120	9 January 1994
Telford	5	113	13 January 1994
Tyneside	4	194	25 August 1991
Wakefield	3	57	31 July 1991
Wellingborough	1	55	26 July 1993
Workington	6	87	4 October 1993

exemption from industrial training levies and from the requirement to provide information to Industrial Training Boards under the Employment and Training Act 1981; a greatly simplified planning regime, in essence meaning that those developments falling within the criteria of the published scheme for each zone do not require individual planning permission; speedy handling of minor administrative details; relaxations in processing procedures providing greater speed in dealing with customs matters for firms in Enterprise Zones; and reduced government requests for statistical information.

Rates

Within Enterprise Zones, any hereditament is exempt from local authority business rates unless it is a dwelling house, a private garage or private storage premises. Consequently there is a general exemption for industrial and commercial property (including retail), but not for water services or other charges. Notification of the rates that would have been payable is issued to owners for record purposes and to indicate the usual assessment of rateable value which is required for other purposes.

In those few instances where there are mixed domestic and business properties the rateable value is apportioned between the two elements, with the business part exempt. No special application for rates exemption is needed as the rating authority will apply a blanket policy. However, the exemption of hereditaments from rates within Enterprise Zones will result in a consequential loss of revenue to the local authority for the area in which the zone is located. To cover this loss, the Secretary of State, with Treasury consent, must compensate the local authority for their rate revenue loss (Schedule 32, Local Government Planning and Land Act 1980). Research indicates that the benefit of the rates 'holiday' is shared between the landlord and the tenant as in many instances rents inside the zones are normally higher than those outside.

Development land tax

Subsequent to the introduction of the Enterprise Zone concept, development land tax has been abolished. However, during the period in which this exemption was effective, it provided a valuable incentive to develop within Enterprise Zones as the rate at which the tax was levied was usually 60%. Hence this incentive and benefit was primarily targeted at the developer.

Capital allowances

A special scheme, broadly similar to that of industrial building allowances, operates in Enterprise Zones. The provisions of the Capital Allowances Act 1968 were initially applied to Enterprise Zones by Section 74 of the Finance Act 1980 and later updated by the Capital Allowances Act 1990. The legislation provides an initial allowance for corporation or income tax purposes of 100% of the value of the works or capital expenditure incurred on the construction, extension or improvement of industrial and commercial building.

The entire allowance can be taken initially or it can be reduced to any amount the owner wishes, in which instance the balance will be received in straight line, annual writing-down allowances of 25%. For example, if 40% is claimed initially, the writing-down allowances over three years will be 25, 25 and 10%, respectively. If the building is brought into use in the same year as that in which the expenditure is incurred, an initial allowance will be given for that year (Department of the Environment, 1991). On the sale of the building within 25 years of its first having been brought into use, a balancing charge or allowance will be made in accordance with the normal industrial building allowance rules. This is often avoided by the sale of a 'lesser interest', normally a long leasehold interest of, say, 999 years if a freehold is held.

Owners are eligible for the capital allowances whether they occupy their buildings themselves or let the premises. The allowances apply to capital expenditure incurred within the Enterprise Zones' initial ten year period, and also to expenditure incurred later under a binding contract entered into within that period.

In the case of hotels and industrial buildings where other capital allowance provisions exist, the Enterprise Zone allowances apply. Under these other capital allowance provisions the initial allowances are considerably less generous: 4% per annum for industrial buildings and 20% for qualifying hotels. They also apply to all offices and to other commercial buildings used for trading or professional purposes, but not to dwelling houses.

In practice the availability of capital allowances has the effect of reducing the net of tax cost of a property or increasing the gross yield on investments by the marginal rate of income/corporation tax applicable to that particular investor. This is currently 40% for a private taxpayer in the United Kingdom and 33% for a company paying corporation tax. The practical benefits are demonstrated by the following calculation illustrating the impact on an investment acquisition.

In this example it is considered that a project of £1 000 000 is sold with a rental income of £85 000 per annum and an assumed land value of £100 000. The investment return without the Enterprise Zone allowances would be 8.5%; with the allowances the return is 13.28% to an individual paying the highest marginal rate of tax of 40%, and 12.09% to a company paying corporation tax at 33%.

Rental income per annum (£)	85 000	
Purchase price (£)	1 000 000	
Deductible land cost (£)	100 000	
Tax deductible element (£)	900 000	
Tax saving at 40% (£)	(360 000)	33% (297 000)
Land cost to be added back (£)	100 000	100 000
Net purchase price (£)	640 000	703 000
Investment return on net price	13.28%	12.09%

Industrial Training Boards

Industrial Training Boards can impose a levy on employers and demand information from them. These powers do not apply to establishments in

Enterprise Zones. Grants and advice on training may, however, still be available from Industrial Training Boards.

Simplified planning regime

When an Enterprise Zone is designated an approved planning scheme is published. This sets out the types of development for which planning permission is deemed to be granted, without an individual planning application being required. The automatic granting of planning permission will, however, be subject to such conditions or limitations as are specified in the Enterprise Zone scheme. Health, safety, parking and pollution standards are normally included and a limited number of matters are reserved for approval by the Enterprise Zone authority. Any development proposal which does not conform with the conditions of the particular scheme will require individual planning permission in the normal way. Where individual applications are needed, there are special arrangements to ensure that these are determined speedily.

As most forms of development in Enterprise Zones are granted planning permission by virtue of the Enterprise Zone scheme, there should in general be less cause for appeals to the Secretary of State within the designated area compared with elsewhere. However, where appeals do arise, the parties involved may obtain from the Department of the Environment a copy of an advice note on the operation of the Enterprise Zone Planning System in England and Wales.

Speedier administration

Every effort is made to ensure that administrative matters in Enterprise Zones are handled as quickly as possible. Most Enterprise Zone authorities have set themselves the target of deciding any residual planning applications and building regulation approvals within 14 days wherever possible. The local authority will deal with queries on land availability and release, highways, access and public transport as a matter of priority. Likewise the suppliers of gas, electricity, water, sewerage and telecommunications services have put in place special arrangements to promptly consider requests from operators within Enterprise Zones. Specifications on adoption standards and other requirements relating to water and sewerage mains can be obtained from the appropriate authorities.

Customs facilities

Applications from firms within Enterprise Zones for 'inward processing relief' and from general customs warehouses will be processed as a matter of priority by Customs and Excise. The criteria applying to decisions on private customs warehouses will also be relaxed. Inward processing relief is an arrangement which allows goods to be imported for processing and subsequently exported outside the European Community without payment of customs charges. General customs warehouses which are independently owned and operated can be established with authorization from Customs and Excise for the storage of imported goods, again without payment of customs charges. In private customs warehouses traders are allowed to store their own goods; normally such facilities are granted only where a substantial proportion of export trade can be shown. Applications for customs relief are dealt with by local offices of the Collector of Customs and Excise.

Reduction in statistical requirements

Firms' activities within Enterprise Zones are excluded from the scope of compulsory government statistical requirements. The only exception is the Census of Employment, which is simple to complete and is no longer held annually. Normal administrative returns, such as those required for the collection of VAT, do, however, continue.

16.4 DEVELOPMENT ACTIVITY

Development activity within Enterprise Zones has attracted a wide range of use categories. Of particular significance, however, is the level of new office accommodation. The following three examples from London, Tyneside and Salford demonstrate the ability of inner city areas to promote themselves as quality office locations.

London Docklands

London Docklands has been the most important and publicly visible of all the Enterprise Zones. Since its designation in July 1981, the 195 ha within the Enterprise Zone comprising redundant wharves, dockyards and associated areas have attracted continuous attention. The designated zone is situated approximately 3 km to the east of the city centre. However, the proximity belies the problem of transport in east London. Consequently, substantial infrastructure projects have been required, including the Docklands Light Railway which links the area to the London Underground network, and a dual carriageway linking the City with the A13.

The main development and the largest commercial project in Europe, Canary Wharf, is located within the Enterprise Zone. Over 380 000 m² have been completed, with the capability of increasing this to nearly 1 200 000 m² of commercial space. Although the Canary Wharf scheme and the London Docklands area in general have been the victim of poor transportation links and the depressed property market of the early 1990s, considerable achievements have nevertheless been made in attracting companies to the area. Development activity has been on a massive scale with 700 000 m² of new offices having been completed since the inception of the Enterprise Zone (London Docklands Development Corporation, 1992).

Tyneside

This Enterprise Zone, also designated in 1981, consists of several parcels of land. The most significant of these, an area to the south-west of Newcastle city centre, displayed considerable urban deprivation with associated industrial decay and high unemployment. The zone has been developed in a unified manner to provide a high quality business park attracting office occupiers, including a government department, the Automobile Association and the British Airways ticketing office.

Salford Quays

The shoreline of the 19th century industrial waterway, the Manchester Ship Canal, was the choice for the Salford Quays Enterprise Zone. Although situated close to Manchester city centre this area, characterized by high unemployment and industrial malaise, was one of the most difficult environments in north-west England for private sector investment. However, since designation, the zone has witnessed over 100 000 m² of high specification office development including some of the most prestigious projects outside of London.

16.5   INVESTMENT ACTIVITY

In promoting the Enterprise Zone scheme the intention of government was to encourage new investors and occupiers to areas which would, in all likelihood, have remained otherwise unattractive. The initial response was characterized by a high degree of scepticism. It was considered that investors (mainstream developers and financial institutions) might be deterred from having to undertake large scale land acquisition and investment in places they hitherto tended to avoid. However, Cadman (1982) argued that long term institutional investors could be persuaded to abandon their conventional criteria and invest in areas which do not justify expectations of security of

Table 16.2 Investments and trust sales in Enterprise Zones

	Investments available/sold (£ million)		
	1989–90	1990–1	1991–2
London Docklands	302/69	175/91	249/3
Manchester	247/105	112/87	27/22
Remainder	196/76	203/119	192/175
Total of all zones	745/250	498/302	468/200
Trust sales/percentage of sales	135/54	145/48	169/80

income and rental growth. The time-scale of the incentives, and the quality or image of the areas designated, were seen by McDonald and Howick (1982) as being crucial to the Enterprise Zone concept.

Although scepticism was justified to some extent, the volume of investment activity generated within Enterprise Zones has been remarkably high. New money has been invested in real estate, most of which has come from property companies and from individuals through Enterprise Zone unit trusts (Table 16.2). The impact of these unit trusts has been especially influential, dominating the market from 1988 to the end of the tax year 1991–2 (Johnson, 1991). Comprehensive analysis of the sources and destinations of investment flows in Enterprise Zone markets undertaken by St Quintin's (Chartered Surveyors) indicates that the depression which afflicted the institutional investment markets during the late 1980s did not leave the flow of investment into Enterprise Zones undiminished.

Investors in Enterprise Zones are broadly divisible into three categories: private individuals, the corporate sector and financial organizations. Private individuals either make investments directly, by participation in syndicates, or as investors in Enterprise Zone trusts. These are now the largest participants in the market. In comparison the corporate sector has traditionally focused on the opportunities presented in Enterprise Zones to buy property investments at enhanced yields. This route was especially popular at a time when large corporate profits were being made and with relatively few opportunities to shelter from corporation tax. Banks and other financial organizations have also participated in the market by the provision of long term finance through leasing.

Approximately £150 million per annum has been invested in the Enterprise Zone property unit trusts. These are unauthorized unit trusts regulated by the Financial Services Act 1986, enabling private individuals and companies to invest, in units of £1000, in substantial properties located within Enterprise Zones. Benefits attributable to owners of property in Enterprise Zones are also available to the trusts and thereby to the individual unit holders. In addition, further benefits are often gained as investors will frequently borrow the non-tax element of the purchase price of the units with the result that any interest due on these borrowings can be offset against the rental income.

16.6   CASE STUDY: SUNDERLAND

Doxford International is a 32 ha site of which 20 ha lie within the Sunderland Enterprise Zone. In response to the decline of the shipbuilding and steel-making industries four areas of Sunderland were granted Enterprise Zone status in April 1990, with Doxford being the largest. Enterprise Zone des-ignation has helped in the economic restructuring of Sunderland and the surrounding region. Significant financial services employment has been attracted and Nissan has recently chosen Washington, which is within Sunderland's boundaries, as their new European headquarters. This has resulted in an investment of £900 million with over 3000 jobs created directly and a further 10 000 jobs indirectly. About 33 American and 40 Japanese companies have opened in the last decade.

Doxford International is a greenfield site located to the west of Sunder-land city centre. Development on the site has been commissioned to Doxford International plc, a joint venture company, following open competition in early 1991. The marketing programme for the scheme, which began in mid-1991, identified a considerable latent demand for high quality office buildings. Occupiers were attracted by rates exemption together with the facilities provided in a landscaped business park and the excellent communications. Furthermore, as negotiations with potential occupiers became much easier once construction had begun on site, Doxford therefore identified the need to fund substantial speculative development to maintain progress. The finance to achieve this was raised by selling off the first phase, consisting of four office buildings with a total net area of 10 500 m^2, to an Enterprise Zone property unit trust (Brodtman, 1992).

Marketing and detailed negotiations resulted in an early conclusion of terms with Property Enterprise Trust, the originator of the Enterprise Zone property unit trusts. The contract for the sale, development and income guarantee was completed in February 1992 and on the same date Doxford received the full proceeds of sale, the sum of £18 080 000. Consequently, the next phase of the construction programme also began in February 1992, with anticipated completion in March 1993.

Under the terms of the transaction the developer is obliged to construct the buildings to pre-agreed plans and specification, and to obtain a bank guarantee to secure completion of the works. The developer is also to seek out end-users at a minimum rent of £120/m^2 on modern institutional 25 year lease terms. In recognition of the early payment of the full proceeds, the developer will provide income to the trust at £120/m^2, secured by means of guarantee leases from practical completion. These leases are to be supported by a minimum five year bank guarantee from practical completion, although all leases and guarantees may be surrendered when granted to suitable occupational tenants. The trust receives a return of 7.5% per annum payable quarterly in advance, of which 0.25% is deducted by the trust managers, providing a net yield to investors of 7.25%. This equates to a net post-tax yield to personal tax investors of 11.7%, and to high rate corporation tax-payers of 10.6%. Borrowing facilities were arranged by the trust with the Bank of Scotland, whereby the full amount of the non-tax element of the purchase price of units could be borrowed on a floating or fixed rate basis.

Doxford agreed terms with the trust in November 1991, and the trust's sponsors began seeking subscriptions from private and corporate investors immediately thereafter. The sponsors also obtained full underwriting to enable the trust to be formed on a pre-agreed date whether or not sufficient subscription had been raised by that date. In the event, the trust was approximately 70% subscribed at the date of closure, and underwritten units were marketed to investors thereafter with the full availability of capital allowances.

Third party underwriting allowed the developer to place the building contract before the trust was formed, in the knowledge that full subscription would be available to allow the development to proceed. The proceeds of the trust sale are sufficient to enable the developer to complete the works and provide the necessary guarantees; profit will be taken when the buildings are let to occupational tenants.

Hence the sale of Phase I at Doxford International allowed a specially formed development vehicle to undertake a substantial project in response to the demands of occupational tenants. Funding was made available on a speculative basis by using 100% first year capital allowances available in Enterprise Zones to attract about 500 private investors in a specifically created Enterprise Zone property unit trust.

Although complex, and at present only available to the developers of Enterprise Zone property, the transaction clearly demonstrates the benefits of tax allowances to local economies, and the demand from the private sector both for a tax shelter and for property investments. In an era of recession and limited liquidity from banks and traditional institutional investors in property, such mechanisms have far wider applications. Such case study evidence demonstrates the need for government to consider extending Enterprise Zone regulations as an effective method of promoting economic development.

16.7 CONCLUSIONS

In the 1990s, with the Enterprise Zones coming to the end of their designation period, transitional arrangements have been embodied in legislation.

With respect to the key issue of transition arrangements for capital allowances, the solution has been for owners of sites to enter into building contracts before the expiry of the zone, thus enabling a sale with allowances to an eventual purchaser after the zone has ended (Watson, 1991).

In all Enterprise Zones, immediately following the expiry of benefits, a period of consolidation can be expected to allow on- and off-zone rental and capital value differentials to be eliminated (McDougall and Filer, 1990). It is argued that alternatively a lowering of values in the zones to eliminate these differentials is unlikely to materialize because of a reluctance on the part of most occupiers, owners and investors to sell property at a perceived loss. Furthermore, the Inland Revenue (in March 1992) also introduced regulations to ensure that those investing in trusts after the termination of an Enterprise Zone would be entitled to the allowances available as if the trust had purchased the property before the expiration of the zone (Inland Revenue, 1992). In addition, the Government has designated new Enterprise Zones at Inverclyde and Lanarkshire with the specific objective of dealing with industrial closures and alleviating the long term problems in each of the respective areas.

Where an adequate infrastructure, a sufficiently vibrant local economy and taxation advantages are available, Enterprise Zone designation can contribute to the early and rapid redevelopment of the economic base of an area. The physical improvement within designated areas can have an important economic and physiological impact, with real benefit being provided both within zones and to their surrounding local economies. However, the cost effectiveness of the experiment could be improved, particularly with regard to reducing the amount of deadweight on both capital allowances and rate relief. This could be differentiated across zones and between economic sectors or tapered downwards through time (Department of the Environment, 1987).

REFERENCES

Brodtman, M. (1992) The funding of an Enterprise Zone: Doxford International, Phase 1, *Journal of Property Finance*, **3**(1), 24–27.

Bruinvels, P. and Rodrigues, D. (1989) *Investing in Enterprise*. Basil Blackwell, Oxford, pp. 156–216.

Cadman, D. (1982) Urban change, Enterprise Zones and the role of investors, *Built Environment*, **7**(1), 13–19.

Department of the Environment (1987) *An Evaluation of the Enterprise Zone Experiment*, HMSO, London.

Department of the Environment (1991) *Enterprise Zone Information, 1988–1989*, HMSO, London.

Heap, D. (1991) *An Outline of Planning Law*, Sweet & Maxwell, London.

Inland Revenue (1992) *New Regulations defining Enterprise Zone Property Trusts,* Inland Revenue Press Office, London.

Johnson, R.A. (1991) To invest or not to invest? *Estates Gazette,* **9115**, 76–77.

London Docklands Development Corporation (LDDC) (1992) *Isle of Dogs Enterprise Zone,* LDDC, London.

McDonald, I. and Howick, C. (1982) Monitoring the Enterprise Zones, *Built Environment,* **7**(1), 31–37.

McDougall, B. and Filer, A. (1990) What happens when the benefits go? *Estates Gazette,* **9015**, 20–22.

Watson, J. (1991) Capital allowances and the maturity of EZs, *Estates Gazette,* **9118**, 105.

17

Evaluation of Urban Development Corporations

M. Bintley

Since the 1930s the United Kingdom has experienced difficulties associated with economic restructuring. This has manifested itself in the inability of traditional manufacturing industry to compete, together with increased rates of unemployment among particular sectors of the population. Although new employment opportunities have emerged in the service sector, the demands in terms of skills, premises and location are markedly different. Physically and economically this restructuring has resulted in vacant and under-used docks and factory premises, an outdated infrastructural base unable to meet the needs of modern enterprise and a general loss of confidence in urban areas by potential investors. Consequently, the traditional centres of industry and employment in the United Kingdom found themselves in the difficult position of requiring major investment to adapt premises and provide the necessary infrastructure needed by modern industry. For the most part, the private sector has found this scale of investment difficult to finance.

After the Second World War, central government attempted to address these problems through the auspices of regional policy by influencing the location of employment investment, through the use of incentives, in the declining industrial areas. However, an unintentional consequence of regional policy has been its contribution to inner city decline. For example, between 1974 and 1979 the Department of Industry gave £250 million in regional assistance to Merseyside, most of which went for development in greenfield locations (Lawless, 1989). The problems of industrial decline, combined with the location and relocation of industrial investment in peripheral greenfield sites has had a marked impact on the inner areas of towns and cities. Planned redevelopment in outer areas exacerbated the problem further by encouraging the outmigration of the younger and more skilled sectors of the population. Thus the inner city became synonymous as an area of dereliction suffering from congested roads with a poor environmental image, populated by the elderly, low skilled and disadvantaged sectors of society. Central government started to address the problem in the late 1960s through the Urban Programme. At that time the Urban Programme had a social focus, although by the late 1970s policy had shifted to an economic emphasis, culminating in the Inner Urban Areas Act 1978.

In 1979 urban policy experienced a further change in emphasis with the election of Margaret Thatcher and a right wing Conservative Government, committed to free enterprise by rolling back the powers of the state. The basic tenets of Thatcherism were that government was too big, too powerful and too involved in economic affairs and should be restricted in favour of the private sector. In essence, it was considered that a more effective and sensitive guidance of growth could be exercised by market forces compared with the planned intervention of the state (Barnekov et al., 1989). Therefore, the private sector was encouraged to take the lead in inner city regeneration, with the public sector acting in a facilitating capacity. The Conservative Government considered that public agencies directly controlled by the state were a more appropriate mechanism to assist in levering private sector investment. Urban Development Corporations (UDCs) articulate this vision most dramatically (Parkinson, 1990).

17.1   CONCEPT OF URBAN DEVELOPMENT CORPORATIONS

The proposal to establish UDCs was announced in September 1979 as part of a review of inner city policy undertaken by Michael Heseltine, the then Secretary of State for the Environment. The first two development corporations were established in London and Merseyside Docklands. The Minister's justification for these was as follows: '. . . the existing machinery streamlined and adjusted will be capable of carrying developments forward in the inner cities and enable local government and the private sector to fulfil their respective roles. For London Docklands and the Merseyside Dock Area I do not think that the present arrangements can meet the particular problems and opportunities of these areas. In both there is a need for a single-minded determination, not possible for the local authorities concerned, with their much broader responsibilities'.

In short, it was contended that the creation of single-minded agencies with specific objectives, operating in a clearly defined area, could achieve regeneration quicker than by providing the local authorities with the necessary resources. Furthermore, UDCs would be able to adopt administrative procedures to facilitate the speedy implementation of projects. Perhaps more importantly, the UDCs offered the private sector greater political stability, which was perceived to be an incentive to investment (Adcock, 1984). These single purpose agencies are to have a life expectancy of 10–15 years.

London Docklands and Merseyside Development Corporations were established in 1981 under the provisions of the 1980 Local Government, Planning and Land Act. This Act charged the UDCs with the regeneration of their designated area by: bringing land and buildings into effective use; encouraging the development of existing and new commerce; creating an attractive environment; and ensuring that housing and social facilities were available to encourage people to live and work in the same area.

The Act gave UDCs extensive powers of land acquisition, not only by compulsory purchase, but also in acquiring the freehold interest of public sector land by means of a vesting order agreed between the Secretary of State for the Environment and the relevant Minister.

Urban Development Corporations have extensive land use planning powers in relation to development control and forward planning. Although UDCs are not allowed to produce statutory local plans for their areas, they can produce development strategies and planning briefs. A peculiar anomaly of this legislation is that the local authorities, when preparing the statutory unitary development plan for their administrative area, must take into account the non-statutory policies and proposals of the UDC. Finance for UDCs is obtained through grant-in-aid from central government, by borrowing from the National Loan Fund and by using their own income raised from the letting and sale of land and premises. UDCs are accountable to Parliament, via the Secretary of State for the Environment, and to the Treasury.

17.2   DESIGNATION OF URBAN DEVELOPMENT CORPORATIONS

A total of 13 UDCs have been designated to date (1992) in three principal waves. The first two, London and Merseyside, were designated in 1981. In 1987 a further five were designated: Trafford Park, the Black Country, Cardiff Bay, Teeside and Tyneside. The following year saw the declaration of Manchester, Leeds, Sheffield and Bristol. Laganside in Northern Ireland was designated in 1989 and in March 1992 Birmingham Heartlands was the latest UDC to be established (Figure 17.1).

However, UDCs have been the subject of a considerable degree of controversy. One of the key issues is that, although they are directly responsible to central government, they are not accountable to the people in their area. As such, they are considered by many to be undemocratic with powers to impose initiatives on the locality. They have been further criticized for their short term planning horizons, and at times have carried out arrogant or non-existent public consultation (Coulson, 1990). A major criticism

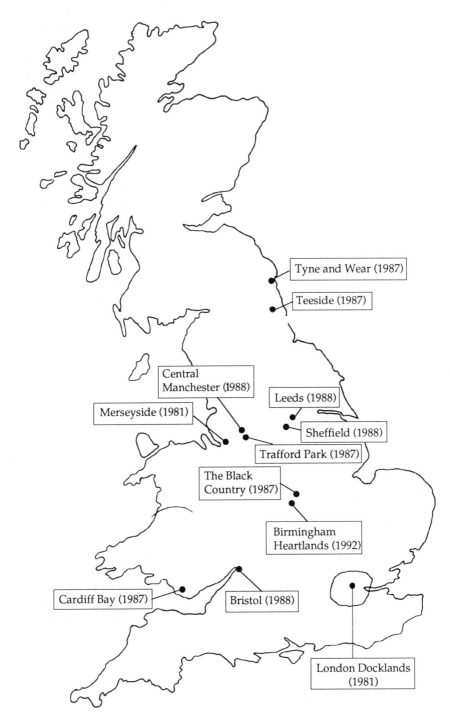

Figure 17.1 Urban Development Corporations in England and Wales: location and date of designation

levelled against central government, in using UDCs as an instrument of urban policy, is that an evaluation of the two initial corporations in London Docklands and Merseyside was not undertaken before the second generation had been declared. Indeed, to date there has still not been a systematic monitoring and evaluation of all of the UDCs by central government. Consequently, the basic rationale for choosing the areas of the 13 UDCs remains uncertain.

A spatial examination of UDCs reveals a geographically dispersed pattern: 11 are located throughout England, one in Wales and one in Northern Ireland, yet there are none in Scotland. A report by the Centre for Local Economic Strategies (1990) identifies certain characteristics, with each designated area containing a large degree of industrial dereliction, often including stretches of waterfront. All of the UDCs incorporate part of, or are adjacent to, the city centre and most exclude areas of existing inner city housing, although most have a significant employment base. The first and second generation of UDCs have large areas of land in public ownership, usually in a derelict state, and have subsequently adopted a policy of land acquisition, reclamation and infrastructure provision to lever private sector investment. The third generation of UDCs are rather different in that they have a specific city centre focus but have very little land in their ownership (Centre for Economic Strategies, 1990). Consequently, it is not envisaged that this last generation of UDCs will become major landowners; instead, their main role is to facilitate the private sector in the regeneration process.

However, notable differences can be discerned among UDCs; they vary in size and reveal significant contrasts in local economic circumstances. The first two UDCs illustrate this point very clearly. London Docklands Development Corporation is charged with regenerating an area located approximately 2.5 km from one of the world's largest financial centres, whereas Merseyside Development Corporation is charged with regenerating an area which is not only physically isolated within an urban context but is also located in one of the most depressed cities in Europe (Parkinson and Evans, 1990). These differences are not just a north/south issue; in fact, there are significant variations between the physical, social and economic circumstances of the UDCs for Merseyside and Central Manchester and, indeed, between Central Manchester and Trafford Park. The latter is a rather unique case in that it is a very large industrial estate showing a great deal of commercial wasteland following its demise in the 1960s. These contrasting circumstances can be further illustrated by analysing the characteristics of the various UDCs.

17.3   PROFILES OF THE DESIGNATED CORPORATIONS

The following profiles provide a discussion of the salient characteristics, problems, development and other objectives of the designated corporations.

London Docklands Development Corporation

The London Docklands Development Corporation (LDDC) came into operation in July 1981, consisting of 2226 ha, a resident population of 40 000 and an employed population of 27 213. Part of the declared area receives additional benefits under Enterprise Zone status. The London Docklands Strategic Plan was prepared in the 1970s by the Greater London Council, although the local authorities of Newham, Southwark and Tower Hamlets had previously embarked on a programme of land acquisition and reclamation in the dock area.

The establishment of the LDDC proved controversial, mainly because of opposition from the existing communities and constituent local authorities. Over £1 billion of grant-in-aid had been given to the corporation, three-quarters of which has been spent on infrastructural developments such as the Docklands Light Railway and the docklands highway (London Docklands Development Corporation, 1991a). Among the flagship schemes are Hays Wharf Office Development, St Katherine's Dock Marina, Surrey Docks, London City Airport and Canary Wharf. The latter is alleged to be the largest development of its kind in the world. Located in the Enterprise Zone, it has benefited from a range of incentives including the favourable tax regime. Most of the Canary Wharf development is unlet (1993), although a potential move by some civil service departments, including the Department of the Environment, is currently under negotiation. When the office space is fully let, Canary Wharf should provide employment for 50 000 people. However, a daily influx of commuters of this magnitude is thought to be beyond the capacity of Docklands Light Railway (London Docklands Development Corporation, 1991b).

The LDDC has adopted the policy of acquiring and reclaiming land which is then sold on to the private sector for development. Owing to the proximity to the City of London, the corporation has been very successful in securing both developer interest and development capital. However, the nature and type of the development attracted has been the subject of much criticism. The jobs provided are largely in the service sector and the existing local communities lack the educational and skill levels to gain meaningful employment in these activities. Similarly, much of the initial housing was built for the private sector, and the luxury end of the market was well beyond the means of the indigenous population (Docklands Consultative Committee, 1990). However, the LDDC has been making efforts to redress this situation by embarking on initiatives to improve the skills base of the local population, and in seeking to attract an element of low cost social housing.

Furthermore, concern has been expressed on the lack of strategic and integrated planning within the designated area. Development has been piecemeal, often taking place in advance of the infrastructure, with the result that the overall effect on the townscape has become unharmonious.

The Docklands Light Railway is constructed to a different gauge to the underground system and as such cannot be easily integrated. The financing of the Jubilee line extension is uncertain, as Olympia and York (the developers of Canary Wharf) have gone into administrative receivership and their financial contribution to both the development and the funding of the Jubilee line is now in doubt (although the prospect of government funding was implicit in the Chancellor's Autumn 1992 statement). Furthermore, with land values and sales plummeting and the costs of infrastructure improvements increasing, financial difficulties now face the LDDC. In the circumstances, the realization of its social and community programmes will become increasingly more difficult to achieve (Thomas, 1992).

Merseyside Development Corporation

When designated in 1981 the Merseyside Development Corporation (MDC) comprised 350 ha of derelict dockland, with only 450 residents and approximately 1500 people employed. Grant-in-aid is about £25 million per annum (Merseyside Development Corporation, 1991). A low indigenous and employed population in the area has helped to avoid conflict, but has nevertheless made the task of regeneration more difficult. Although the designated area straddles three local authorities, it is separate from the city centre.

Before designation Liverpool City Council had prepared a development brief for the redevelopment of the docks and negotiated with a number of developers, but for various reasons the schemes failed to materialize. Unrealistic land prices, the costs of land reclamation and associated infrastructural requirements prohibited private sector involvement in the area. Consequently, Liverpool City Council recognized the need for a large injection of public sector finance to upgrade the infrastructure if redevelopment was to take place (Liverpool City Council, 1987).

In 1981 the MDC prepared an initial development strategy for the area, which placed an emphasis on industrial development (Merseyside Development Corporation, 1981). This document made use of existing plans and proposals prepared by the constituent local authorities. However, with the failure to attract new industry, the focus changed in 1984 to a tourism/ leisure dominated strategy. The Audit Commission were highly critical of the industrial-led strategy, as Liverpool never had a strong industrial base. The MDC's main schemes in the original designated area include the International Garden Festival site, Albert Dock refurbishment and Brunswick Business Park. This phase of redevelopment has involved a massive injection of public sector funding, with relatively little attraction of private sector capital. The MDC have argued that this is due to the nature of the designated area, yet in terms of achievements the land has been brought into a condition capable of development and opportunities and markets have been created where none hitherto existed. There was some initial difficulty in encouraging a long term operator for the International Garden Festival site, although one was eventually secured after an injection of £1 million by the Department of Trade and Industry and the site reopened in May 1992.

The MDC's inability to lever private sector investment led the Audit Commission to suggest that the UDC should be wound up. Instead, the government decided to extend the designated area in 1988 and MDC now consists of 960 ha, a three-fold increase in size, including part of the city centre. The extended area contains a resident population of 7000 and an employed population of 36 000. Consequently, the nature of the urban development area has changed dramatically and the remit for MDC has been widened to include the needs of a much larger population base in terms of housing and employment provision. One of the first tasks undertaken by the MDC was to prepare an overall strategy for the urban development area, which placed emphasis on community and social policy, including efforts to improve the skills base of the resident population (Merseyside Development Corporation, 1990).

Black Country Urban Development Corporation

Established in May 1987, the urban development area consists of 2598 ha and at the time of designation contained a resident population of 35 400 and an employed population of 53 000. The UDC's grant-in-aid is approximately £33 million per annum. As the second largest UDC area in Britain it includes a mix of uses, namely industry, derelict land, opencast mining and housing. The original designation was for seven years with a budget allocation of £160 million. However, in 1988 the urban development area was extended to incorporate land close to Wolverhampton town centre (Centre for Local Economic Strategies, 1990).

The Black Country UDC has prepared development strategies for the north, central and south areas. The acquisition and reclamation of land is a major priority, together with the provision of supporting infrastructure. The most ambitious infrastructural project is the Black Country spine road at a cost of £130 million, while Sandwell 2000, a 1 500 000 m^2 retail and leisure development is to be constructed as an important flagship project.

Cardiff Bay Urban Development Corporation

Designated in 1987 the urban development area, which was formerly part of Cardiff Docks, covers 1089 ha. At the time of designation 5180 people were residing and 15 000 people were employed in the area. Although the docks are still active, they now occupy a much smaller area. Since 1974 the

County Council have been anxious to redevelop the dockland area, with linkages into the city. Indeed, the council was instrumental in working with the Welsh Office to set up the UDC as a means of obtaining government money towards redevelopment. The two largest schemes in the urban development area, Atlantic Wharf and Penarth Docks, were already under way when the UDC was set up, whereas Cardiff Bay Barrage is a more recent flagship scheme.

Trafford Park Urban Development Corporation

This UDC, designated in February 1987, consists of 1267 ha and, although the local population was only 40 people, Trafford Park provided 25 000 jobs at the time of designation. Grant-in-aid has averaged approximately £16 million per annum (Trafford Park, 1991). A notable feature of this urban development area is that designation was received by request from employers in Trafford Park and the local authorities rather than by imposition. Trafford Park was originally established as the world's first industrial estate and in its heyday in 1896 contained a resident population of 600 and an employed population of 75 000. As new technology replaced traditional industry, Trafford Park went into decline. Before designation Trafford Borough Council embarked on a range of environmental improvements using Urban Programme funding, whereas firms committed major investments in plant and machinery. However, infrastructure development was required for Trafford Park to reassert its competitiveness.

The task of the Trafford Park UDC is to improve the environment, engage in special area projects and attract 16 000 additional jobs in its lifetime (Law, 1992). In the early years, the UDC concentrated on planning/feasibility works, infrastructure and environmental improvements. Major projects include a link to the M602, which involves bridging the Manchester Ship Canal; a road link to Manchester city centre; access to the Euro terminal which is due to open in 1993; and improvements to public transport. The Village, Hadfield Street area improvements, Irlam industrial estate and Wharfside are key flagship developments. Although significant progress has been made in the Hadfield and Irlam areas, the Wharfside scheme, by far the most ambitious in Trafford Park, is currently in abeyance due to financial difficulties caused by the property recession.

Teeside Urban Development Corporation

The Teeside UDC, designated in May 1987, consists of the largest land area of any UDC (4858 ha). At the date of designation the local population consisted of only 400 people with few employment opportunities in the area. Grant-in-aid received by the UDC amounts to approximately £36 million per annum. The urban development area, which straddles the administrative boundaries of five local authorities, is characterized by industrial decline, with vast areas of derelict/vacant land and under-used factory premises.

The UDC's regeneration strategy is based on a small group of flagship projects, which were identified in a consultant's report, commissioned by the Department of the Environment before designation. One of the key projects is Teesdale, a 100 ha site for which land acquisition, reclamation and environmental improvements are estimated at a cost of £60 million to the public sector. A development plan prepared for the site proposes a mix of uses; to date the Teeside UDC has been successful in attracting commercial and housing investment together with university facilities (Teeside Development Corporation, 1991). In addition, significant infrastructural investments include a barrage between Stockton and Middlesbrough to enhance the environmental attraction of the area.

Tyne and Wear Development Corporation

Established at the same time as the Teeside Corporation (May 1987), the Tyne and Wear Development Corporation consists of 2375 ha of land left derelict due to the decline of three staple industries: heavy engineering, coal mining and shipbuilding. At the time of designation about 4500 people were resident and 40 115 were employed in the area. Grant-in-aid averages approximately £36 million per annum (Tyne and Wear Development Corporation, 1991).

The UDC sees its task as bringing the river banks of the Tyne and Wear back to life by introducing a range of mixed uses. There are a number of flagship schemes which include Newcastle Business Park, St Peter's Basin, Closegate Hotel and a major land assembly scheme at East Quay, which has £250 million of private sector development committed (Tyne and Wear Development Corporation, 1990). The urban development area is divided into North and South Tyneside and Sunderland, areas targeted for industrial development. In this context the UDC is seeking to build on its recent successes at Sunderland by continuing to target south-east Asia as a source of inward investment (Tyne and Wear Development Corporation, 1989).

A notable feature of the Tyne and Wear UDC is the desire to secure an element of social housing within the urban development area. The UDC is prepared to fund 25% of the development, with housing associations providing 40% and the private sector financing the remainder. This illustrates its commitment in securing investment of direct benefit to the local community. A further example of this policy has been to embark on a training programme to provide skills for inward investment. Nevertheless concern has been expressed that Tyne and Wear UDC is concentrating too much on its flagship schemes and leaving vast areas of industrial land with little or no activity (Centre for Local Economic Strategies, 1990).

Bristol Urban Development Corporation

Designated in December 1988 and consisting of 360 ha, Bristol UDC includes a major employment area containing 13 800 jobs. Bristol City Council, in recognition of the importance of retaining existing industry, had prepared a draft local plan for the area and consequently challenged the initial designation order in the House of Lords, arguing that there was no need for a UDC on the grounds that the land would be eventually developed. The outcome of the court's decision resulted in the designation area being considerably reduced in size.

The corporation has characteristics more akin to third generation UDCs in that it owns very little land and has a relatively small budget of £7 million per annum, primarily aimed at levering private investment. Infrastructure improvements which are required to open up the area, including the M32 spin road, will entail additional expenditure. Major developments within the designated area include St Anne's Board Mills and Temple Mead/Kingsley Village.

Central Manchester Development Corporation

Established in June 1988, the urban development area consists of 187 ha on the edge of Manchester city centre with a resident population of 500 and 19 500 people in employment. Although the area does not contain a cohesive community, it borders the residential developments of Hulme and Moss Side, both of which have very high unemployment and social stress characteristics. Before the designation of the urban development area Manchester City Council, in conjunction with the private sector, was engaged in renewing parts of the area under the auspices of the Phoenix Initiative. Manchester City Council initially opposed the designation of the UDC but eventually reached a compromise and now has an agency agreement to process planning applications on behalf of the corporation.

The strategy for the area aims to extend the city centre both functionally and geographically by introducing new and under-represented uses. Major projects include the Great Bridgewater Initiative – International Concert Hall, Piccadilly Village, Grand Island and major environmental improvements particularly along the waterways (Central Manchester Development Corporation, 1991). The corporation is also involved in training and community initiatives. However, progress with two of the flagship schemes, the Refuge Building and Great Bridgewater Initiative, has been slow. Although the former, which is a listed building, has been converted into a hotel and funding has been secured for the latter. The corporation has been relatively successful in levering private sector capital, compared with other development corporations, with the exception of London, almost certainly reflecting the relative buoyancy of the Greater Manchester economy (Sherman, 1990).

Leeds Urban Development Corporation

Declared in June 1988, the Leeds UDC consists of 500 ha of derelict or under-used land to the south of the city centre. Approximately £15 million grant-in-aid is received per annum (Leeds Development Corporation, 1992). Before designation the council had adopted local plans for the central and south Leeds areas. A measure of continuity has been achieved by the UDC adopting a similar strategy to that contained in the local plans. However, the policies of the City Council and Leeds UDC differ with regard to Kirkstall Valley, for which the council proposed an industrial use on the site of the former power station and open space in the rest of the valley, whereas the UDC proposed a mixed leisure and residential use.

The aim of the corporation is to extend the city centre southwards. Priorities include upgrading property, land assembly, highway improvements (including a link to the M1), environmental improvements particularly along gateway areas, sustaining existing employment/creating new jobs, encouraging new commercial housing and implementing training schemes (Leeds Development Corporation, 1988). Development progress has been affected by the recession of the early 1990s with the result that some of the larger schemes have been temporarily postponed (Leeds Development Corporation, 1992). Flagship schemes include Clarence Dock to which the Royal Armouries Museum has been attracted, Hunslet Business Park, Hunslet housing development and the Kirstall Valley proposal.

Sheffield Urban Development Corporation

The Sheffield UDC, designated in June 1988, consists of an area of 900 ha. At the time of establishment the area contained a resident population of 300 and employed 18 000 people. Grant-in-aid amounts to approximately £15 million per annum (Sheffield Development Corporation, 1992). The area focuses on the Don valley, which was traditionally associated with steel and metal industries. However, industrial decline prompted Sheffield City Council to undertake a feasibility study from which emerged a five year regeneration programme for the valley (Sheffield Development Corporation, 1990).

The overall strategy of the UDC has been to provide infrastructure, support industry and commerce, and to attract inward industrial investment. Flagship schemes include the 120 000 m² Meadowhall Regional Shopping and Leisure Complex, Cutlers Wharf, and a link to the M1 and to Sheffield airport. However, the recession of the early 1990s has slowed the pace of implementation and although the corporation have secured a new developer for the Canal Basin scheme, the Cutlers Wharf redevelopment has been a casualty of the current slump in property development. Sheffield UDC has also supported local infrastructure development; for example, a contribution of £800 000 was made to the South Yorkshire Passenger Transport Executive's Supertram scheme to link Meadowhall with the city centre.

Laganside Development Corporation

Laganside occupies a location immediately east of Belfast city centre. The land within the designated area covers about 120 ha, of which 48 ha have potential for development. Most of the land (95%) is in public ownership. Under the Laganside Development (Northern Ireland) Order 1989, the corporation was given responsibility to oversee development, encourage investment and marketing. Its statutory powers are broadly similar to the British UDCs, except that the Laganside Corporation does not possess any devolved planning powers. Responsibility for planning matters in the designated area remains with central government.

The key infrastructural schemes being undertaken in Laganside include a cross-harbour road – rail bridge and a weir at a capital investment of £87 million and £14 million, respectively. These developments are heavily dependent on a high capital expenditure from the public sector, with support from the European Regional Development Fund (Berry *et al.*, 1991). In terms of development opportunity eight key sites are targeted for private sector investment which will incorporate a mixture of commercial, residential, recreational and cultural uses. Development has started on several sites with plans agreed for others. The key development site within the designated area is Laganbank, which will include a flagship 2500 seater concert/ conference hall for which European Community funding will augment central and local monies. The scheme will also include an international hotel, office accommodation and a transportation terminus at a total projected cost of £100 million. A consortium of Ewart plc, O'Hare and McGovern and the US based Enterprise Development Corporation has been appointed as the preferred developer for the scheme (Laganside Corporation, 1991).

Birmingham Heartlands Urban Development Corporation

In November 1989 Birmingham City Council, the Chamber of Commerce and several private companies established a development agency charged with the task of regenerating 1000 ha of land in east Birmingham, containing a resident population of 16 000. The agency's main role is to produce and oversee the implementation of a development framework and to bring resources and services. The area suffered major job losses between 1981 and 1985, housing conditions were poor, yet there was a demand for accommodation, although the quality of the environment had deteriorated due to land dereliction and vacancies in industrial premises. A development plan was prepared based on four key elements: a physical development strategy, a marketing strategy, an investment strategy and measures to ensure that benefits accrue to the area. Principal achievements include 23 000 m² of industrial development, 17 000 m² of offices, 800 houses refurbished, 600 homes built, and education and training initiatives.

In March 1992 UDC status was granted to the area in agreement with the City Council. Indeed the Birmingham Heartlands UDC has a 'tailor-made' constitution, with the council able to nominate half of the development board (Birmingham City Council, 1992). Furthermore, the existing development strategy has been carried forward with funding to be £50 million over a five year period.

17.4   URBAN DEVELOPMENT CORPORATIONS: SIMILARITIES AND DIFFERENCES

The profiles of the various UDCs show a commonality of approach to the regeneration of inner city areas. Development strategies often build on the proposals adopted by the local authorities responsible for the area before UDC designation. Furthermore, major infrastructural projects constitute an integral part of these strategies. The proposals are then supplemented by individual planning briefs/development plans for key sites together with design guidelines.

Each corporation has its flagship schemes which Parkinson and Evans (1990) suggest are prompted by the need to produce immediate action and visible results. These high profile schemes are aimed at improving the environment and changing the image of an area, as illustrated by the refurbishment of St Katherine's Dock (LDDC) and Albert Dock (MDC). Flagship schemes are perceived as being necessary to create confidence in an area for private sector investment. Simultaneously, environmental improvements are required by the UDC on major corridors in the area, such as along the waterfront, canalside or major highway routes. These flagship schemes and environmental improvements are then used to support high profile marketing exercises to lever private sector funding. Indeed, private sector investment may require further leverage through the Urban Programme or by City Grant. In addition, the UDCs outside London, and more recently the LDDC, have all identified a need to support employment training and community based projects.

Most UDCs have adopted a similar organizational approach, run by a board which is chaired by a person from local industry with members drawn from both the public and private sectors. The day to day work of a UDC is undertaken by a small team of staff, headed by a chief executive. The UDCs employ consultants to carry out much of the technical feasibility, design and project management work (Ward, 1990). Indeed the Audit Commission has criticized both the LDDC and MDC for their use of consultants in that they did not appoint on the basis of competitive tendering often enough.

Perhaps when the organizational structure of UDCs and their approach to regeneration are considered, it is not surprising that there is an element of 'sameness' in the physical results. There is similarity in the mix of uses, consisting of housing, office, retail, cultural (often public sector) and leisure development, whereas manufacturing industry is seldom included within development schemes. Even more striking is the similarity of architecture. Although indigenous buildings give a strong sense of place and local identity, new construction often lacks this local vernacular. This is a formidable task which requires to be addressed more urgently by UDCs.

17.5   EVALUATION OF URBAN DEVELOPMENT CORPORATIONS

Urban Development Corporations have benefited favourably from government funding, having received considerably more money each year than the 57 Urban Programme authorities combined (Centre for Local Economic Strategies, 1990). This favourable financial treatment has been at a time when the local authority block grant has declined. However, among the UDCs the spread of resources has been uneven. The LDDC, located in the nation's capital close to one of the world's major financial centres, receives over half of the total UDC budget and indeed, since establishment, has received over £1.5 thousand million in grant-in-aid from central government.

Given this large allocation of resources, the Department of the Environment has been criticized for not undertaking a systematic monitoring of UDCs. Reviews of UDCs have been undertaken by the Audit Commission (National Audit Office, 1988), the House of Commons Employment Committee (1988) and the House of Commons Select Committee on Public Accounts (House of Commons, 1989). The Audit Commission argued that UDC corporate plans should place more emphasis on strategic issues and provide a basis for monitoring. Co-ordination with other development bodies and government departments needs to be considered, and social and environmental factors borne in mind from the outset. The House of Commons Committee on Public Accounts emphasized the importance of systematic monitoring of UDC performance, not only in terms of inputs and outputs but in achieving wider and longer term objectives.

Urban Development Corporations operate to a number of performance indicators, which are reported in returns to the Department of the Environment and to the general public through annual reports and accounts. These indicators include the amount of private sector money which UDC spending has levered; the number of kilometres of new road created; the environmental improvements undertaken; the amount of commercial floorspace created through new building or refurbishment; the number of housing units built and the number of jobs created. These indicators convey a physical definition which raises the issue of whether the achievement of such performance targets will result in regeneration in the true sense. The Public Accounts Select Committee is of the opinion that improving local recruitment to jobs in the London Docklands is important if regeneration is to secure the full benefits intended. This suggests a wider definition in that regeneration should not just rest on creating physical change in an area but should also include social change by improving the circumstances for the whole of the population within the urban development area.

In assessing the impacts of social change as a consequence of the UDC programme, the government should be examining not just how many jobs have been created but also the targeting of those jobs. However, Barnekov *et al.* (1989) advise that such targeting is not only difficult and expensive to monitor but sanctions are problematic to implement. It is alleged that at present over 50% of those employed in Manchester city centre are from outside the administrative boundary (Sherman, 1990). Perhaps it is unreasonable to expect a UDC, which has a specific remit, to be responsible for changing such trends. Doubt has also been expressed as to whether jobs 'created' in the urban development area are actually new or just relocation of existing employment. This accusation has been levelled at the LDDC where firms were relocating from the City, leaving vacant floorspace behind. Even if it was possible to establish that jobs created in UDC areas are new, the fact remains that many inner city residents or workers with traditional manufacturing skills would need extensive training/retraining to gain access to this employment. Most UDCs are aware of the issue and are currently engaged in skill enhancement schemes. However, the scale of the problem in these areas is so great that their impact is likely to be marginal at best. Such schemes are no substitute for an effective education and training programme, which is clearly within the remit of central government policy. In improving the prospects of local employment, job creation needs to be matched with an appropriate programme of skill training.

An indirect impact of regeneration is that success can create its own problems. Much of the existing employment in many of the city centre UDCs is marginal and benefits from cheap premises. Regeneration and redevelopment can raise property values and rents, with the result that increases in costs can affect the viability of existing industry and employment. This is clearly a critical issue, the effects of which require careful monitoring.

Most of the UDCs now support community schemes. However, with falling land and property prices affecting UDC finances, doubt has been expressed as to whether these will be implemented. There is also concern that the policies and proposals contained in UDC development strategies, which are for the benefit of local communities, may not be honoured, especially in times of development pressure (Dawson and Parkinson, 1990). Much of the housing which has been built is private, although some UDCs are making concerted efforts to secure provision of social housing. Housing tenure is, therefore, a useful indicator to monitor, particularly in areas of housing stress. However, these indicators do overlook some of the wider benefits which UDCs have brought to their local areas, such as opening up water-fronts and creating facilities which local residents can enjoy.

The strategic planning impact of UDCs raises further concern. Within urban development areas the flagship projects and the site by site approach leads to incrementalism which may not necessarily produce a cohesive plan. Regarding the wider urban context, the development areas may not link in with other parts of the city. For example, the new infrastructure serving an urban development area may not integrate with the existing transportation networks elsewhere in the city because the latter has not been designed to a comparable standard. Liverpool City Council (1987) has also questioned whether the resources of the UDC would have been better targeted in areas where people live rather than in empty wastelands. Alternatively, there is the argument that if regeneration targets are achieved, UDCs will create 'islands of excellence', and the benefits will not filter down to other parts of the city. The outer council estates of many of our urban areas, which manifest some of the starkest social and economic problems, are unlikely to benefit from UDC activity.

The present recession has also highlighted that UDCs do not have a magic answer to regeneration. Schemes in urban development areas have been affected by the downturn in the economy, some have required to be re-negotiated, whereas others have been postponed indefinitely. Those projects which have been implemented have, for the most part, required a massive injection of public sector money up front. This has led to many questions concerning whether local authorities could not have achieved the same results with a similar injection of funding. The financial resources involved have been so large that it is debatable whether the public sector is levering, or in essence subsidizing the private sector (Barnekov *et al.*, 1989). Experience shows that, where a local economy lacks buoyancy, the task of regeneration is extremely difficult.

17.6 CONCLUSIONS

The Urban Development Corporations were created as single purpose agencies charged with the task of assisting the private sector to carry out urban regeneration. The UDC was developed as a concept by a government which felt that the private sector would be more capable of achieving this task. Even though the first two corporations were established in the early 1980s with a further eleven in subsequent years, the government has not carried out a systematic evaluation of their achievements at any stage. Many local authorities have learnt to live with the UDCs, and in some areas they are now working together and achieving some success. The UDC initiative has demanded a massive injection of public funding, at a time when local authority expenditure has been cut. However, it is clear that the UDC model offers no easy solution to the task of urban regeneration. Given the same allocation of resources, the local authorities would, in all probability, have achieved results comparable with those of UDCs and possibly ensured that regeneration programmes were more effectively linked into the rest to the city. There is grave doubt whether the regeneration successes of development areas will filter into the rest of the urban hinterland. Achieving urban regeneration in its widest sense demands a co-ordinated national programme of infrastructural development, together with investment in education and skills training.

REFERENCES

Adcock, B. (1984) Regenerating Merseyside docklands, *Town Planning Review*, **55**(3), 265–288.

Barnekov, T., Boyle, R. and Rich, D. (1989) *Privatism and Urban Policy in Britain and the United States*, Oxford University Press, Oxford.

Berry, J.N., Deddis, W.G. and McGreal, W.S. (1991) Waterfront regeneration in Ireland: public and private sector partnerships, *Journal of Property Finance*, **2**(2), 179–184.

Birmingham City Council (1992) Birmingham Heartlands: a unique story of success, *The Planner*, **78**(11), 15–19.

Centre for Local Economic Strategies (1990) Inner city regeneration: a local authority perspective, *First Year Report of the CLES Monitoring Project on UDCs*, CLES, Manchester.

Central Manchester Development Corporation (1991) *Annual Report 1990/91.*

Coulson, A. (1990) Flagships and fairs assessing the UDC decade, *Town and Country Planning*, November, 299–302.

Dawson, J. and Parkinson, M. (1990) Urban Development Corporations: the Merseyside experience 1981–1990, physical regeneration, political accountability and economic challenge. *Centre for Urban Studies WP No. 13.*

Docklands Consultative Committee (1990) *The Docklands Experiment: A Critical Review of Eight Years of the LDDC.*

House of Commons (1989) *HC-385. Urban Development Corporations. Committee of Public Accounts 20th Report,* HMSO, London.

House of Commons Employment Committee (1988) *The Employment Effects of Urban Development Corporations,* Vols. 1 and 2, HMSO, London.

Laganside Corporation (1991) *Annual Report 1990-91.*

Law, C. (1992) Property-led urban regeneration in inner Manchester. In: *Rebuilding the City: Property-led Urban Regeneration* (Eds P. Healey, S. Davoudi, M. O'Toole, S. Tavsanoglu and D. Usher), E & FN Spon, London, pp. 62–76.

Lawless, P. (1989) *Britain's Inner Cities,* 2nd edn, Paul Chapman Publishing, London.

Leeds Development Corporation (1988) *Strategic Plan.*

Leeds Development Corporation (1992) *Annual Report, 1990/91.*

Liverpool City Council (1987) *MDC: The Liverpool Experience,* Liverpool City Council Planning Department, Liverpool.

London Docklands Development Corporation (LDDC) (1991a) *The Corporate Plan,* LDDC, London.

London Docklands Development Corporation (LDDC) (1991b) *Decade of Achievement 1981–1991,* LDDC, London.

Merseyside Development Corporation (1981) *Initial Development Strategy.*

Merseyside Development Corporation (1990) *Development Strategy.*

Merseyside Development Corporation (1991) *Annual Report 1990/91.*

National Audit Office (1988) *Department of the Environment Urban Development Corporations.*

Parkinson, M. (1990) Merseyside testing the UDC strategy to the limit, *Town and Country Planning,* November, 306–308.

Parkinson, M. and Evans, R. (1990) Urban Development Corporations. In: *Local Economic Policy* (Ed. M. Campbell), Cassells, London.

Sheffield Development Corporation (1990) *Turning Vision into Reality.*

Sheffield Development Corporation (1992) *Report and Accounts 1990/91.*

Sherman, P. (1990) Greater Manchester centrefolio, *Chartered Surveyor Weekly,* 29 March.

Teeside Development Corporation (1991) *A Partnership in Renewal.*

Thomas, H. (1992) Understanding London Docklands. *The Planner,* 20 March, 6–9.

Trafford Park (1991) *Annual Report 1990-91.*

Tyne and Wear Development Corporation (1989) *A Vision for the Future.*

Tyne and Wear Development Corporation (1990) *Corporate Plan 1990-94.*

Tyne and Wear Development Corporation (1991) *Annual Report 1990-91.*

Ward, C. (1990) Seeking a formula, *Town and Country Planning,* November, 293.

18

Holistic regeneration: the experience of Calderdale, United Kingdom

Economic restructuring is taking place in many regions of the developed world and the likelihood is that local economies will be increasingly subject to change due to factors such as international trading policies, rising energy costs and the impact of new technologies, to mention but a few. The pace of economic and technological change will affect company structures and life spans, and people may expect to retrain a number of times during their working lives. Therefore, when framing planning policies relating to the local economy, the only thing that can be planned for with certainty is uncertainty.

Many older towns and cities which grew out of the industrial revolution now find that they are struggling with the problems of an over reliance on traditional manufacturing activities, ageing infrastructure and a legacy of buildings which are often viewed as unattractive and difficult to use when compared with modern purpose-built developments. How are such communities to cope with change? Are they powerless in the face of market forces to influence the trends, or are there effective strategies which can be applied at the local level which can assist them to promote their own economic well-being?

In 1983 these were the questions that faced the business and civic leaders in Calderdale, a district of 200 000 people, in West Yorkshire, United Kingdom. Faced with the virtual collapse of its textile and engineering industries the local authority, supported by local businesses, created a remarkably successful community based regeneration programme. Within a period of less than five years this programme had a dramatic effect on the future of the area: the appearance of the main centre, Halifax (population 90 000), was significantly improved; considerable resources were drawn into the general area; and there was evidence of a restoration of investment confidence. The methods used were effective in harnessing local willpower and resources, and in triggering a myriad of positive decisions and actions. Thus regeneration occurred as a result of the community using what was available from within itself and, as a consequence of this experience, the term 'holistic regeneration' was coined to describe the processes which created 'regeneration by the community from within the community' (Lockwood, 1989).

This programme was successful despite, and indeed, strange as it may seem, because of, limited public sector funding. In fact, at the beginning informed commentators expressed the criticism that the project was seriously underfunded. Sir Ronald Dearing (Chairman of the Post Office), adjudicating in a national competition for management innovation, said 'If the prize had been for . . . attempting great things with small resources, then it would have gone to Calderdale' (RIPA, 1986). Projects in Calderdale do not qualify for major government financial assistance and the latter half of the 1980s was a period during which local government expenditure was severely restricted. However, the paucity of resources actually had beneficial effects, producing a community based response and demonstrating an effective technique for stimulating change. The programme proved to be remarkably effective: as described later, for every £1 of local authority investment nearly £13 has been attracted from external sources.

This success is a result of the way in which the programme was managed and, particularly, the processes that were used as a vehicle for promoting improvements to the fabric of the area and to encourage investment. However, before describing these methods it is appropriate to take a closer look at the economic and environmental circumstances which led to the adoption of this approach.

18.1   BACKGROUND TO THE PROJECT

Calderdale, located in the Pennine hills, lies at the centre of the classic textile manufacturing region of the north of England. Its settlements are typified by sandstone buildings clinging to steep valley sides, rows of attractive cottages and terrace houses together with impressive multistorey mills and soaring chimneys. This industrial heritage, which includes the Halifax Piece Hall (a cloth hall built in 1779) with its vast central quadrangle, stands as a testimony to its former industrial heyday. However, the very things which give the area its attractive character – the nature of the buildings and its dramatic landscape – impose major constraints on its future physical and economic development.

In common with the other textile and engineering areas of the region, from the 1960s onwards Calderdale suffered from a gradual decline in traditional employment opportunities. Urban planning policies were based on the expectation of further slow decline in manufacturing industries accompanied by a shift towards employment in under-represented service industries. Economic development programmes encouraged industrial diversification and the growth of new enterprises, whereas the service sector was left to grow in response to market forces. In reality, during the 1970s, the economic strength of the area was slowly bleeding away which, in the recession of the early 1980s, grew into a massive haemorrhaging as company after company went into liquidation or withdrew from the area. Unemployment in Calderdale increased from 1% in 1971 to 4% in 1978 and leaped to 14% in 1982.

In addition to high levels of unemployment the recession was bringing other alarming features.

1. The amount of vacant industrial floorspace rose to the unprecedented level of 250 000 m^2 and this was increased by a further 125 000 m^2 when, in 1982, the closure was announced of the giant Dean Clough carpet mills (a complex of 13 multistorey buildings dating from the 19th century).
2. In 1983 the Woolshops shopping centre, consisting of a large supermarket and chain stores (with integral car parking), had opened in Halifax. Therefore, when the local economy went into unprecedented decline, the survival of shops in the peripheral parts of the town was threatened as trade was drawn to this new centre.
3. Railway patronage was reduced and, as a result, the future of the line through the district was under review. Halifax station fell into a state of disrepair; in May 1986 a national journalist writing about Halifax described the station as a 'dreadful wreck' (Pedley, 1986).

There was a realization that the area faced a changed situation: whereas the shedding of labour in hard times was a process that would normally be reversed when more favourable economic conditions returned, the closure of many companies in the early 1980s meant that the potential for regrowth was severely curtailed. Thus the existing intervention mechanisms such as building small industrial estates, encouraging the subdivision of building complexes for multi-occupation, offering businesses advice and access to new technology and training, no longer had any appreciable impact on the local economy.

It was in response to these trends that, in 1983, the Chief Executive of Calderdale Council called for a report to be prepared to discuss ways in which negative perceptions of the area could be transformed into something that would attract investors and help reinvigorate the local economy. It was realized that, although a great deal had been done in the past to clean up the area, its image to many people was that of a dirty, depressed, declining, northern industrial area. Furthermore, as the recession deepened the evidence of a depressed economy was apparent in the empty mills and the run-down appearance of the district's centres and their approaches.

The report which was presented to the council contained seminal ideas from which the holistic regeneration strategy eventually grew. Entitled 'Advertising the Attractions of Calderdale' it proposed initiating an environmentally orientated programme and marketing campaign aimed at encouraging investment in the area by those people who, both locally and nationally, controlled property and capital. It recommended that selected features of the district, particularly the town centres, should be enhanced by the creative development of their character and that these and other attractions of the area should be advertised to create a new image. This work was to involve cleaning buildings, the removal of modern plastic shop fascias, the re-creation of traditional signs and the comprehensive restoration of one of Halifax's fine streets of Victorian buildings. The rationale was that it should be a showpiece (and be named 'Quality Street' after the famous Halifax chocolates of the same name). It is interesting to note that these ideas had strong similarities to the methods being used to attract trade back into downtown shopping areas in the USA through the Main Street Programme, and the successful regeneration strategy pursued at Lowell, Massachusetts, although at the time there was no linkage of ideas. These seminal proposals were well received by the council which then commissioned the Civic Trust (a national body with a remit to safeguard and enhance the urban environment of Britain) to formulate a comprehensive plan for the improvement of the built environment and economy of the area. This led to the council establishing a new initiative to be known as the Inheritance Project, out of which developed the community based processes on which the holistic regeneration approach is founded.

18.2 CREATING A FRAMEWORK FOR ACTION

The commissioning of the Civic Trust to undertake a study of the area was an important step in establishing a rationale on which community based regeneration grew because (1) as an external organization it was able to take an objective view of the problems and potential of the area and (2) its status as a national authority in environmental and town enhancement work gave credence to its findings.

The Civic Trust produced two reports under the general title of 'A Strategy for Prosperity' (Civic Trust, 1984; 1986) which presented ideas ranging from strategic proposals and detailed designs, to methods of implementation for each of the towns of the district.

Six main policy strands were identified.

1. Regeneration aims: making the area more attractive to new industry, boosting trade in town centres and improving quality of life for local people.
2. An environmental programme: treating the inherited natural and man-made environment as an asset and using it as a basis for regeneration.
3. Changing preconceptions: changing the negative image of the area and creating a high profile to present the area in a truer and better light.
4. Creating a partnership approach: recognizing the limited availability of public expenditure and aiming to share the responsibility for achievement between the private sector, voluntary agencies and the council.
5. Building on success: recognizing, complementing and developing local achievements.
6. Cost effectiveness: developing a range of schemes, many of which would be low key but which, cumulatively, would change the appearance of the area, raise confidence and attract external funding and investment.

The Civic Trust's advice confirmed the importance of the enhancement of Halifax's architectural heritage through the restoration of period shopfronts, the cleaning and repairing of stonework, the refurbishment of prominent industrial buildings and rejuvenation of neglected areas. A high degree of involvement was to be encouraged from local community groups, traders and business interests to form 'nothing less than a great community movement to take Halifax and Calderdale into a new and prosperous future' (Civic Trust, 1984).

The Civic Trust suggested that, as the financial resources available to the council were insufficient to sustain the kind of programme suggested, the support of government sponsored agencies such as English Heritage (the National Monuments and Historic Buildings Commission), the Rural Development Commission and the Manpower Services Commission should be sought. Nevertheless, the council would be required to invest about £3 million in the programme over a five year period (Civic Trust, 1986), but in return it was suggested that for every pound the local authority invested, seven pounds might be attracted from national government agencies and the private sector. It advised that to achieve this goal the council would have to provide the essential leadership for the initiative. The Civic Trust commented: 'If the policies and programmes indicated in this report are to be realised, a specially constituted project orientated team, with no other responsibilities than to execute an agreed programme, has to be created.' 'Consideration should be given to seconding appropriate staff from the departments concerned, to form a new integrated team for the purpose, reporting directly to the Chief Executive' (Civic Trust, 1984).

Calderdale Council adopted the Civic Trust's proposals as the guidelines for a strategy rather than a blueprint for action. It then took two important steps. First, it recognized that the support of the community for the regeneration initiative would be essential and therefore carried out a public consultation exercise. An exhibition of the proposals was mounted in each town of the district, followed by a series of public meetings where local people were invited to offer their ideas on the form that the programme should take. One point stood out – the emphasis the Civic Trust placed on the promotion of tourism produced public scepticism because it was felt that job creation in tourism and retailing was a poor substitute for the employment in manufacturing that had been lost. As a result, the programme which was created did not directly involve itself in tourism promotion. Second, the council established a small multidisciplinary team to lead the new programme but it also took the crucial step of inviting local companies to provide staff to create a joint project team.

Positive responses to the programme initiated by the council were received from a number of local companies: the Halifax Building Society and Rowntree Mackintosh plc both agreed to second staff for up to three years; the Department of the Environment provided a secondee for a year; and as the project developed several other companies made secondments. The business secondees had no professional experience in urban regeneration, conservation or design but, working with planners, architects and a marketing expert from the council, they were able to make valuable contributions to the programme. The decision to create a joint project team supported the concept of partnership in a concrete way and this proved to be a key factor in drawing further businesses into the programme. The project team had the support of the council's technical departments to provide expertise and advice.

The community based regeneration programme was launched in February 1985 under the title the Inheritance Project, a name that implied using the past to create a new future. It was to be a comprehensive strategy for urban revival which would use heritage to advantage but promote new buildings as appropriate. The project was given a high profile: the launch took place in the Upper Waiting Hall at the House of Commons and a project office was established in the centre of Halifax to serve as a meeting place and an elegant shop window for the initiative. A strong identity separate from that of the council was established by the creation of its own distinctive symbol and letterheading.

18.3   INITIAL PROJECTS

The project team started with the aim of transforming the appearance of Halifax town centre: removing dereliction, reversing years of property neglect and stimulating high quality design in property development and refurbishment.

To promote the initiative and pump-prime private sector action, the council decided to use one of its Halifax shops as a centre for the Inheritance

Project. As an exemplar to show what could be achieved, the plastic and plywood cladding was stripped off the building to reveal an elegant Victorian shopfront, which was renovated and repainted with detailing highlighted in gold leaf to achieve a truly stunning transformation (Figure 18.1). As a further step in pump-priming and promoting the initiative the council restored 12 small properties in and around the Borough Market (a substantial and ornate building dating from 1896). Although some original material was renovated, much of the work involved creating accurate replicas. The total cost of these schemes amounted to £151 000 of which £43 000 was provided as grant aid by English Heritage. The tenants' agreement was necessary and the contractors had a strictly curtailed period for the main on-site installation to prevent disruption of trade. The refurbishment work aroused considerable public interest and, instead of losing business, one trader actually reported a rise in his monthly takings, despite the disturbance caused by a longer than usual contract period. On completion of each scheme the Inheritance Project arranged for the Mayor to perform an official re-opening which benefited the trader and raised the profile of the programme.

As the programme developed, difficulties were encountered and a problem-solving approach was adopted; for example, it became apparent that shop proprietors were only interested in fine architecture if it would attract more income to their businesses. Therefore, during 1986, the project team responded by establishing the Retail Action Group with a few far-sighted retailers. The group worked with the Inheritance Project's marketing officer to develop a co-ordinated programme of retail promotions which emphasized the Victorian character of the town. Thus the method of attracting more trade gave retailers a reason for undertaking property improvements which emphasized the town's special character.

During 1986 the project team started to take an interest in frontage renewals by national retailers. Although these were initially few, they increased in number due to the impact of the programme and the national consumer-led boom. However, most designs involved the installation of a new shopfront of ubiquitous design: slab fronted with aluminium frame and a plastic fascia with tiled stall riser. Therefore, following consultation with the Town Planning Department, the Inheritance Project would contact the company's chief executive and seek to gain the organization's interest in the aims of the programme and explain the commercial basis and advantages of working with the Inheritance Project. The objective was to persuade the company's decision-makers to change the proposals so that the frontage would complement the design of the upper levels of the building, incorporating traditional or other appropriate signage. A high degree of co-operation was obtained despite the fact that the re-design and revised method of construction incurred additional costs.

Another feature of the programme was the Project Centre, which contained high quality displays illustrating the work of the project and operated as an

Figure 18.1 Photographs of Halifax shop used as the centre for the Inheritance Project before (upper photo) and after (lower photo) renovation

information bureau and contact point. Property owners, architects and developers used it to obtain advice on design and grant-aid matters. The Inheritance Project commissioned a graphic designer, who had worked on the Covent Garden project in London, to produce a poster illustrating typical design features of the Victorian buildings of Halifax including lettering styles and embellishments appropriate to the period. A second poster illustrating traditional applied (wooden) shopfronts was subsequently produced. These proved to be valuable in assisting architects and shopfitters to produce authentic and appealing designs. In some instances grant aid of 25% towards the cost of structural repairs and restoration work was available from English Heritage and the project team advised property owners on how to obtain it. However, although this grant was helpful in a few instances its impact on the programme was limited as larger companies were not eligible.

The Inheritance Project was also instrumental in bringing about other important improvements. British Rail was persuaded to improve visitors' first impressions of Halifax by refurbishing the semi-derelict station, and the project team promoted the creation of an attractive precinct in what was derelict backland adjacent to the main street of the town. To encourage the surrounding property owners to participate, an artist's impression of the scheme was prepared to illustrate how the area could be transformed; and Marshalls Mono, local manufacturers of paving products, were persuaded to support the partnership by donating the paving materials for the scheme. Negotiations were successful in achieving the donation of land to allow new pedestrian routes to be created, including a new arched link through one of the properties. The public house on one side of the new square was totally refurbished, a new frontage to the space was constructed, and other property improvements followed. The Inheritance Project organized a team of people on a government sponsored training scheme to construct the paved precinct which was completed in 1988. The cost of the scheme to the council was £49 000 (at 1988 prices), whereas the total investment in the surrounding buildings, which included shops, an amusement arcade, a cafe and the reconstructed public house, amounted to approximately £1 million. (The scheme has further potential for expansion into an adjoining backland area and tentative proposals have been prepared for its development as a small speciality shopping centre at an estimated cost of £2.5 million at 1991 prices.)

18.4   STRENGTHENING BUSINESS COMMITMENT TO THE PROGRAMME

At the end of 1986 Business in the Community (BITC), a national organization sponsored by many national companies with the aim of stimulating enterprise and initiative at a local level, was looking for a suitable location for a pilot initiative that would aim to regenerate a whole area. Calderdale Council saw the opportunity of further strengthening the successful partnership programme which was operating through the Inheritance Project and secured the interest of BITC in supporting the programme. As a result, in February 1987 HRH The Prince of Wales visited Halifax in his dual capacity as President of BITC and Patron of the Civic Trust, and saw the progress being made by the Inheritance Project. Later the same day he visited Dean Clough Mills, which by now was becoming a centre for new businesses and small firms, and at a seminar attended by local and national business figures he launched the 'Calderdale Partnership' on behalf of BITC.

The involvement of BITC gave greater prominence to the Inheritance Project both locally and nationally and strengthened business support for the programme. At the Prince's request senior executives from 60 of the most influential business organizations and companies visited the district in a series of day-long tours to make a personal appraisal of the area's potential. Experts in successful regeneration strategies from Lowell, Massachusetts also came and advised the Calderdale Partnership on experience in the USA. This high level exposure of the area and the sharing of regeneration techniques assisted the Inheritance Project in a number of important ways.

1. Rowntree Mackintosh plc established a £200 000 revolving loan fund to assist owners to improve the appearance of buildings in prominent locations.
2. The Inheritance Project was introduced to a small number of national and commercial organizations who were persuaded to join in the property enhancement programme.
3. The trustees of Eureka! (a proposed interactive learning centre for children) were introduced to Halifax and decided, following presentations on the area, to locate their £8 million development on vacant land next to Halifax railway station.
4. The Department of the Environment announced a pilot scheme for the treatment of neglected land in conjunction with private landowners. It operated to streamlined procedures with a budget of £50 000 per annum.
5. JCB Ltd gave the free loan of an excavator for a period of 15 months, which worked on a series of environmental improvements and amenity projects in the Halifax area.

18.5   WIDENING THE PROGRAMME

The Metropolitan District of Calderdale was created in 1974 as part of the national reform of local government and represented an amalgam of nine separate communities, each of which formerly had its own administration. Therefore, as the programme developed successfully in Halifax there was pressure from these communities for improvements to be started in the other towns of the district. As a result individual project team members were assigned to work on a range of projects as follows.

1. At Hebden Bridge (a small town of 8000 people, higher in the Pennines, 11 km from Halifax) a scheme was promoted for the restoration and improvement of the square which forms the historic core of the settlement. This involved repaving the square and cleaning and restoring the buildings, including the replacement of modern signs and shopfronts with traditional features. This work was promoted with the help of joint council and English Heritage grant aid (at a rate of 40%) and loans from the Rowntree Mackintosh Fund.

2. At Todmorden (a town of 14 000 people, 18 km from Halifax) a scheme similar to that in Hebden Bridge was promoted for the restoration of a prominent group of shops and repaving of the street opposite the Town Hall. However, because economic conditions in Todmorden were among the most depressed in Calderdale, backing for the grant aid scheme was also obtained from the Rural Development Commission and the local town council. This enabled a grant of 60% to be offered to property owners.

3. At the small town of Sowerby Bridge (population 12 000, 3 km from Halifax), a new team member was appointed to manage a scheme for the restoration of a large complex of semi-derelict riverside mills.

4. At Ripponden, a village near Sowerby Bridge, the project team was given the task of remodelling the village green and an adjoining area of dereliction to create a site for a development of small workshops. Using European Community aid with small contributions and gifts of land from surrounding property owners, and the support of the Rural Development Commission, the area was successfully transformed. As a result local entrepreneurs were stimulated to undertake extensive property renovations for further craft workshops.

5. At Elland (population 8000, 5 km to the south of Halifax), European Community aid was used to build a landscaped access road through an area of terraced housing and textile mills, replacing roads and tracks from the era of the horse and cart. The adjoining factory owners were persuaded to support the regeneration partnership and donate all the land required for the road construction.

It should be noted, however, that although most of these satellite programmes successfully achieved their immediate objectives, none stimulated a community ground swell of support or set a wider process of investment and improvement in motion. Therefore, when Grand Metropolitan provided the project team with a new secondee in 1989, preparations were made for the launch of a new initiative in Brighouse (population 34 000) which would project the idea of partnership and through marketing create the conditions for business confidence and participation. It would build on the success of the Halifax initiative rather than repeat the mistake of only pursuing a project orientated approach.

A carefully planned strategy was put into effect with the slogan 'Build a Better Brighouse' to give the programme a separate identity. To pump-prime the programme the council restored a group of four Edwardian shops (about 1910), creating a high quality exemplar to encourage others to follow suit. A project centre was opened in a vacant shop provided rent-free by a local business, with the furniture donated by a local office furniture supplier. Following the pattern of the successful programme in Halifax a high profile launch was organized. In May 1990, Rocco Forte, the Chief Executive of Forte plc, arrived by horse-drawn barge to a media event involving street theatre, a children's orchestra and the release of hundreds of balloons, followed by the official launch at the Forte Crest Hotel with 120 local business people.

The business secondee again promoted the idea of partnership, raising over £30 000 in donations from local and national companies for landscaping and repaving the canal towpath and persuading the operator of the open-air market to invest £120 000 in replacing the existing concrete, timber and tar-felted structure with a more attractive building. To encourage community participation and enhance the profile of the project the Brighouse project officer (a council employee) promoted the idea of local schools producing murals to be placed on the outside walls of the new market as a community art project.

Progress was such that, just one year later in June 1991, Brighouse was the focus of the Prince of Wales's fifth visit to the district, when he was able to see the rebuilt market with stone walls and poppy red roof, admire the six large murals prepared by junior school children depicting aspects of the town's history, and walk along the partially completed canalside walk. Since that time the private sector secondee and his council officer counterpart have continued to maintain a high profile and stimulate interest and activity in the town.

18.6   WHAT THE PROGRAMME ACHIEVED

When the Inheritance Project was launched it was perceived as an environmental improvement and image-building project. It was anticipated that its effectiveness would depend on the amount of business and community participation achieved. However, in the event, the methods that were developed through the work of the Inheritance Project have achieved direct business investment in the programme and stimulated activity beyond the forecasts made when the project was conceived.

Looked at from the local authority's point of view, in purely financial terms, the project has been very cost-effective. The total council investment in

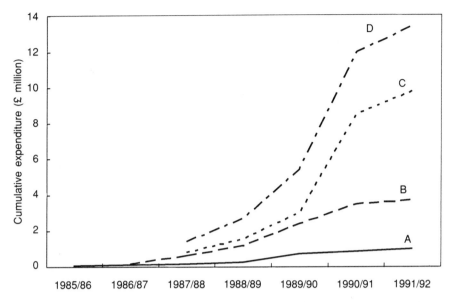

Figure 18.2   Progress of Calderdale Inheritance Project 1985 to 1992: expenditure and generation of resources. (A) Council expenditure; (B) external resources attracted; (C) private sector investment influenced by Inheritance Project programmes; and (D) total investment attracted

capital projects between 1985 and 1992 was £1 million, whereas investment attracted to the programme and funded by external organizations amounts to almost £13.5 million. This compares well with the Civic Trust's recommended budget of £3 million and the forecasted 1:7 return on investment. The graph (Figure 18.2) shows how the growth in investment occurred. Of particular interest is how the council's pump-priming activity over the first two years started to stimulate investment in similar, small scale projects and after three years this was followed by other more significant investment activity (speculative property refurbishment, hotel development and new business investment). Although the rate of investment growth slowed as a result of the recession in the United Kingdom, prospects for further growth are indicated by numerous schemes in the pipeline. It can therefore be confidently predicted that as the programme expands the levels of investment attracted will also continue to grow.

The impact is most apparent in Halifax where the programme has operated for the longest. The railway station has been transformed into an attractive entrance to the town and visitors are surprised by the high quality environment of the town centre, including, for example, the new McDonald's restaurant in a splendidly refurbished art deco building with its imposing

Table 18.1   Calderdale Inheritance Project. Sources of funding April 1985 to March 1992

(A) Public sector agencies	£
English Heritage	399 100
British Rail/Passenger Transport Executive	453 800
Department of the Environment	191 000
Rural Development Commission	331 000
Department of Transport	28 000
European Commission	273 000
Manpower Services Commission	80 000
Total	1 755 900
(B) Calderdale Council capital expenditure	1 091 700
(C) Private sector	11 654 700
Total public sector (A+B)	2 847 600
Total external resources (A+C)	13 410 600

frontage sympathetically designed in white palatine marble. Contrary to expectations before the programme began, that trade in the town centre would decline, retailers now consistently report sales performance which is as good as, or better than, that achieved in comparable centres.

The effectiveness of the programme in Halifax is indicated by the ratio of council expenditure (capital) to that of the private sector, which is 1:40 (£263 000:£10 478 000) and the ratio of capital investment made by all public agencies to that of the private sector, which is 1:9 (£1 172 000:£10 478 000). A breakdown of the sourcing of the whole programme in Calderdale is set out in Table 18.1. In terms of its revenue costs the local authority has also had to fund the overheads for the five team members (salaries and accommodation) and budgets for marketing, consultants and feasibility studies, which has averaged £130 000 per annum over the seven years of the programme.

18.7   WIDER IMPACT

When the programme began it was evident that if there was to be metaphorical gold at the end of the rainbow, it would require the creation of the right conditions to produce an economic rainbow. Although the Inheritance Programme benefited from the consumer-led boom of the late 1980s, its progress was made more difficult as the local economy continued to suffer from company closures and job losses (Figure 18.3). However, there is evidence that the programme had a beneficial effect on industrial and commercial attitudes towards the area.

1982	1983	1984	1985	1986	1987	1988	1989	1990	1991
2757	1241	1111	1296	928	468	505	2315	2103	1987

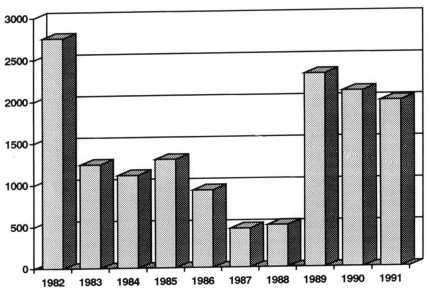

Figure 18.3   Job losses in Calderdale: figures collated from press reports

Before the programme started local companies such as Bradford Pennine Insurance (part of the Sun Alliance group), with offices in various parts of the country, experienced difficulty in persuading key workers to move to Halifax, in part due to the image associated with the area's industrial character. There is anecdotal evidence that negative images of the area were widely held. To illustrate, when a large retail chain asked its store manager from the Welsh coastal town of Llandudno to move to Halifax, his wife was totally opposed to the idea and it was only after a reluctant visit that her attitude to the area softened. That this negative attitude to industrial towns in the north of England is entrenched was recognized in research carried out for the Ministry of Labour as far back as 1968 (House *et al.*, 1968) and in the latter half of the 1970s media advertising, promoting investment in the new town of Milton Keynes, featured photographs of industrial townscapes in the West Yorkshire region. The message associated with the pictures of dirty houses, factories and chimneys was in effect 'you can't be successful in this sort of environment'.

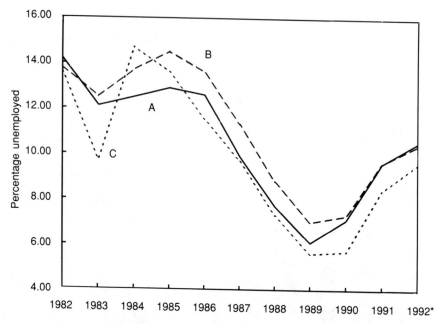

Figure 18.4 Comparative unemployment rates. (A) Calderdale; (B) West Yorkshire; and (C) Great Britain. All October figures except *April 1992. Data derived from Department of Employment published statistics

The image and profile of the area has improved dramatically and this has had an effect on industrial and commercial investment. The number of outside enquiries received by the council for land or buildings for new industrial and commercial projects has increased and, despite job losses, unemployment levels have kept parity with regional trends (Figure 18.4). Major gains in new employment have been from the rapid expansion of the Halifax Building Society (increased from 970 to 2900 employees between 1985 and 1992), the growth of a number of insurance and financial service operations, and from the Dean Clough Business Park (increased from 200 to 2500 employees between 1985 and 1992). Companies and institutions are investing and consolidating operations in the area indicating the shift in attitudes that has occurred and the confidence of decision-makers in the area's future. Therefore the effects of the programme measured in terms of investment are significantly more than those indicated by the figures earlier in the chapter.

18.8   PROCESSES WHICH CREATE A DYNAMIC PROGRAMME

When the Inheritance Project was established in 1985 the scale and complexity of the economic problems facing the area were daunting. Critics argued that the proposed programme was concerned with superficial window dressing rather than dealing with the fundamental economic and employment issues facing the area. Those criticisms are no longer valid. The Inheritance Project has actually produced a proactive method of working which has had a major influence on market forces and improved the economic prospects of Calderdale.

It has taken time to demonstrate the effectiveness of the approach (although in urban regeneration terms, five years is relatively short) because, by its very nature, in the initial stages it only affects the prevailing economic conditions at the margins. In fact, in its early stages the programme was extremely vulnerable to the criticism that little of significance was being achieved. However, as the graph (Figure 18.2) indicates the cumulative effect of many tiny changes acts as a pump-primer attracting further investment until a threshold in external confidence is reached when investment starts to flow into the area from outside. This is a classic example of how the whole can be greater than the sum of its parts.

This community based approach to regeneration was a response to difficult local conditions. Three factors were significant in influencing its development.

1. The shock of a collapsing local economy as symbolized by the closure of Dean Clough Mills, which concentrated the minds of community leaders.
2. The limitations of the area, particularly the scarcity of flat land for new development and its legacy of old buildings.
3. The paucity of resources available for urban renewal or economic regeneration programmes.

However, it was the last of these factors which produced key ideas forming the basis of the holistic regeneration method. First, the people of the area are its main resource and through them there is the potential to influence the use of capital, properties and activities for the good of the area. Second, small scale pump-priming can stimulate large scale change. Third, processes are more important than projects in the regeneration strategy, i.e. projects should be a means to an end, not an end in themselves.

The fundamental objective of the programme was to create a self-sustaining process of regeneration and to achieve this it was necessary to obtain the support of businesses and property owners to harness the latent resources which existed in the area. However, a major obstacle to achieving this was a prevailing negative attitude that the community was trapped in a spiral of decline and was powerless to influence the market forces which affected the area's prosperity. Therefore, the programme had to involve and inspire people, lifting them out of the inertia created by market forces and the economic restructuring which gripped the district. This was achieved by the development of three interlinked campaigns: partnership, exemplar projects and promotion (forming the acronym PEP), which became the *modus operandi* of the project team. These three campaigns create and sustain the dynamic processes which are responsible for the success of holistic regeneration in Calderdale.

The partnership campaign has proved to be a powerful vehicle for accelerating the process of change. The first step was to establish a jointly funded team. The fact that two major companies seconded staff to the new initiative made it special in the eyes of the community. It also enabled the team to project the idea of partnership to property owners, developers and businesses who had to be drawn into the programme. The message was: 'this is not just another local government programme, but something in which you need to play a part; it makes business sense, is capable of bringing in more trade and it will transform the image and economic potential of the area'.

Business sponsorship for the project team and for projects (a word processor, an excavator from JCB and paving materials are three examples) has been evidence of an active partnership which has helped to break the mould of stereotyped relationships between business and local government. The project team has been remarkably effective in achieving a rapport with decision-makers in both local and national companies. This has both stimulated significant new investments and substantially modified existing schemes so that they achieve the quality of design necessary to contribute to the transformation of the area.

The partnership between the council and local companies has also had an effect on the way in which the council operates. Often departments will be particularly helpful or will respond quickly to a request for action from the project team. This enables the team to project an image of efficiency which assists in strengthening the rapport with the business community.

The idea of partnership is expounded by the project team at every opportunity and is the means by which resources are directly drawn into the programme. Through this approach the council has been able to achieve things which would not normally be possible and has concertinaed the time-scale of urban improvements: what would have taken ten years has been accomplished in five.

The exemplars campaign has demonstrated how dramatic improvements to the built.environment can be made by the application of good design principles. It started with the stylish restoration of a prominent Halifax shop to provide a project centre for the Inheritance Team and was followed by pump-priming projects involving high quality restorations of relatively small groups of council owned properties. Later there were small town centre repaving schemes, feasibility studies into the refurbishment of old industrial buildings and access road projects, all of which were intended to promote further changes and improvements by the private sector.

The exemplars campaign has triggered off numerous improvement projects that, although insignificant individually, create a feeling of quality – particularly in Halifax where the work is well advanced. It has demonstrated how improvements can be made and has set high standards which the project team have used to encourage the private sector to follow suit. The process is slow at first but gathers momentum until a 'critical mass' is achieved when outside investment interest starts to be generated. The modest scale of council spending did not enable a major impact to be made on the appearance of any particular area and therefore the initial progress was slow, but the beneficial effect is that private sector spending has dominated the improvement work and has encouraged other businesses to follow.

The promotional campaign creates confidence in, and a high profile for, the programme. A great deal of effort has to be put into this area of activity, which has three dimensions: public relations, creating a high profile and image building.

1. Public relations: the aim is to inform and involve a wide cross-section of the community in the early development of the programme through exhibitions and public meetings and workshops. Once work is under way public confidence has to be sustained by regular press reports and talks to local societies and amenity groups. The direct involvement of the community is also encouraged through schools and local groups undertaking community art projects, preparing town trails and brochures and undertaking small amenity projects.
2. Creating a high profile: the aim is to keep the project in front of the business community and opinion formers locally and nationally. This has been achieved through the establishment of the project centre as a shop window for the initiative, the creation of a distinctive symbol and letterheading, newsletters to a select mailing list, presentations to business organizations and the encouragement of national media coverage and articles in business and professional publications.
3. Image building: the aim is to create and project new images relating to the project and the area. This has involved working with retailers to establish promotions which use images created by the town centre enhancement work as the basis for building up local pride and attracting trade. It also involves producing high quality exhibitions and publications for consumption by business people and opinion formers.

There may appear to be little that is remarkable about the separate elements of the programme; however, the way in which they were used in concert, as a balanced and co-ordinated strategy, created an effective tool for the promotion and management of urban change. It would be inappropriate to claim that the programme has influenced all the positive developments in Calderdale. The urban and economic systems of the district are extremely complex and people in many walks of life are working to improve the well-being and quality of life of the area. However, without the holistic regeneration programme many opportunities to bring about change would have been lost.

The principles on which holistic regeneration is based means that the process is applicable to other areas because: (1) it grows from local resources and is not dependent to any significant extent on external capital in its early stages; (2) it uses small scale improvements which involve, and are easily replicated, by the local community; (3) it is not reliant on special factors (as demonstrated at Brighouse which does not have the architectural features of Halifax); and (4) it is cost effective.

It is easy to forget what conditions were like in Calderdale in the early 1980s when the first ideas for a regeneration programme were being formulated. However, when the Inheritance Programme was in its infancy, the potential for wide application of the methods being used was recognized. In 1988 at an international conference on urban regeneration organized by the Council of Europe, the architect and broadcaster Patrick Nuttgens told delegates 'the way that the local authority, businesses, groups and individuals are working together to make Calderdale a better place in which to live and work is a shining example to be followed in the whole of Europe. In the coming years people will beat a pathway to see what is going on here'.

Now, after seven years, the processes which are the basis of holistic regeneration have been effectively demonstrated as a tool for the management of urban change.

REFERENCES

Civic Trust (1984) *Halifax in Calderdale – A Strategy for Prosperity*, Civic Trust, London.

Civic Trust (1986) *Calderdale the Challenge – A Strategy for Prosperity*, Civic Trust, London.

House, J.W., Thubron, I.M., Ruddy, S.M. and Storer, C.E. (1968) *Mobility of the Northern Business Manager. Report to the Ministry of Labour, Papers on Migration & Mobility in Northern England No. 8*, Department of Geography, University of Newcastle upon Tyne.

Lockwood, J.I. (1989) The Calderdale Inheritance Project – a holistic approach to urban regeneration, paper presented to the *Law & Business Forum, Urban Regeneration Conference, London, 24th October 1989*, unpublished.

Pedley, F. (1986) Calderdale tells story of industrial revolution, *Municipal Journal,* 9 May, 765.

RIPA (1986) *Newsletter,* Royal Institute of Public Administration. London.

19

Evaluation of regeneration projects in small towns

_____ *R. Lawton*

In recent years there has been a steady growth in initiatives to revitalize run-down areas. These vary widely in terms of the geographical size of the area in question, the financial resources of the initiative and the type of organizational structure established to tackle the problem. The well resourced Urban Development Corporations with cross boundary remits to tackle the inner cities contrast sharply with the charitably based Development Trusts and Community Partnership Schemes that operate in similar areas with comparable objectives and yet are in receipt of only a fraction of the resources.

Deprivation is not, however, limited to inner cities. There are an increasing number of schemes being established to revitalize areas that traditionally fall through the net of central government funded initiatives. These smaller community based initiatives are to be found in very diverse circumstances (Civic Trust, 1989). The project in Wirksworth, Derbyshire, which started in 1978 and went on to win a Europa Nostra Award, set the scene for such initiatives (Civic Trust, 1984). Subsequently, projects were established in seaside towns such as Hastings, Ilfracombe and Ramsgate, in heritage towns such as Ripon, Brigg and Halifax, in mining settlements such as Thorne and Loftus and inner cities in Deptford, Tower Hamlets and Glasgow among others.

Despite this diversity of place there are common elements to be found in most of them, and yet there is no one single solution which can be applied to all, no common prescription. Each place will have its own set of ills, each locality its own political flavour, and each project its own leader to put a particular slant on the solution. Thus one may find a 'community' approach or a 'property investment' approach reflecting in part the expertise of the project leader. Any evaluation of these approaches to regeneration will by definition need to allow for a degree of subjectivity. Furthermore there are important elements of achievement that will remain difficult to measure and yet will be crucial to the project's success. Community spirit arguably is the most important but the most difficult to quantify.

The Brigg Regeneration Project, a Civic Trust initiative which started in 1989, provides an excellent case study of the operation of town regeneration schemes. In considering this example issues to be discussed include a review of progress against defined objectives, sponsorship, political support and good development practice.

19.1 BRIGG REGENERATION PROJECT

Brigg, a traditional market town dating back to the 13th century, has a compact linear layout along its main shopping streets. At the outset of the regeneration project several problems were identified including a general lack of confidence, physical deterioration, a lack of investment, loss of major retail occupiers and the occurrence of heavy traffic with about 15 000 vehicles per 12 hour day passing through the town centre.

The initial stimulus for the project came from Glanford Borough Council who in 1987 employed consultants Nathaniel Lichfield to look at the future for Brigg. Three possible roles were identified for the town, namely a speciality shopping centre, a high quality residential suburb or a location for small businesses/some larger industry. In addition, it was recommended that a project based approach should be adopted to give a focus to the regeneration process. The Civic Trust was seen by the council as the natural body which could best provide the expertise and prestige to ensure this focus. In particular the Civic Trust's special qualities in physical regeneration is appropriate given Brigg's rich historical legacy, with over 100 listed buildings in the four main streets of the town centre. These properties comprise one of the greatest strengths of the town but many have suffered neglect (Civic Trust, 1990).

The stated objectives of the Civic Trust project in Brigg are to: establish a partnership of national and local organizations concerned with the well-being of the town; encourage practical schemes of development, environmental enhancement and building repair; encourage a greater pride in, and awareness of, the heritage and special qualities of Brigg; encourage, wherever possible, the creation of new job opportunities; and provide a forum and focus for the exchange of views between townspeople and the local authorities on all matters affecting the well-being of Brigg.

19.2   COMMON ELEMENTS IN REGENERATION PROJECTS

Regeneration projects are by definition found in places beset by a number of ills. Each place will have its own particular set of problems, dictated by such influences as political persuasion, economic base, ethnic make-up and geographical position. However, there are certain elements that appear with some regularity and in a differing combination of circumstances depending on the size, scale and complexity of the urban environment.

Environmental degradation

The outward expression of this problem is often in terms of empty and semi-derelict shops. At the commencement of the Brigg Project many properties were vacant or under-utilized; empty upper floors exhibited dirty, broken windows and peeling paintwork; furthermore, fly posting, graffiti and litter had become a problem. In general an air of decay had settled over the town, a manifestation of the collapse of market investment and confidence. This in turn was influenced by the poor environment of the town centre with heavy through traffic, small and poorly maintained retail units and a dwindling economy. Indeed, a self-perpetuating spiral of decline was clearly evident.

Physical remoteness from the seat of local government

After the 1974 local government reorganization, many towns used to self-government were disfranchised of their powers and found themselves in some instances locationally detached from the new seat of power. Indeed, this was a common feature of several towns, a number of which are the subject of regeneration projects, namely Ripon, Ilfracombe and Loftus. In some instances resentment of the 'new' authorities still runs high, and in part no doubt contributes to the general lack of public investment that they receive as a result.

Paradoxically Brigg is not one of these towns in so far as it has retained its position as a centre of local administration. Rather the problems of Brigg are more of a physical nature. The project did, however, try to pull together the Borough Council and Town Council, bodies that traditionally viewed each other with some suspicion.

Collapse of private investment

Market confidence is essential for investment to take place. When that confidence is threatened by economic or physical change the fortunes of the community take a downturn. The impacts of such changes are often only apparent in the longer term. In the case of Brigg, the spiral of decline set in motion the departure of a number of national retailers who rationalized their outlets in favour of the larger neighbour, Scunthorpe. A contributory factor in their decision was the congestion and heavy through traffic in Brigg town centre. The challenge which now faces Brigg is to repackage its future without the support of national retailers, at least in the short term.

Closure of the staple employer

Many small towns owe their existence to the operations of a large single employer who may have exploited a local raw material such as coal, potash, fish or agricultural products. Rationalization of plants due to mergers or the depletion of the raw material may result in that employer closing. This can have catastrophic effects on communities. Consequently training needs to become a feature of regeneration efforts, together with a diversification of the economic base. Agencies involved in the regeneration process need to target their activities to reflect such needs.

In Brigg (population 5500), the British Sugar factory closed its manufacturing operation with the loss of 106 full-time jobs. However, the true position needs to consider the several hundred seasonal jobs lost and the unknown knock-ons into transport related businesses and agriculture. Such investment decisions taken at boardroom level are remote from the community affected and heighten the sense of isolation. They also contribute to the spiral of decline by casting a shadow of doubt over the viability of the town's remaining business base.

Loss of a traditional role

Decline may arise when a town is eclipsed by the rise of a neighbour. Iron was discovered in Scunthorpe at the turn of the century, thus ensuring the rapid growth of what was at that time a collection of hamlets. Brigg, the traditional market town about 16 km away, could not compete. Effectively from that stage the implications for and the eventual demise of Brigg were apparent.

Hence the regeneration project needs to cast a new role for Brigg, one that builds on its historical attractions whilst at the same time respecting its long tradition in a still largely agricultural economy. The role which is envisaged is a slightly upmarket, traffic-free retail and service centre with speciality shops and restaurants. Diversification of the employment base will be facilitated by a new business park, and in an effort to increase the base population substantial areas have been allocated for new housing development. The aim is to provide a robust but flexible economy that reflects the demands of the 1990s.

Heavy through traffic

This is an issue that afflicts many communities with noise, air pollution and danger accompanying traffic within the town centre. The problem, however, is particularly severe given the medieval street pattern within Brigg. Surprisingly, many towns remain antagonistic towards the concept of pedestrianization despite the experience of investment growth which has accompanied such schemes elsewhere. An essential part of the Brigg package, as indeed in Ripon and other project towns, is the removal of through traffic from its medieval town centre.

Poor communications

Certain projects are located in towns that suffer from remoteness with inadequate communication infrastructure provision. If modest investment is one of the objectives of regeneration, account must be taken of the need for accessibility. Any realistic programme therefore will be heavily dependent on proposed public transport expenditure plans, or the likelihood of influencing those through mobilizing political support. In this respect it is essential that the project's objectives are pragmatic and achievable if further disillusionment is not to be caused.

Lack of community pride

Frequently discounted or omitted as a consideration of the regeneration process, this factor can have significant benefits in the sustainability of the proposals. A community that lacks pride in its surroundings will treat them with disdain. A regeneration project must project a positive and attainable image of the future. Likewise the community must have a share in formulating this image, either through direct workshop sessions or more formal consultation procedures. It is argued that if the community feels a sense of ownership for the plans thus produced they are more likely to support them through the cycle of political and economic life. The Brigg experience shows, by working with the community and the schools, that the incidence of vandalism has declined and graffiti all but disappeared. The approach is essentially bottom-up.

19.3   APPROACHES TO OVERCOMING COMMUNITY PROBLEMS

The nature of the place where a project is operating tends to dictate the approach. Each town/project has an unique flavour, and yet common experience has shown that there are tools that have proved useful in promoting concepts and overcoming potential problems. Key ingredients in this process include partnership and community involvement, public sector expenditure programmes, government grant regimes, charitable grant sources and the role of planning.

Partnership and community involvement

It is essential, from the outset, that all parties are involved in the process of setting up and formulating proposals for the project. A true spirit of partnership between the community, the local authority and business interests is required, which may be formalized by the setting up of a forum for debate or a steering group to review progress, or both. Indeed, for the sustainability of any development it is essential that it is patronized. There is a vested interest in involving the community at an early stage in the process of identifying opportunities, as the same people who will patronize the development will have initially helped to shape the proposals and arguably feel a degree of ownership. This provides a positive illustration of how the bottom-up approach of local regeneration initiatives can offer developers a chance to tease out problems before expensive submissions are required. Furthermore, the process offers the developer early market analysis.

Other factors that have helped generate community support include local groups such as the Civic Society or Brigg's Don.K.E.Y Group (an environmental youth group). Hand-holding helps to get groups established, creates confidence and generates funding. For example, the Don.K.E.Y Group in Brigg have raised over £5500 from charitable and government sources to undertake small scale environmental schemes around the town.

Public sector expenditure programmes

Stemming from initial discussions and feasibility studies it should become apparent at an early stage what policies are to be pursued by the project. An agreed vision of the future that adopts a realistic and pragmatic view of the town's limitations and financial constraints is essential. In Brigg, as elsewhere, studies were conducted to test future proposed models and to gain the support of all the partners. This may be achieved by various means such as professional consultants or community workshops, but at the end of the day any proposal must be achievable if credibility is not to be lost. Overly ambitious developments with long lead-in times make it difficult to deliver on the ground and risk losing community and hence political support.

Given the scale of problems affecting regeneration projects, large amounts of public expenditure in the form of infrastructure provision, may be required to prime the private sector. Political support for these concepts is a prerequisite for action on the ground. This often involves both county and district tiers of government, particularly with respect to the provision of infrastructure, with the project providing the focus of co-ordination between the differing levels of administration.

Government grant regimes

These may take various forms ranging from central government schemes such as the incentives offered to industrialists in Development Areas/Assisted Areas, the initiatives offered by the Rural Development Commission to promote jobs; for instance, the conversion of redundant buildings/promotion of community schemes, or Townscheme grants from English Heritage with up to 40% allowances for eligible costs on building works. The latter has proved invaluable in Brigg in triggering private sector monies and promoting property refurbishments. Equally there may be available local government grant schemes such as the Brigg Shopfront Grant, which offers 50% towards the repair or reinstatement of a traditional softwood shopfront, or the Conservation Area Enhancement Grant which assists in laying traditional paving schemes and reinstating iron railings. In marginal investment areas such as small towns the proportion of grant may be the carrot that is needed to swing the decision whether to develop or not. Where several schemes of grant are packaged the amounts of money are not inconsiderable.

Charitable grant sources

In those circumstances where the project is set up with charitable or voluntary status, funds are available from independent charitable sources that will match pound for pound in some instances monies raised from elsewhere. This provides an additional source of finance and can greatly assist in achieving projects on the ground, particularly during periods of monetary constraint. A particularly good example of the use of such monies comes from Ilfracombe, where the conversion of a redundant chapel into community use was generously grant-aided from the Tudor Trust.

Planning

Given recent central government guidance concerning the importance of and legal weight of a local plan in guiding and promoting development, it is essential that the document agrees in a large part with the ambitions of the project. The ability to tap into and influence local policy will ultimately be reflected in the achievements of the project. In this respect the regeneration of Brigg and the work of the project was enhanced by the existence of the Brigg Local Plan (Glanford Borough Council, 1989), which the Brigg Urban Design Study has been capable of interpreting in a graphic and visually exciting way.

19.4 METHODS OF EVALUATION

Methods of evaluating the progress within a project may need to draw on a wide range of sources, including access to data normally of a confidential nature. In circumstances where such information is not available, subjectivity and 'best guess' estimates may need to be relied on when approaching future sponsors. Analysis and evaluation does, however, need to consider the client base, needs and interests. For instance, the local authority may wish to utilize the ratio of public grant aid to private gross investment figures as this will give a pump-priming ratio of interest to future investors. Similarly, the Rural Development Commission may like to see a return on investment with specific reference to the number of jobs created.

Total gross investment

Confidentiality of individual investments, assuming that they are known or obtainable, means that such figures are often aggregated to an annual amount with subdivision into gross private sector development and gross public sector development. Allowing for these constraints it is estimated that over the initial three years of the Brigg project, the private sector has invested £3 million in property refurbishments. This includes schemes as diverse as an internal refit of the Nottingham Building Society offices, a re-roofing of a domestic cottage and the construction of a 17 bed hotel complex. Expenditure levels can, however, quickly add up. In Brigg the average small commercial/domestic re-roofing in slate or pantile works out at £4000; ten such schemes therefore give an aggregate of £40 000 gross development costs. In contrast, the public sector gross development figure in Brigg over the same three year period is nearer to £9 million. This is indicative of a local authority committed to the concept of regeneration, with its programme of capital expenditure tied in to help prime follow-on investment by the private sector.

The type of public sector schemes that are benefiting Brigg include: a £6 million link road that will open up land for a business park and remove through traffic from the town centre; pedestrianization of the main shopping areas; and several major refurbishments of public buildings and the releasing of key public sites for redevelopment.

Spatial and numerical quantification

Statistical counts allow the quantification of several variables as diverse as floorspace and tree planting. With respect to the former, new floorspace generated or refurbished, whether it is commercial, retail or industrial, is a relative measure of progress. However, within small towns an over supply of accommodation may occur in a relatively short period of time, hence it is important that the local planning authority monitors the rate of uptake and input. In contrast, environmental enhancement projects offer the opportunity of evaluation by the production of statistics such as the number of trees planted, area of dereliction tackled and lengths of footpaths improved or cleared. In either instance such data will have a bearing on future work programmes and funding sources and offer reassurance to existing sponsors concerned with value for money.

Grant-aided contributions

The amount of grant aid paid out is potentially more difficult to evaluate than gross development costs due to problems of accessing data and the potentially misleading nature of information where invariably the grant is offered for particular elements of the building work only. For instance, English Heritage Townscheme monies will pay in the main for structural works, namely roofs, windows, repointing, rain water goods and damp-proof courses, at a proportion not exceeding 40%, yet the full programme of building work will obviously encompass decoration and other repairs to heating, lighting and basic amenities. Nevertheless, this provides an indication of leverage which may prove helpful in securing further funding and investment. The Brigg Townscheme has committed £20 000 per annum over the past three years and is presently over-committed. Thus the £3 000 000 of private sector investment has been triggered by £60 000 of Townscheme grants, although not every scheme has benefited from grant aid.

Press cuttings file

Local publicity and media coverage is vital in creating community awareness, in establishing a profile and maintaining a presence in the local area. Indeed, to be taken seriously by local politicians and potential sponsors a project needs to have 'clout'. A simple measure of credibility which can be utilized effectively by a project is the amount of newspaper coverage that has been generated. In this respect the Brigg Project in its initial three years attracted 3700 column centimetres of newspaper coverage alone. Likewise radio and television interviews also impart credibility, as well as giving an indication of the effectiveness of the project's proposals.

Cost per head of population

A statistic used by the Audit Commission, cost per head of population, is a simple indicator of cost effectiveness derived from the total project budget divided by the total population. In the case of Brigg, a project budget of £50 000 per annum divided by a total population of 5500 produces a figure of £9 per head of population. Comparisons are difficult to make but, for example, Task Forces, comparable area based initiatives, each have a budget of between £20 and £40 per head of population on top of operating expenses (Annabel Jackson Associates, 1990). In value for money terms the Brigg Project can thus point towards economy, effectiveness and efficiency at a relatively low per capita cost set against the £3 million of investment levered from the private sector.

Vacancy rates

The number of vacant premises or voids in the town at the outset of the project on the ground floor and/or upper floors provides a basis against which progress may be evaluated. Subsequent monitoring on an annual cycle will allow an assessment of the rate of uptake which will help to show the efficacy of policies aimed at remedying the situation and any modifications necessary to allow for evolving circumstances. In particular, changes in prime retailing positions caused by development elsewhere may be picked up using this void register.

Regarding Brigg at the commencement of the project, the town centre was characterized by a large number of voids in the principal retail areas and to compound the problem many of the properties were semi-derelict. In the life of the project all but one of these premises have been refurbished. However, due to the downturn in the macroeconomy, voids, albeit refurbished voids, remain ready for occupation once the economic climate improves.

Property values and rental levels

In the case of small towns, national or regional property performance indices have little validity. In the absence of national multiple retailers database records are not held by the major property firms as there is generally little perceived retailer demand. However, the commercial study of Brigg conducted on behalf of the project by Hillier Parker (1990) used local estate agent details in their investigation of property yields and rental levels. The study offered some positive solutions and has helped to raise the profile of the town in terms of advice on investment opportunity.

One of the difficult issues that town regeneration projects face is to balance the competing and justifiable requirements of agencies. For example, English Heritage demand the use of high quality materials in repairs while the owner has to recoup development costs on a low rental income derived from traders who may only be 'ticking over' in volume terms. The gamble is that regeneration will create a new market or recapture a previous one, thus increasing turnover and supporting future rental growth. However, the perspective is inevitably long term.

Unemployment levels

Normally a key indicator in any evaluation, unemployment levels, however, have undergone a great many changes in recording practice and computational procedures making it difficult to compare current levels with earlier figures. Nevertheless it is important that some assessment of the number and type of job opportunities created is carried out. Indeed, partners in projects, particularly the Rural Development Commission, will be interested in seeing lower unemployment figures in return for their financial involvement.

In Brigg the employment generated as a result of the project has been mainly for part-time women as most schemes are retail orientated. Jobs in construction have also been maintained, if not created, with the use of local labour and trades. The unemployment figures, until the recession, bore this out. However, with the collapse of several major employers the employment situation has since deteriorated.

Third party interviews

This technique, carried out in Brigg by Annabel Jackson Associates, requires an independent third party to assess local opinion by interviewing businessmen, community leaders and councillors who may or may not have had an involvement with the project. The approach seeks to determine attitudes to the project and perceptions of achievements or otherwise. It provides an excellent means of appraising project direction, generates the impetus to remedy any recognized defects and enables quantification of the more intangible aspects of a project.

Head counts

This technique simply involves logging all visitors to the project office, though volume will be dependent on factors such as the location and hours of attendance. Arguably this provides an indication of public acceptance and support; however, the results can be skewed. The Brigg Project Office for its first three years was a shop on the main shopping street and during the year 1991–2 logged 3000 visitors through the door. A further measure of public interest, but difficult to rationalize, is the distribution of leaflets by the project office. Although experience shows that these are very much in demand, whether this truly reflects the level of public interest in the regeneration activities of the project is questionable.

19.5 MEASURING THE SOCIAL ELEMENTS

Much of the foregoing discussion has been concerned with the physical effects of regeneration and attempts at quantification. However, an essential element of regeneration, particularly in the smaller town, is the transformation of social attitudes and expectations. In Brigg at the start of the project there was a prevalence of apathy and complacency. Many years of neglect had taken their toll not only on the fabric of the town, but also on the aspirations of a community that saw businesses open and close with monotonous regularity. If investment was to return to the town, clearly there was a need for a change in attitude.

With respect to the regeneration initiative the requirement was not only an injection of capital but a future based on an attainable solution and one in which the community shared. The traditional approach in the inner city, a massive injection of capital channelled through an organization superimposed over existing agencies, creates its own problems. The Urban Development Corporation approach often alienates local communities by development activities which are not compatible with existing centres. Thus in the economic downturn of the early 1990s their sustainability is becoming questionable. The smaller market town can ill afford non-patronized development. Clearly the top-down approach will not work; rather, by working with and through the local community it is possible to identify proposals that are deemed locally important and sustainable. Within the latter, key influencers include local organizations and societies, councillors, schools and the impact of outside agencies.

Local organizations and societies

In communities where regeneration projects are established it is often apparent that local organizations are struggling to maintain membership. This is indicative of a community that has lost heart. For example, in Brigg the local Chamber of Trade had become very negative and critical of the Borough Council. The project, however, was viewed in a substantially different light and was offered a seat on the executive committee. Resulting from the stimulus of the project the Chamber of Trade now has a much more positive view of the future, and enjoys a much higher level of knowledge of local affairs than previously.

As the regeneration momentum grows the number of people wishing to set up new societies increases. In Brigg the first attempt to launch a Civic Society early in the life of the project met with apathy and the attempt was abandoned. However, nine months later, when changes on the ground had started to appear and media interest had stimulated awareness of the project, a second attempt attracted over 100 people. Currently the membership stands at over 150, which for a community of 5500 people represents a very high proportion.

New councillors

The interest and focus generated by a project often encourages those within the community who share the vision to participate more actively, thus new faces appear on the local council and these supporters in turn generate more interest. This process of democratic change has been witnessed in Brigg, ultimately bestowing benefits to the community and the town.

School visits

Likewise once the regeneration process becomes more widely appreciated, approaches for information or visits are forthcoming from educational establishments offering a further indication of the growing community interest. In this context the Brigg experience is worthy of consideration. With respect to requests for talks and materials the project office has become a regular venue for children doing project work including environmental enhancement schemes. The children in turn talk to their parents and school open days display project work, all a valuable form of information dissemination.

Visits from outside agencies

A measure of the success of either the project's progress on the ground or its media campaign is reflected in the number of visits from outside agencies and interested professionals. Indeed, the latter stages of a project can be characterized by the project leader spending more of his time as a tour leader. However, the impressions gained are invaluable in helping set up projects elsewhere. In addition, such wider based networking is essential for achieving national recognition and central government support.

19.6   CONCLUSIONS

Regeneration projects play an important part in small towns and as demonstrated by the Brigg case study provide value for money, showing a reasonable return for a relatively modest outlay. Yet a characteristic of most projects is the desperate nature of short term core funding and chronic undermanning. Taken together these offer a recipe for short term expediency, time spent chasing funding and a consequent loss of efficiency in promoting the project's objectives and even less so evaluating them. Given the magnitude of the task that many projects are set, this must seem at times a contradiction to the project staff. Projects politically are 'nice to have' but are not statutory essentials, therefore they suffer from the swings of funding policy.

Evaluation is being increasingly requested from all funding sources. It therefore becomes imperative that information is available to supplement approaches to new sponsors, and similarly to placate the present ones. Inevitably it is hard data that will attract the attention of the media or the sponsor; however, the project must not lose sight of the community it purports to serve. Indeed, the ultimate test of a project's success will be the way the community feels about itself.

REFERENCES

Annabel Jackson Associates (1990) *Evaluation of Regeneration Unit Projects*, report commissioned by Civic Trust Regeneration Unit, London (unpublished).

Civic Trust (1984) *The Wirksworth Story: New Life for an Old Town*, Civic Trust, London.

Civic Trust (1989) *Regeneration: New Forms of Community Partnership*, Civic Trust, London.

Civic Trust (1990) *Brigg Regeneration Project Report*, Civic Trust, London.

Glanford Borough Council (1989) *Brigg Local Plan*, The Council, Glanford.

Hillier Parker (1990) *Brigg Town Centre Study of Development Potential*, report commissioned by Civic Trust Regeneration Unit, London (unpublished).

20

Piccadilly Village, Manchester: a case study in waterside urban renewal

_____ *P. Syms*

Any urban renewal project will, almost certainly, bring with it a multiplicity of problems. It should always go without saying that, when contemplating the redevelopment of a site which has previously been used for some other purpose, great care should be taken so as to overcome any problems which may remain hidden from sight. Fleming (1991) observed that in an industrialized community such as Europe, much of the land used for redevelopment has a history of previous uses and went on to point out that the state of such land is often so poor as to be unsuitable for continued use or re-use without major land engineering works. The cost of such works will, in many instances, have a significant effect on the viability of a redevelopment project. Such costs may well be far in excess of the reclaimed value of the land in question and, in such circumstances, the balance of a potentially successful urban regeneration project may well be tipped from profit into substantial loss.

It follows, therefore, that it is of benefit to gain as much knowledge as possible about a redevelopment site before any commitment is made to the project. McEntee (1991) describes four basic stages to be followed in undertaking an investigation of a derelict or potentially contaminated site: a desk study; identification of materials underlying the site; measurement of the geotechnical and chemical properties of these materials; and recommendations for development of the site.

In the pre-acquisition stage of a property development it is often not possible to undertake a full site investigation and the prospective developer has to base the investment decision on limited information. This should include, at the very least, a desk study of both the available geological data and records (e.g. town planning, building regulations, waste regulations, health and safety) relating to past uses of the land. Even a study of old Ordnance Survey maps will indicate where site levels have been changed, indicating the possible presence of fill materials. All too often, however, these fundamental first steps are completely overlooked, or are given only cursory attention.

Where sites have been occupied by structures which are no longer required, whether they be old factories, houses, gasworks or chemical works, these are usually demolished down only to ground level. Often the rubble left behind from the demolition process is either spread over the surface of the site or left around the perimeter, in a continuous mound, to deter vehicular access. Alternatively, it may be used to fill voids, such as basements and old mineral workings, with any surplus material simply being mounded on the site. Whatever method is used in disposing of demolition rubble the end result, with the introduction of topsoil, grass seed and a few shrubs, may be the creation of a green and pleasant visual environment. Even if the former industrial site is left to vegetate naturally in the post-demolition period, the end result may not be unattractive. In reality, however, many of the problems associated with the former use may be hidden from sight beneath the green sward and will present major problems for the future redevelopment of the area.

Add to the problem of adverse ground conditions the inadequacy of an outdated infrastructure and a multiplicity of ownerships, then an understanding may be gained of the wide range of problems likely to face the prospective developers of inner city sites. Other issues, such as the un-neighbourliness of remaining industrial users and the demographics of the area, will also have to be addressed in considering redevelopment proposals. Land adjacent to commercial waterways, docks, canals and rivers in industrialized locations, introduce a further set of problems which must be taken into account. Such problems have been considered in some detail by Hoyle *et al.* (1988).

Considerable as they may seem, the physical problems attaching to an urban renewal site may become relatively unimportant when compared with the problem of perception and this is especially true of urban watersides, which are frequently regarded as 'no-go' areas and often with good reason. Typically urban waterside sites are in the most run-down, and very often crime-ridden, parts of inner cities, the areas from which industry has departed and in which no-one wishes to live. High technology firms and service industry companies are reluctant to relocate into such areas and therefore they become abandoned. Law (1988) refers to a process of cumulative decline with a lack of investment producing further obsolescence, which has in turn discouraged investment. An important part of a waterside urban renewal project must therefore be the changing of perceptions to encourage new investment.

The location of what is now Piccadilly Village, close to the centre of Manchester, contained all of these problems and more besides. It was also bisected by a run-down canal and suffered from major changes in level across the site as well as containing a number of old cobbled streets. Although close to Manchester centre, the site was in a highly depressed area of the city, regarded in a poor light by property professionals and potential occupiers alike. This chapter examines the development of Piccadilly Village from its inception through to completion of the development process.

20.1   INNER CITY ENVIRONMENT

Lying immediately north of Piccadilly Station, Manchester's mainline railway terminus, there used to exist an area of industrial dereliction. The area in general is bisected by the Manchester and Ashton Canal, including its junction with the Rochdale Canal. In years gone by, this was an important traffic hub, both in connection with the canal system and later with the introduction of the railway. As a transport interface, development of the area predated by about 100 years the better known and larger Manchester Docks, the redevelopment of which to form Salford Quays has been described by Law (1988). In the post-war era the area fell into a typical state of industrial decline; the canal had lost its commercial traffic by 1957 and fell derelict in 1961, when the last pleasure boat made a passage with the greatest difficulty (McKnight, 1975). The former cotton mills became disused or passed into alternative uses, many of which were unneighbourly; most of the other manufacturing concerns either went out of existence or managed to subsist at the economic margin. Such residential accommodation that had existed in the area, mostly in the form of back-to-back housing, has been demolished as a result of slum clearance programmes.

Situated within the defined inner area of Manchester (Manchester and Salford Inner City Partnership, 1979), the locality suffered from physical, economic and social dereliction. According to the Manchester and Salford Inner Area Study (published in September 1978) the area encompassed by the partnership had the largest concentration of employment in the Greater Manchester Conurbation, and yet contained the largest concentration of poor and disadvantaged people. A lack of investment had also resulted in the inner area containing the bulk of the vacant industrial buildings and derelict land in the two cities.

Poorest housing stock conditions were perceived as being in the private sector but some physical problems, for example, associated with walk-up and deck access flats, were to be found among council dwellings, often housing the poorest and most disadvantaged people. Of all the problems found in the inner city the public considered vandalism to be the most serious.

Such was the situation which existed before 1985 and the formation of the Manchester Phoenix Initiative. The Phoenix Initiative was promoted by the 'Group of Eight', industry, manufacturing, professional and trade union organizations representing the building industry. Originally it was intended that the area north of Piccadilly Station would be excluded from the Phoenix Initiative area. Not only was it a 'forgotten area' in terms of economic activity, it was also overlooked as far as urban renewal proposals were concerned. On further reflection, however, the area was included within the Phoenix Initiative as it was seen to present an opportunity for early redevelopment, owing to the fact that many of the older buildings had already been demolished and those which remained were grossly under-utilized. The Phoenix Initiative, together with two of the major landowners in the area, sponsored a land use study, encompassing an area of about 13 ha. From this initial study the Piccadilly Village concept emerged as one of a mix of uses providing an environment in which people would wish to 'live, work and play'.

The general environment of the area was not conducive to any form of new development and it was recognized that any project would have to produce an end product which was in itself a total contrast to the run-down aura of the inner city location. A genuine exercise in urban renewal was called for, not simply some new buildings on a former industrial site. The development would also have to be capable of existing in isolation from the surrounding area, although it was the hope of the study team that the example provided by the Piccadilly Village concept would encourage other landowners to redevelop, or at least upgrade, their properties. The objective of trying to create an environment which transformed the site from a scene of total dereliction into something modern and refreshing was later condemned by some as the creation of a 'yuppie village'. Such an intention was far from the minds of the promoters and, as will be shown later, has proved not to be the case in reality.

The concept produced by the study team called for a high density urban development, preferably one which would be vibrant, with a mix of uses ensuring activity throughout the day and evening. Although intended as a high density development it was considered most important to retain the human scale, therefore the height of the development was to be limited to four storeys. Public access and security for the occupiers of properties were to be given prominence, especially bearing in mind the poor public and professional perceptions of this run-down part of the inner city.

20.2   SITE ASSEMBLY

The initial land use study identified a site of approximately 1.62 ha, bisected by the Ashton Canal which, due to the lack of existing buildings, could be developed at an early date. The canal itself was in use as part of the Cheshire Ring of the leisure waterways, although it was in need of dredging. The canal structure, in the form of its walls and adjacent footpaths, was in an unsound condition and totally unsuitable for the new development. The two parts of this first site had, during the commercial lifetime of the canal, contained a total of three canal basins but these had been filled in at some point during the past.

The southern part of the site had previously been occupied by a mill building and timber yard as well as stabling used by British Rail. With the exception of a small beerhouse, which was by then occupied by a rag sorter, all of the existing buildings had been demolished. Some problems had been encountered with the unauthorized use of the site by itinerant travellers and extensive fly-tipping had also taken place. On the north side of the canal the former wharves had long since fallen into disuse; once again all buildings had been demolished. During the 1960s and 1970s (Figure 20.1) the site had been in use as a car breaker's yard but more recently had been used by British Waterways for the tipping of canal dredgings. Some environmental improvement work had taken place under the auspices of the Manpower Services Commission along the north bank, creating a footpath with landscaping and seating. Unfortunately this had not been very well maintained and was becoming overgrown.

At the time of the land use study the initial site (Figure 20.2) was in approximately 18 or 19 different ownerships, which included bodies such as British Waterways, Manchester City Council and British Rail. Fortunately, the first two of these bodies agreed to include their land in a comprehensive redevelopment scheme and the City Council also made a compulsory purchase order in respect of a number of the ownerships along the Great Ancoats Street frontage for the purpose of widening the street so that it could form part of the city's inner relief road. British Rail, on the other hand, decided that it could not wait for a comprehensive regeneration scheme to be put together and made the decision to sell, by auction, its totally derelict portion of the site. At the auction this small piece of land, crucial to the comprehensive scheme, was bought by National Car Parks, which already owned land in the area, used as surface car parking. Eventually the car park company agreed to sell the site for the purpose of redevelopment, but at a price approximately twice that received by British Rail, the additional cost being eventually met by the Department of the Environment.

During this early stage of the project no developer was committed to carrying out the urban regeneration of the area, but one of the landowners, Moran Holdings plc of London, had indicated a willingness to proceed with

Figure 20.1 Photograph of site taken in the 1960s showing previous usage

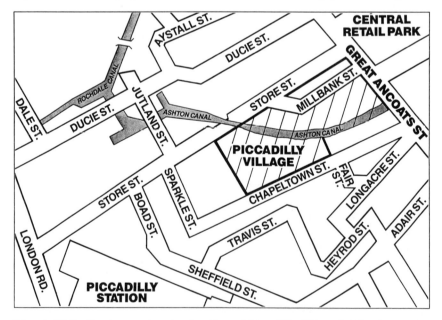

Figure 20.2 Street map showing location of Piccadilly Village in Manchester city centre. Initial phases are shown as hatched

a project subject to it being financially viable. British Waterways had also held discussions with a north-west based developer, Trafford Park Estates plc, regarding the possible development of the land owned by the waterway. It was therefore decided that these two companies would form a joint development company, Piccadilly Village Limited, to carry out the urban renewal project.

Following the formation of the development partnership, negotiations started to acquire the other land ownerships, all of which were eventually obtained by agreement. The total cost of the site was just in excess of £187 800/ha. This relatively low price for land close to the city centre was attributable to the fact that major changes in level existed between the canal and the adjoining streets, the configuration of the plots themselves made redevelopment extremely difficult and ground problems were anticipated.

The site acquisition stage extended over a period in excess of one year and indeed work started on some areas of the site before legal formalities had been completed. In addition to site assembly, the first phase of the project involved two street closures, as well as the diversion of existing services and the installation of new services for the development itself.

20.3   PROFESSIONAL TEAM

Other than the development consultants no other professionals were employed by the joint development company in the early stages of the project and it was therefore necessary to assemble a full team, capable of undertaking a project of this size and nature. A development brief was prepared, setting out the requirements for a mixed commercial and residential development which would encourage visitors to this part of the city, while at the same time preserving the privacy and security of the residents. Five architectural practices were invited to submit their proposals and, following interview, Halliday Meecham Architects of Alderley Edge, Cheshire were selected.

This firm had already designed several very successful urban waterside residential projects, in Bristol and Swansea, and this was an important factor in the decision-making process. The development which eventually emerged closely followed the architects' original competition entry (Figure 20.3), subject to some elevational changes requested by the city's planning department. A number of modifications were, however, made to the mix of uses, both in the early design stages and as the project proceeded.

In addition to the architects, it was necessary to appoint quantity surveyors and consulting engineers. These were appointed from firms with which the joint venture partners had worked on previous occasions. So far as the water related engineering aspects were concerned, it was decided to appoint British Waterways' own civil engineering department for their expertise

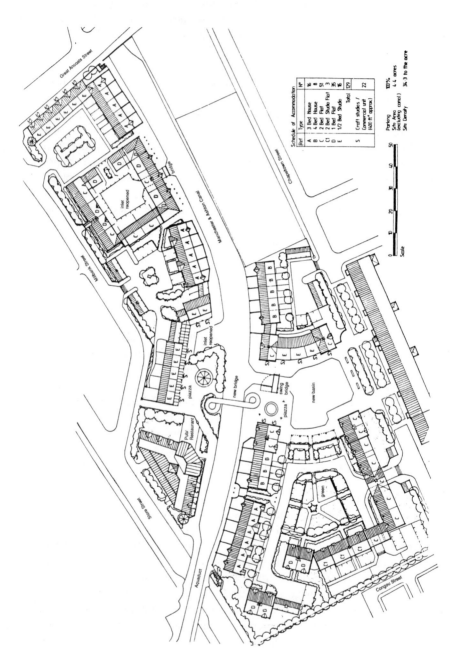

Figure 20.3 Layout of Piccadilly Village from winning entry in architectural competition

in the design of canals and bridges. In return for this, and a share in the development profits, British Waterways agreed to accept future responsibility for the repair and maintenance of engineering structures within three metres of the water.

20.4 SITE CONTAMINATION AND RECLAMATION

A major consideration in planning the redevelopment of an inner city industrial site, such as that to be occupied by Piccadilly Village, is the possibility of ground contamination. This is of particular importance where residential occupation is the proposed end use, especially when the site has been in a multiplicity of uses. So far as this site was concerned past uses were known to have included a timber yard, coal yard, engineering factory, car breakers, stables, car sales, dredgings tip and a rag sorter. In addition much of the site had been the subject of fly-tipping and so the diversity of potential contaminants was considerable.

Currently (1992) no set standard exists in the United Kingdom for the reclamation of contaminated sites, although some guidance is available. The Interdepartmental Committee on the Redevelopment of Contaminated Land (ICRCL) was established in 1976 with representatives from the Department of the Environment, Department of Health, the Welsh Office, the Health and Safety Executive and the Ministry of Agriculture, Fisheries and Food. Subsequently, the Scottish Development Agency was also represented on the committee. Since its formation the ICRCL has produced guidelines for the redevelopment of contaminated sites to a number of different end uses. Guideline information is presented in the form of 'trigger concentrations' which, together with an appreciation of local background levels, are intended to be of assistance during the interpretation of data derived from site investigation (Harris, 1987).

The ICRCL guidelines do not cover all circumstances and, although of assistance, are not mandatory; nor should they be regarded as minimum standards to be achieved. Valuation implications are disregarded so far as the ICRCL guidelines are concerned; consequently there are arguments in favour of seeking a clean site solution, in which all contaminants are removed from the land so that it may be redeveloped for any purpose.

Reclamation of the site was carried out in 1988–9, before the introduction of the Environmental Protection Act 1990. Nevertheless the site was reclaimed in a controlled manner, with the contaminated material being removed to a licensed tip. Thus the clean site option was chosen to render the site suitable for any end use. Where contaminated material was contained in voids, such as old canal basins, these were excavated and either refilled with clean material or re-opened to the canal. Following reclamation the ground was left with a high sulphate level, probably no different to that found in the surrounding area, and therefore special precautions were taken in the construction of foundations and ground floor slabs.

The two re-opened canal basins were found to be in surprisingly good condition and, except for some alterations to fit in with the proposed development, required very little in the way of restoration. The canal walls themselves, on the other hand, were a totally different proposition.

On the south side of the canal the wall was in a very poor state of repair, necessitating total removal and rebuilding. Instead of replacing this wall in masonry, as the original, it was decided to use sheet steel piling, capped with concrete and finished above water level with stone copings. The problems on the north side were less severe and thus was possible to retain much of the existing wall, pressure cleaned and grouted where necessary, with a new mass concrete wall poured in behind the existing structure.

The new basin was constructed with sheet piling at the same time as the rebuilding of the south wall of the canal and finished in a similar manner. Traditional puddle clay was used to waterproof the bed of the basin and behind the rebuilt and refurbished canal walls. All of the canal restoration works were undertaken during the winter season, with the canal closed and drained between November and March (1988–9).

The new canal bridges were constructed: one across the canal itself and the other two crossing the mouths of basins. The main canal bridge, with spiral ramps, was based on the design of a traditional Macclesfield Canal roving bridge, to provide disabled access between the two halves of the development. The canal was narrowed at this point to reduce the span of the bridge and to provide a lay-by for the mooring of boats.

20.5   PROJECT FINANCE

When the Piccadilly Village project was conceived in 1987 the property development industry was fairly buoyant and, in particular, urban renewal was receiving a great deal of attention from both government and media. As a result the banks were prepared to bid against each other for the privilege of providing competitive finance rates for what they perceived to be prestige projects. Thus it was possible for the development partnership to obtain a very attractive package of lending.

Private sector funding on its own, however, was not sufficient to ensure the commercial success of the project. Public sector support was necessary to provide the right environment for urban renewal by overcoming the ground and water engineering problems. Initial discussions with the Department of the Environment centred around two possible sources of public sector support, the Urban Development Grant and private sector Derelict Land Grant. During the course of these discussions two important events occurred.

In May 1988 City Grant was introduced to replace the Urban Development Grant and the Urban Regeneration Grant, as well as subsuming (in the 57 invited authority areas to which City Grant was applicable) the private sector Derelict Land Grant scheme. The rationale for introducing City Grant was described by the then Minister in the Department of the Environment as 'firstly, to simplify the existing grant structure (UDG, URG and DLG) which many people found confusing; and secondly to speed up delivery of assistance.' The Minister went on to say that 'City Grant is available . . . for private sector projects which benefit our inner cities. It attracts private investment by supporting projects which would not go ahead without grant and which provide jobs or private housing and help rebuild investors' confidence' (Bruinvels and Rodrigues, 1989).

The second event occurred in July 1988 with the setting up of the Central Manchester Development Corporation and the inclusion of the Piccadilly Village site in the urban development area. The Department of the Environment's appraiser thereafter acted as agent for the fledgling development corporation and, within six weeks of submission of the formal application, a City Grant of £1.13 million was agreed. This equated approximately to the estimated costs of reclaiming the site and the restoration works to the canal. The new development itself did not receive any commercial subsidy.

20.6   NEW HOMES AND COMMERCIAL ACCOMMODATION

Initially the project was to provide 125 residential units, 15 craft studios, six shops and 1486 m^2 of office accommodation. During the course of construction a number of changes were made which increased the number of residential units to 150 and omitted the craft units. These changes were made in response to market conditions; although tenants could be found for the craft units the rents which most were able to afford were uneconomic and none appeared able to purchase units. At the same time there was found to be a demand for bedsitting room units; the only one originally provided by the design had sold very quickly. Hence the craft units were converted, very successfully, into residential use. The ground floor units in Figure 20.5 are therefore bedsitting rooms, with two storey apartments above.

Originally the development company intended to let the construction contract for the development by competitive tender, in the same way that the site reclamation work had been procured. However, following problems with the successful tenderer, the decision was taken by the two partners for Piccadilly Village Limited to act as its own contractor.

Moran Holdings plc, through its subsidiary company Moran Homes Limited,

Figure 20.4   Photograph of part of Piccadilly Village (same view as Figure 20.1) showing residential accommodation

was already actively involved in house-building projects in south-east England. Therefore the expertise was available within the partnership for the control and supervision of the construction programme using consultants to assist on the cost control and purchasing aspects. Trafford Park Estates plc provided local management and accounting facilities.

20.7   MARKETING AND FUTURE MANAGEMENT

The acquisition of additional land subsequently increased the potential size of the development to around 200 residential units, with a site for a public house and the possibility of increasing the office content to as much as 9290 m^2, subject to there being sufficient demand. Although intended to provide a mix of differing uses, the new development was to be essentially driven by residential occupation and it was in this respect that the greatest problems of perception lay.

The intention was that new housing would be for sale to owner occupiers, yet the site lay close to a fairly notorious local authority housing estate and, unlike many other cities, Manchester did not have a history of people living in the city centre. At the time that the Central Manchester Development Corporation was designated, a survey revealed that less than 200 people

lived in the central area of the city. Virtually no new residential development had taken place in recent years, the last new building scheme having
been St John's Gardens, developed by Wimpey in the 1970s. One former
warehouse building had also been converted into residential use to provide
low cost housing accommodation, but neither of these schemes compared
in any way with the type of development envisaged for Piccadilly Village.

A view of the market, which had arisen out of the original study, was the
need for good quality accommodation in a pleasant environment, yet within
a few minutes' walk of the city centre. Potential purchasers were seen as
people working in the centre of the city, often during unsocial hours, in
hospitals, media industry, restaurants and entertainment businesses. In
addition, due to the close proximity of the universities and Manchester
Polytechnic, another potential market was academic staff and students.

One of the most important aspects to be considered in respect of an
urban renewal project of this nature is the methods used in selling and
letting the accommodation produced by the project. In one respect this
comes down to a decision of whether real estate agents should be employed
and, if they are, which firm should be appointed. So far as central Manchester
is concerned, there are very many well known and competent estate agents
located in the city centre. For the most part, however, these firms are only
involved with the marketing of commercial and industrial properties and
the sale of development sites. Thus such firms had little feel for urban
renewal and their perceptions of the Piccadilly area of the city were extremely
poor.

So far as residential estate agents were concerned, these were few in
number, mostly located in the run-down areas of east Manchester where the
bulk of their business was in older terraced housing. These practices were also
considered to be unsuitable for the marketing of this type of product. In
addition, most of the prospective purchasers envisaged for the development
were also considered unlikely to make enquiries of east Manchester agents.

Therefore the decision was taken to establish a direct selling operation
from the site, initially with a staff of one, later increased to two. A temporary
sales office was established, to be followed later as construction proceeded
by a more permanent sales suite and show units. During the first 18 months,
from release of the first units onto the market, sales averaged approximately
one and a half units per week, running contrary to the local and, especially,
national house sales trends which were in deep depression for most of that
period. The general malaise of the housing market did eventually catch
up with the development, with a resultant slowdown of sales in the later
stages.

An early sale of half the phase one office buildings to a housing association
gave a good boost to the commercial side of the project, followed by the
sale of a second building to a firm of quantity surveyors. An over-supply of
offices in the Manchester market, the 'off pitch' location of the development

and the poor state of the economy resulted in some resistance from prospective purchasers. The development company, having been set up specifically for this one project, also had a firm desire to sell buildings, rather than to enter into leases and retain the investment on a long term basis. To assist sales, therefore, one of the city centre firms of commercial estate agents was subsequently engaged to assist in the marketing.

The future maintenance of the completed development is of greatest concern to all who live and work in an urban renewal project such as Piccadilly Village. A dedicated management company was therefore set up, Piccadilly Village Management Limited, administered on a day to day basis by Trafford Park Estates plc. The full-time manager is responsible for ensuring the cleanliness and security of the village; for example, keypad control vehicle entry gates have now been installed for additional security, and for ensuring that maintenance and repair works are undertaken. All of the properties are occupied on leases for 125 years, at peppercorn rents, and all occupiers contribute to the ongoing costs by way of management charges.

20.8 CONCLUSIONS

In terms of transforming a run-down former industrial area of the inner city, Piccadilly Village has undoubtedly proved to be successful. The same can also be said of the architectural appearance of the project although, with the benefit of hindsight, occupiers, developers and architects alike would probably wish to make a number of changes to the internal layout of the buildings.

Having once been accused of creating a 'yuppie village', the developers can now point to the very broad mix of people who have taken up residence, from students to semi-retired, manual workers to professionals, people working in medicine and entertainment, and from a mix of ethnic backgrounds. Many of the purchasers have been attracted by the presence of the restored waterway; although few residents are boat owners several are fishermen and the quality of the water means that the canal is well stocked with fish.

Even in one of the worst markets for residential property, a good level of sales was achieved. During the 18 month period following the release of the first phase, a selling programme was maintained three to four months ahead of completions, averaging 1.5 units sold each week. Although the residential properties had to be priced at full market value, a requirement of the City Grant, they were fixed at a realistic level to attract purchasers into this previously untested part of the inner city. Prices ranged from £39 950 for a bedsitter and £50 000 for a one-bedroomed apartment up to £140 000 for a four-bedroomed house, all on 125 year leases. At these prices it is not difficult to understand why people are willing to consider moving back to the centre (Hanson, 1989). Sales of the commercial properties were slower than the residential units, much more in line with the prevailing market conditions of that period, although half of the first phase office building was sold during construction to a housing association as its head office.

Problems have certainly occurred, not least of all concerning security. The existence of a major new development has not, in itself, succeeded in entirely reversing the high incidence of crime in the neighbourhood. A number of car thefts have taken place from the village, which has resulted in the fitting of keypad controlled vehicular gates. There have been a number of attempted burglaries and several fairly minor crimes against the person. Nevertheless the police have reported that there has been an overall reduction in the incidence of crime and that, compared with other areas of the inner city, a serious crime problem does not exist.

Considered as an entirety the development has so far been a success. The presence of water has played an important, but perhaps not, an essential part; good design and proximity to the facilities of the city centre have been of equal importance. As an exercise in urban renewal the project has transformed a run-down area of the city and is having a catalytic effect in encouraging adjoining landowners to embark on other development projects.

REFERENCES

Bruinvels, P. and Rodrigues, D. (1989) *Investing in Enterprise: A Comprehensive Guide to Inner City Regeneration and Urban Renewal*, Basil Blackwell, Oxford.

Fleming, G. (Ed.) (1991) The marginal and derelict land problem. In: *Recycling Derelict Land*, Institution of Civil Engineers, London.

Hanson, M. (1991) Manchester revives its city centre, *Estates Gazette*, **9120**, 84–85.

Harris, M.R. (1987) Recognition of the problem. In: *Reclaiming Contaminated Land* (Ed. T. Cairney), Blackie, Glasgow, pp. 1–29.

Hoyle, B.S., Pinder, D.A. and Husain, M.S. (Eds) (1988) *Revitalising the Waterfront*, Belhaven Press, London.

Law, C.M. (1988) Urban revitalisation, public policy and the redevelopment of redundant port zones. In: *Revitalising the Waterfront* (Eds B.S. Hoyle, D.A. Pinder and M.S. Husain), Belhaven Press, London, pp. 146–166.

Manchester and Salford Inner City Partnership (1979) *New Life for the Inner Cities – the Inner Area Programme 1979/80*, joint report by central government and the local authorities.

McEntee, J. (1991) Site investigation. In: *Recycling Derelict Land* (Ed. G. Fleming), Institute of Civil Engineers, London.

McKnight, H. (1975) *The Shell Book of Inland Waterways*, David and Charles, Newton Abbot.

Index